DRAMACON

Volume 3

Created by
Svetlana Chmakova

HAMBURG // LONDON // LOS ANGELES // TOKYO

Dramacon Vol. 3
Created by Svetlana Chmakova

Digital Toning Assistant - J. Dee Dupuy
Lettering - Erika "Skooter" Terriquez
Graphic Designer - Chris Tjalsma
Cover Art - Svetlana Chmakova

Editor - Lillian Diaz-Przybyl
Digital Imaging Manager - Chris Buford
Pre-Production Supervisor - Erika Terriquez
Production Manager - Elisabeth Brizzi
Managing Editor - Vy Nguyen
Creative Director - Anne Marie Horne
Editor-in-Chief - Rob Tokar
Publisher - Mike Kiley
President and C.O.O. - John Parker
C.E.O. and Chief Creative Officer - Stuart Levy

A **TOKYOPOP** Manga

TOKYOPOP Inc.
5900 Wilshire Blvd. Suite 2000
Los Angeles, CA 90036

E-mail: info@TOKYOPOP.com
Come visit us online at www.TOKYOPOP.com

ISBN: 978-1-59816-131-1

First TOKYOPOP printing: December 2007
10 9 8 7 6 5 4 3 2 1
Printed in the USA

CONTENTS

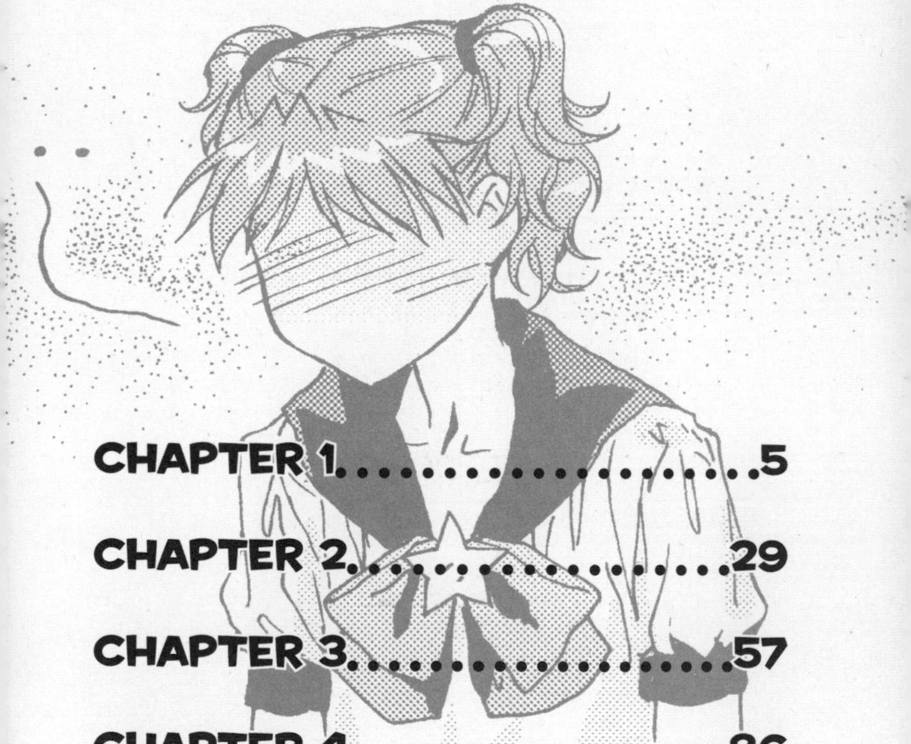

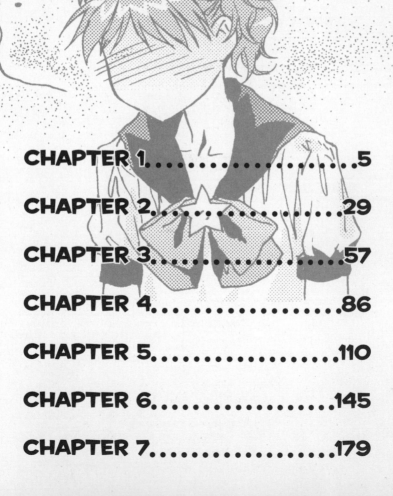

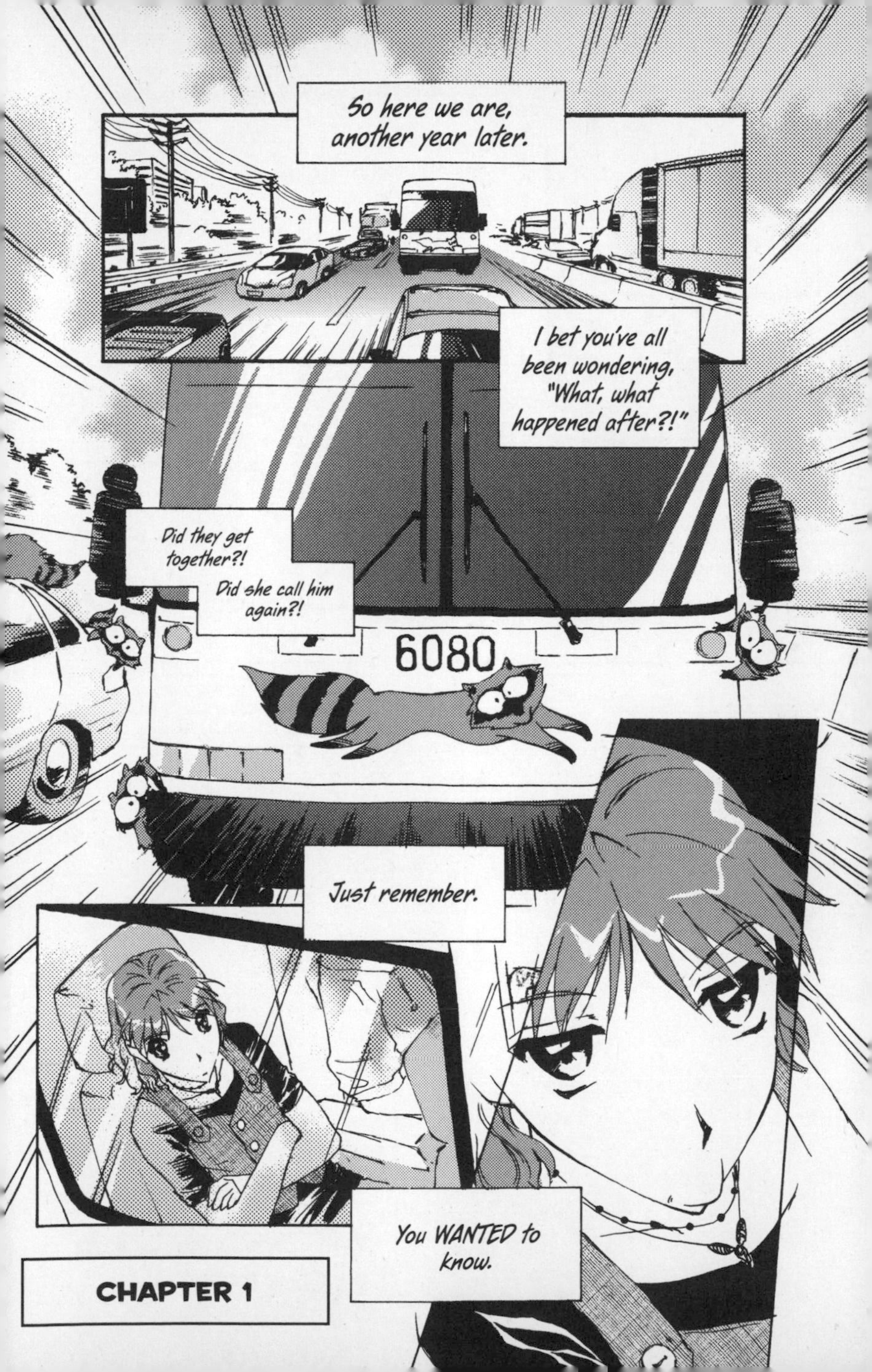
So here we are, another year later.
I bet you've all been wondering, "What, what happened after?!"
Did they get together?!
Did she call him again?!
6080
Just remember.
You WANTED to know.
CHAPTER 1

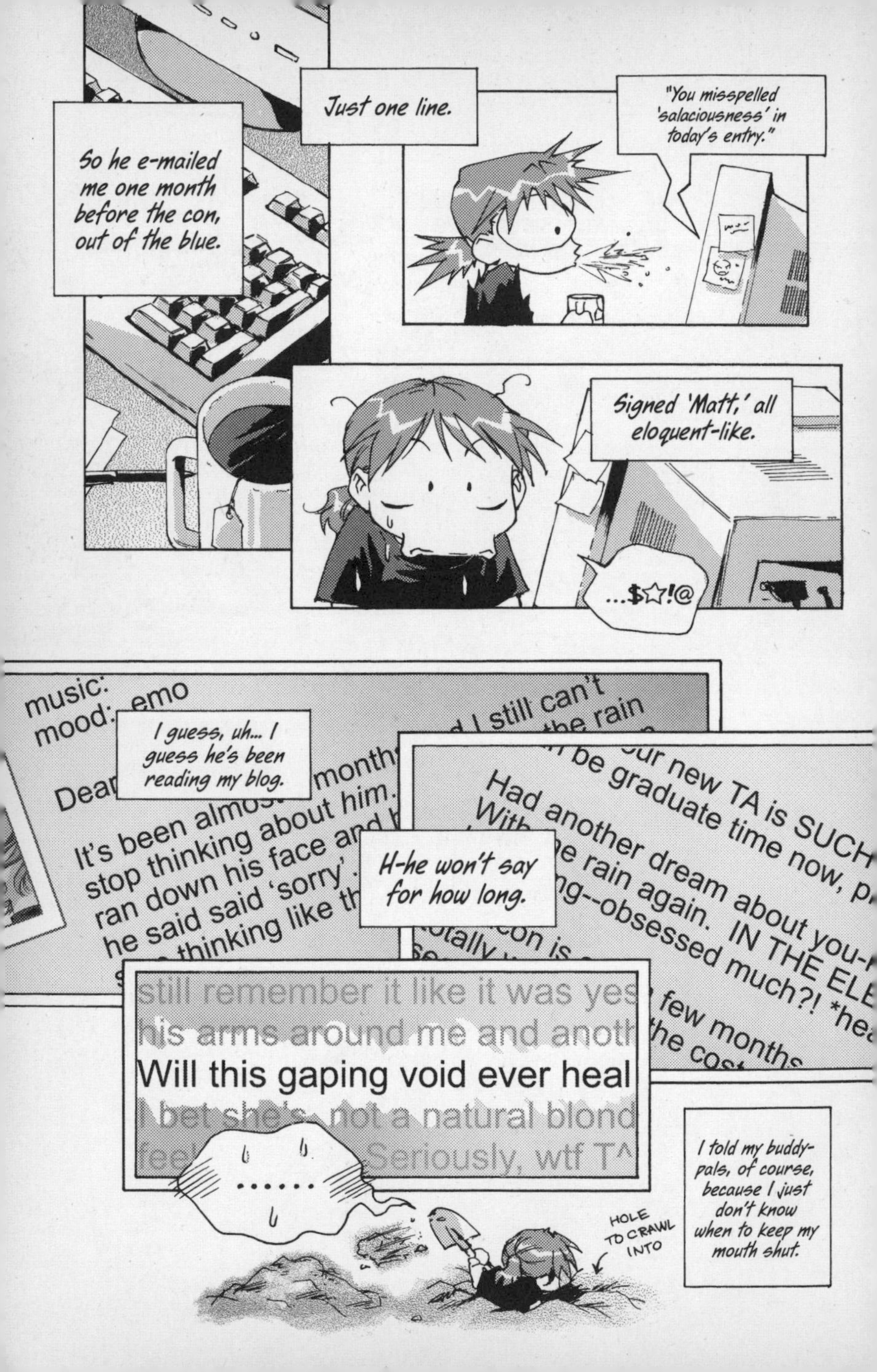

So he e-mailed me one month before the con, out of the blue.
Just one line.
"You misspelled 'salaciousness' in today's entry."
Signed 'Matt,' all eloquent-like.
...$☆!@
music:
mood: emo
I guess, uh... I guess he's been reading my blog.
stop thinking about him.
ran down his face and
he said said 'sorry'.
be graduate time now,
Had another dream about you-
rain again. IN THE ELE
g--obsessed much?! *hea
few months
H-he won't say for how long.
still remember it like it was yes
his arms around me and anoth
Will this gaping void ever heal
I bet she's not a natural blond
Seriously, wtf T^
......
HOLE TO CRAWL INTO
I told my buddy-pals, of course, because I just don't know when to keep my mouth shut.

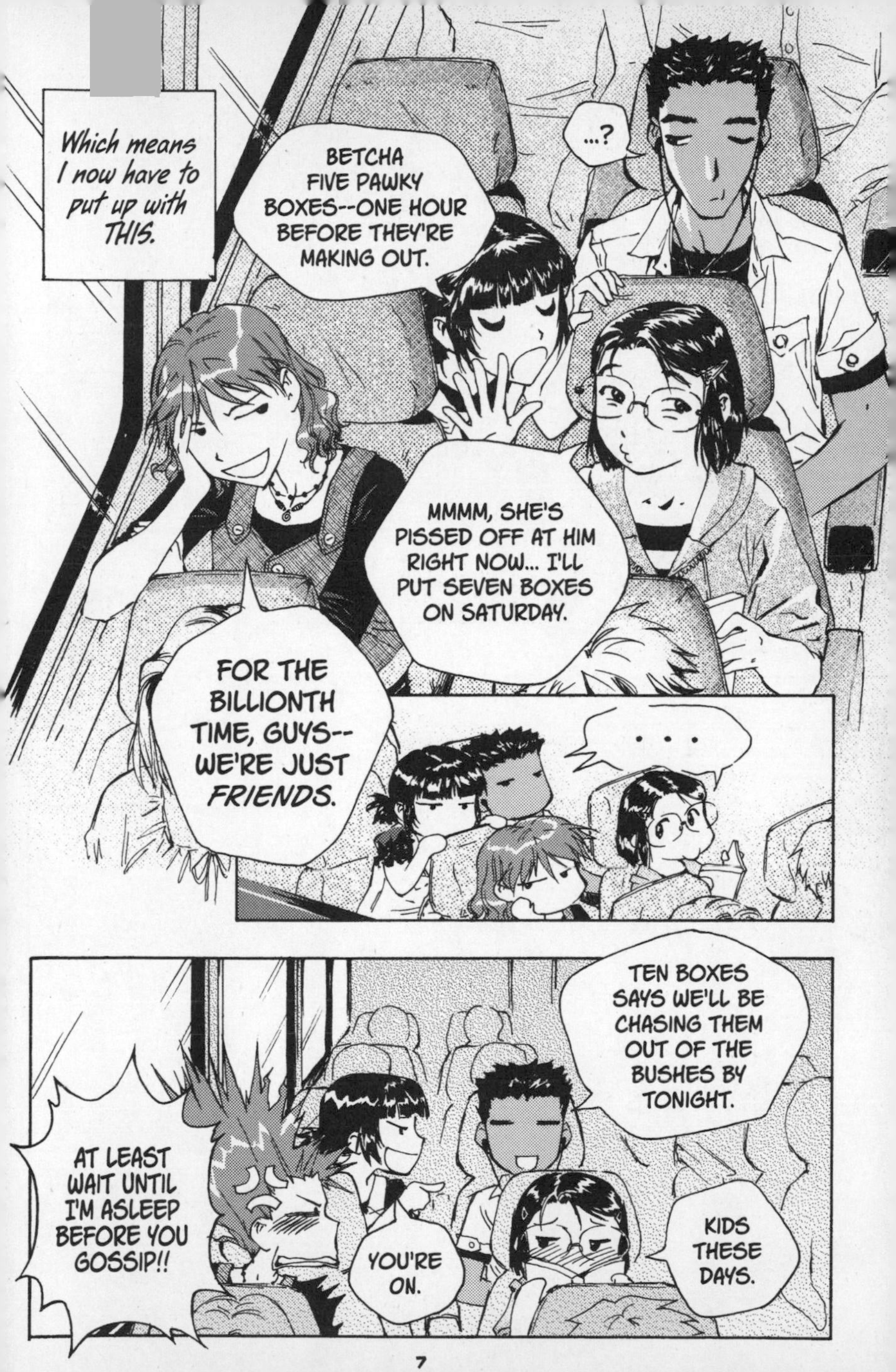
Which means I now have to put up with THIS.
BETCHA FIVE PAWKY BOXES--ONE HOUR BEFORE THEY'RE MAKING OUT.
...?
MMMM, SHE'S PISSED OFF AT HIM RIGHT NOW... I'LL PUT SEVEN BOXES ON SATURDAY.
FOR THE BILLIONTH TIME, GUYS-- WE'RE JUST FRIENDS.
. . .
AT LEAST WAIT UNTIL I'M ASLEEP BEFORE YOU GOSSIP!!
TEN BOXES SAYS WE'LL BE CHASING THEM OUT OF THE BUSHES BY TONIGHT.
YOU'RE ON.
KIDS THESE DAYS.

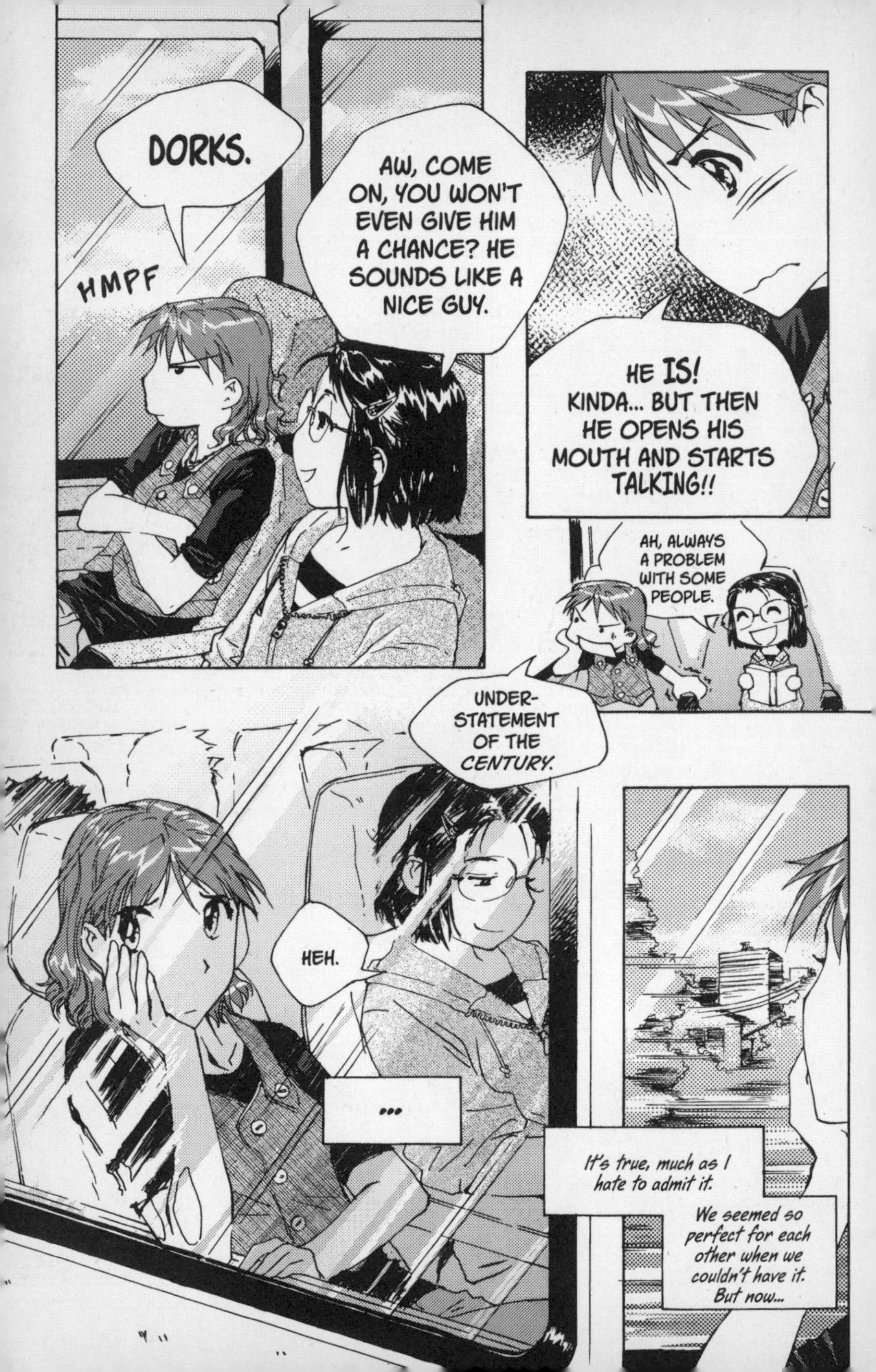
DORKS.
HMPF
AW, COME ON, YOU WON'T EVEN GIVE HIM A CHANCE? HE SOUNDS LIKE A NICE GUY.
HE IS! KINDA... BUT THEN HE OPENS HIS MOUTH AND STARTS TALKING!!
AH, ALWAYS A PROBLEM WITH SOME PEOPLE.
UNDER-STATEMENT OF THE CENTURY.
HEH.
...
It's true, much as I hate to admit it.
We seemed so perfect for each other when we couldn't have it. But now...

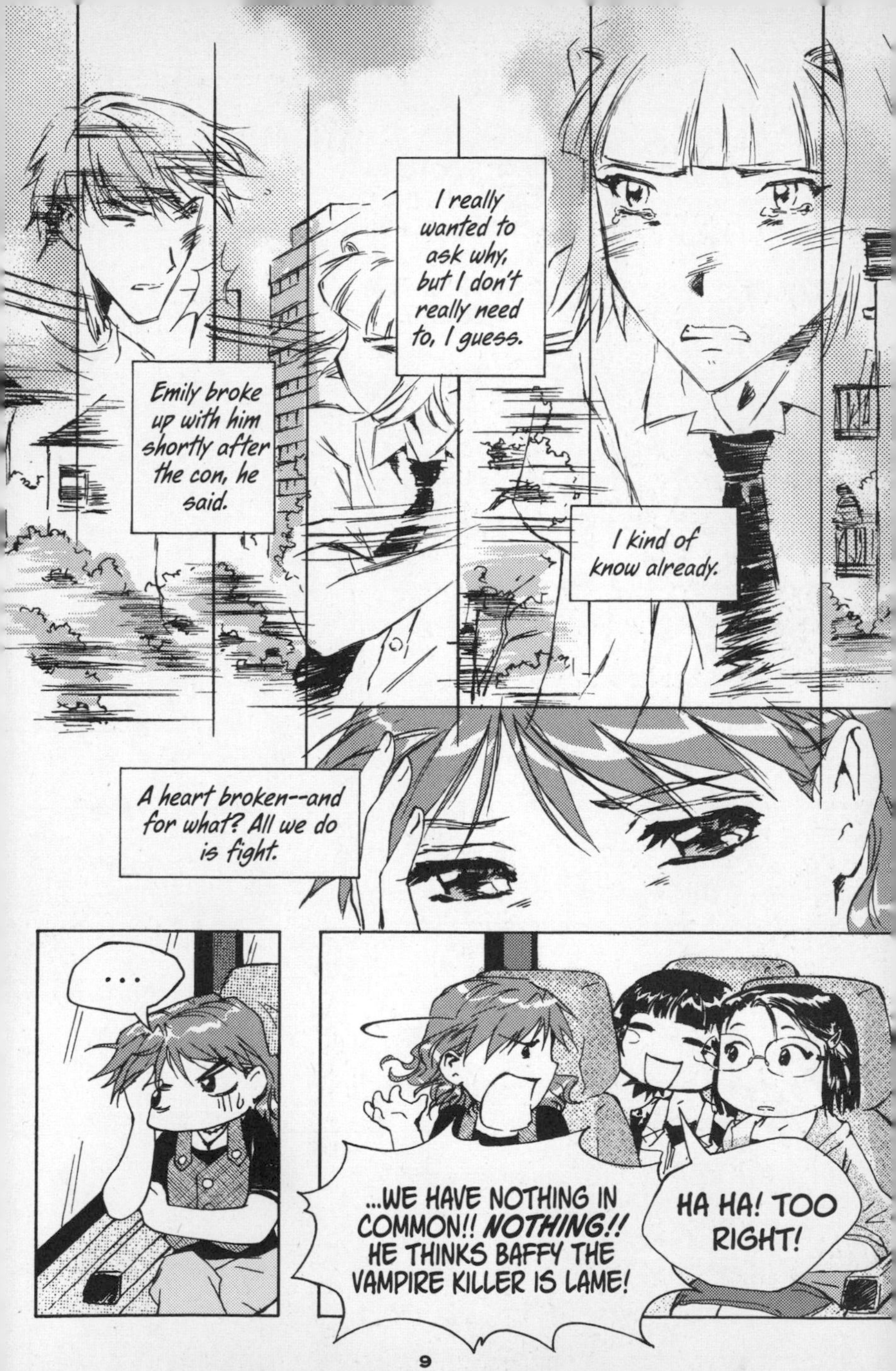
Emily broke up with him shortly after the con, he said.
I really wanted to ask why, but I don't really need to, I guess.
I kind of know already.
A heart broken--and for what? All we do is fight.
...
...WE HAVE NOTHING IN COMMON!! ***NOTHING!!*** HE THINKS BAFFY THE VAMPIRE KILLER IS LAME!
HA HA! TOO RIGHT!

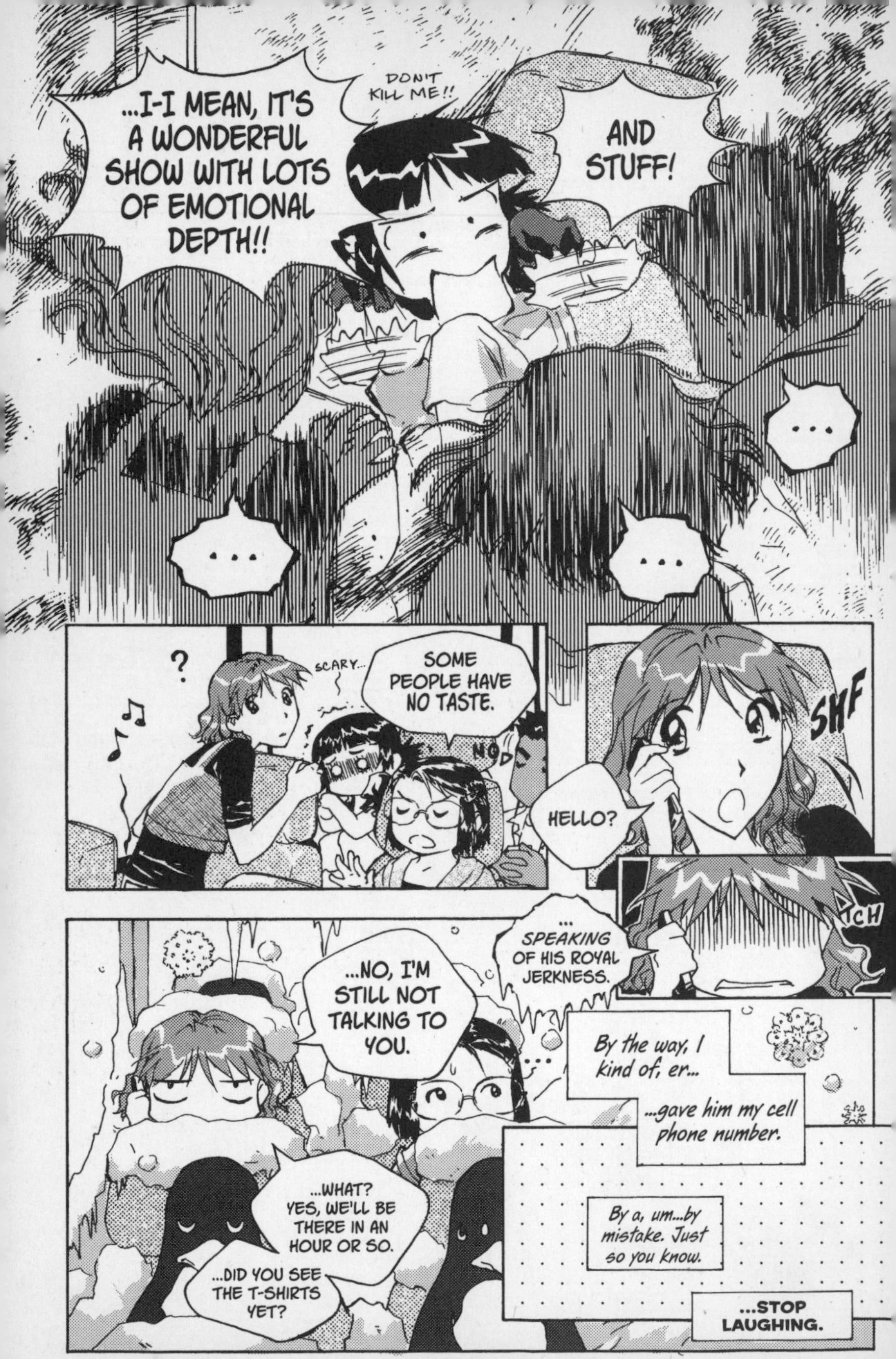

...I-I MEAN, IT'S A WONDERFUL SHOW WITH LOTS OF EMOTIONAL DEPTH!!
DON'T KILL ME!!
AND STUFF!
...
...
...
?
SCARY...
SOME PEOPLE HAVE NO TASTE.
NOD
SHF
HELLO?
...NO, I'M STILL NOT TALKING TO YOU.
... SPEAKING OF HIS ROYAL JERKNESS.
By the way, I kind of, er...
...gave him my cell phone number.
...WHAT? YES, WE'LL BE THERE IN AN HOUR OR SO.
...DID YOU SEE THE T-SHIRTS YET?
By a, um...by mistake. Just so you know.
...STOP LAUGHING.

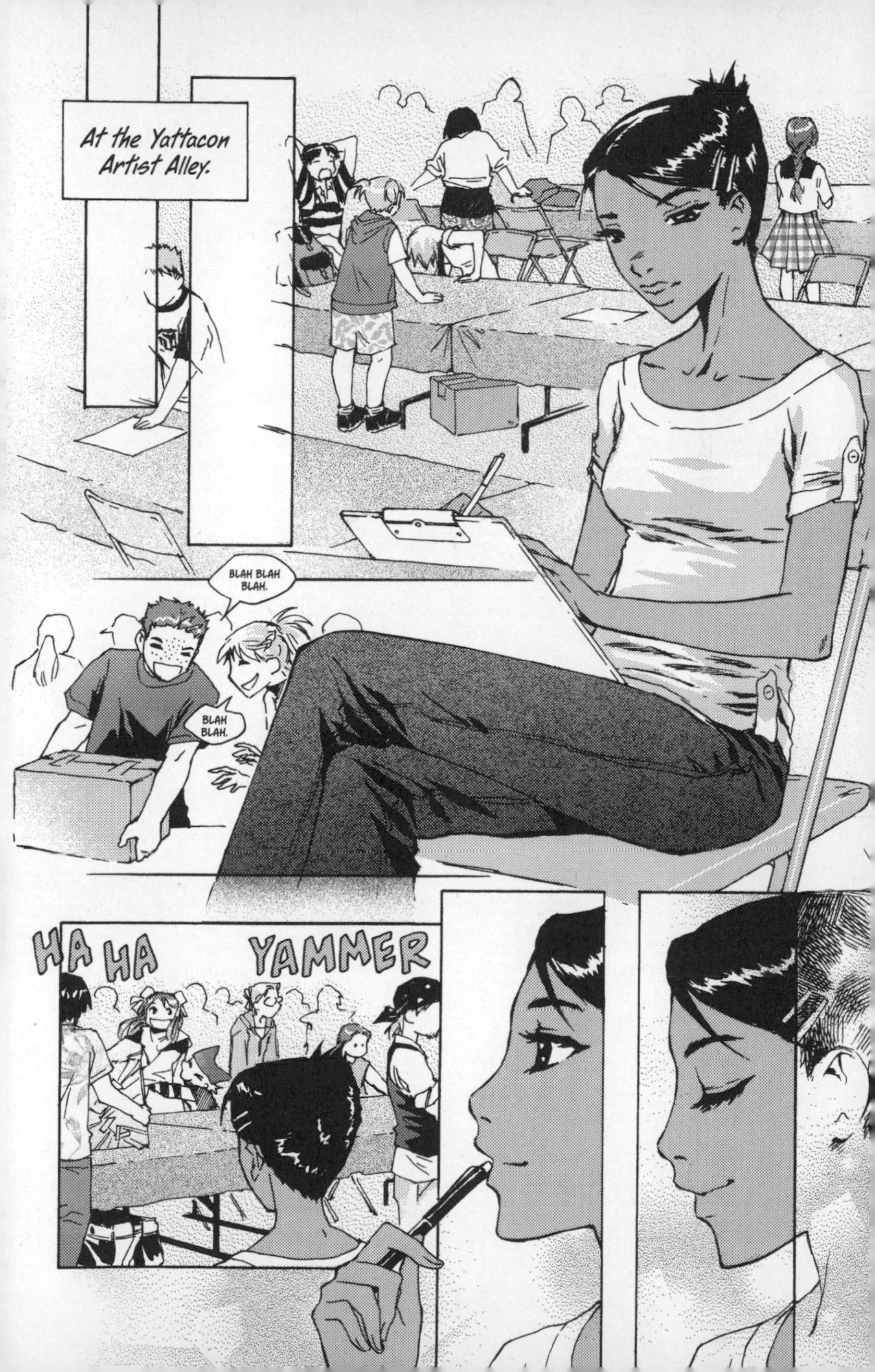
At the Yattacon Artist Alley.
BLAH BLAH BLAH.
BLAH BLAH.
HA HA
YAMMER

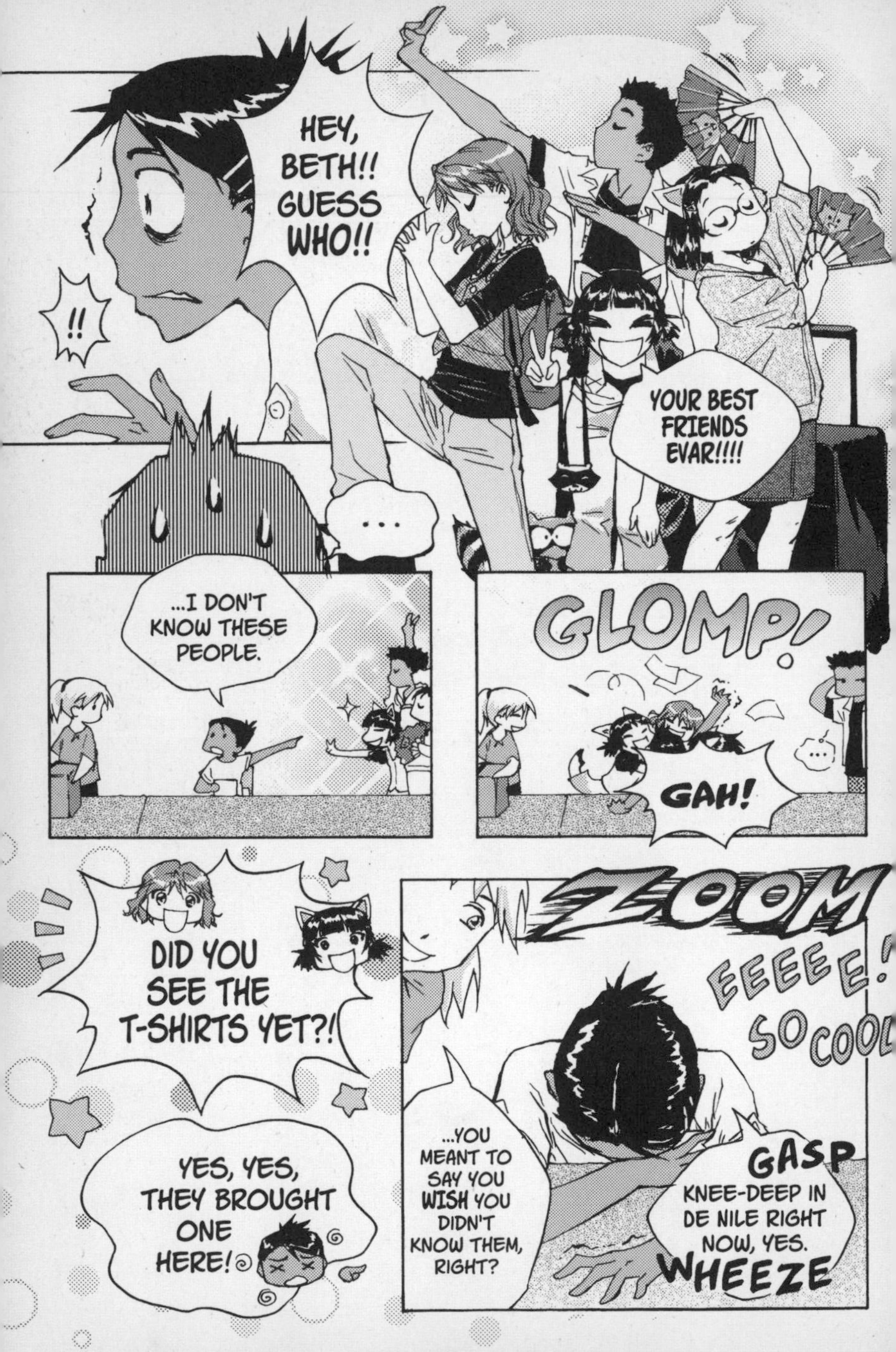

!!
HEY, BETH!! GUESS WHO!!
YOUR BEST FRIENDS EVAR!!!!
...
...I DON'T KNOW THESE PEOPLE.
GLOMP!
...
GAH!
DID YOU SEE THE T-SHIRTS YET?!
YES, YES, THEY BROUGHT ONE HERE!
ZOOM
EEEEE!
SO COOL
...YOU MEANT TO SAY YOU WISH YOU DIDN'T KNOW THEM, RIGHT?
GASP
KNEE-DEEP IN DE NILE RIGHT NOW, YES.
WHEEZE

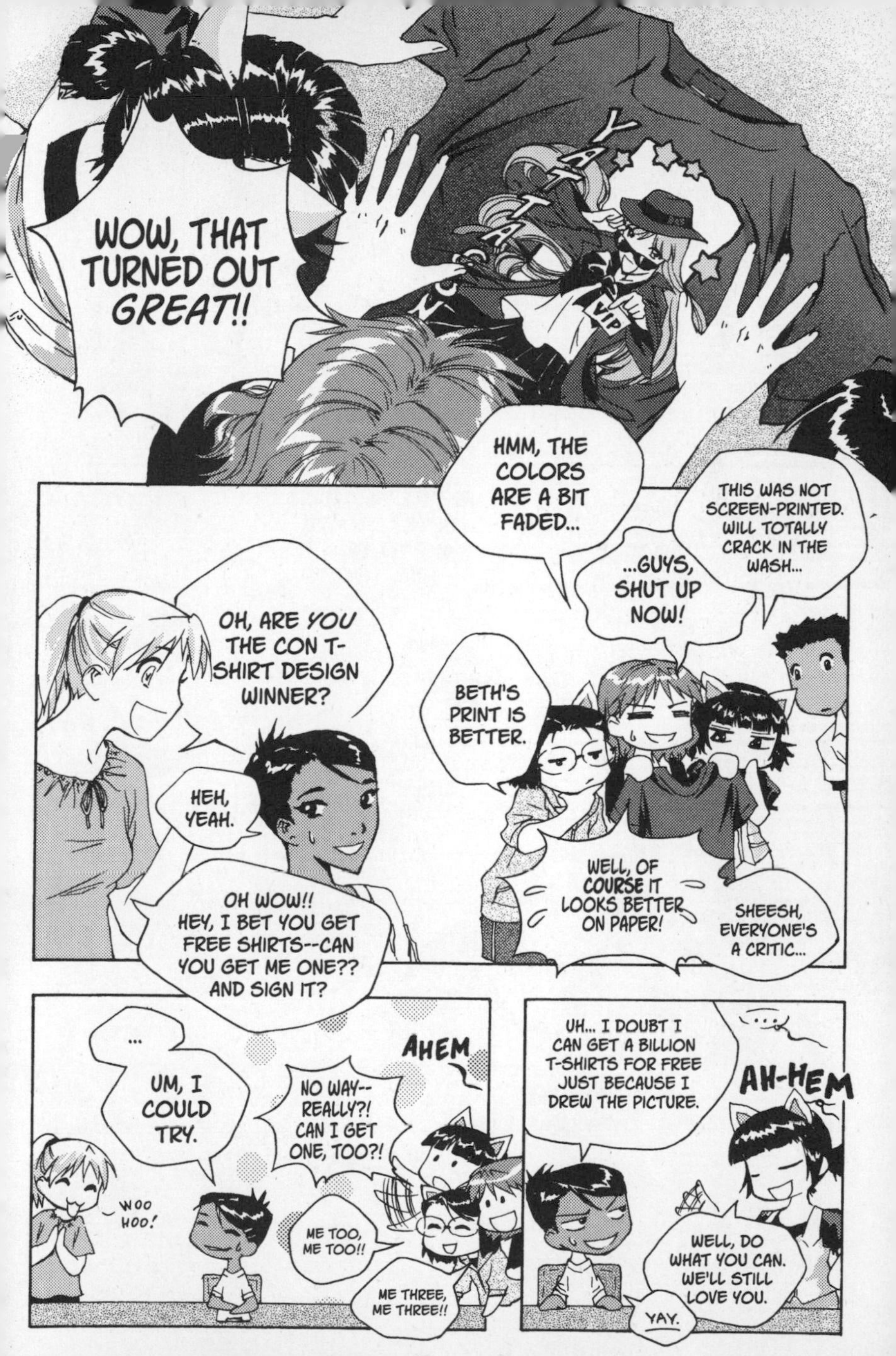
WOW, THAT TURNED OUT GREAT!!
VIP
HMM, THE COLORS ARE A BIT FADED...
OH, ARE YOU THE CON T-SHIRT DESIGN WINNER?
HEH, YEAH.
OH WOW!! HEY, I BET YOU GET FREE SHIRTS--CAN YOU GET ME ONE?? AND SIGN IT?
THIS WAS NOT SCREEN-PRINTED. WILL TOTALLY CRACK IN THE WASH...
...GUYS, SHUT UP NOW!
BETH'S PRINT IS BETTER.
WELL, OF COURSE IT LOOKS BETTER ON PAPER!
SHEESH, EVERYONE'S A CRITIC...
...
UM, I COULD TRY.
WOO HOO!
NO WAY-- REALLY?! CAN I GET ONE, TOO?!
AHEM
ME TOO, ME TOO!!
ME THREE, ME THREE!!
UH... I DOUBT I CAN GET A BILLION T-SHIRTS FOR FREE JUST BECAUSE I DREW THE PICTURE.
...
AH-HEM
WELL, DO WHAT YOU CAN. WE'LL STILL LOVE YOU.
YAY.

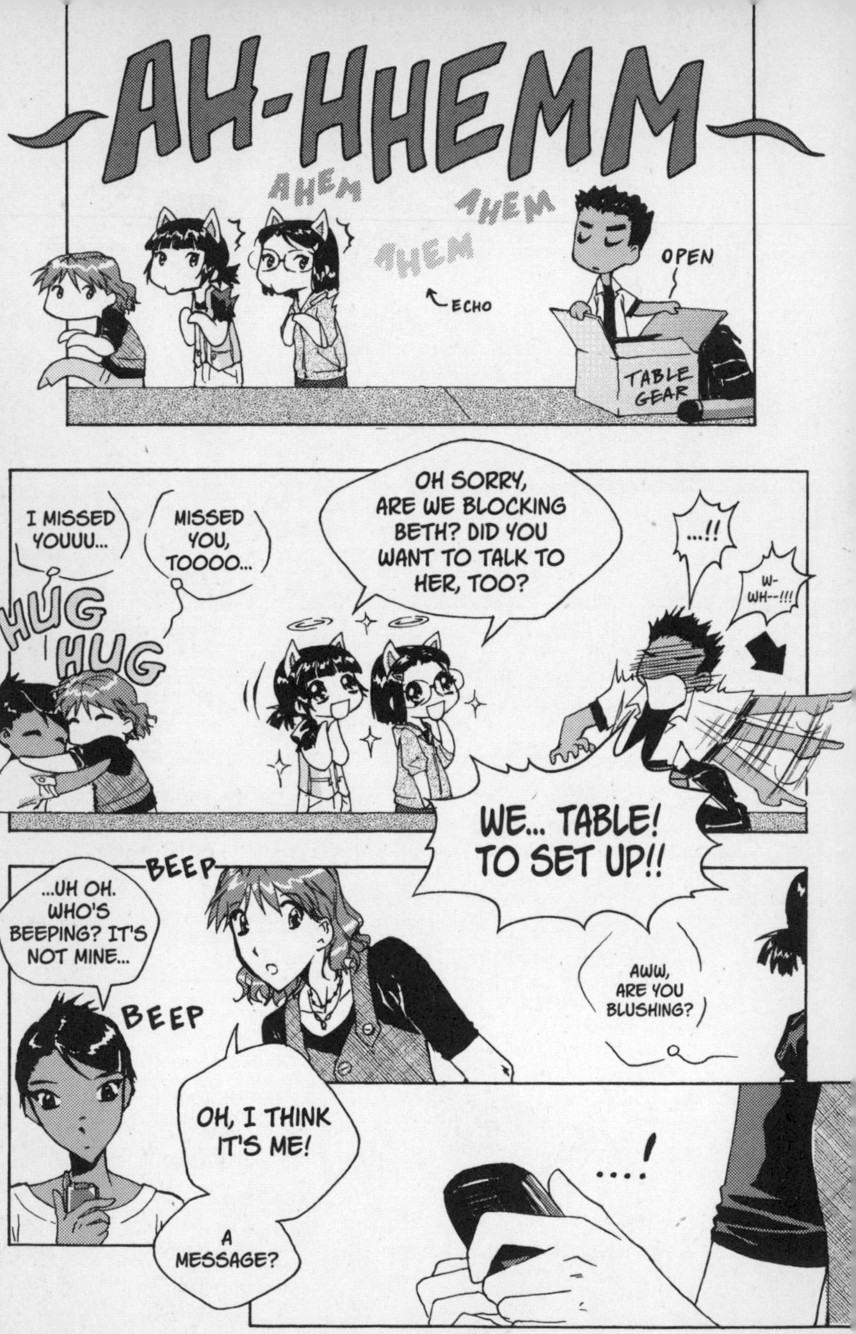
AH-HHEMM
AHEM
AHEM
AHEM
ECHO
OPEN
TABLE GEAR
I MISSED YOUUU...
MISSED YOU, TOOOO...
HUG HUG
OH SORRY, ARE WE BLOCKING BETH? DID YOU WANT TO TALK TO HER, TOO?
...!!
W- WH--!!!
WE... TABLE! TO SET UP!!
BEEP
...UH OH. WHO'S BEEPING? IT'S NOT MINE...
BEEP
AWW, ARE YOU BLUSHING?
OH, I THINK IT'S ME!
A MESSAGE?
...!

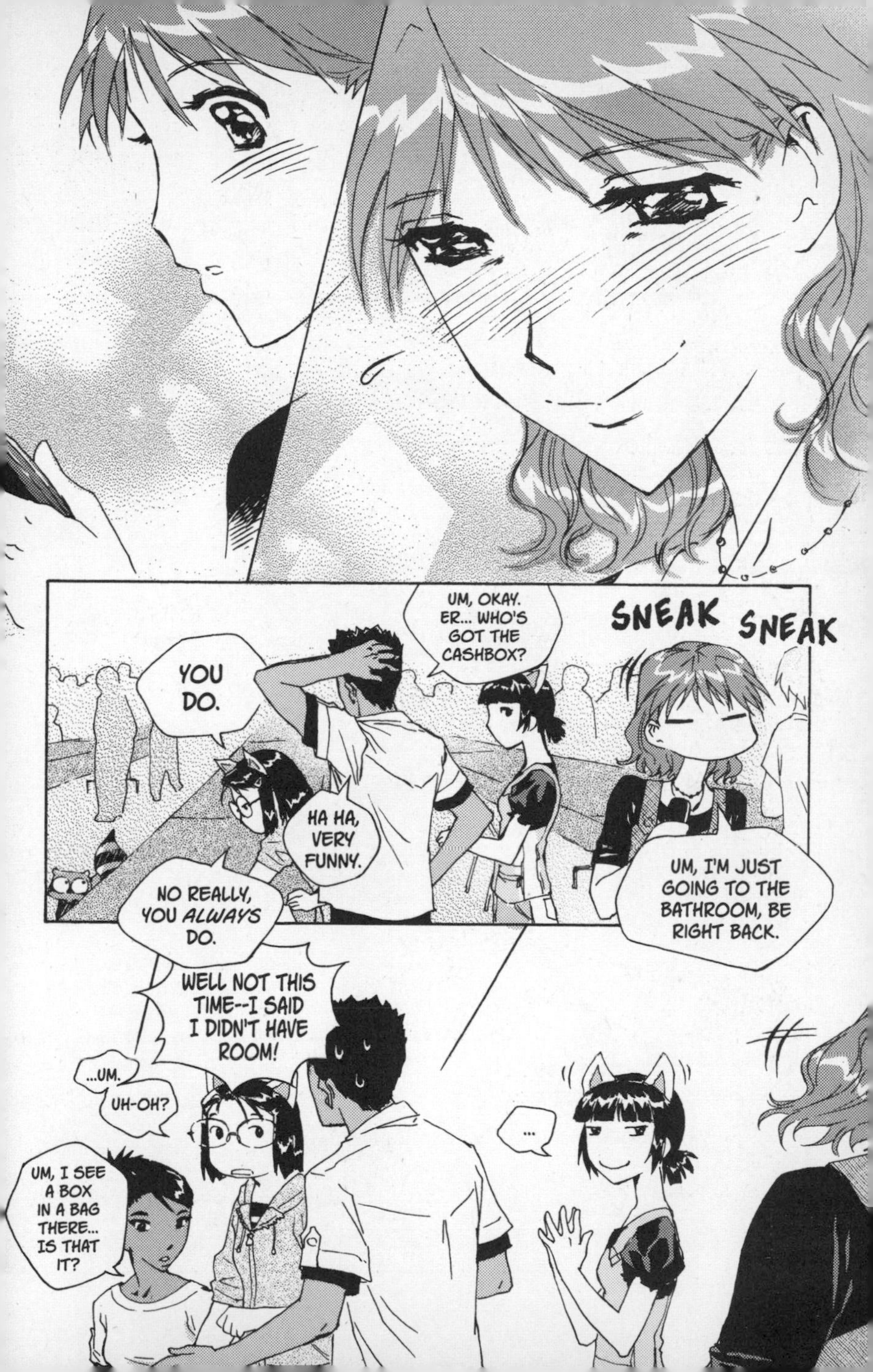
UM, OKAY. ER... WHO'S GOT THE CASHBOX?
YOU DO.
HA HA, VERY FUNNY.
NO REALLY, YOU *ALWAYS* DO.
SNEAK SNEAK
UM, I'M JUST GOING TO THE BATHROOM, BE RIGHT BACK.
WELL NOT THIS TIME--I SAID I DIDN'T HAVE ROOM!
...UM.
UH-OH?
...
UM, I SEE A BOX IN A BAG THERE... IS THAT IT?

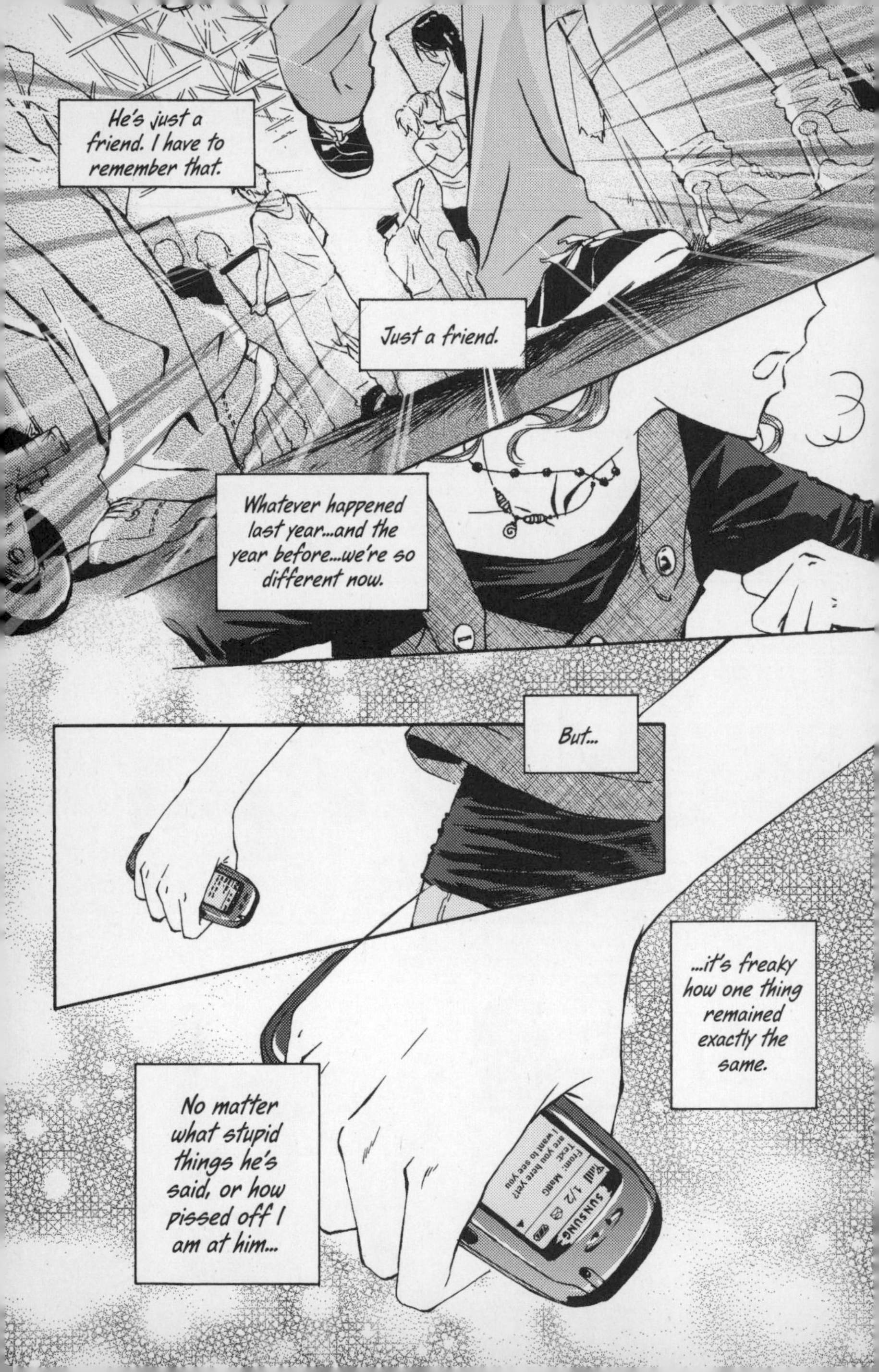
He's just a friend. I have to remember that.
Just a friend.
Whatever happened last year...and the year before...we're so different now.
But...
No matter what stupid things he's said, or how pissed off I am at him...
SUNSUNG
1/2
From: Matt
Text: are you here yet? I want to see you
...it's freaky how one thing remained exactly the same.

SUNSUNG
1/2
From: MattG
Text:
are you here yet?
i want to see you
i want to see you
All it takes is this.
A defenseless admission like that, and I lose myself, head over heels for this guy I still barely know.
P.S. Dear Self-- STOP RUNNING, YOU IDIOT.

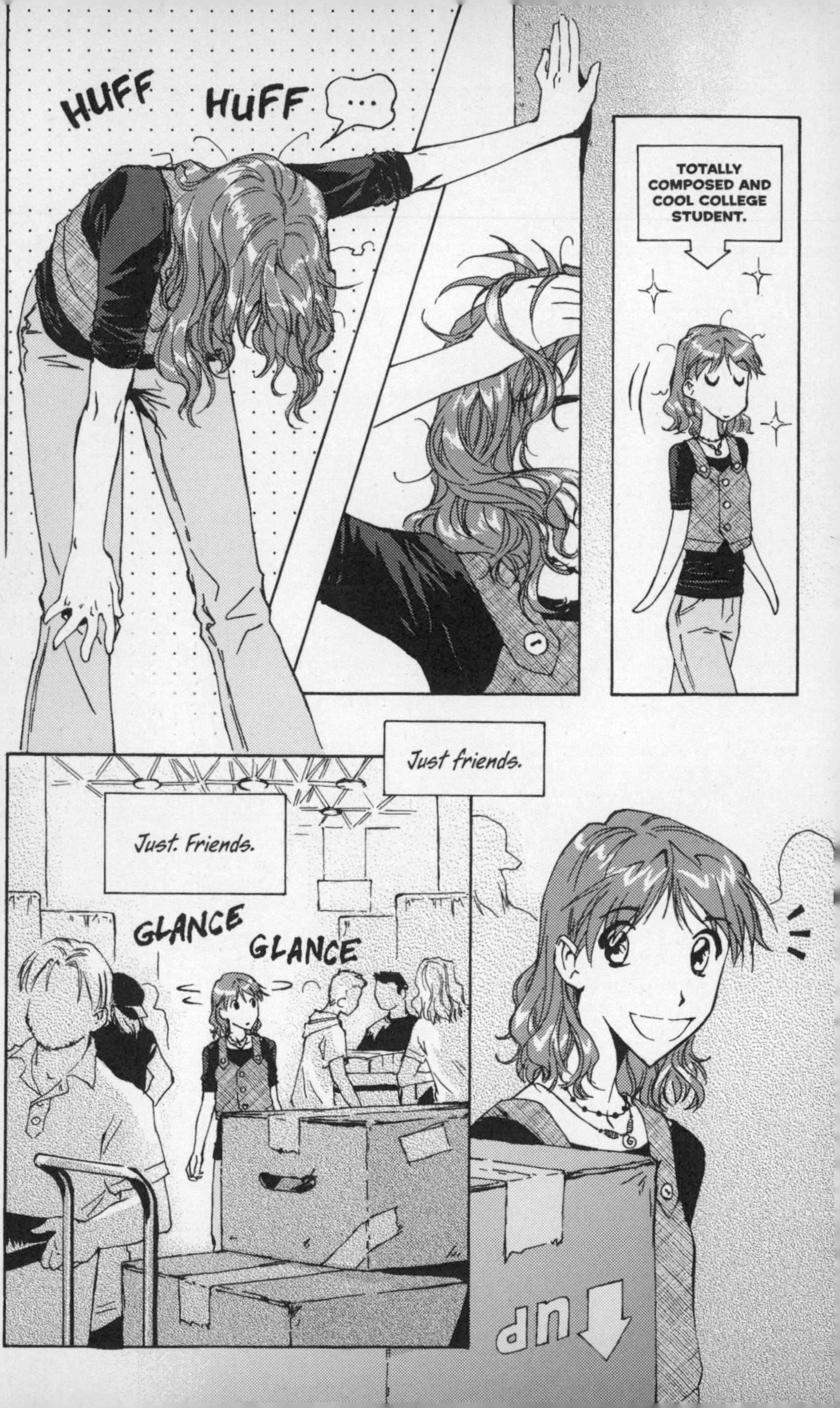
HUFF HUFF
...
TOTALLY COMPOSED AND COOL COLLEGE STUDENT.
Just. Friends.
GLANCE
GLANCE
Just friends.

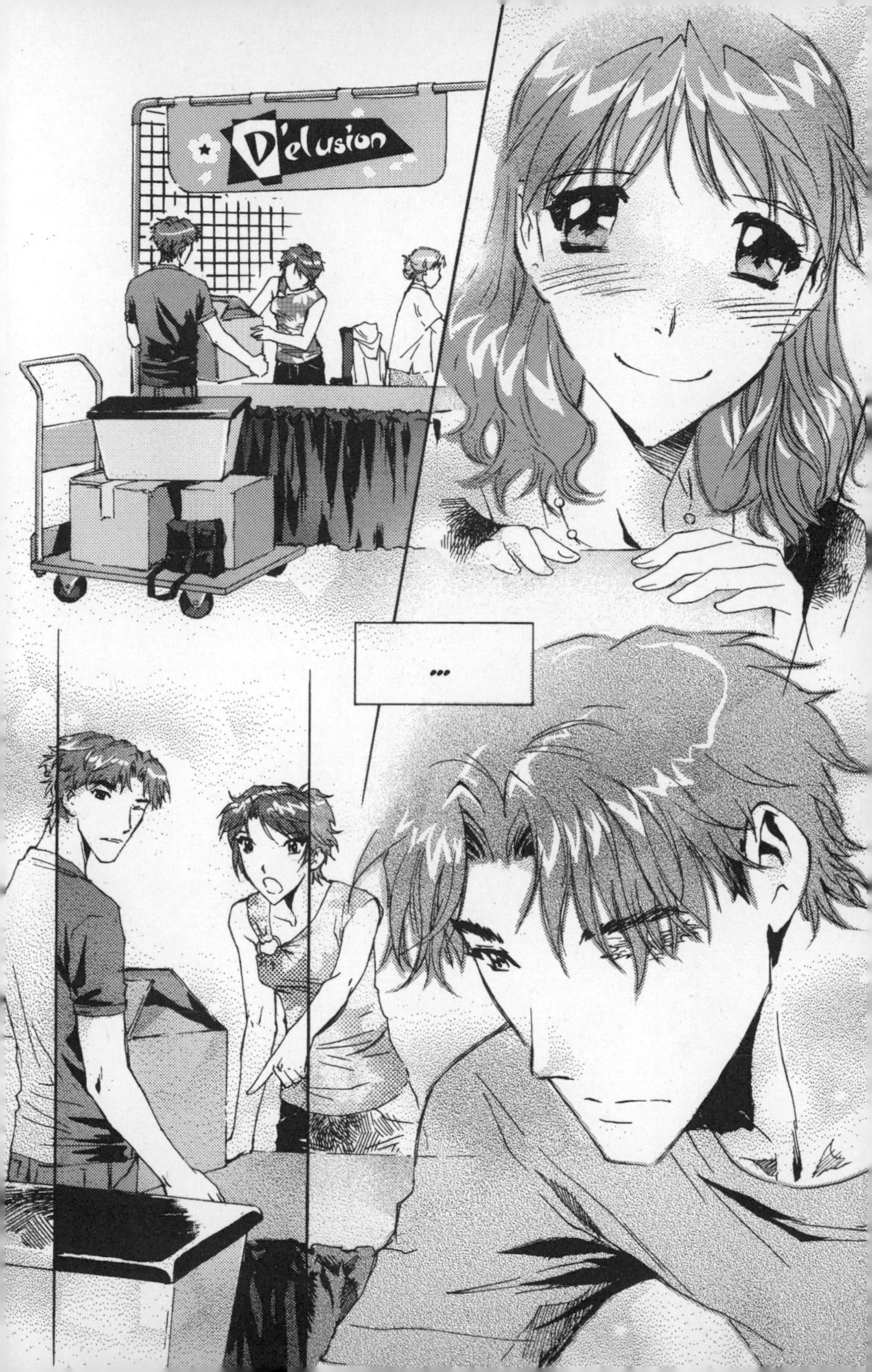
D'elusion
...

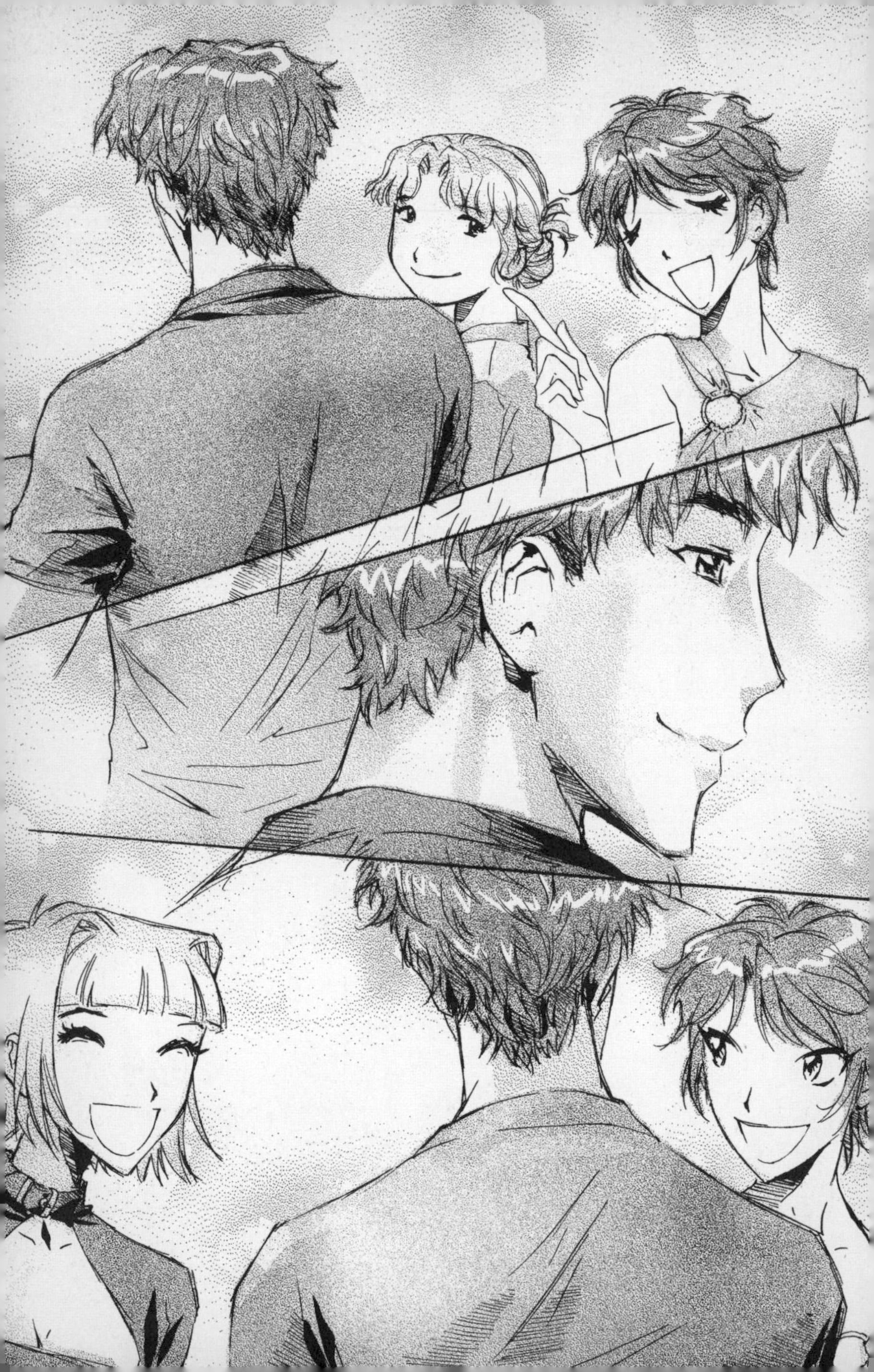

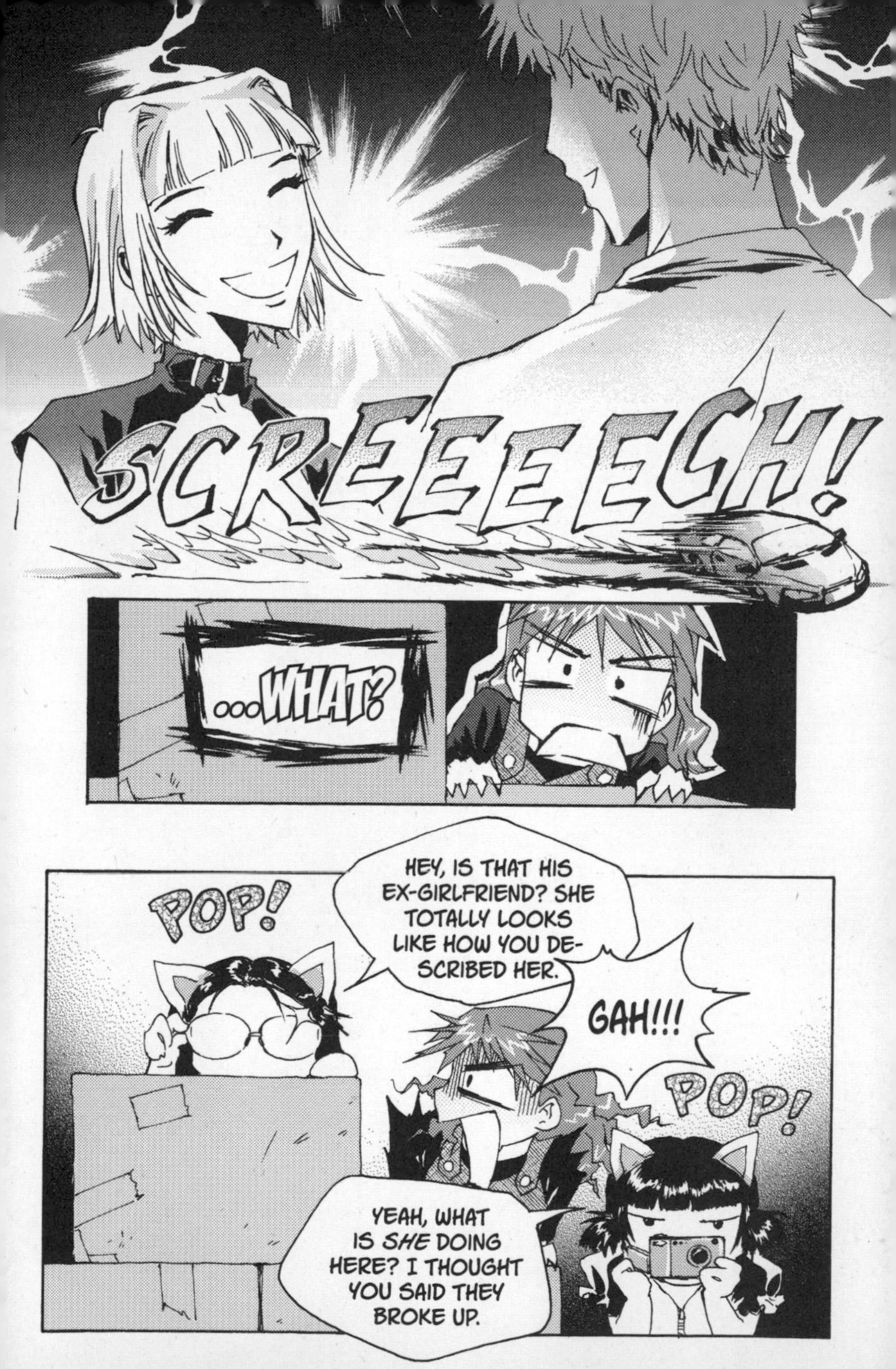
SCREEECH!
...WHAT?
POP!
HEY, IS THAT HIS EX-GIRLFRIEND? SHE TOTALLY LOOKS LIKE HOW YOU DE-SCRIBED HER.
GAH!!!
POP!
YEAH, WHAT IS *SHE* DOING HERE? I THOUGHT YOU SAID THEY BROKE UP.

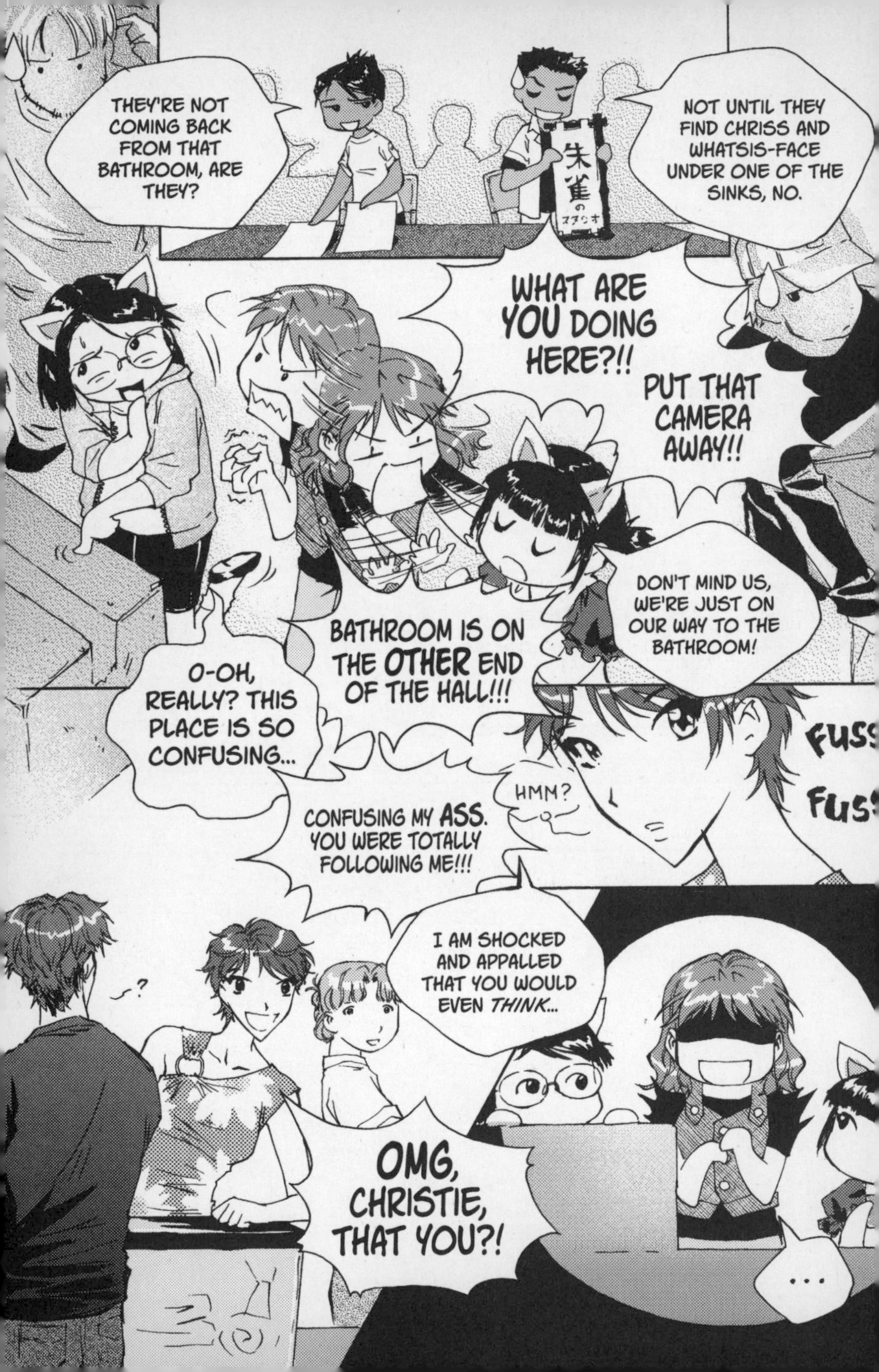
THEY'RE NOT COMING BACK FROM THAT BATHROOM, ARE THEY?
NOT UNTIL THEY FIND CHRISS AND WHATSIS-FACE UNDER ONE OF THE SINKS, NO.
WHAT ARE YOU DOING HERE?!!
PUT THAT CAMERA AWAY!!
DON'T MIND US, WE'RE JUST ON OUR WAY TO THE BATHROOM!
BATHROOM IS ON THE OTHER END OF THE HALL!!!
O-OH, REALLY? THIS PLACE IS SO CONFUSING...
HMM?
FUSS
FUSS
CONFUSING MY ASS. YOU WERE TOTALLY FOLLOWING ME!!!
I AM SHOCKED AND APPALLED THAT YOU WOULD EVEN *THINK*...
OMG, CHRISTIE, THAT YOU?!
...

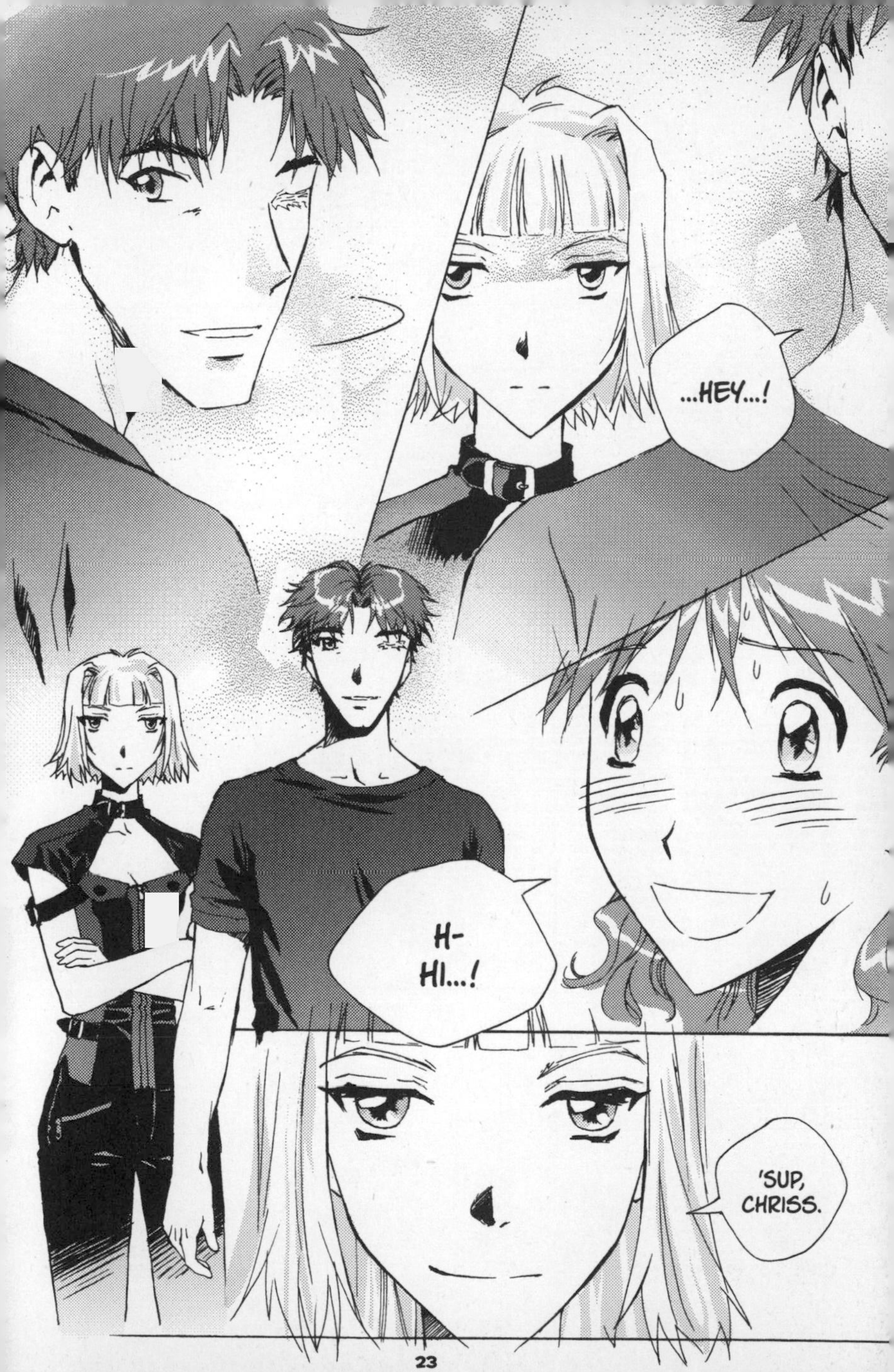
...HEY...!
H-
HI...!
'SUP,
CHRISS.

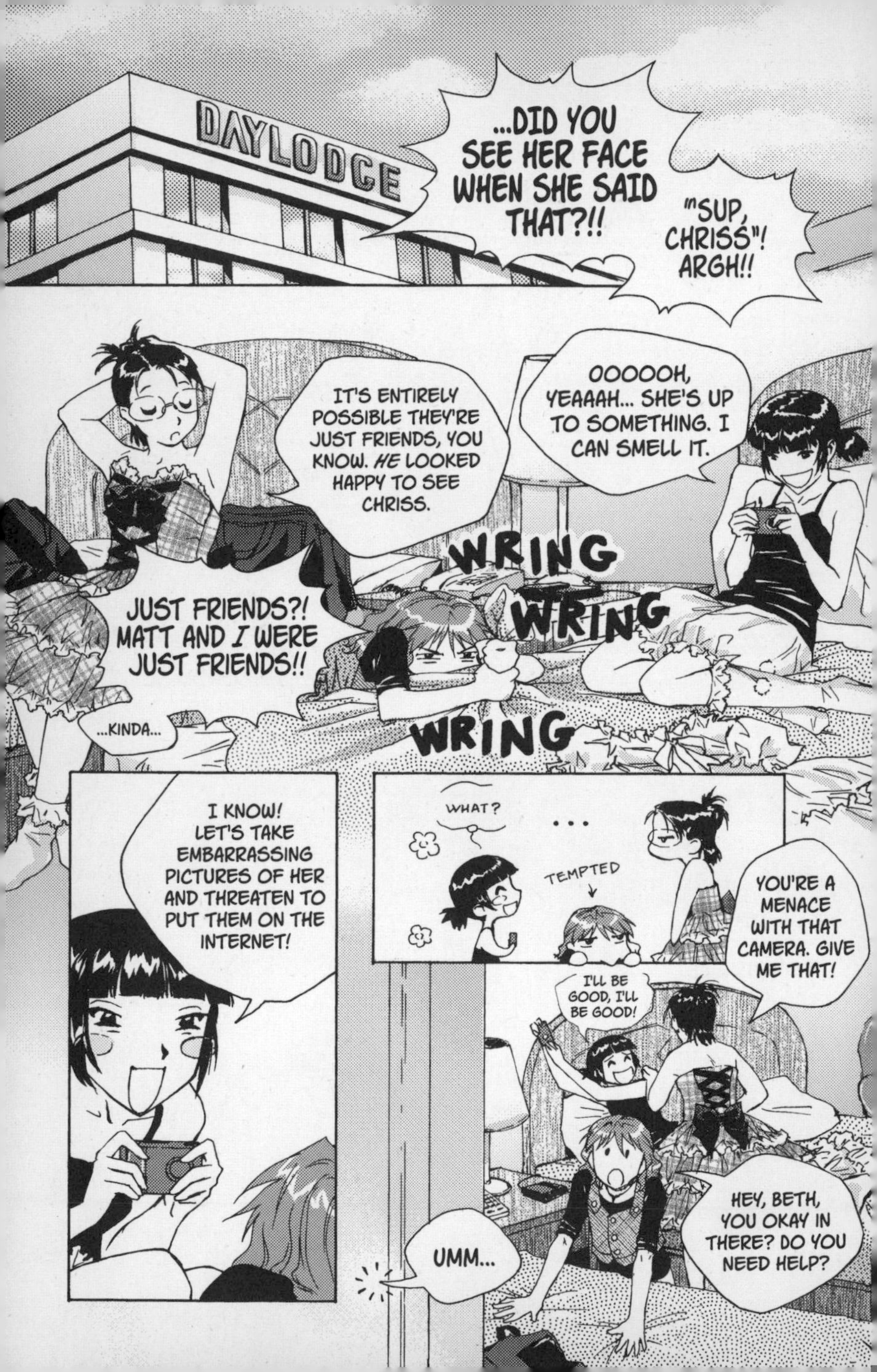
DAYLODGE
...DID YOU SEE HER FACE WHEN SHE SAID THAT?!!
"SUP, CHRISS"! ARGH!!
IT'S ENTIRELY POSSIBLE THEY'RE JUST FRIENDS, YOU KNOW. *HE* LOOKED HAPPY TO SEE CHRISS.
OOOOOH, YEAAAH... SHE'S UP TO SOMETHING. I CAN SMELL IT.
WRING
JUST FRIENDS?! MATT AND *I* WERE JUST FRIENDS!!
WRING
...KINDA...
WRING
I KNOW! LET'S TAKE EMBARRASSING PICTURES OF HER AND THREATEN TO PUT THEM ON THE INTERNET!
WHAT?
...
TEMPTED
YOU'RE A MENACE WITH THAT CAMERA. GIVE ME THAT!
I'LL BE GOOD, I'LL BE GOOD!
HEY, BETH, YOU OKAY IN THERE? DO YOU NEED HELP?
UMM...

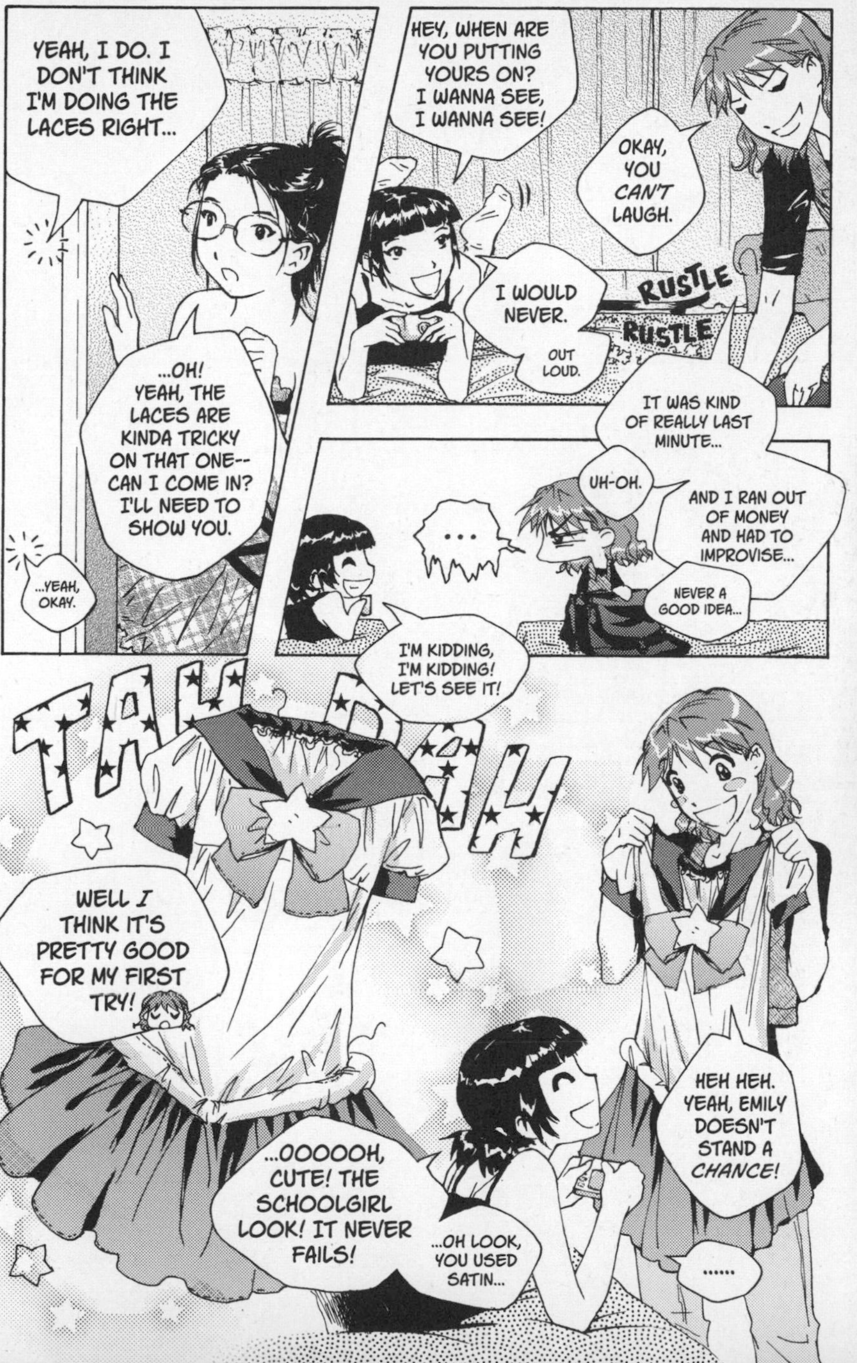
YEAH, I DO. I DON'T THINK I'M DOING THE LACES RIGHT...
...OH! YEAH, THE LACES ARE KINDA TRICKY ON THAT ONE-- CAN I COME IN? I'LL NEED TO SHOW YOU.
...YEAH, OKAY.
HEY, WHEN ARE YOU PUTTING YOURS ON? I WANNA SEE, I WANNA SEE!
OKAY, YOU *CAN'T* LAUGH.
I WOULD NEVER.
OUT LOUD.
RUSTLE
RUSTLE
IT WAS KIND OF REALLY LAST MINUTE...
UH-OH.
AND I RAN OUT OF MONEY AND HAD TO IMPROVISE...
...
NEVER A GOOD IDEA...
I'M KIDDING, I'M KIDDING! LET'S SEE IT!
TAH DAH
WELL *I* THINK IT'S PRETTY GOOD FOR MY FIRST TRY!
HEH HEH. YEAH, EMILY DOESN'T STAND A *CHANCE*!
...OOOOOH, CUTE! THE SCHOOLGIRL LOOK! IT NEVER FAILS!
...OH LOOK, YOU USED SATIN...
......

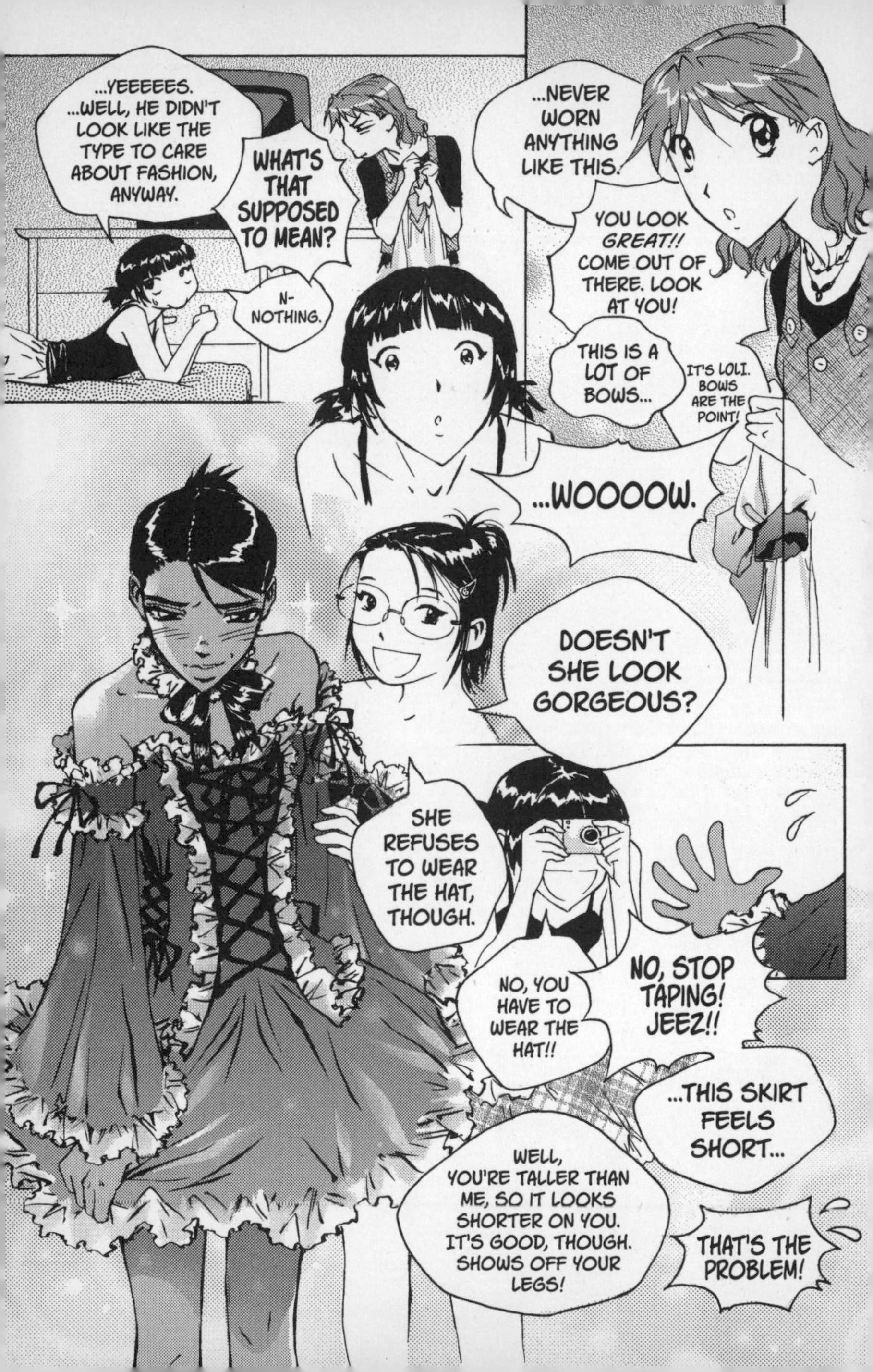
...YEEEEES. ...WELL, HE DIDN'T LOOK LIKE THE TYPE TO CARE ABOUT FASHION, ANYWAY.
WHAT'S THAT SUPPOSED TO MEAN?
N-NOTHING.
...NEVER WORN ANYTHING LIKE THIS.
YOU LOOK *GREAT!!* COME OUT OF THERE. LOOK AT YOU!
THIS IS A LOT OF BOWS...
IT'S LOLI. BOWS ARE THE POINT!
...WOOOOW.
DOESN'T SHE LOOK GORGEOUS?
SHE REFUSES TO WEAR THE HAT, THOUGH.
NO, YOU HAVE TO WEAR THE HAT!!
NO, STOP TAPING! JEEZ!!
...THIS SKIRT FEELS SHORT...
WELL, YOU'RE TALLER THAN ME, SO IT LOOKS SHORTER ON YOU. IT'S GOOD, THOUGH. SHOWS OFF YOUR LEGS!
THAT'S THE PROBLEM!

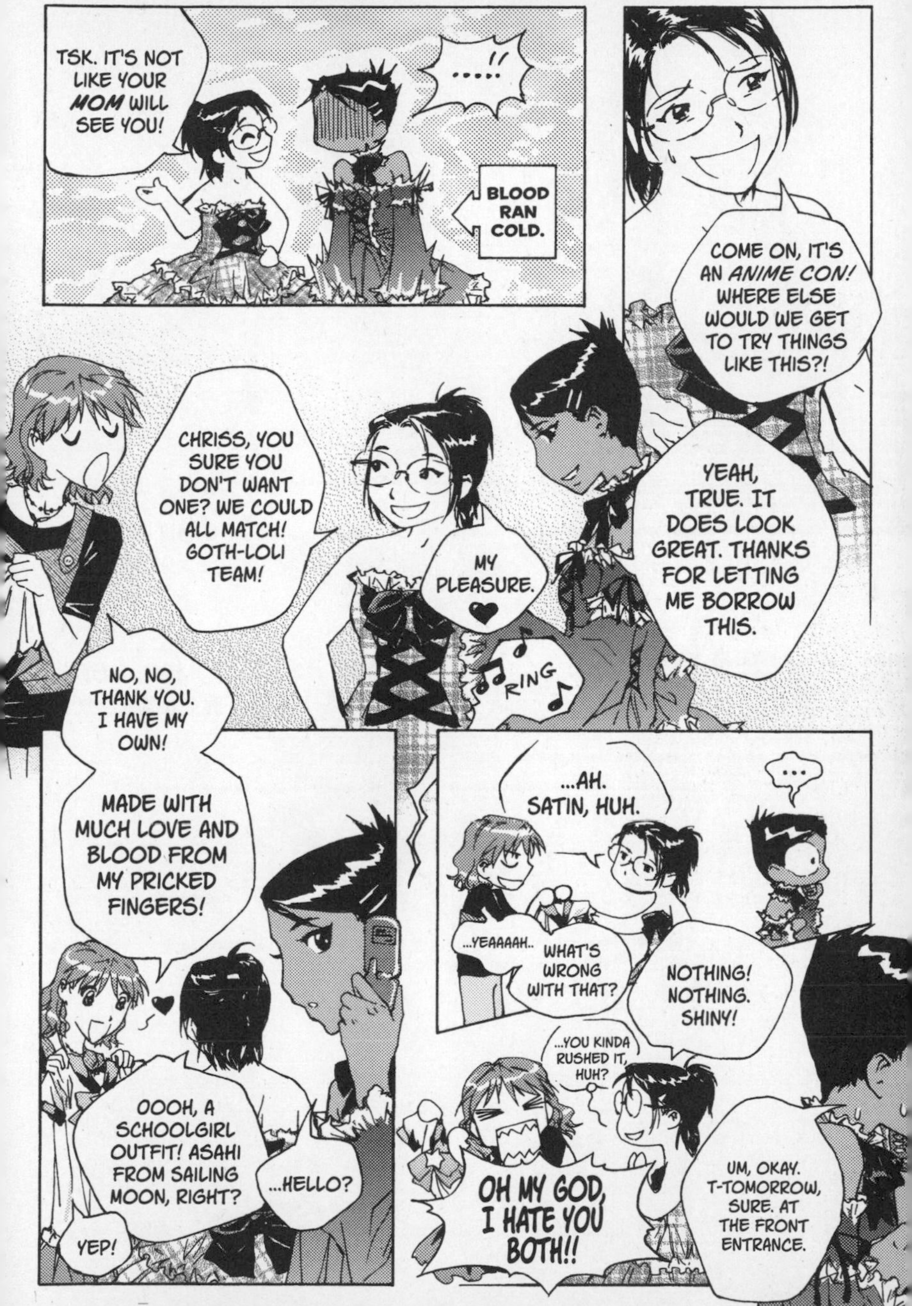
TSK. IT'S NOT LIKE YOUR *MOM* WILL SEE YOU!
....!!
BLOOD RAN COLD.
COME ON, IT'S AN *ANIME CON!* WHERE ELSE WOULD WE GET TO TRY THINGS LIKE THIS?!
CHRISS, YOU SURE YOU DON'T WANT ONE? WE COULD ALL MATCH! GOTH-LOLI TEAM!
MY PLEASURE. ♥
YEAH, TRUE. IT DOES LOOK GREAT. THANKS FOR LETTING ME BORROW THIS.
RING
NO, NO, THANK YOU. I HAVE MY OWN!
MADE WITH MUCH LOVE AND BLOOD FROM MY PRICKED FINGERS!
♥
OOOH, A SCHOOLGIRL OUTFIT! ASAHI FROM SAILING MOON, RIGHT?
YEP!
...HELLO?
...AH. SATIN, HUH.
...
...YEAAAAH..
WHAT'S WRONG WITH THAT?
NOTHING! NOTHING. SHINY!
...YOU KINDA RUSHED IT, HUH?
OH MY GOD, I HATE YOU BOTH!!
UM, OKAY. T-TOMORROW, SURE. AT THE FRONT ENTRANCE.

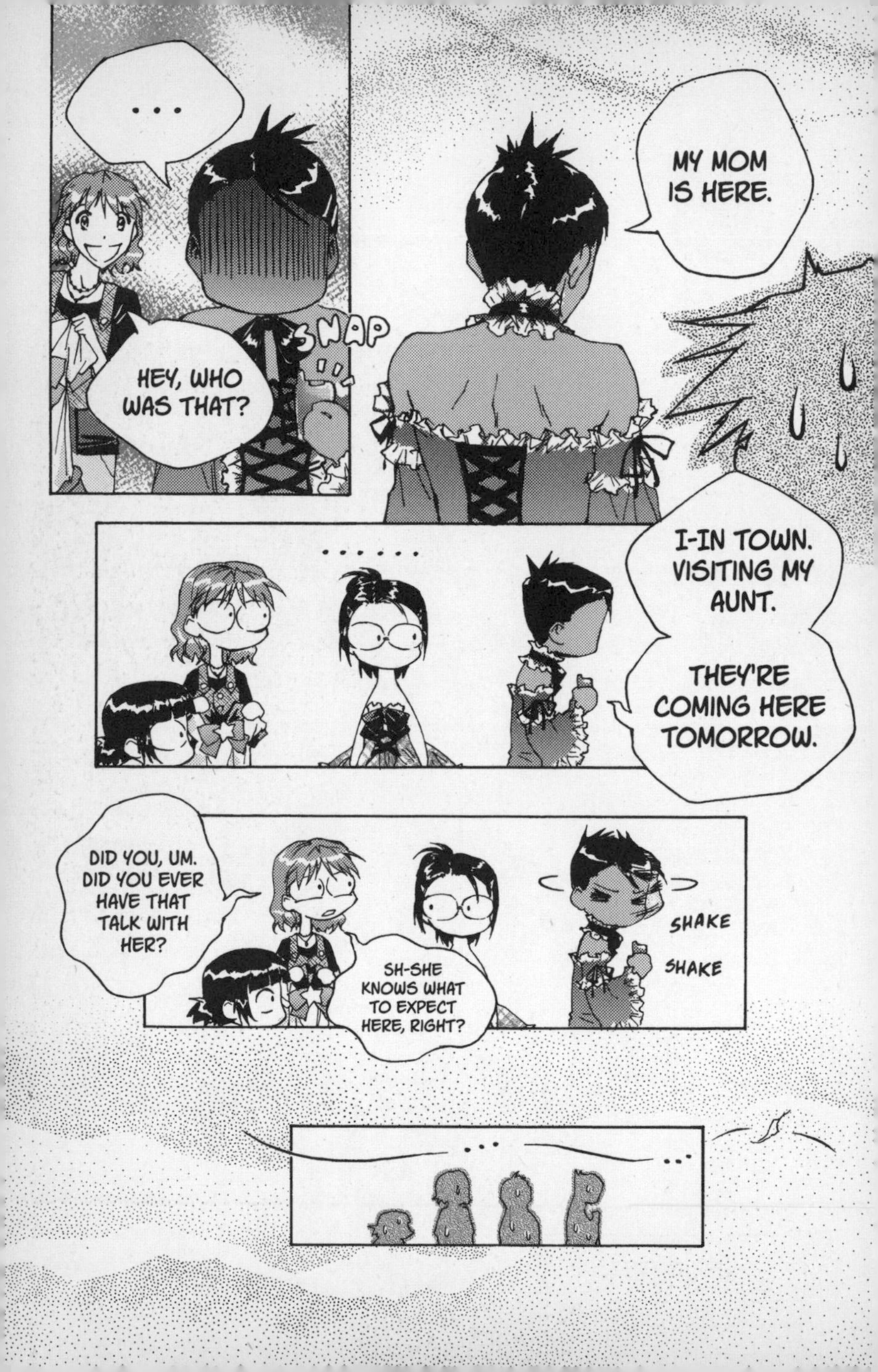
...
HEY, WHO WAS THAT?
SNAP
MY MOM IS HERE.
......
I-IN TOWN. VISITING MY AUNT.
THEY'RE COMING HERE TOMORROW.
DID YOU, UM. DID YOU EVER HAVE THAT TALK WITH HER?
SH-SHE KNOWS WHAT TO EXPECT HERE, RIGHT?
SHAKE
SHAKE
...
..

CHAPTER 2

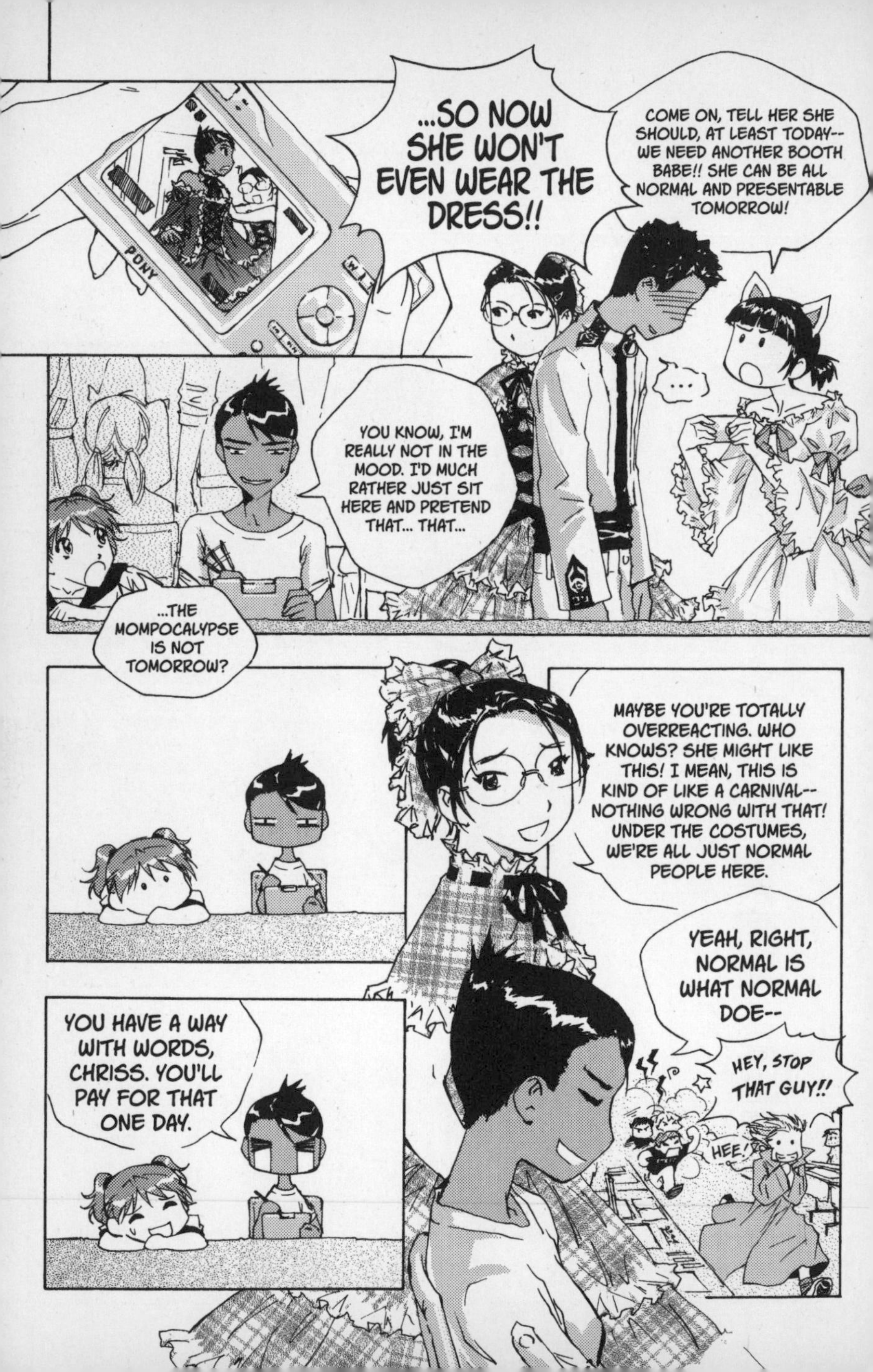
PONY
...SO NOW SHE WON'T EVEN WEAR THE DRESS!!
COME ON, TELL HER SHE SHOULD, AT LEAST TODAY-- WE NEED ANOTHER BOOTH BABE!! SHE CAN BE ALL NORMAL AND PRESENTABLE TOMORROW!
...
YOU KNOW, I'M REALLY NOT IN THE MOOD. I'D MUCH RATHER JUST SIT HERE AND PRETEND THAT... THAT...
...THE MOMPOCALYPSE IS NOT TOMORROW?
MAYBE YOU'RE TOTALLY OVERREACTING. WHO KNOWS? SHE MIGHT LIKE THIS! I MEAN, THIS IS KIND OF LIKE A CARNIVAL-- NOTHING WRONG WITH THAT! UNDER THE COSTUMES, WE'RE ALL JUST NORMAL PEOPLE HERE.
YOU HAVE A WAY WITH WORDS, CHRISS. YOU'LL PAY FOR THAT ONE DAY.
YEAH, RIGHT, NORMAL IS WHAT NORMAL DOE--
HEY, STOP THAT GUY!!
HEE!

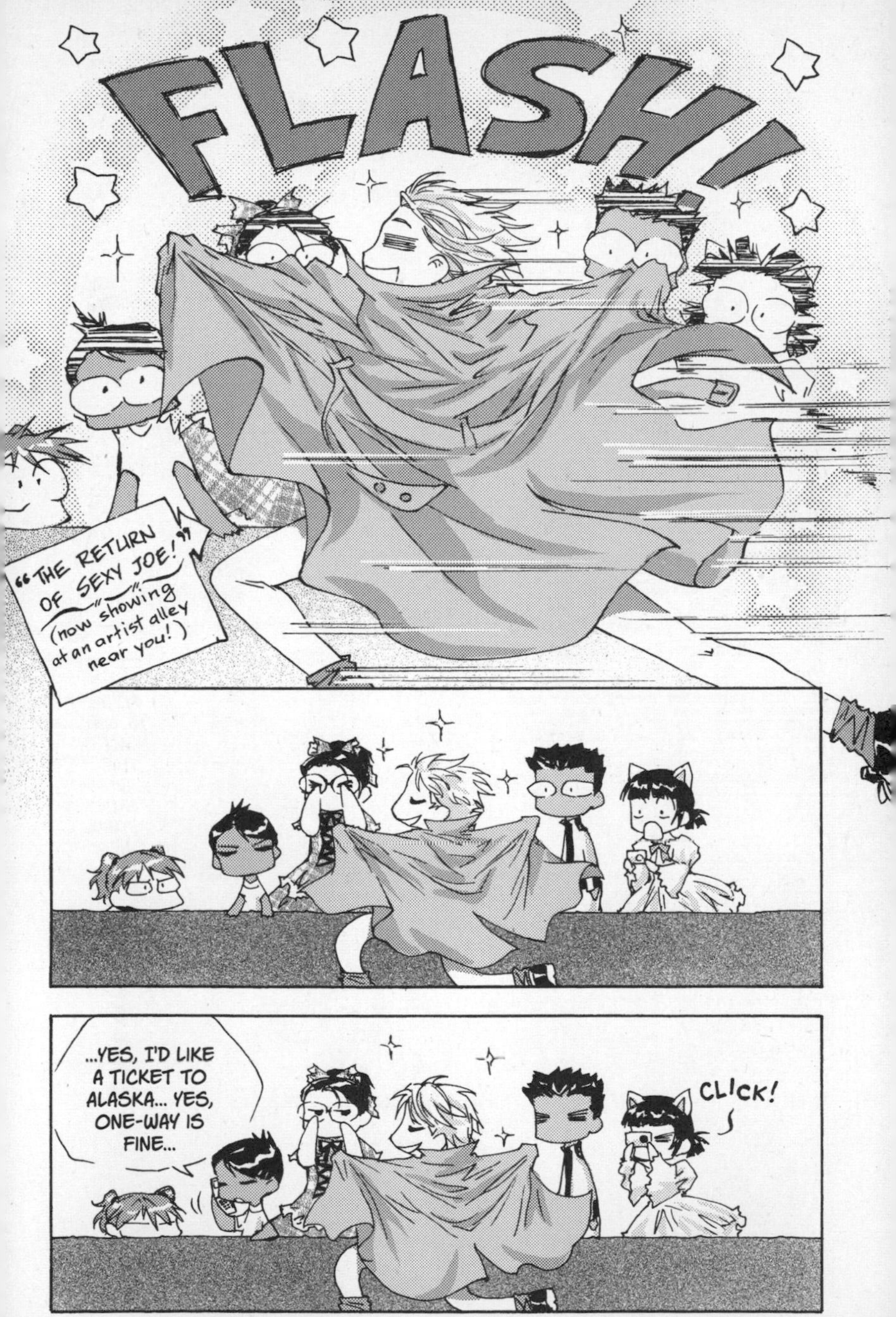
FLASH!
"THE RETURN OF SEXY JOE!" (now showing at an artist alley near you!)
...YES, I'D LIKE A TICKET TO ALASKA... YES, ONE-WAY IS FINE...
CLICK!

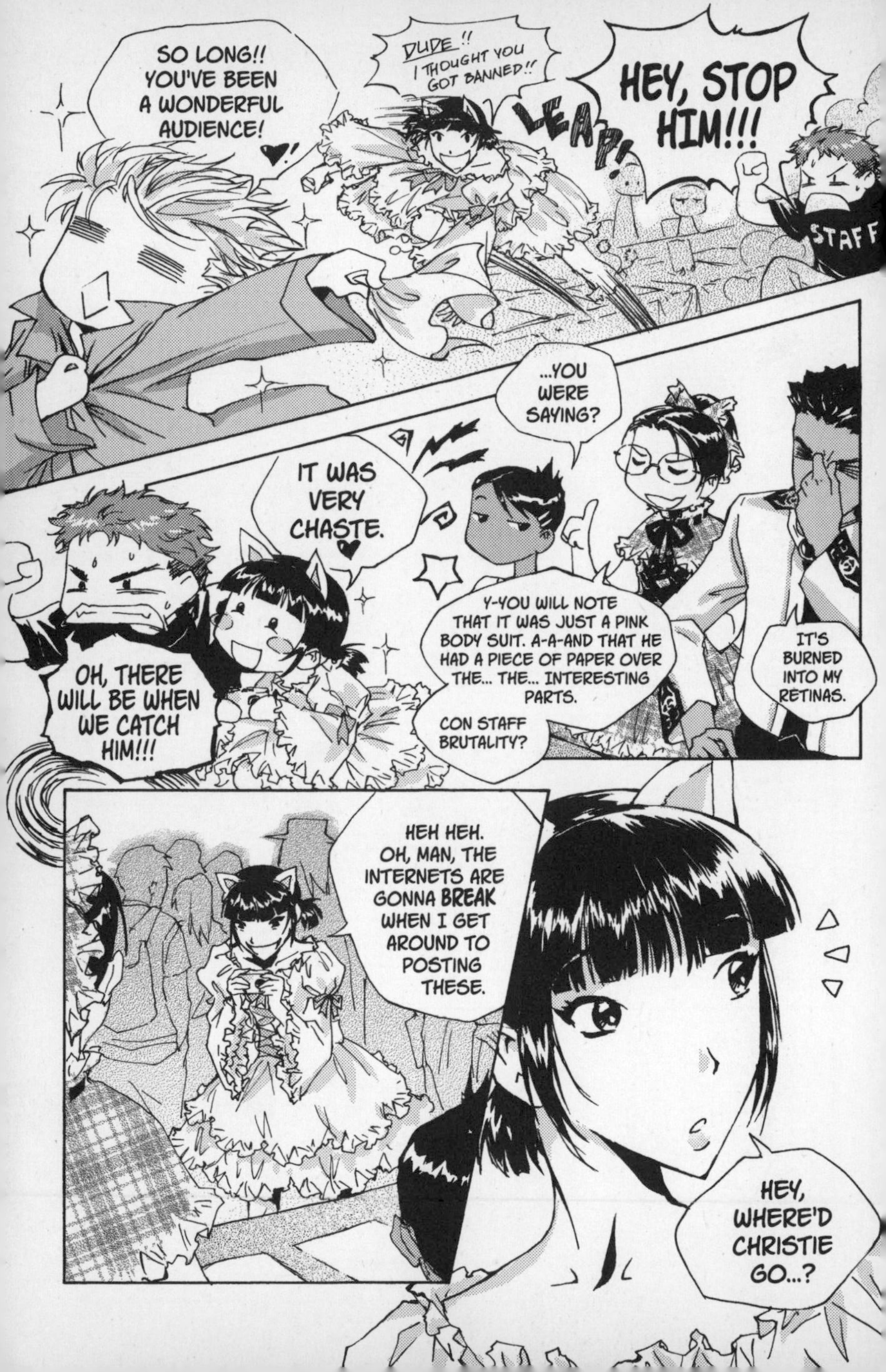
SO LONG!! YOU'VE BEEN A WONDERFUL AUDIENCE!
DUDE!! I THOUGHT YOU GOT BANNED!!
LEAP!
HEY, STOP HIM!!!
STAFF
...YOU WERE SAYING?
IT WAS VERY CHASTE.
OH, THERE WILL BE WHEN WE CATCH HIM!!!
Y-YOU WILL NOTE THAT IT WAS JUST A PINK BODY SUIT. A-A-AND THAT HE HAD A PIECE OF PAPER OVER THE... THE... INTERESTING PARTS.
CON STAFF BRUTALITY?
IT'S BURNED INTO MY RETINAS.
HEH HEH. OH, MAN, THE INTERNETS ARE GONNA BREAK WHEN I GET AROUND TO POSTING THESE.
HEY, WHERE'D CHRISTIE GO...?

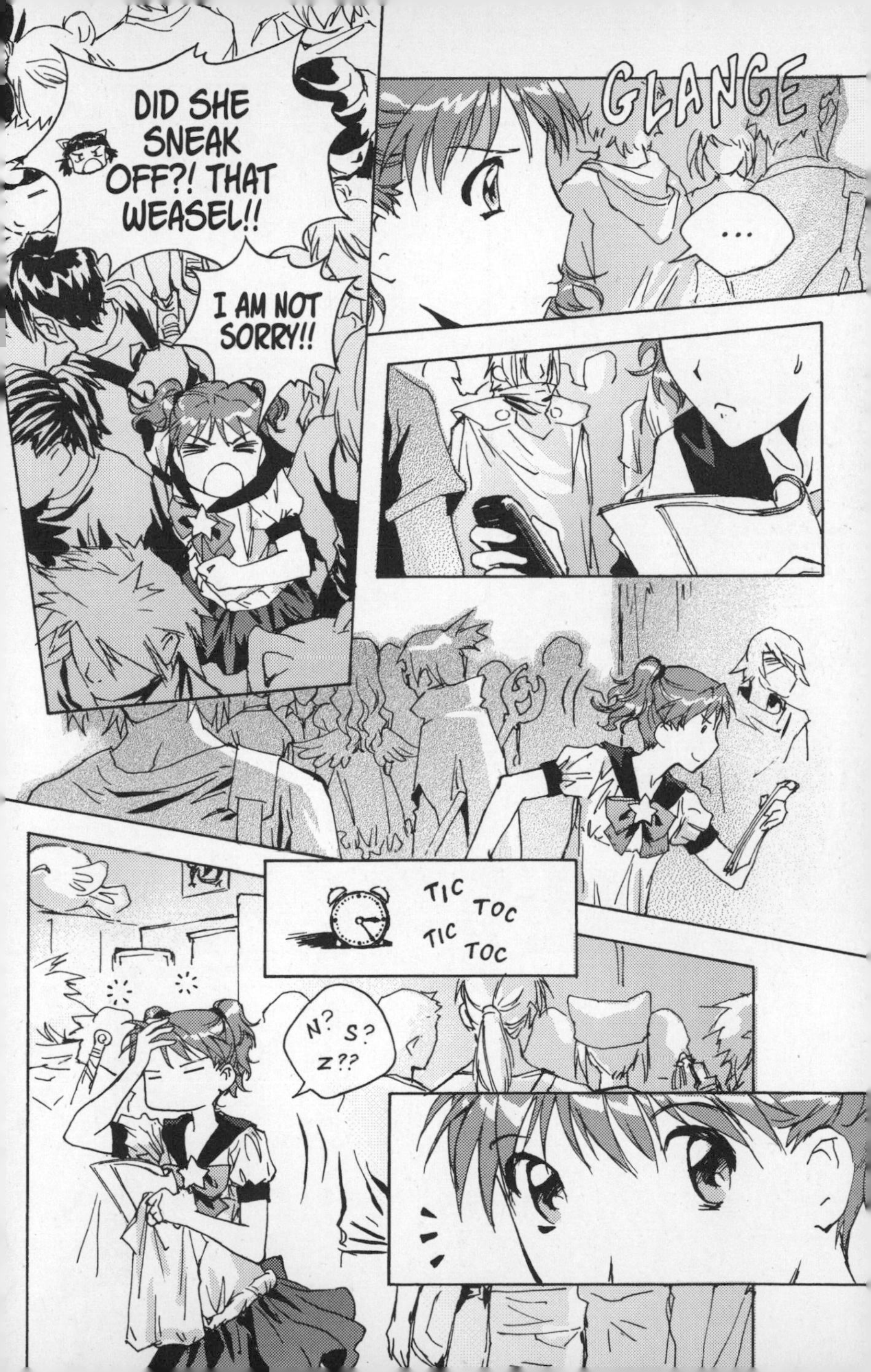
DID SHE SNEAK OFF?! THAT WEASEL!!
I AM NOT SORRY!!
GLANCE
...
TIC TOC TIC TOC
N? S? Z??

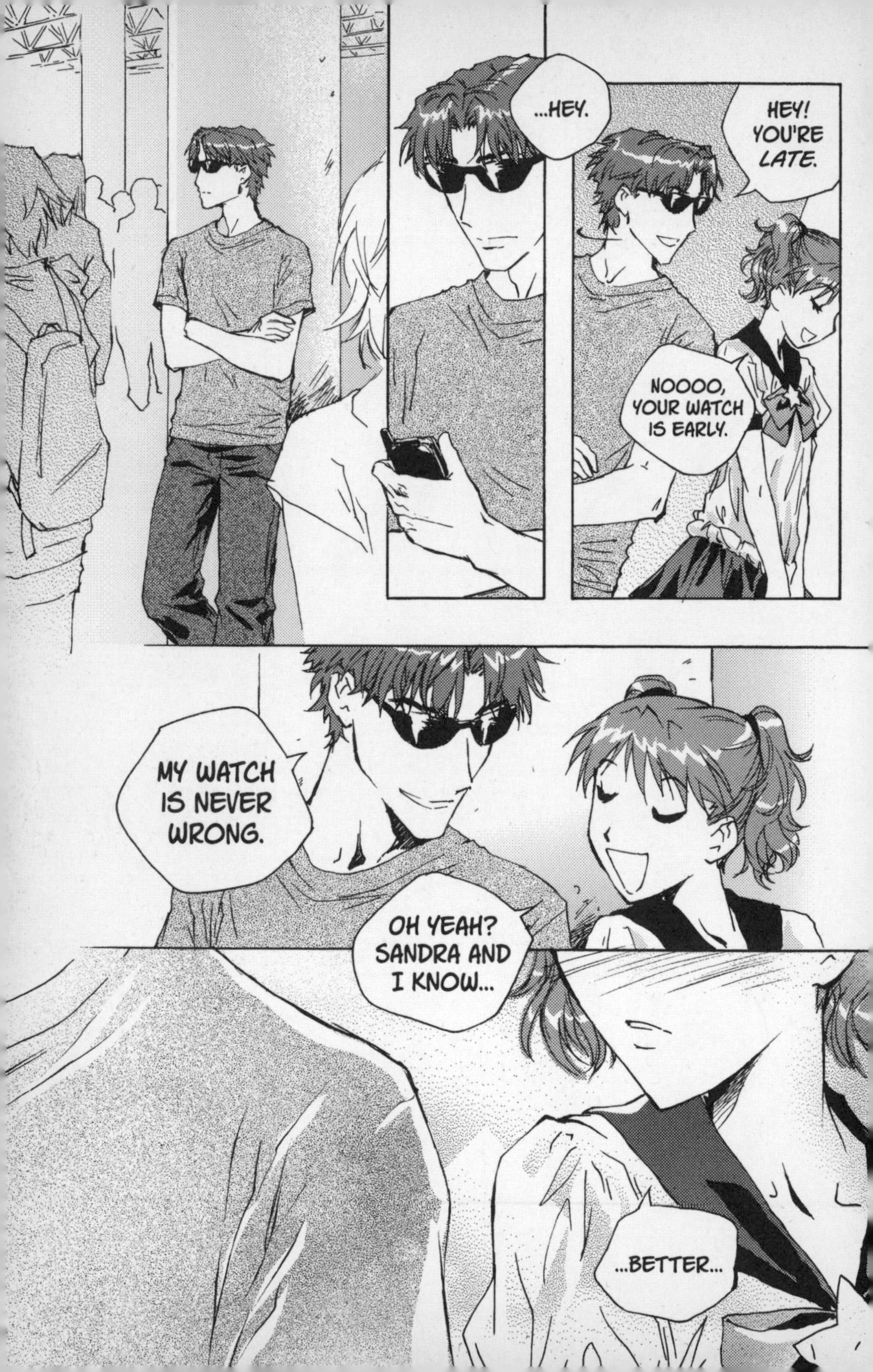
...HEY.
HEY! YOU'RE LATE.
NOOOO, YOUR WATCH IS EARLY.
MY WATCH IS NEVER WRONG.
OH YEAH? SANDRA AND I KNOW...
...BETTER...

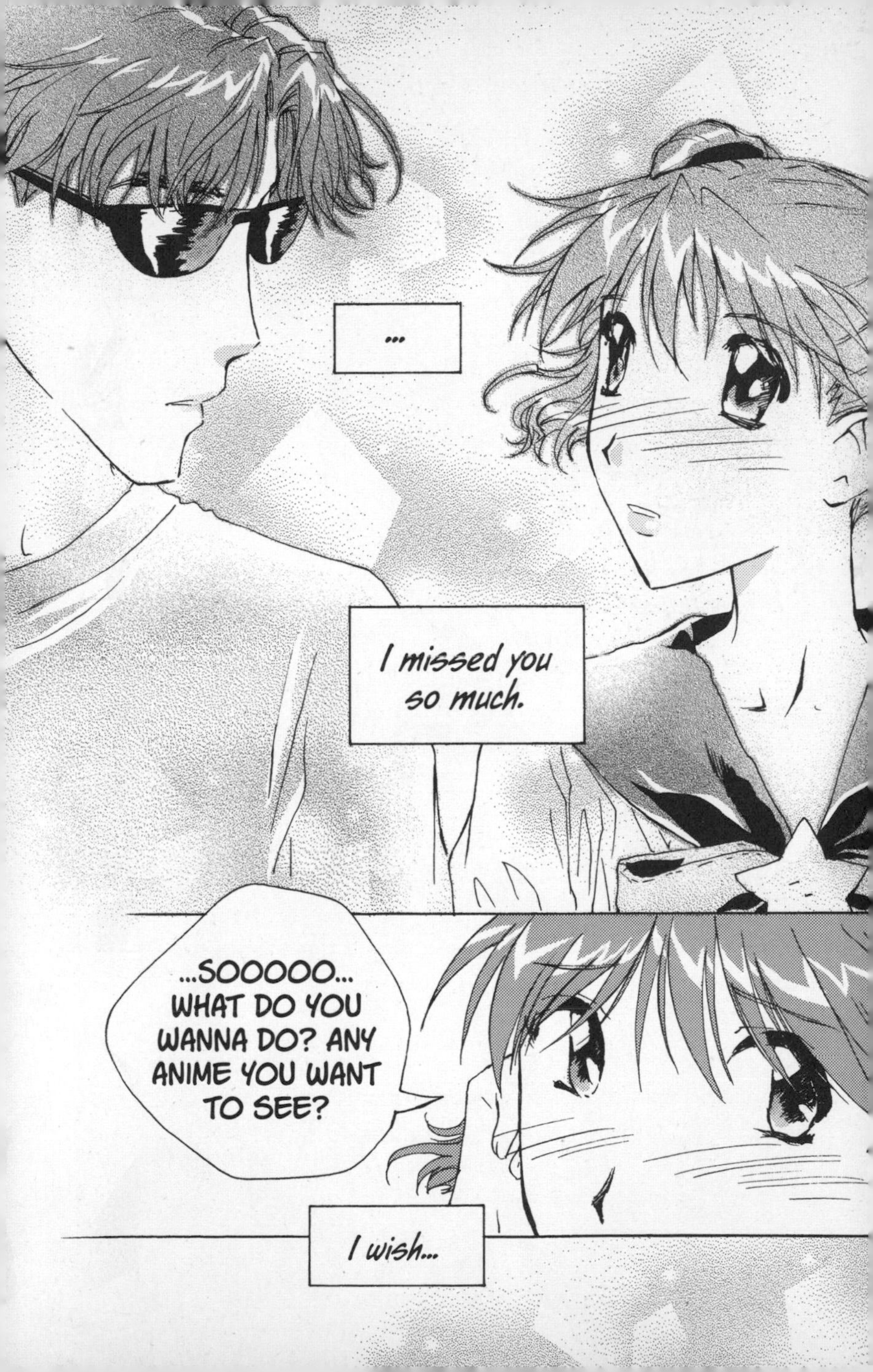
...
I missed you so much.
...SOOOOO... WHAT DO YOU WANNA DO? ANY ANIME YOU WANT TO SEE?
I wish...

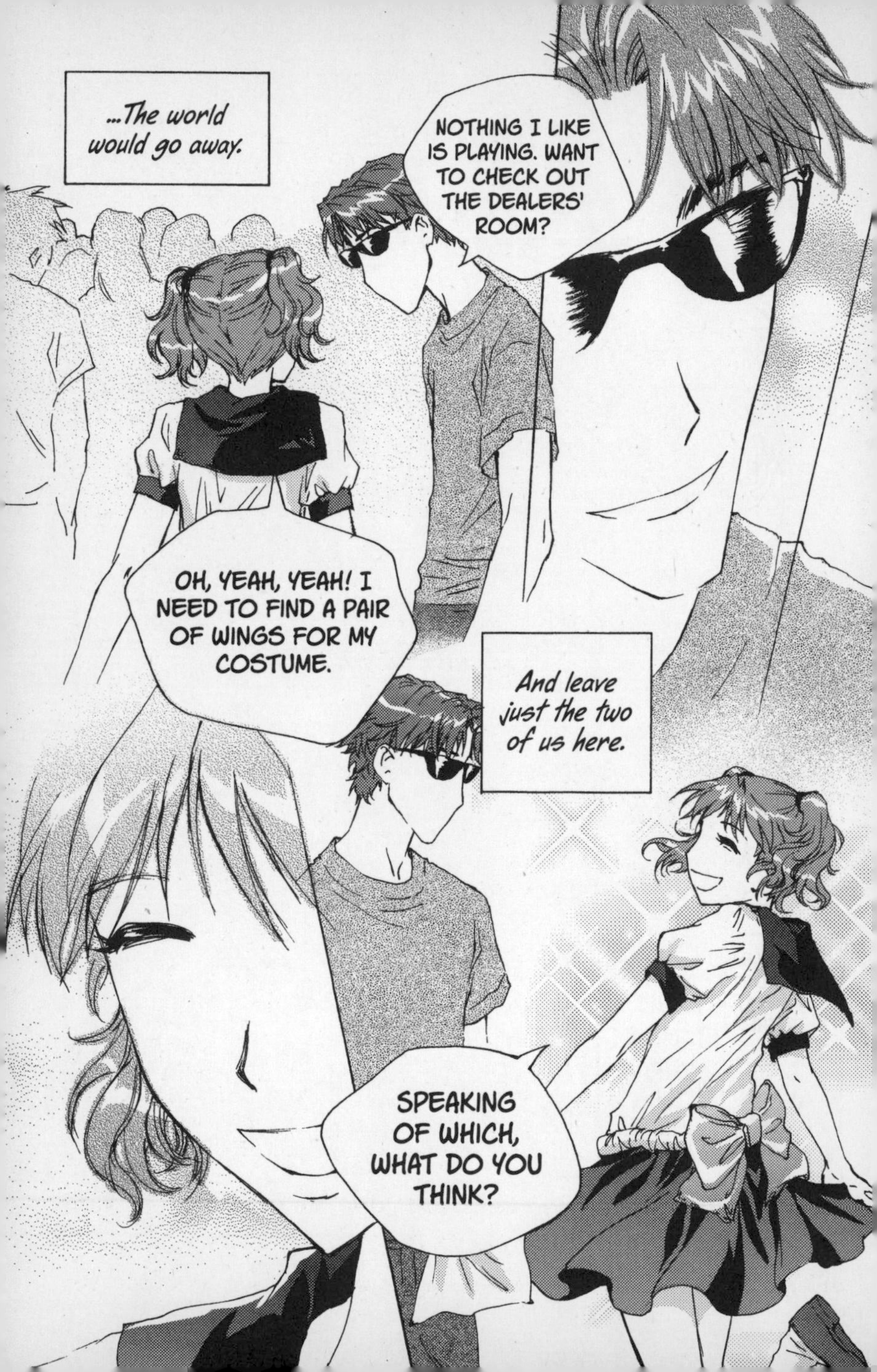
...The world would go away.
NOTHING I LIKE IS PLAYING. WANT TO CHECK OUT THE DEALERS' ROOM?
OH, YEAH, YEAH! I NEED TO FIND A PAIR OF WINGS FOR MY COSTUME.
And leave just the two of us here.
SPEAKING OF WHICH, WHAT DO YOU THINK?

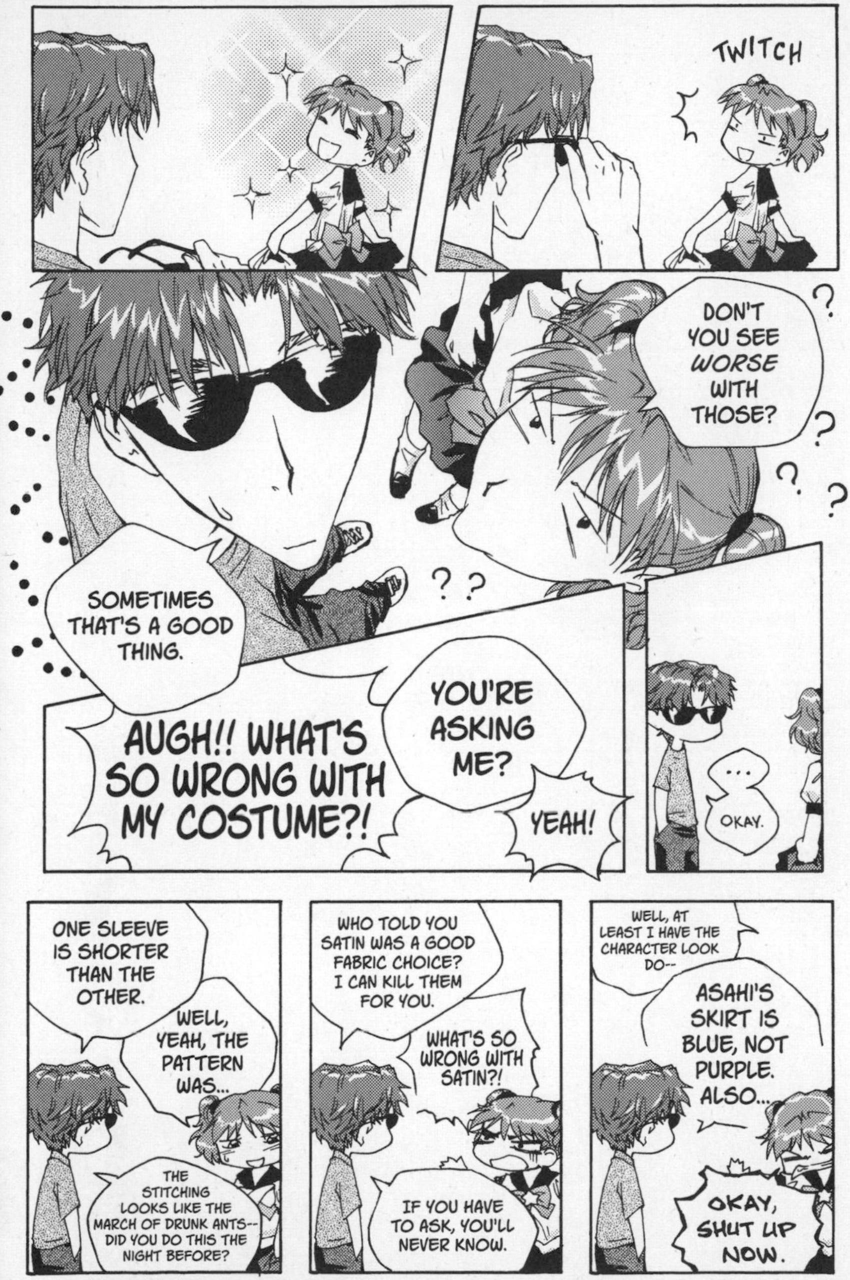
TWITCH
SOMETIMES THAT'S A GOOD THING.
DON'T YOU SEE *WORSE* WITH THOSE?
? ?
? ? ? ?
AUGH!! WHAT'S SO WRONG WITH MY COSTUME?!
YOU'RE ASKING ME?
YEAH!
...
OKAY.
ONE SLEEVE IS SHORTER THAN THE OTHER.
WELL, YEAH, THE PATTERN WAS...
THE STITCHING LOOKS LIKE THE MARCH OF DRUNK ANTS-- DID YOU DO THIS THE NIGHT BEFORE?
WHO TOLD YOU SATIN WAS A GOOD FABRIC CHOICE? I CAN KILL THEM FOR YOU.
WHAT'S SO WRONG WITH SATIN?!
IF YOU HAVE TO ASK, YOU'LL NEVER KNOW.
WELL, AT LEAST I HAVE THE CHARACTER LOOK DO--
ASAHI'S SKIRT IS BLUE, NOT PURPLE. ALSO...
OKAY, SHUT UP NOW.

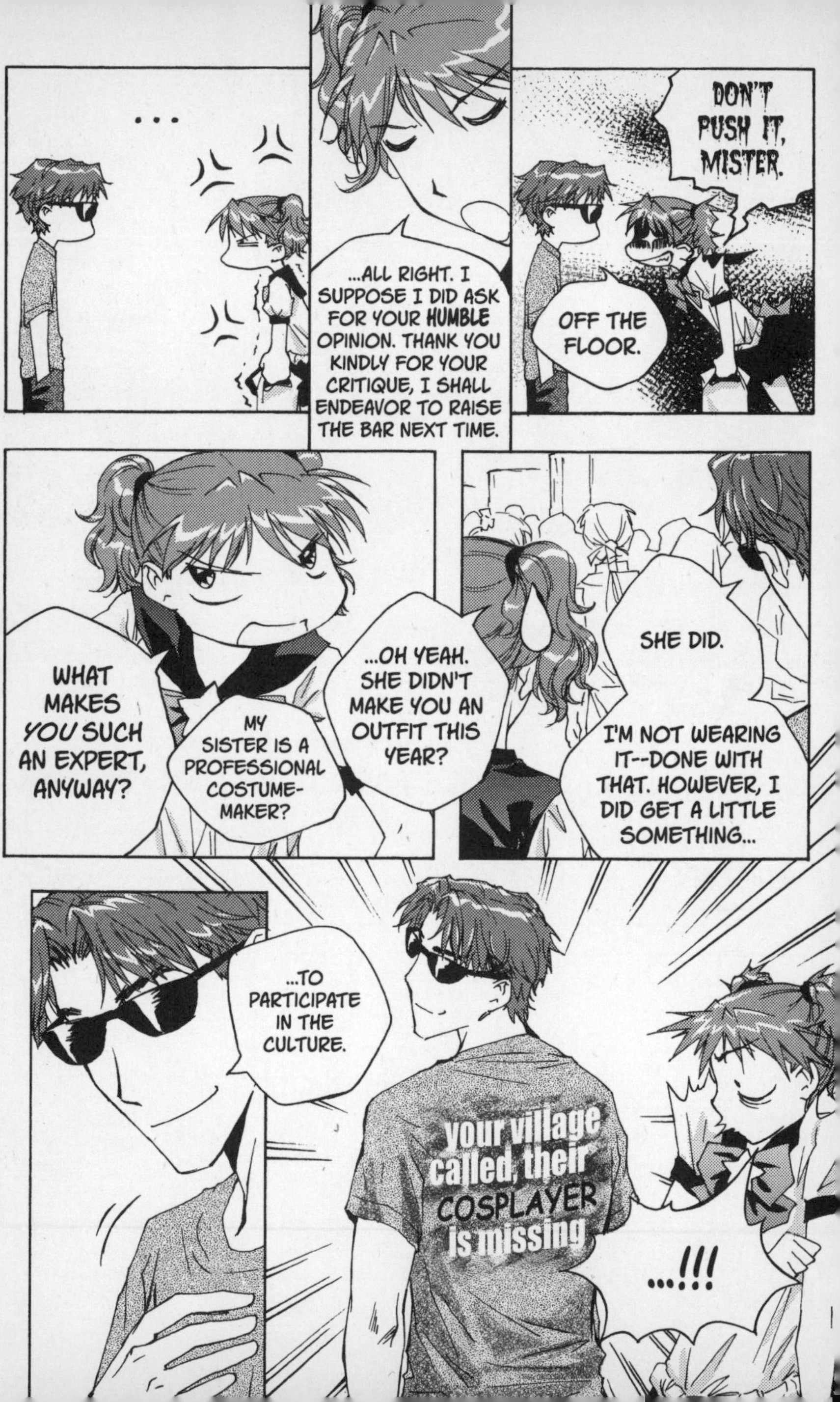
...
...ALL RIGHT. I SUPPOSE I DID ASK FOR YOUR **HUMBLE** OPINION. THANK YOU KINDLY FOR YOUR CRITIQUE, I SHALL ENDEAVOR TO RAISE THE BAR NEXT TIME.
DON'T PUSH IT, MISTER.
OFF THE FLOOR.
WHAT MAKES *YOU* SUCH AN EXPERT, ANYWAY?
MY SISTER IS A PROFESSIONAL COSTUME-MAKER?
...OH YEAH. SHE DIDN'T MAKE YOU AN OUTFIT THIS YEAR?
SHE DID.
I'M NOT WEARING IT--DONE WITH THAT. HOWEVER, I DID GET A LITTLE SOMETHING...
...TO PARTICIPATE IN THE CULTURE.
your village called, their COSPLAYER is missing
...!!!

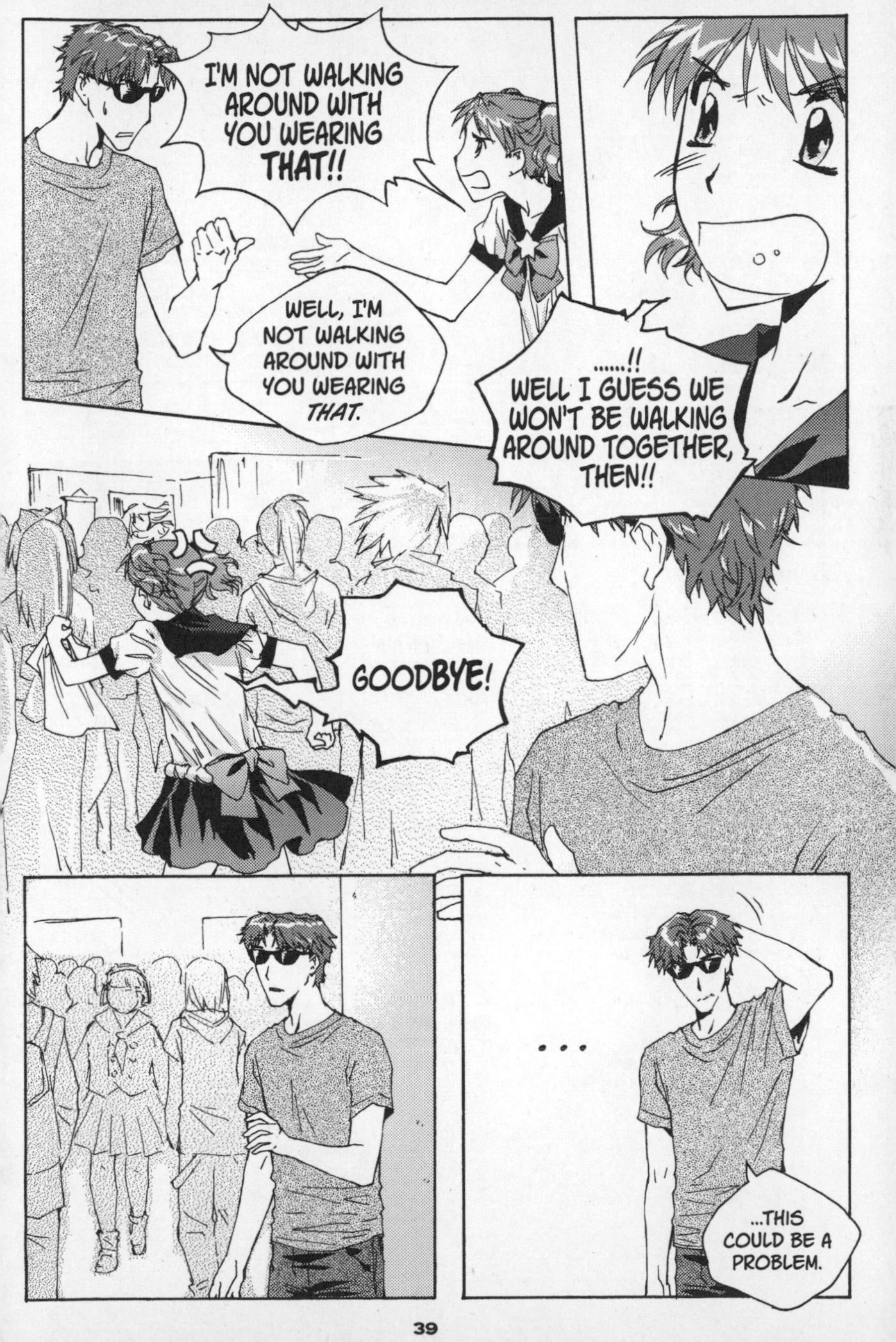
I'M NOT WALKING AROUND WITH YOU WEARING THAT!!
WELL, I'M NOT WALKING AROUND WITH YOU WEARING *THAT.*
......!! WELL I GUESS WE WON'T BE WALKING AROUND TOGETHER, THEN!!
GOODBYE!
...
...THIS COULD BE A PROBLEM.

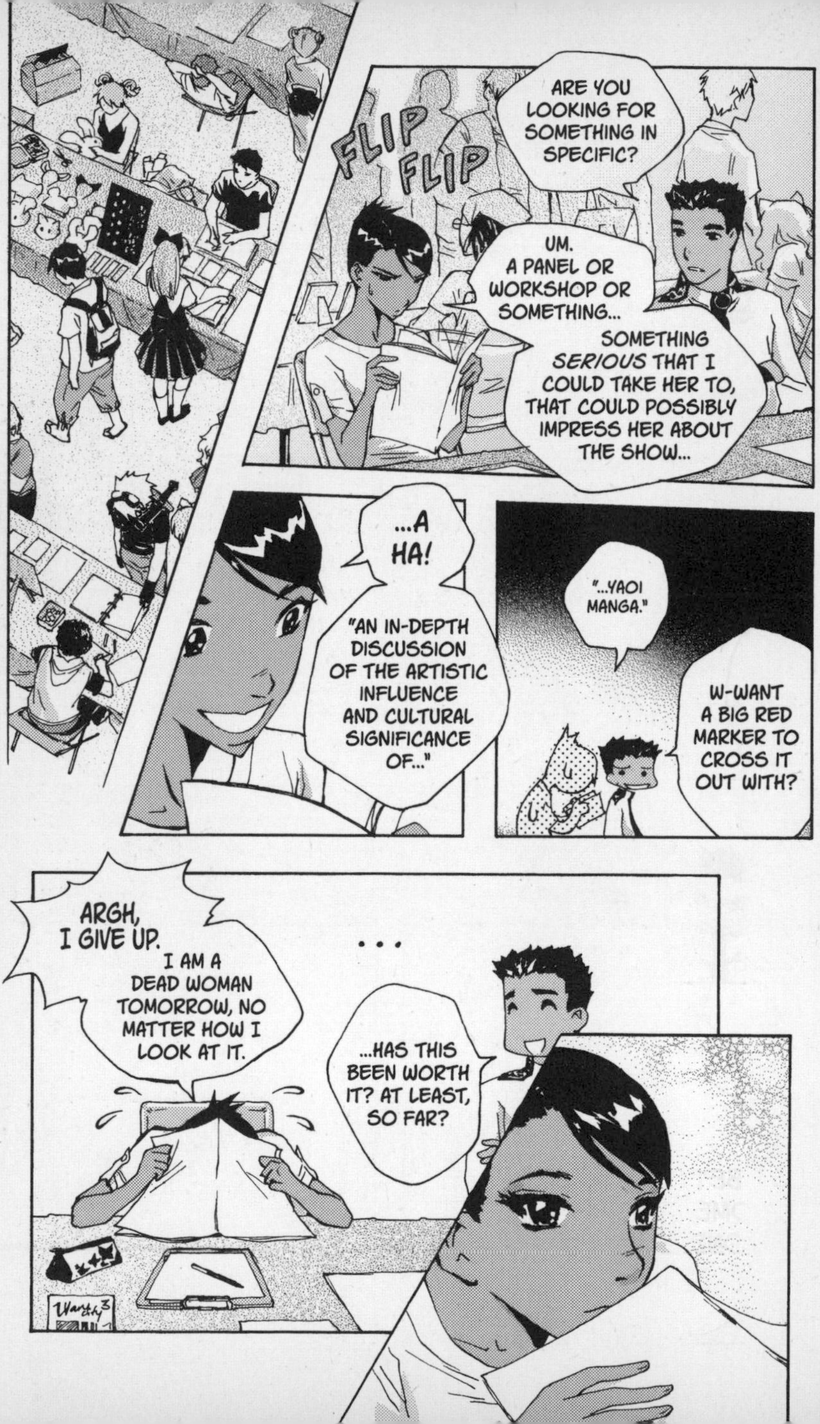
FLIP FLIP
ARE YOU LOOKING FOR SOMETHING IN SPECIFIC?
UM. A PANEL OR WORKSHOP OR SOMETHING...
SOMETHING *SERIOUS* THAT I COULD TAKE HER TO, THAT COULD POSSIBLY IMPRESS HER ABOUT THE SHOW...
...A HA!
"AN IN-DEPTH DISCUSSION OF THE ARTISTIC INFLUENCE AND CULTURAL SIGNIFICANCE OF..."
"...YAOI MANGA."
W-WANT A BIG RED MARKER TO CROSS IT OUT WITH?
ARGH, I GIVE UP.
I AM A DEAD WOMAN TOMORROW, NO MATTER HOW I LOOK AT IT.
...
...HAS THIS BEEN WORTH IT? AT LEAST, SO FAR?

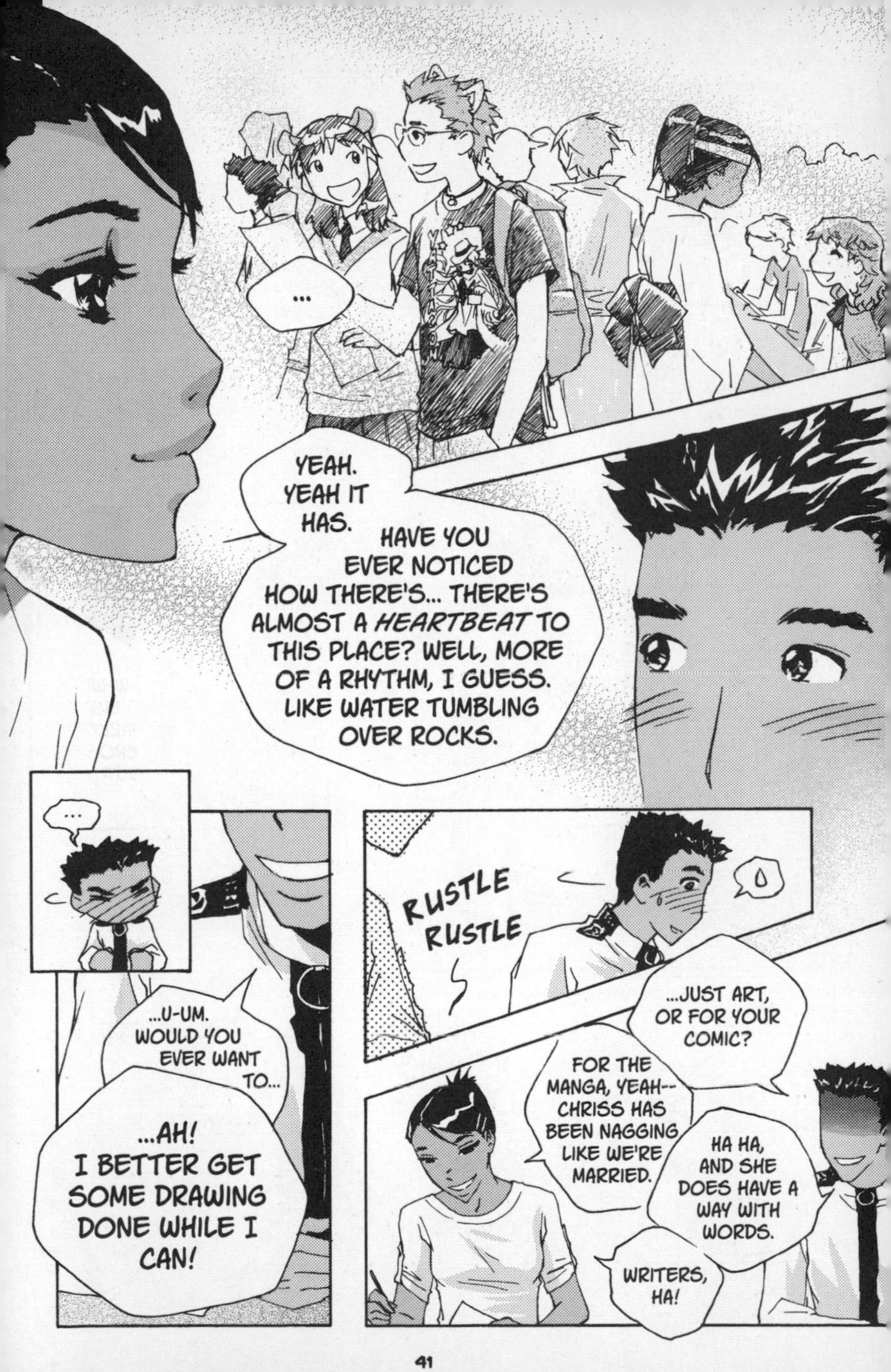
...
YEAH. YEAH IT HAS.
HAVE YOU EVER NOTICED HOW THERE'S... THERE'S ALMOST A *HEARTBEAT* TO THIS PLACE? WELL, MORE OF A RHYTHM, I GUESS. LIKE WATER TUMBLING OVER ROCKS.
...
...U-UM. WOULD YOU EVER WANT TO...
...AH! I BETTER GET SOME DRAWING DONE WHILE I CAN!
RUSTLE RUSTLE
...JUST ART, OR FOR YOUR COMIC?
FOR THE MANGA, YEAH-- CHRISS HAS BEEN NAGGING LIKE WE'RE MARRIED.
HA HA, AND SHE DOES HAVE A WAY WITH WORDS.
WRITERS, HA!

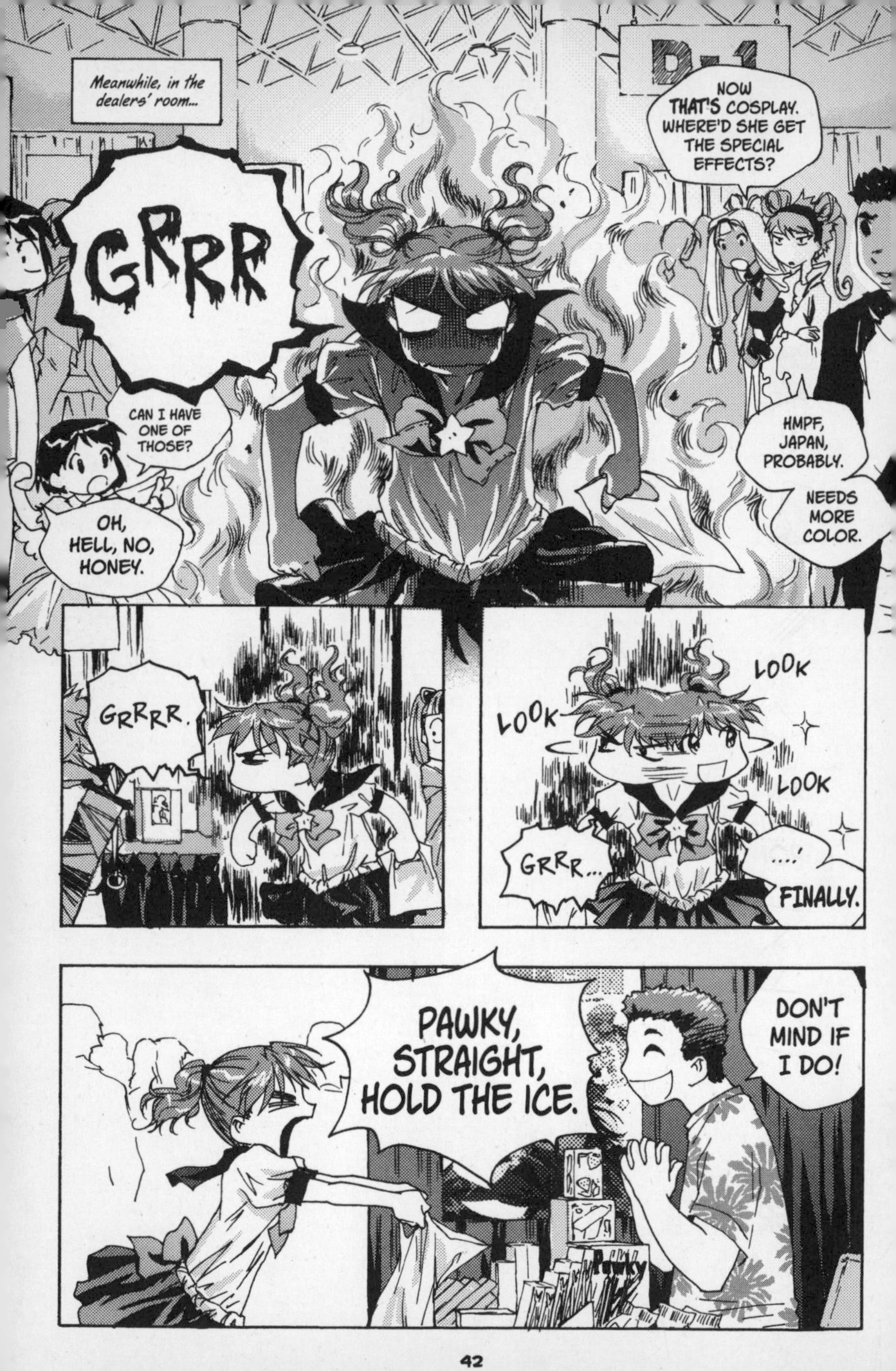

Meanwhile, in the dealers' room...
GRRR
CAN I HAVE ONE OF THOSE?
OH, HELL, NO, HONEY.
NOW THAT'S COSPLAY. WHERE'D SHE GET THE SPECIAL EFFECTS?
HMPF, JAPAN, PROBABLY.
NEEDS MORE COLOR.
GRRRR.
LOOK
LOOK
LOOK
GRRR...
...!
FINALLY.
PAWKY, STRAIGHT, HOLD THE ICE.
DON'T MIND IF I DO!
Pawky

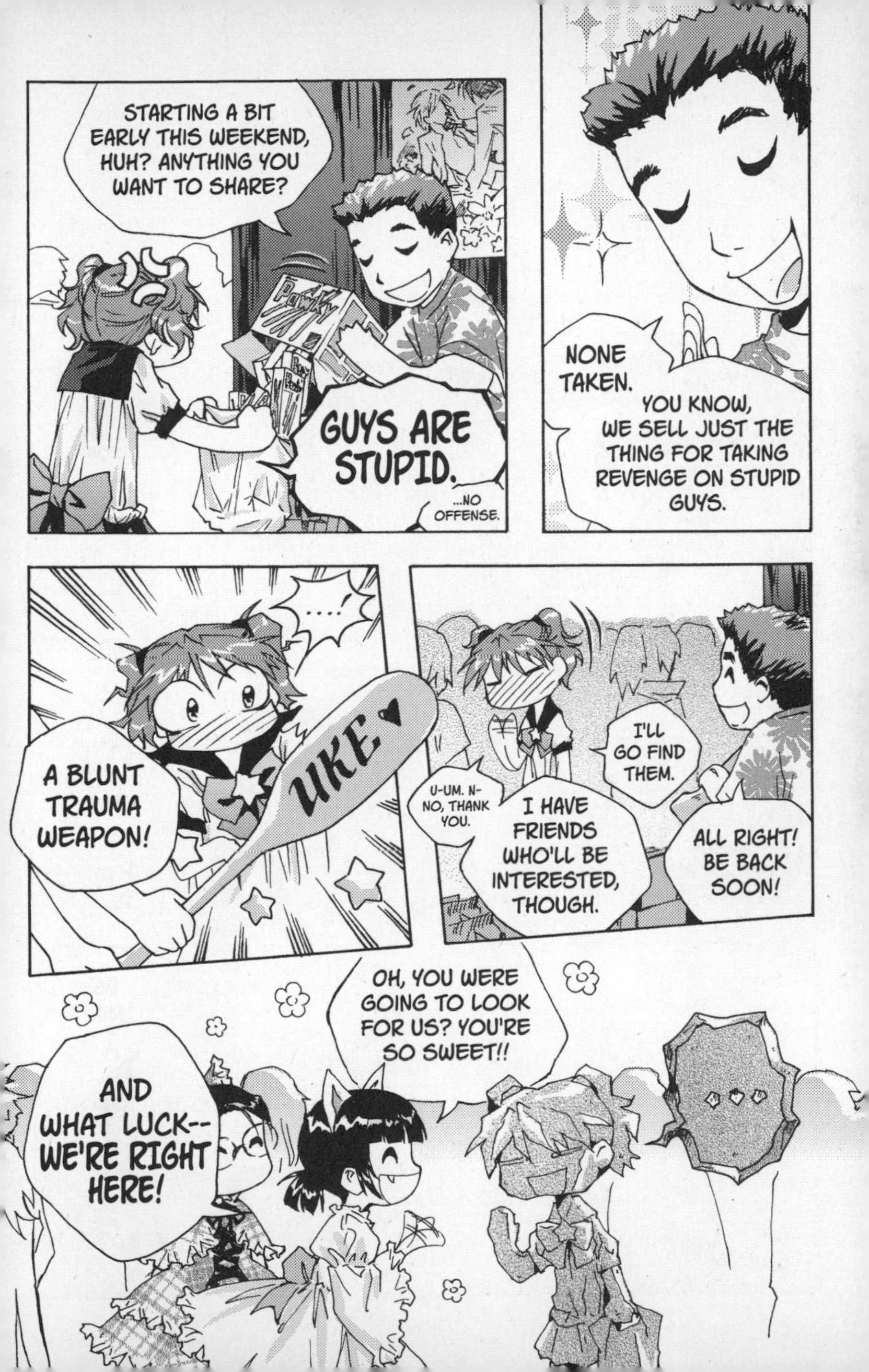
STARTING A BIT EARLY THIS WEEKEND, HUH? ANYTHING YOU WANT TO SHARE?
GUYS ARE STUPID.
...NO OFFENSE.
NONE TAKEN.
YOU KNOW, WE SELL JUST THE THING FOR TAKING REVENGE ON STUPID GUYS.
....
A BLUNT TRAUMA WEAPON!
UKE♥
U-UM. N-NO, THANK YOU.
I HAVE FRIENDS WHO'LL BE INTERESTED, THOUGH.
I'LL GO FIND THEM.
ALL RIGHT! BE BACK SOON!
OH, YOU WERE GOING TO LOOK FOR US? YOU'RE SO SWEET!!
AND WHAT LUCK-- WE'RE RIGHT HERE!

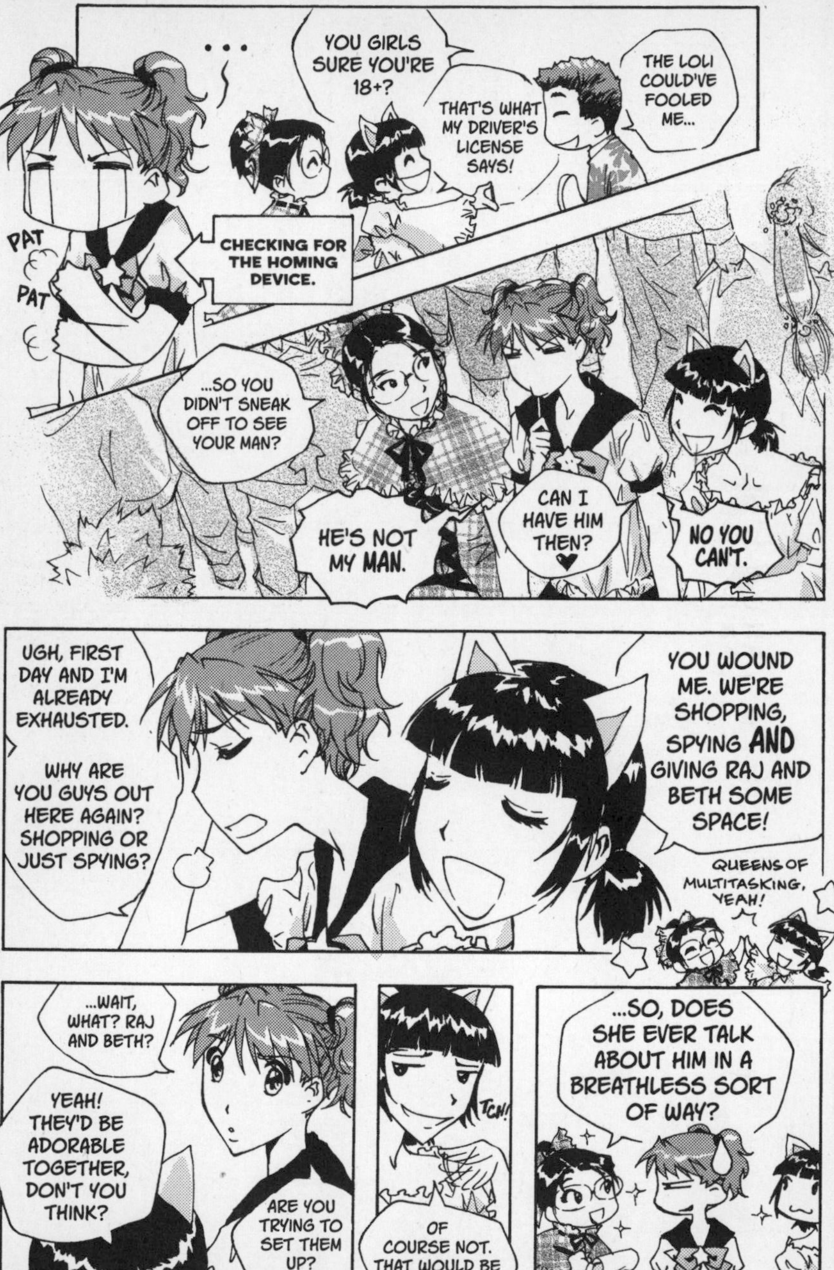
...
YOU GIRLS SURE YOU'RE 18+?
THAT'S WHAT MY DRIVER'S LICENSE SAYS!
THE LOLI COULD'VE FOOLED ME...
CHECKING FOR THE HOMING DEVICE.
PAT
PAT
...SO YOU DIDN'T SNEAK OFF TO SEE YOUR MAN?
HE'S NOT MY MAN.
CAN I HAVE HIM THEN? ♥
NO YOU CAN'T.
UGH, FIRST DAY AND I'M ALREADY EXHAUSTED.
WHY ARE YOU GUYS OUT HERE AGAIN? SHOPPING OR JUST SPYING?
YOU WOUND ME. WE'RE SHOPPING, SPYING AND GIVING RAJ AND BETH SOME SPACE!
QUEENS OF MULTITASKING, YEAH!
...WAIT, WHAT? RAJ AND BETH?
YEAH! THEY'D BE ADORABLE TOGETHER, DON'T YOU THINK?
ARE YOU TRYING TO SET THEM UP?
TCH!
OF COURSE NOT. THAT WOULD BE MEDDLING!
...SO, DOES SHE EVER TALK ABOUT HIM IN A BREATHLESS SORT OF WAY?

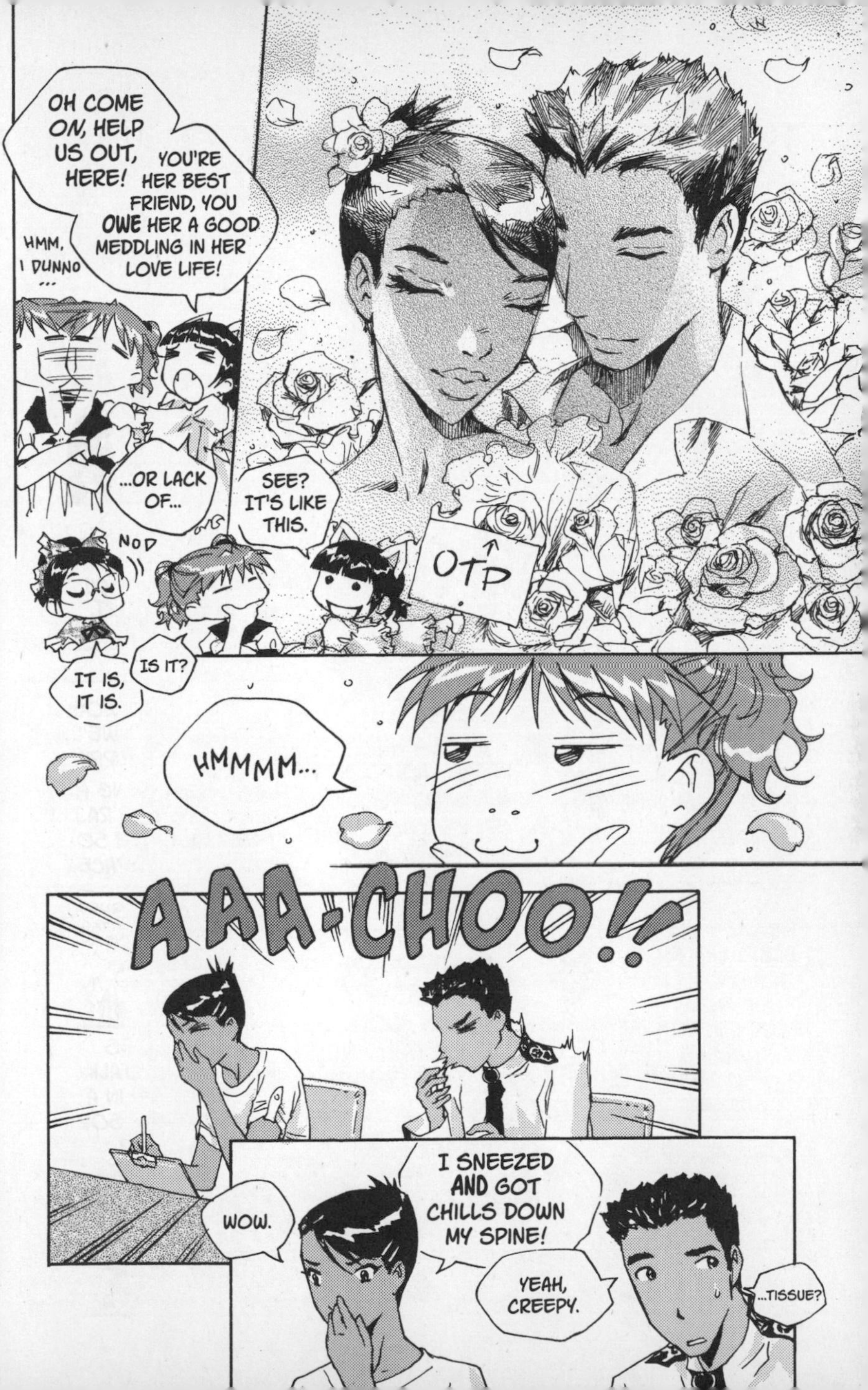
OH COME ON, HELP US OUT, HERE!
YOU'RE HER BEST FRIEND, YOU OWE HER A GOOD MEDDLING IN HER LOVE LIFE!
HMM. I DUNNO ...
...OR LACK OF...
SEE? IT'S LIKE THIS.
OTP
NOD
IS IT?
IT IS, IT IS.
HMMMM...
AAA-CHOO!!
WOW.
I SNEEZED AND GOT CHILLS DOWN MY SPINE!
YEAH, CREEPY.
...TISSUE?

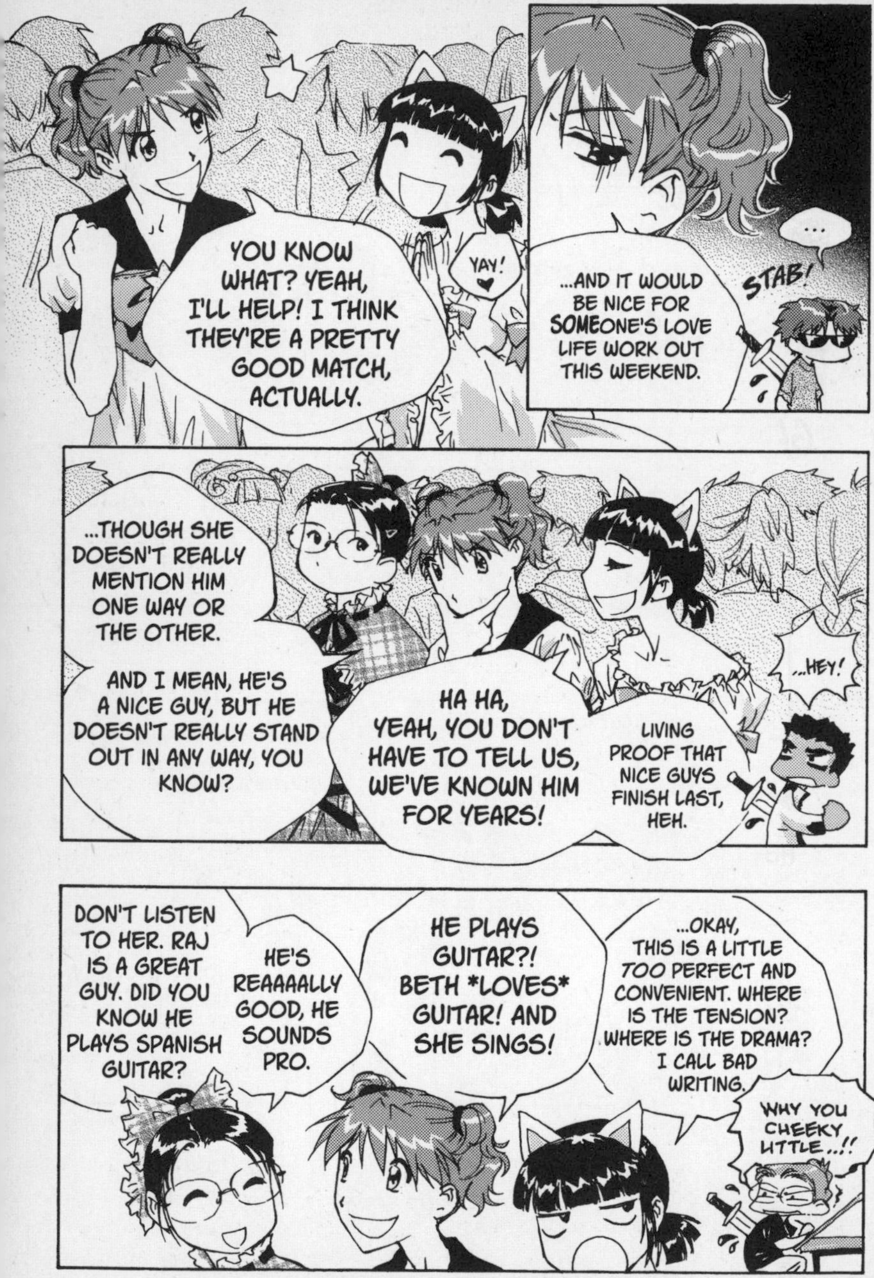
YOU KNOW WHAT? YEAH, I'LL HELP! I THINK THEY'RE A PRETTY GOOD MATCH, ACTUALLY.
YAY! ♥
...AND IT WOULD BE NICE FOR SOMEONE'S LOVE LIFE WORK OUT THIS WEEKEND.
...
STAB!
...THOUGH SHE DOESN'T REALLY MENTION HIM ONE WAY OR THE OTHER.
AND I MEAN, HE'S A NICE GUY, BUT HE DOESN'T REALLY STAND OUT IN ANY WAY, YOU KNOW?
HA HA, YEAH, YOU DON'T HAVE TO TELL US, WE'VE KNOWN HIM FOR YEARS!
LIVING PROOF THAT NICE GUYS FINISH LAST, HEH.
...HEY!
DON'T LISTEN TO HER. RAJ IS A GREAT GUY. DID YOU KNOW HE PLAYS SPANISH GUITAR?
HE'S REAAAALLY GOOD, HE SOUNDS PRO.
HE PLAYS GUITAR?! BETH *LOVES* GUITAR! AND SHE SINGS!
...OKAY, THIS IS A LITTLE TOO PERFECT AND CONVENIENT. WHERE IS THE TENSION? WHERE IS THE DRAMA? I CALL BAD WRITING.
WHY YOU CHEEKY LITTLE...!!

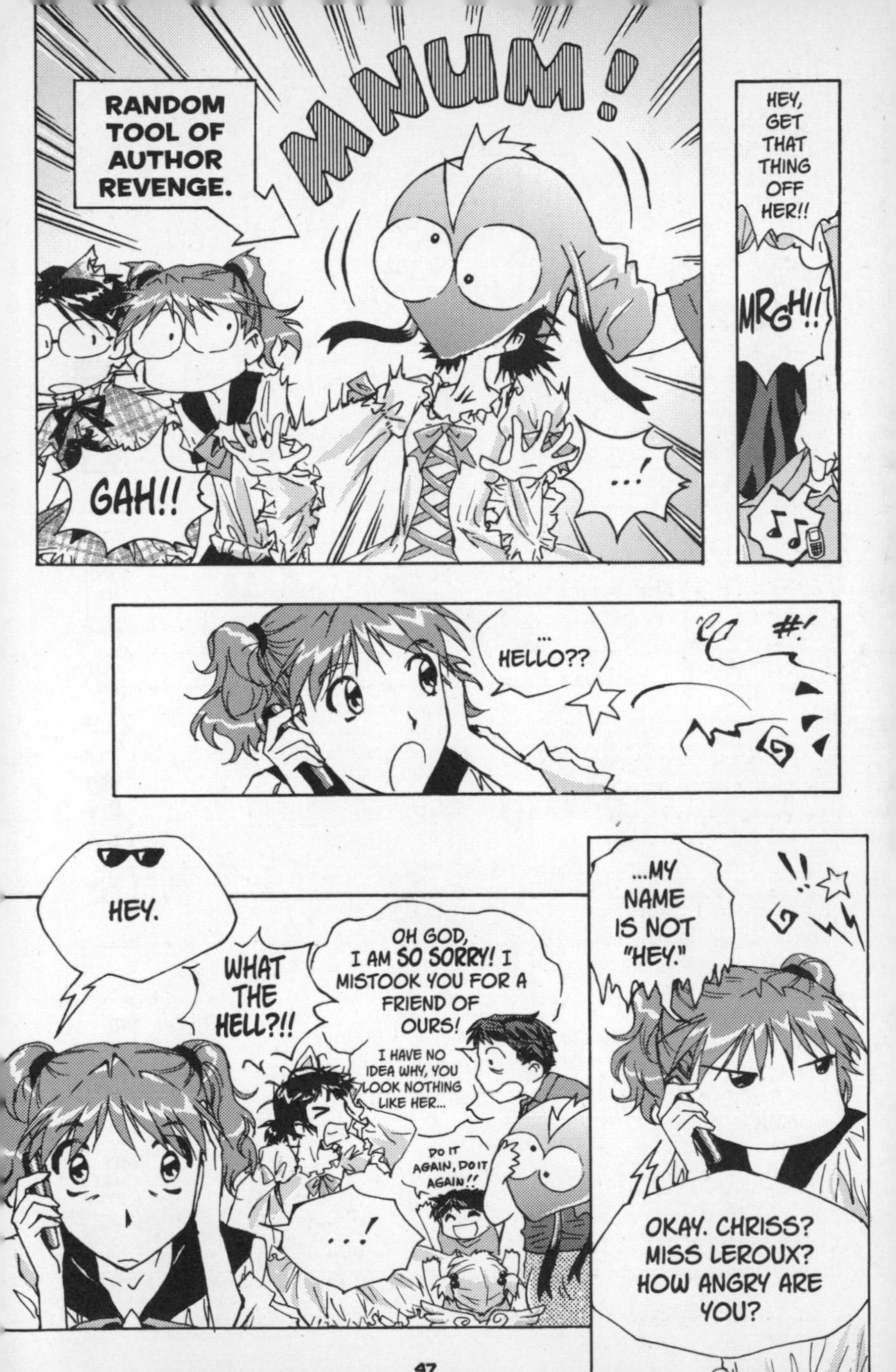
RANDOM TOOL OF AUTHOR REVENGE.
MNUM!
GAH!!
...!
HEY, GET THAT THING OFF HER!!
MRGH!!
... HELLO??
#!
HEY.
WHAT THE HELL?!!
OH GOD, I AM SO SORRY! I MISTOOK YOU FOR A FRIEND OF OURS!
I HAVE NO IDEA WHY, YOU LOOK NOTHING LIKE HER...
DO IT AGAIN, DO IT AGAIN!!
...!
...MY NAME IS NOT "HEY."
!!
OKAY. CHRISS? MISS LEROUX? HOW ANGRY ARE YOU?

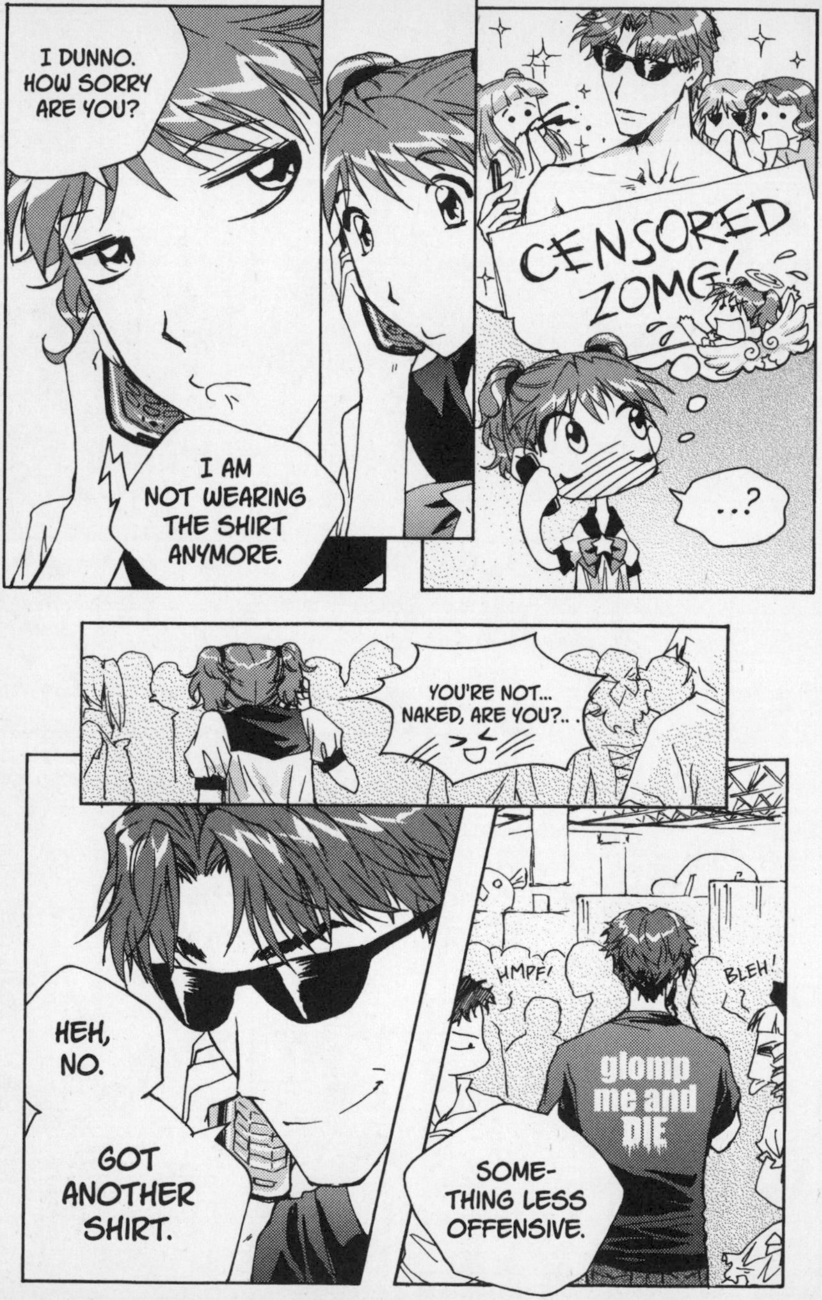
I DUNNO. HOW SORRY ARE YOU?
I AM NOT WEARING THE SHIRT ANYMORE.
CENSORED
ZOMG!
...?
YOU'RE NOT... NAKED, ARE YOU?...
HEH, NO.
GOT ANOTHER SHIRT.
HMPF!
BLEH!
glomp me and DIE
SOME-THING LESS OFFENSIVE.

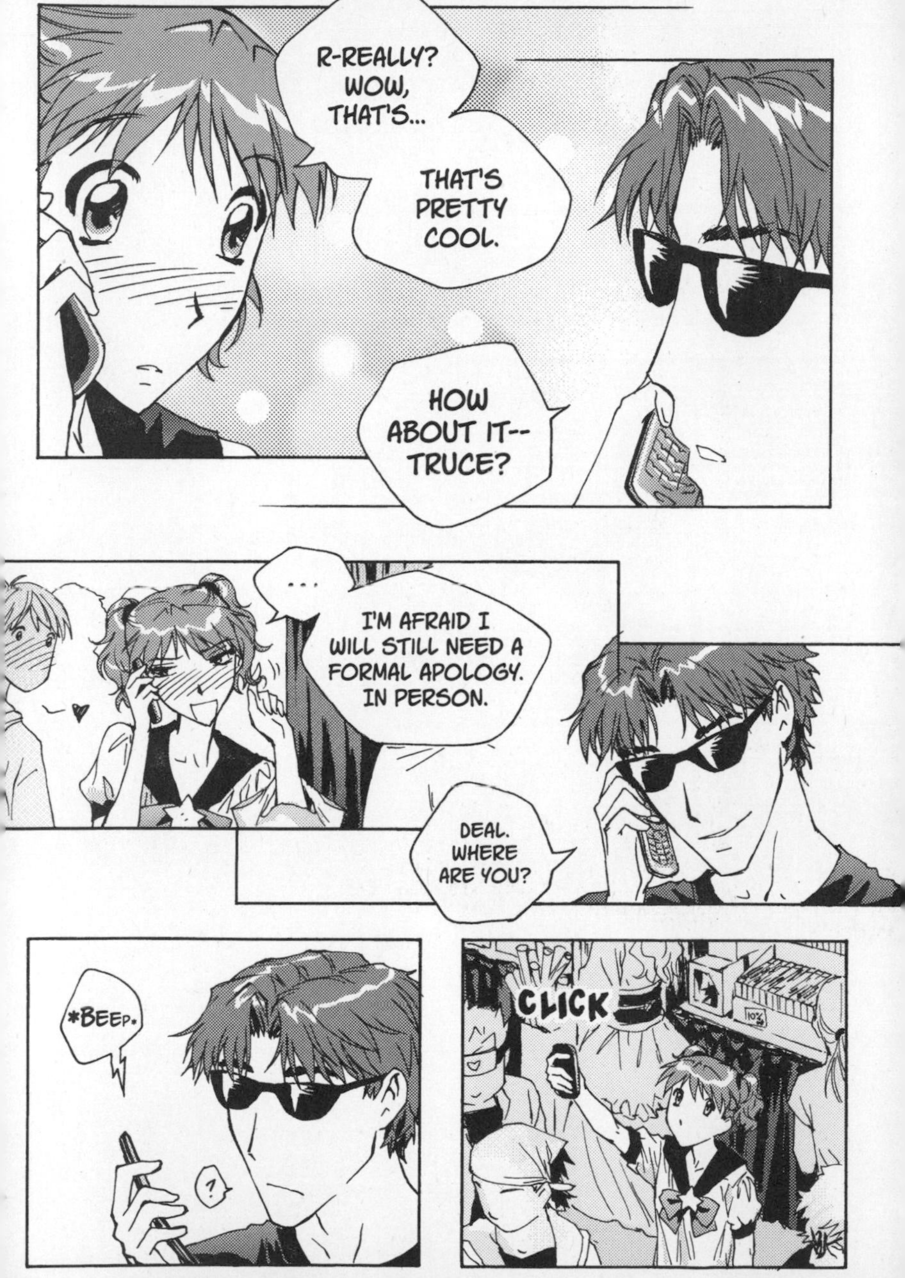
R-REALLY? WOW, THAT'S...
THAT'S PRETTY COOL.
HOW ABOUT IT--TRUCE?
...
I'M AFRAID I WILL STILL NEED A FORMAL APOLOGY. IN PERSON.
DEAL. WHERE ARE YOU?
BEEP
?
CLICK

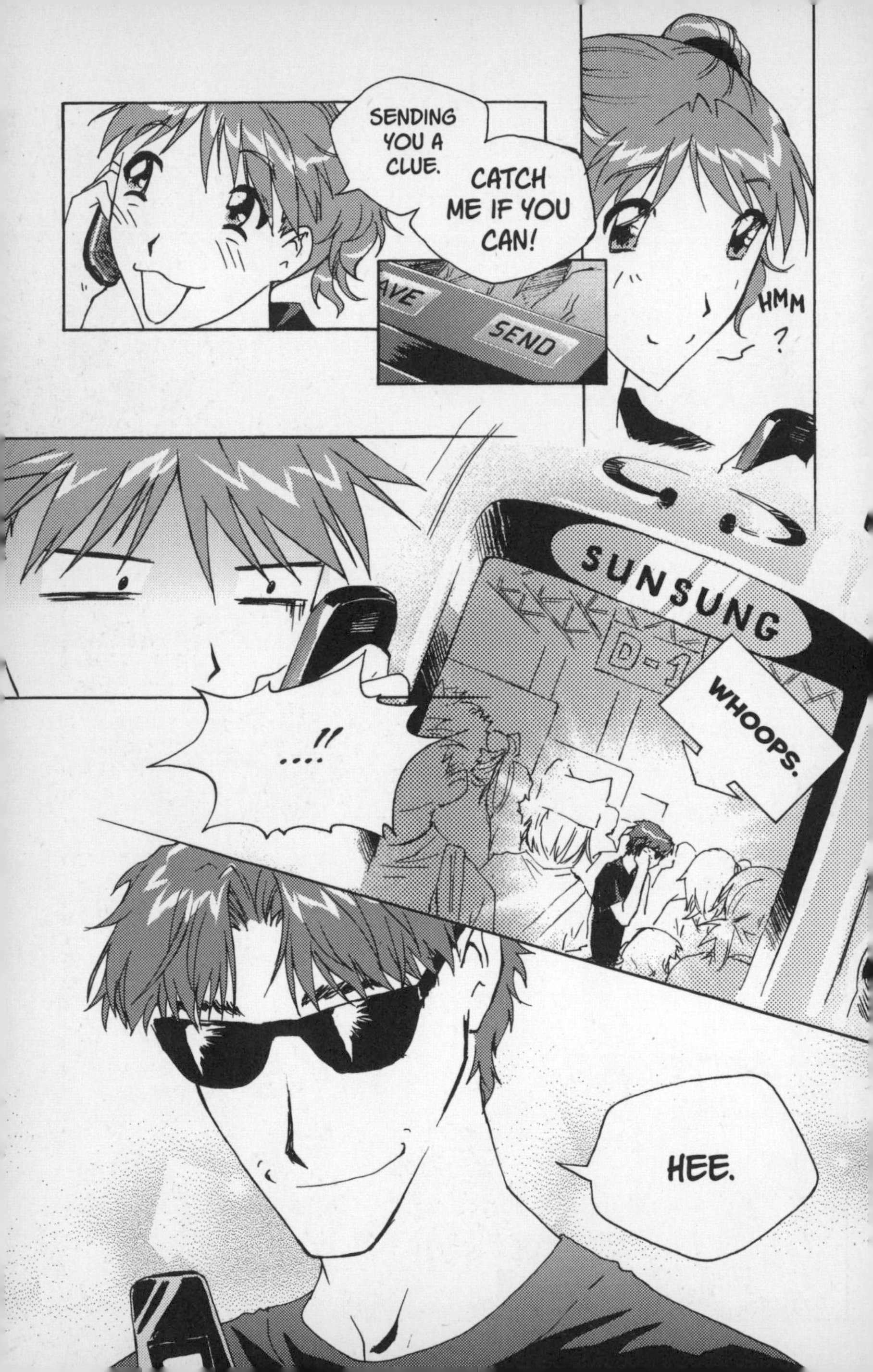
SENDING YOU A CLUE.
CATCH ME IF YOU CAN!
AVE
SEND
HMM ?
SUNSUNG
D-4
....!!
WHOOPS.
HEE.

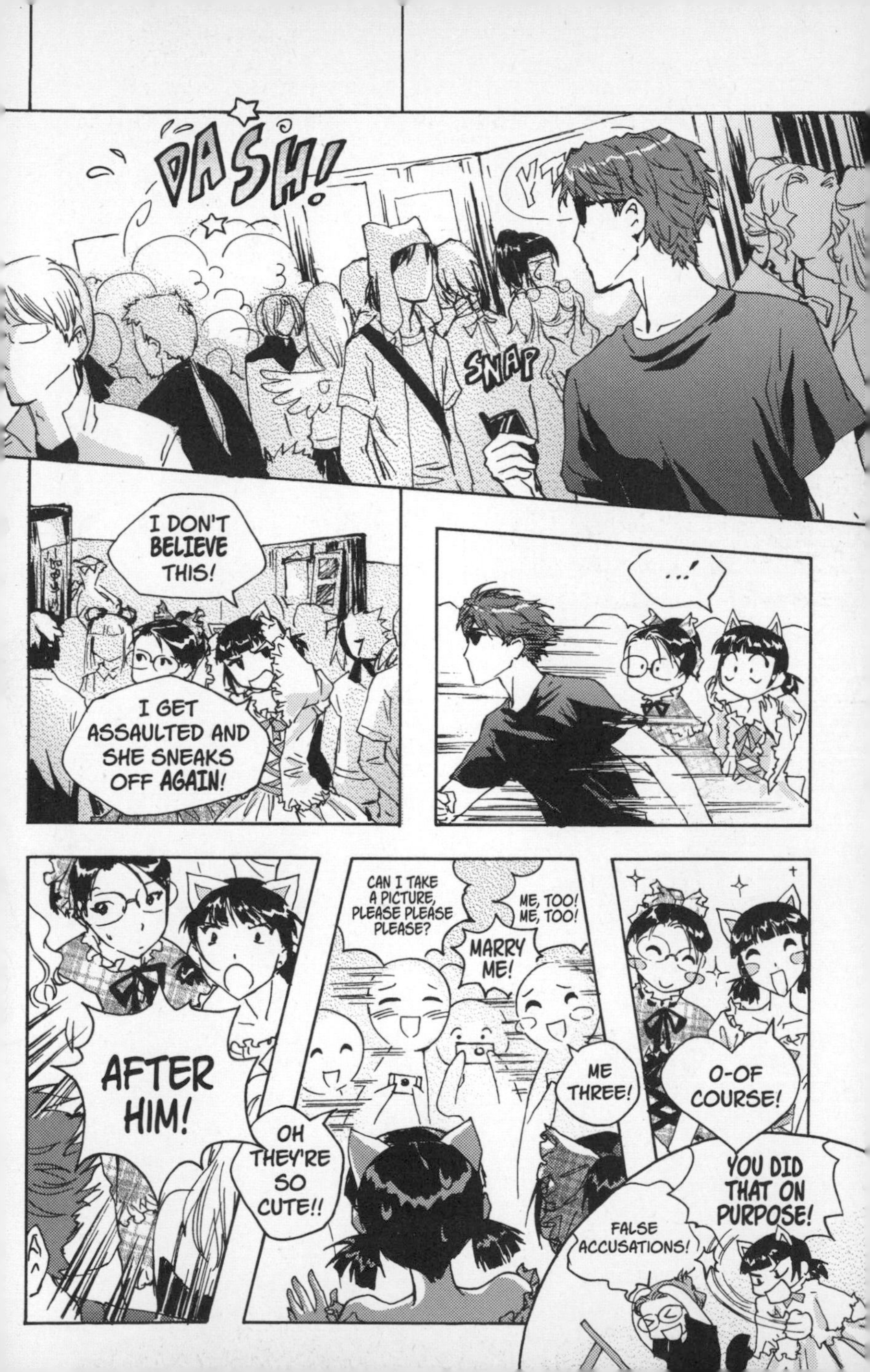
DASH!
SNAP
I DON'T BELIEVE THIS!
I GET ASSAULTED AND SHE SNEAKS OFF AGAIN!
...!
AFTER HIM!
CAN I TAKE A PICTURE, PLEASE PLEASE PLEASE?
ME, TOO! ME, TOO!
MARRY ME!
ME THREE!
OH THEY'RE SO CUTE!!
O-OF COURSE!
YOU DID THAT ON PURPOSE!
FALSE ACCUSATIONS!

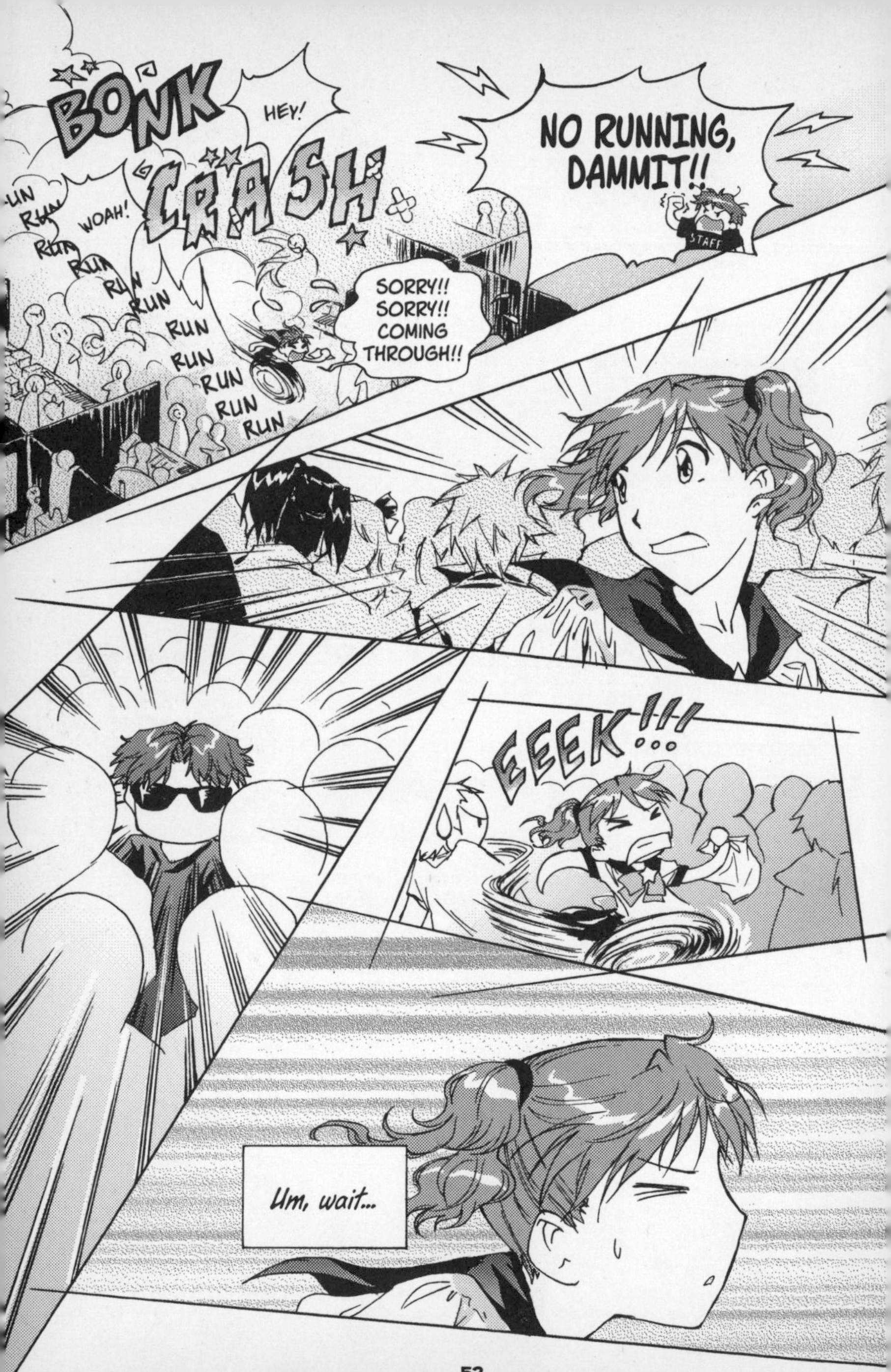
BONK
HEY!
CRASH
WOAH!
RUN RUN RUN RUN RUN RUN RUN RUN RUN RUN
SORRY!! SORRY!! COMING THROUGH!!
NO RUNNING, DAMMIT!!
STAFF
EEEK!!!
Um, wait...

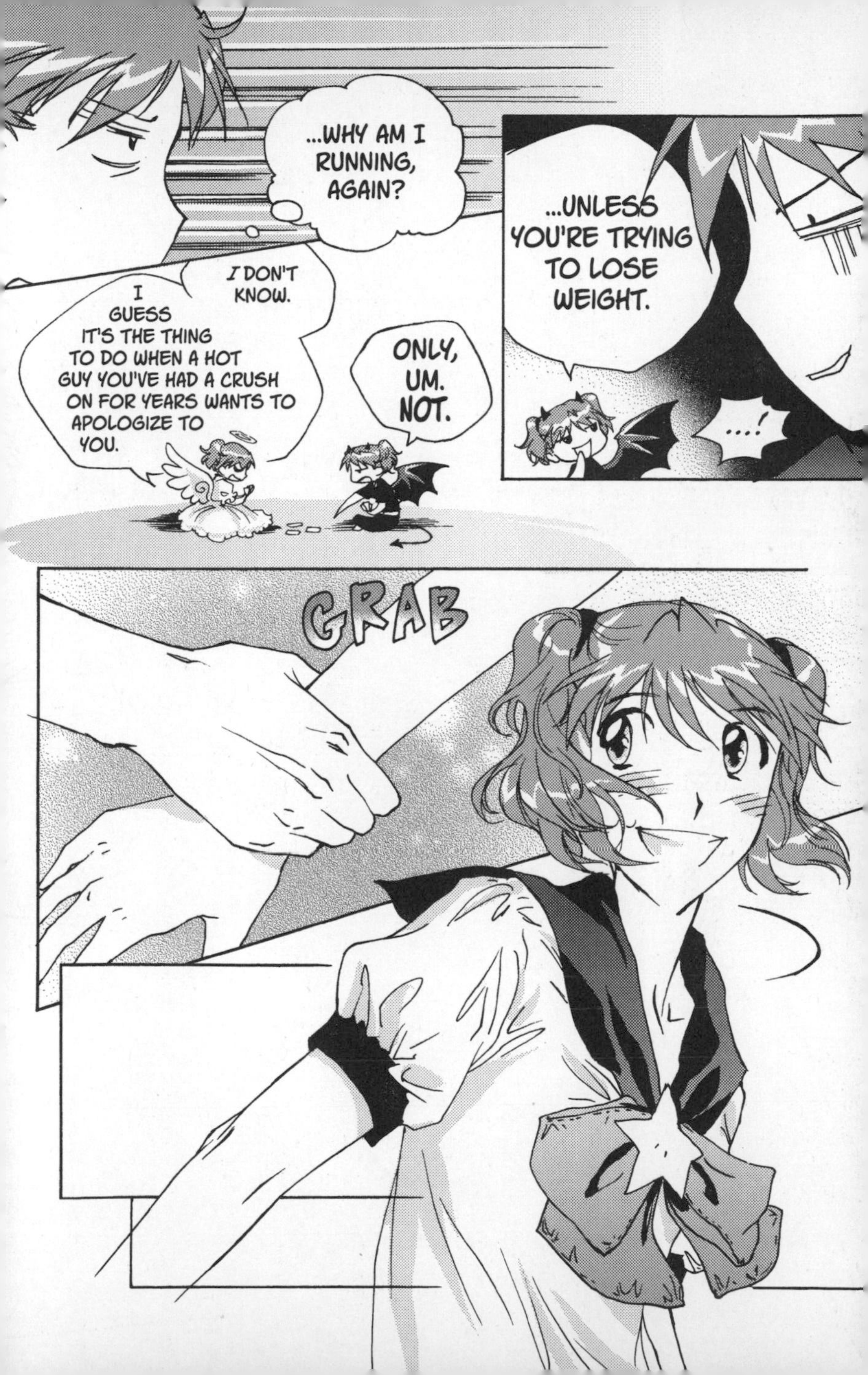
...WHY AM I RUNNING, AGAIN?
I DON'T KNOW.
I GUESS IT'S THE THING TO DO WHEN A HOT GUY YOU'VE HAD A CRUSH ON FOR YEARS WANTS TO APOLOGIZE TO YOU.
ONLY, UM. NOT.
...UNLESS YOU'RE TRYING TO LOSE WEIGHT.
...!
GRAB

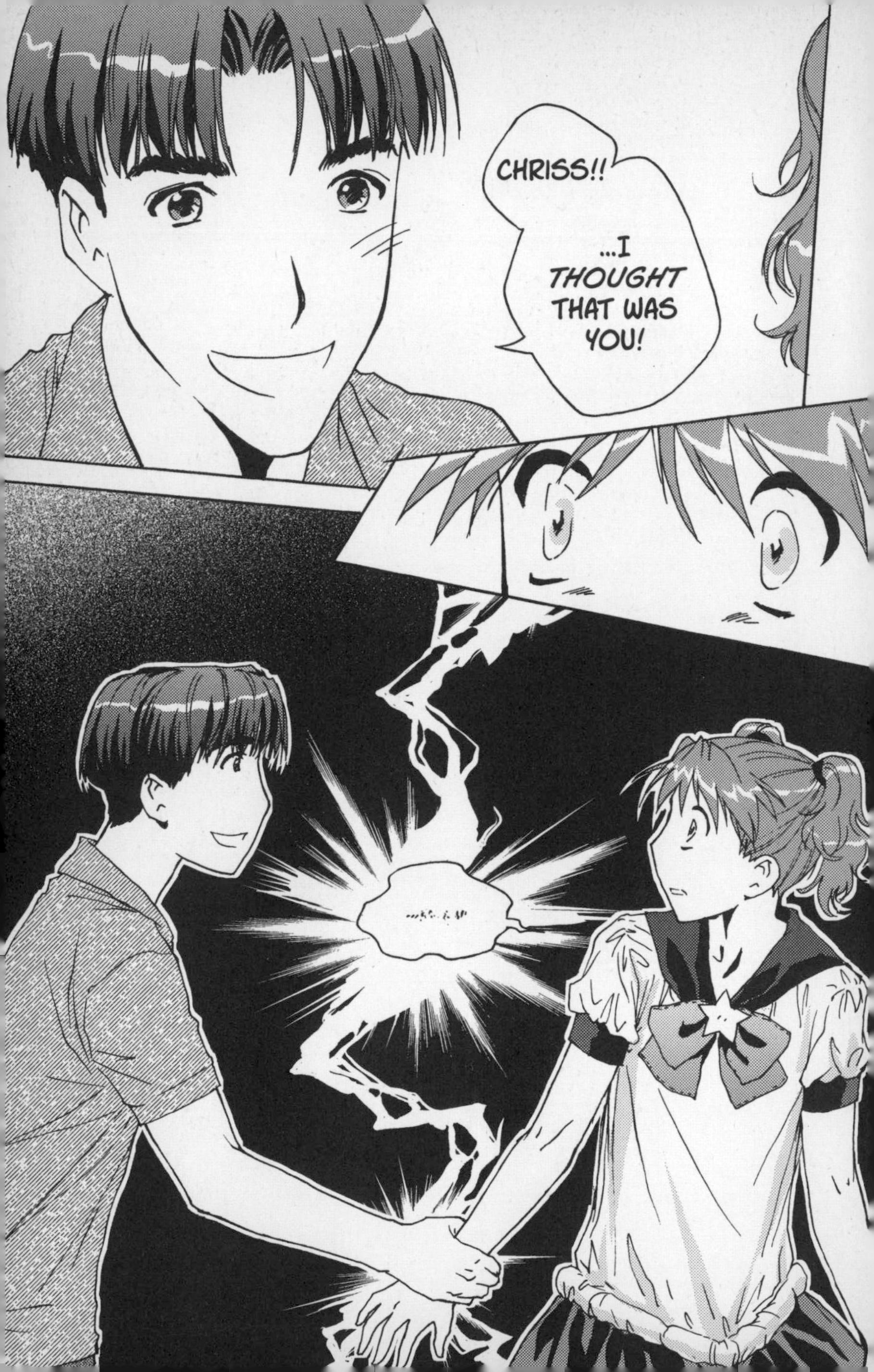
CHRISS!!
...I THOUGHT THAT WAS YOU!

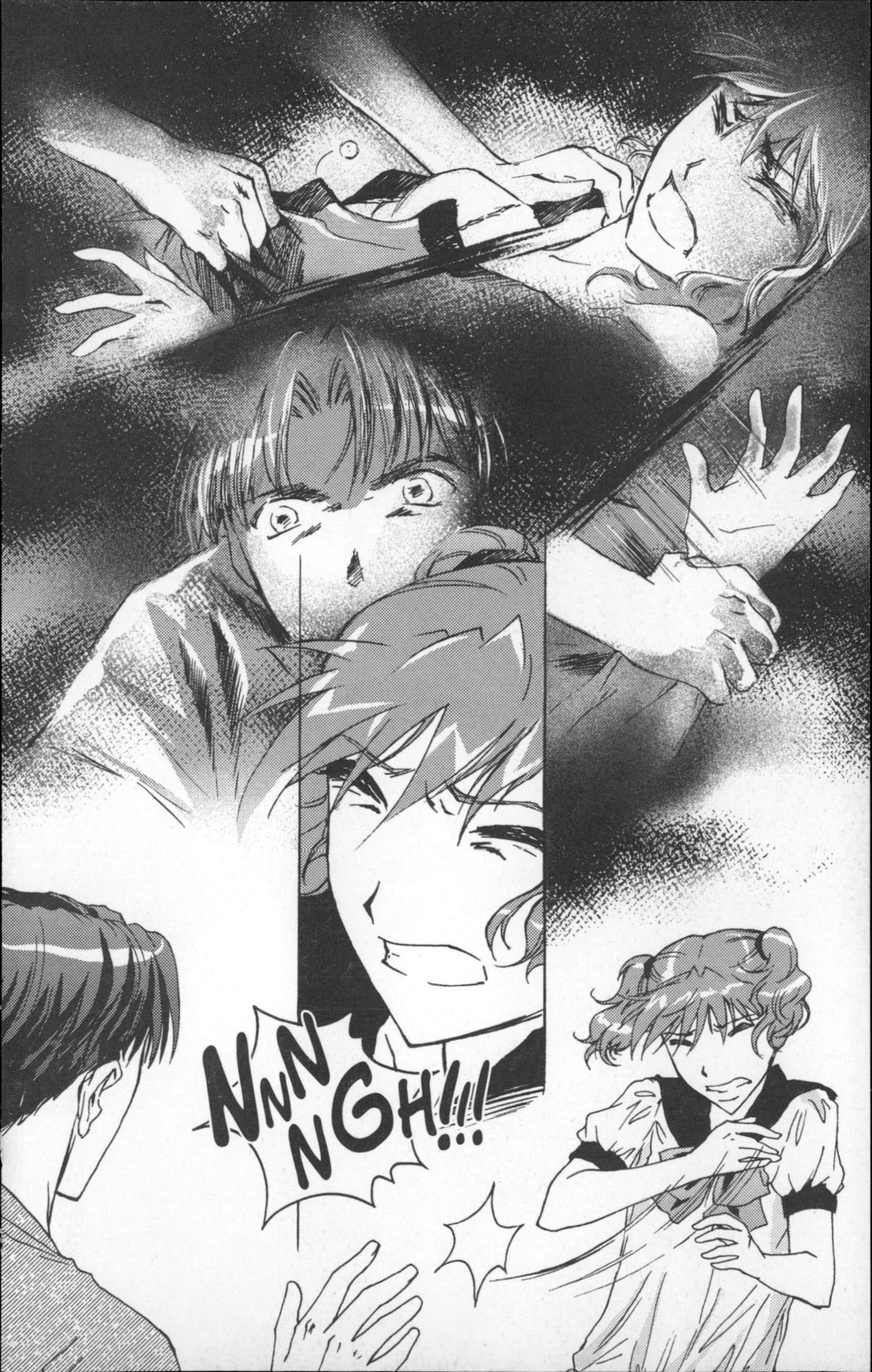
NNNNGH!!!

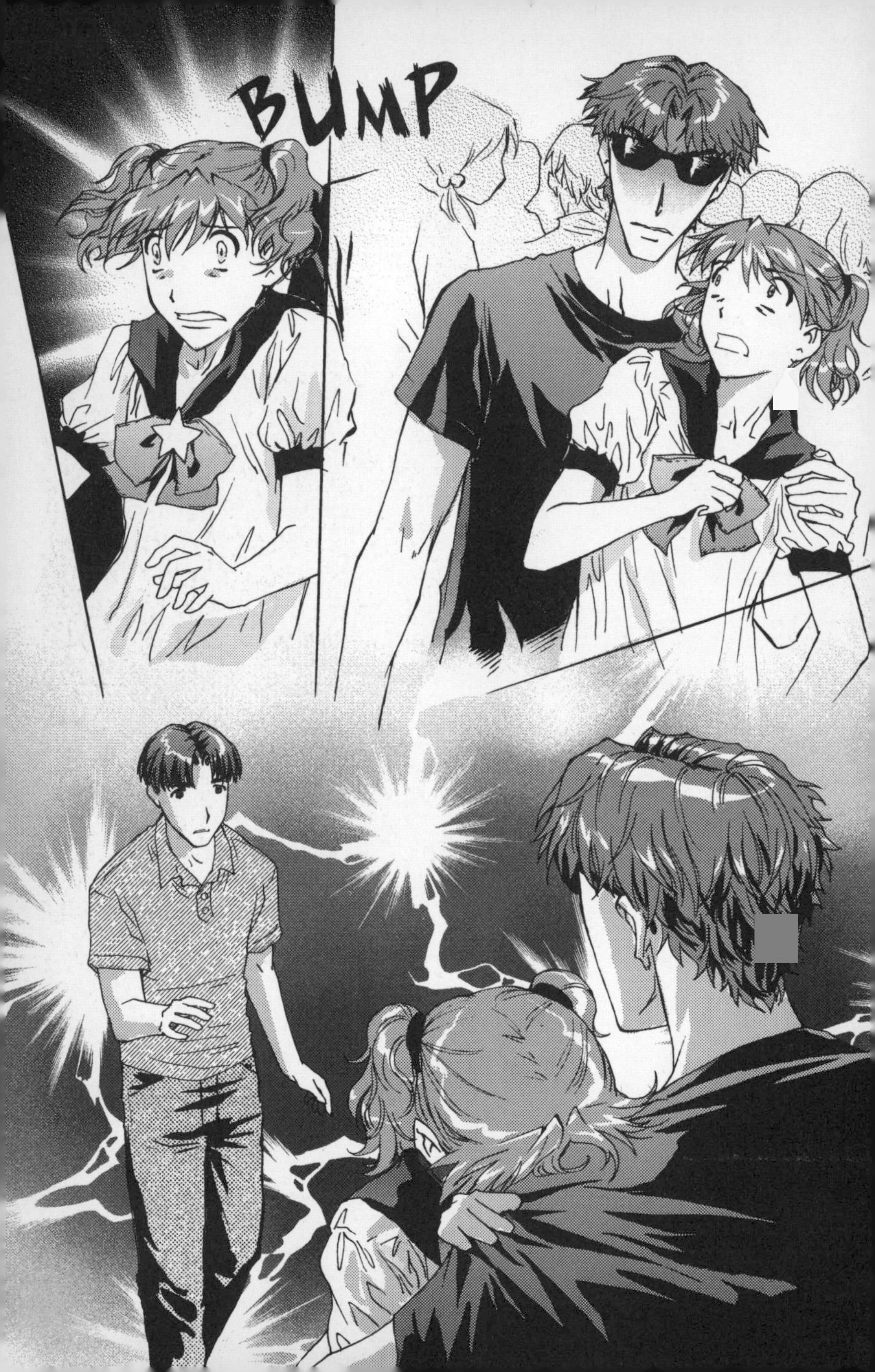
BUMP

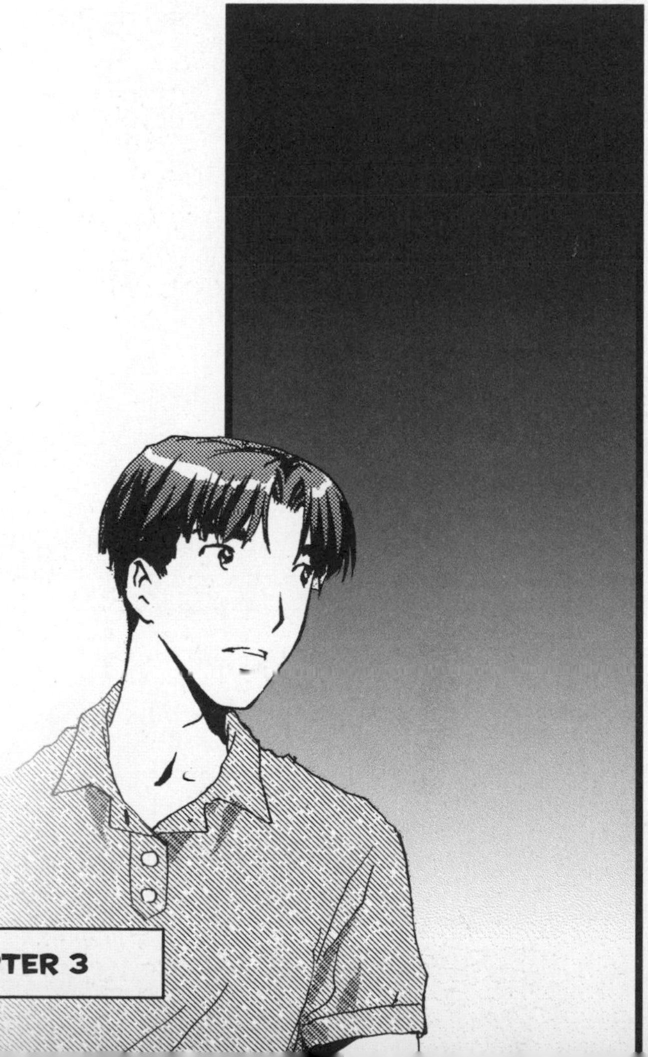

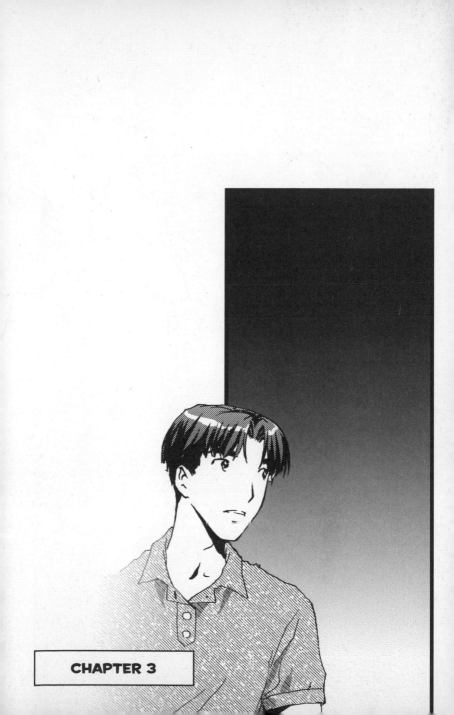

CHAPTER 3

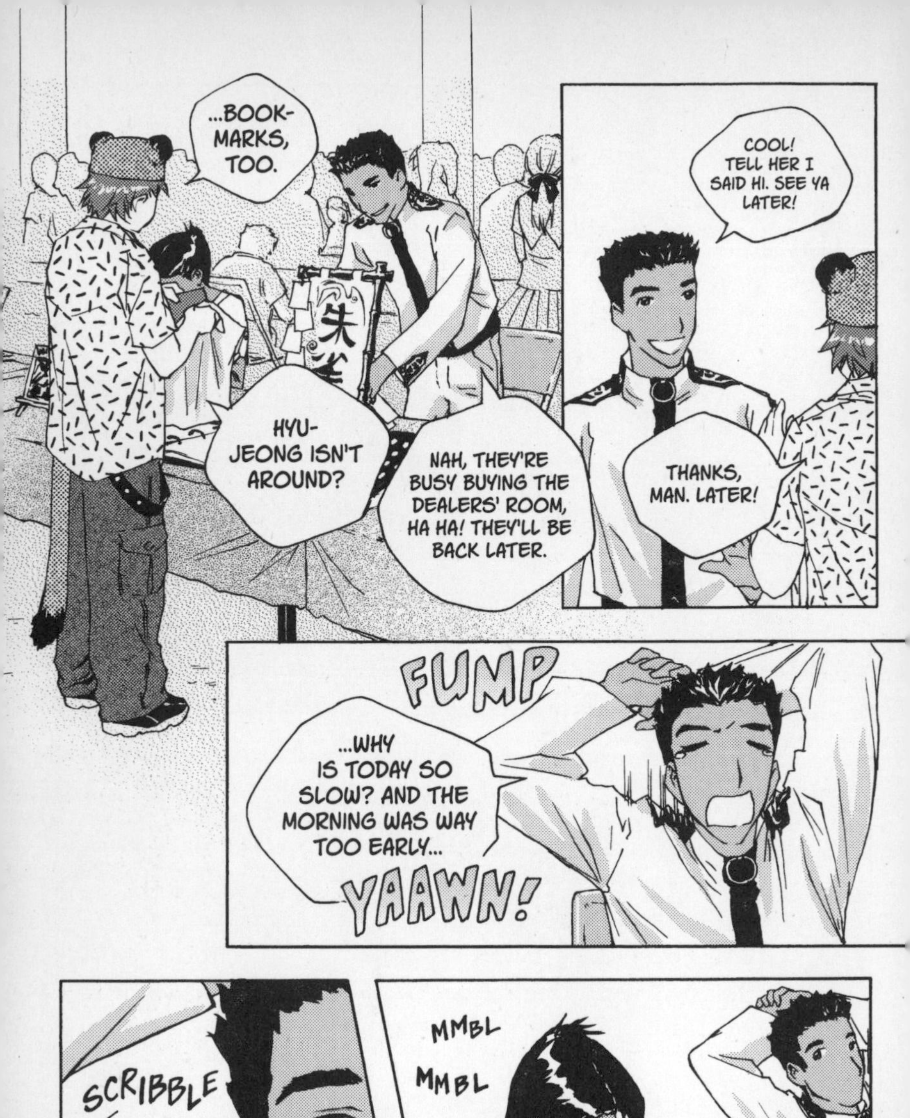
...BOOK-MARKS, TOO.
HYU-JEONG ISN'T AROUND?
NAH, THEY'RE BUSY BUYING THE DEALERS' ROOM, HA HA! THEY'LL BE BACK LATER.
COOL! TELL HER I SAID HI. SEE YA LATER!
THANKS, MAN. LATER!
FUMP
...WHY IS TODAY SO SLOW? AND THE MORNING WAS WAY TOO EARLY...
YAAWN!
SCRIBBLE
SCRIBBLE
MMBL
MMBL
SKRTCH

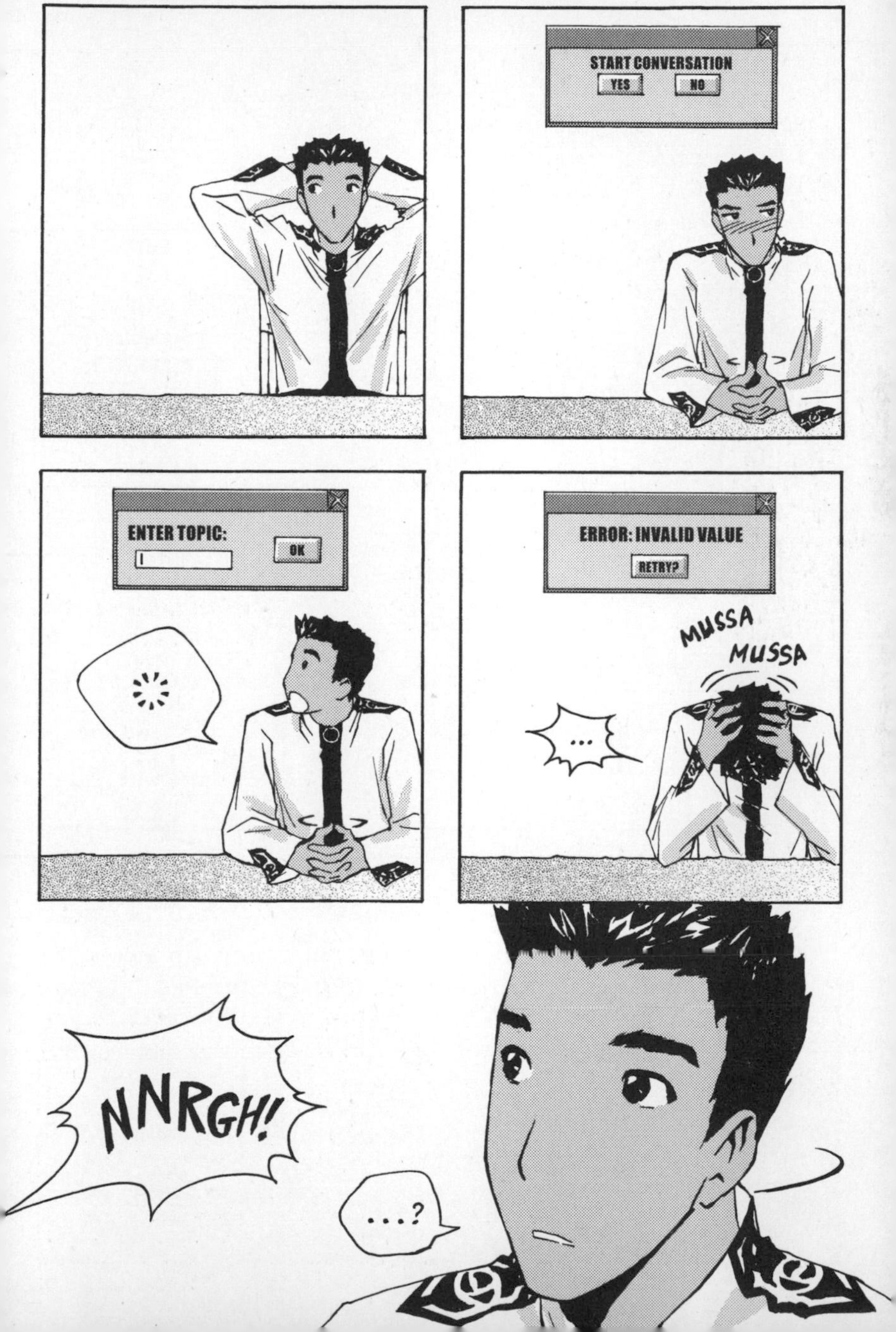
START CONVERSATION
YES
NO
ENTER TOPIC:
OK
ERROR: INVALID VALUE
RETRY?
MUSSA
MUSSA
...
NNRGH!
...?

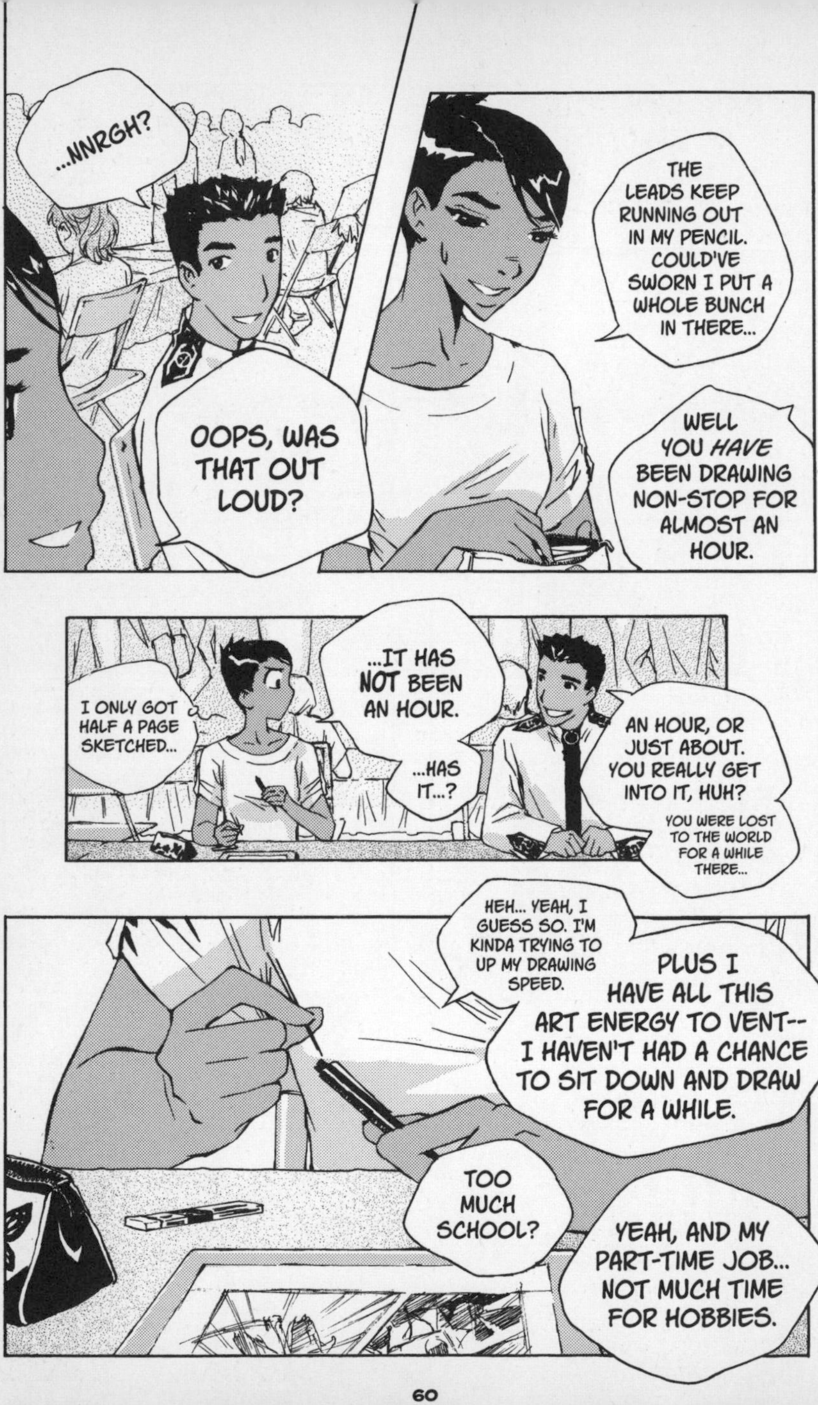
...NNRGH?
OOPS, WAS THAT OUT LOUD?
THE LEADS KEEP RUNNING OUT IN MY PENCIL. COULD'VE SWORN I PUT A WHOLE BUNCH IN THERE...
WELL YOU *HAVE* BEEN DRAWING NON-STOP FOR ALMOST AN HOUR.
I ONLY GOT HALF A PAGE SKETCHED...
...IT HAS **NOT** BEEN AN HOUR.
...HAS IT...?
AN HOUR, OR JUST ABOUT. YOU REALLY GET INTO IT, HUH?
YOU WERE LOST TO THE WORLD FOR A WHILE THERE...
HEH... YEAH, I GUESS SO. I'M KINDA TRYING TO UP MY DRAWING SPEED.
PLUS I HAVE ALL THIS ART ENERGY TO VENT-- I HAVEN'T HAD A CHANCE TO SIT DOWN AND DRAW FOR A WHILE.
TOO MUCH SCHOOL?
YEAH, AND MY PART-TIME JOB... NOT MUCH TIME FOR HOBBIES.

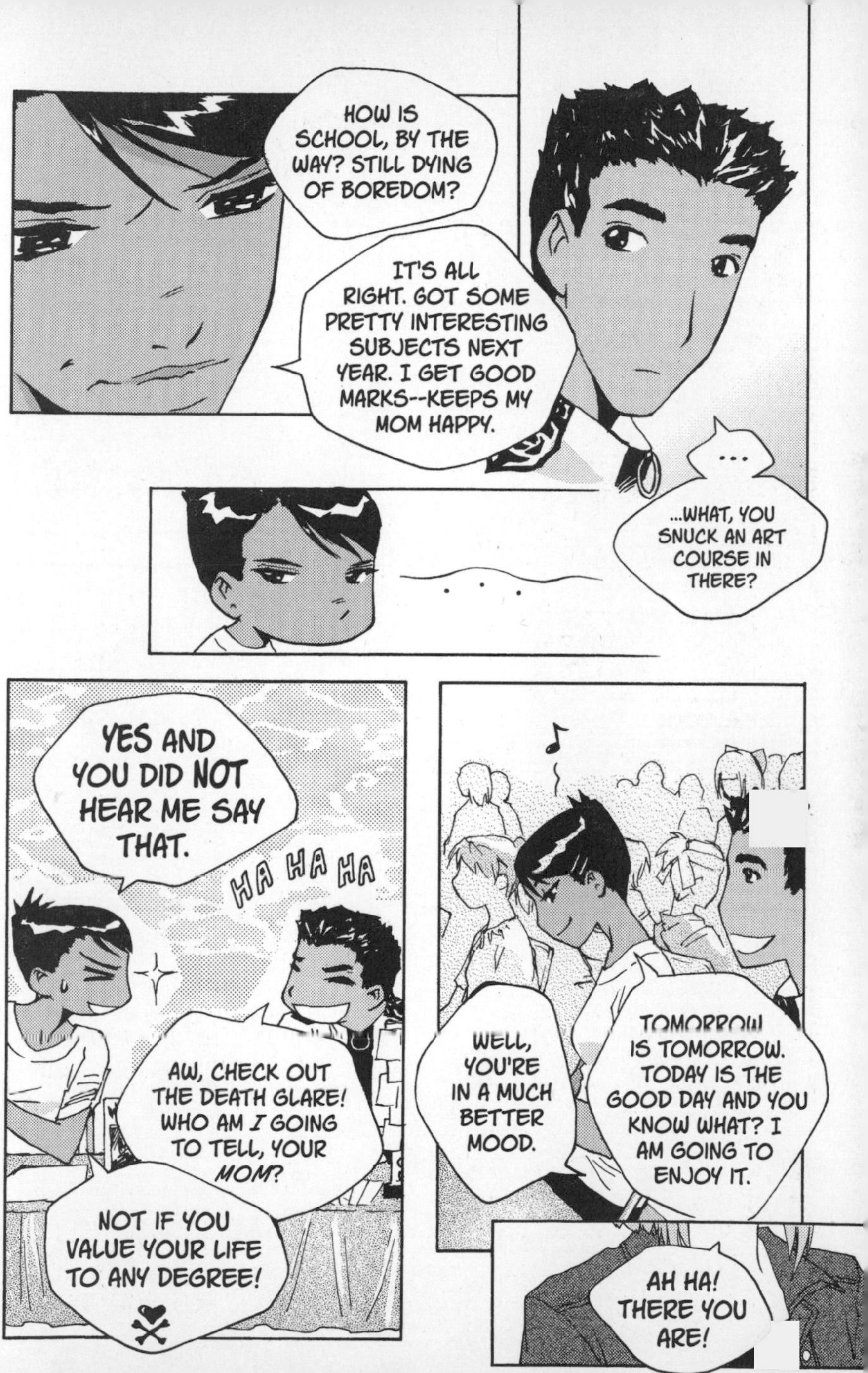

HOW IS SCHOOL, BY THE WAY? STILL DYING OF BOREDOM?
IT'S ALL RIGHT. GOT SOME PRETTY INTERESTING SUBJECTS NEXT YEAR. I GET GOOD MARKS--KEEPS MY MOM HAPPY.
...
...WHAT, YOU SNUCK AN ART COURSE IN THERE?
YES AND YOU DID NOT HEAR ME SAY THAT.
HA HA HA
AW, CHECK OUT THE DEATH GLARE! WHO AM I GOING TO TELL, YOUR MOM?
NOT IF YOU VALUE YOUR LIFE TO ANY DEGREE!
WELL, YOU'RE IN A MUCH BETTER MOOD.
TOMORROW IS TOMORROW. TODAY IS THE GOOD DAY AND YOU KNOW WHAT? I AM GOING TO ENJOY IT.
AH HA! THERE YOU ARE!

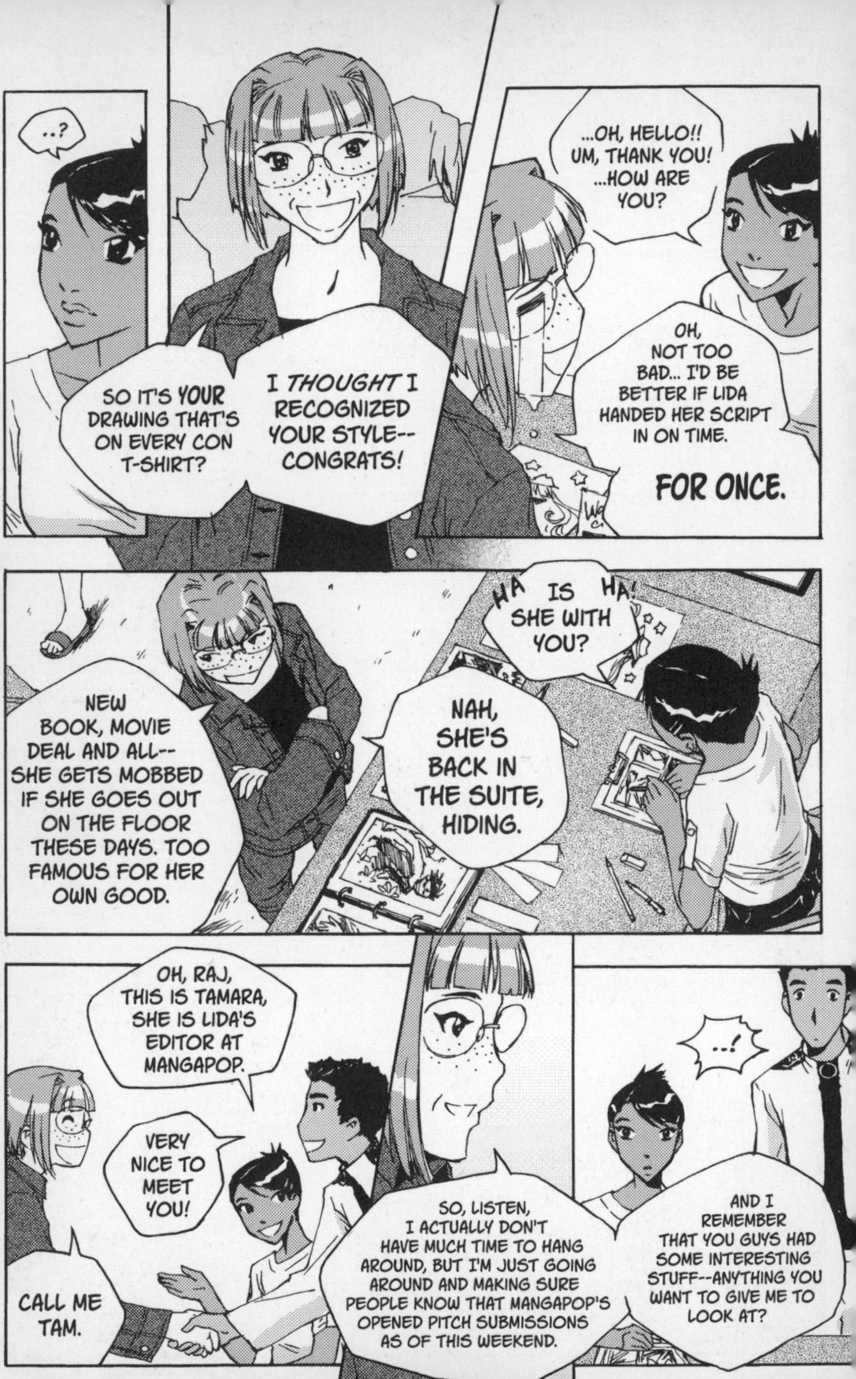

..?
I *THOUGHT* I RECOGNIZED YOUR STYLE--CONGRATS!
SO IT'S **YOUR** DRAWING THAT'S ON EVERY CON T-SHIRT?
...OH, HELLO!! UM, THANK YOU! ...HOW ARE YOU?
OH, NOT TOO BAD... I'D BE BETTER IF LIDA HANDED HER SCRIPT IN ON TIME.
FOR ONCE.
NEW BOOK, MOVIE DEAL AND ALL-- SHE GETS MOBBED IF SHE GOES OUT ON THE FLOOR THESE DAYS. TOO FAMOUS FOR HER OWN GOOD.
HA HA!
IS SHE WITH YOU?
NAH, SHE'S BACK IN THE SUITE, HIDING.
OH, RAJ, THIS IS TAMARA, SHE IS LIDA'S EDITOR AT MANGAPOP.
VERY NICE TO MEET YOU!
CALL ME TAM.
SO, LISTEN, I ACTUALLY DON'T HAVE MUCH TIME TO HANG AROUND, BUT I'M JUST GOING AROUND AND MAKING SURE PEOPLE KNOW THAT MANGAPOP'S OPENED PITCH SUBMISSIONS AS OF THIS WEEKEND.
...!
AND I REMEMBER THAT YOU GUYS HAD SOME INTERESTING STUFF--ANYTHING YOU WANT TO GIVE ME TO LOOK AT?

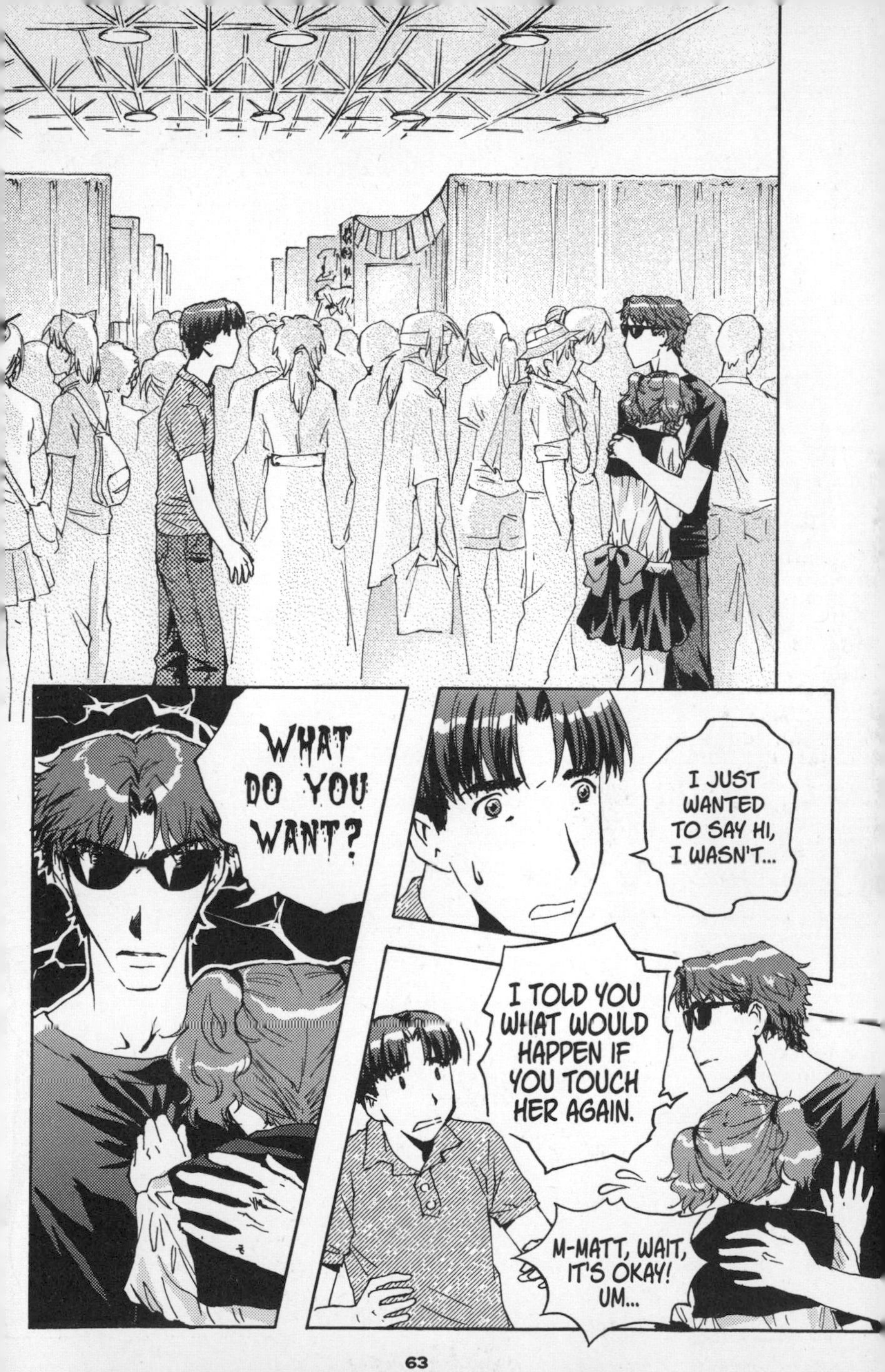
WHAT DO YOU WANT?
I JUST WANTED TO SAY HI, I WASN'T...
I TOLD YOU WHAT WOULD HAPPEN IF YOU TOUCH HER AGAIN.
M-MATT, WAIT, IT'S OKAY! UM...

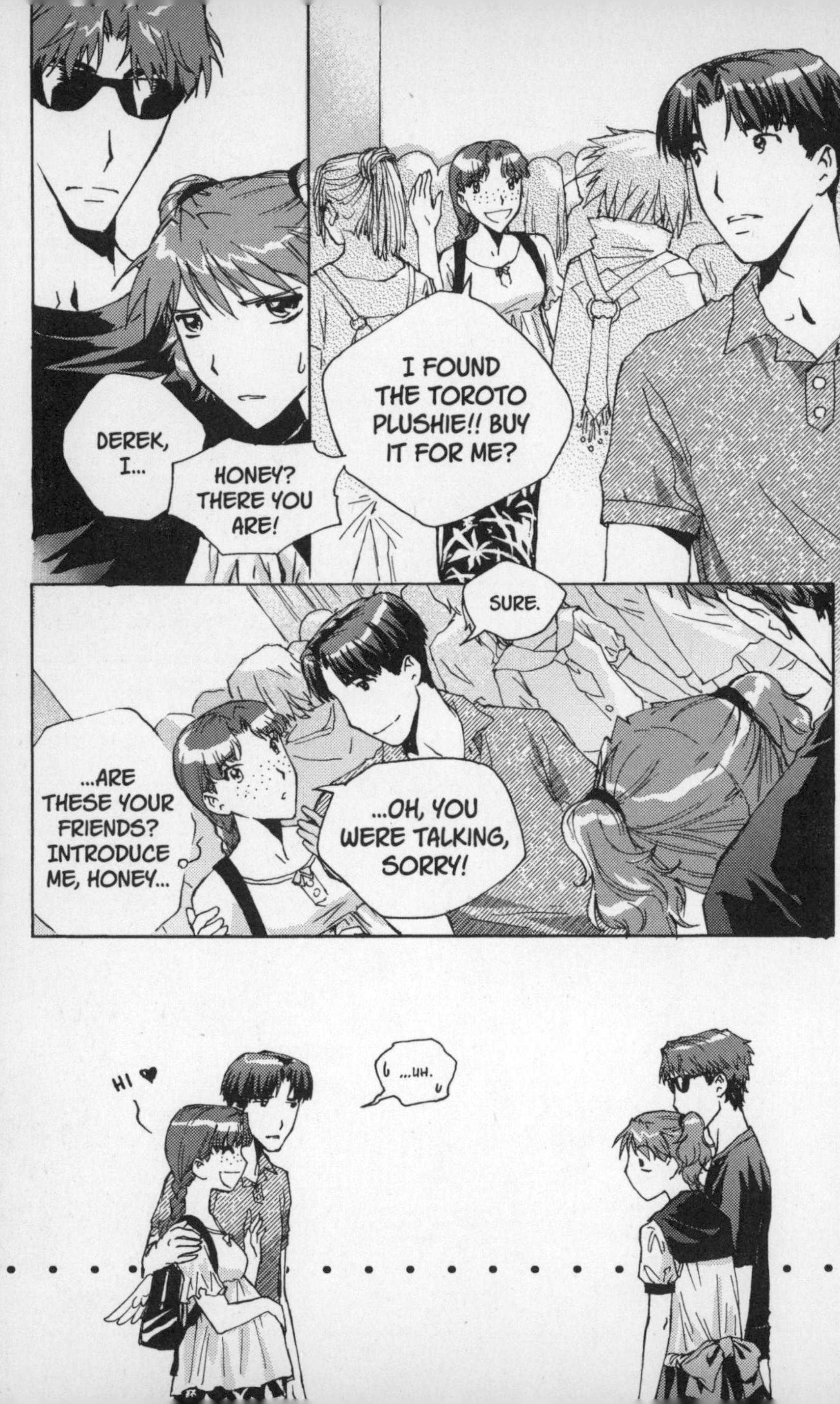
DEREK, I...
HONEY? THERE YOU ARE!
I FOUND THE TOROTO PLUSHIE!! BUY IT FOR ME?
SURE.
...ARE THESE YOUR FRIENDS? INTRODUCE ME, HONEY...
...OH, YOU WERE TALKING, SORRY!
HI ♥
...UH.

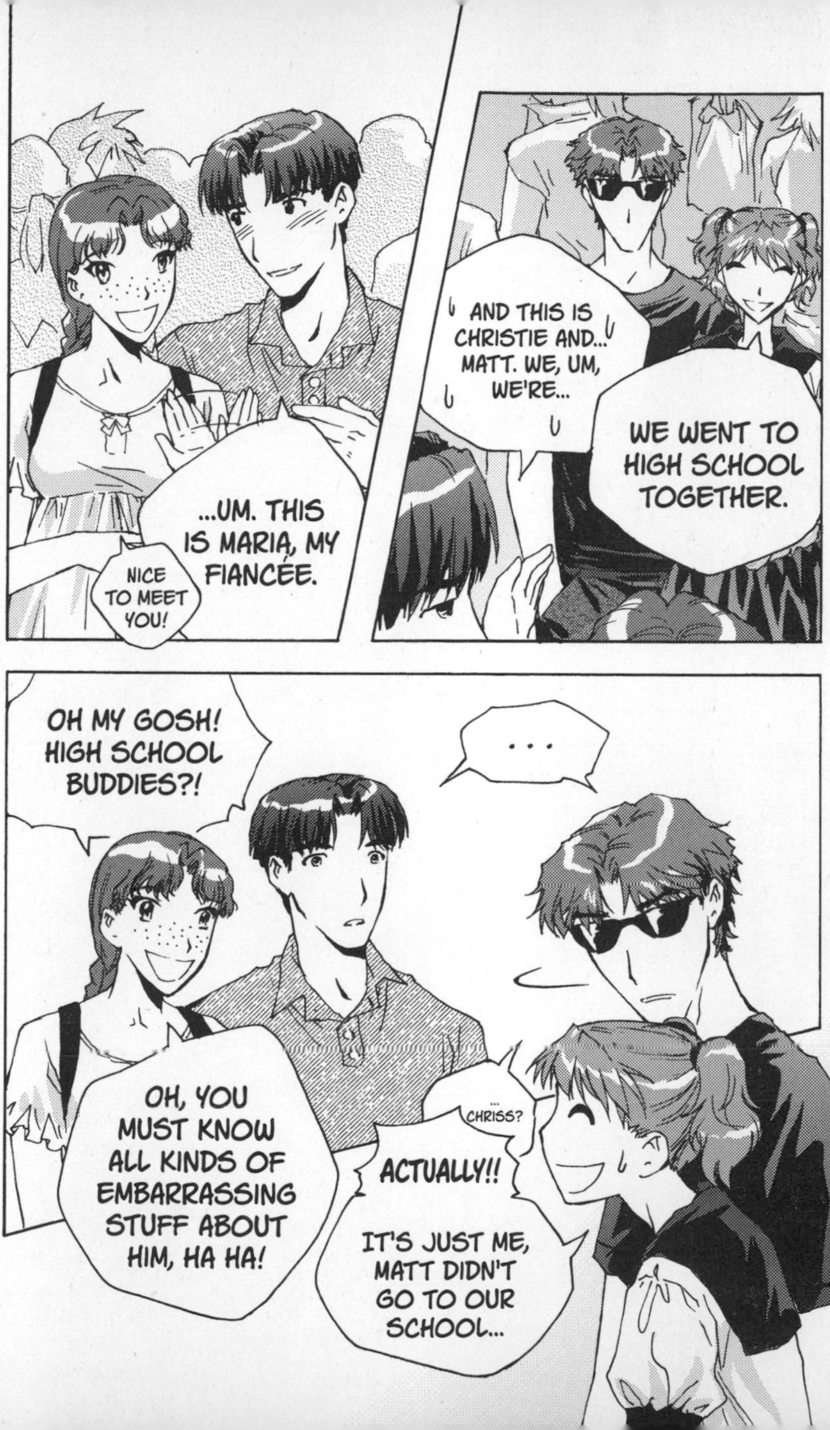
...UM. THIS IS MARIA, MY FIANCÉE.
NICE TO MEET YOU!
AND THIS IS CHRISTIE AND... MATT. WE, UM, WE'RE...
WE WENT TO HIGH SCHOOL TOGETHER.
OH MY GOSH! HIGH SCHOOL BUDDIES?!
...
OH, YOU MUST KNOW ALL KINDS OF EMBARRASSING STUFF ABOUT HIM, HA HA!
...CHRISS?
ACTUALLY!!
IT'S JUST ME, MATT DIDN'T GO TO OUR SCHOOL...

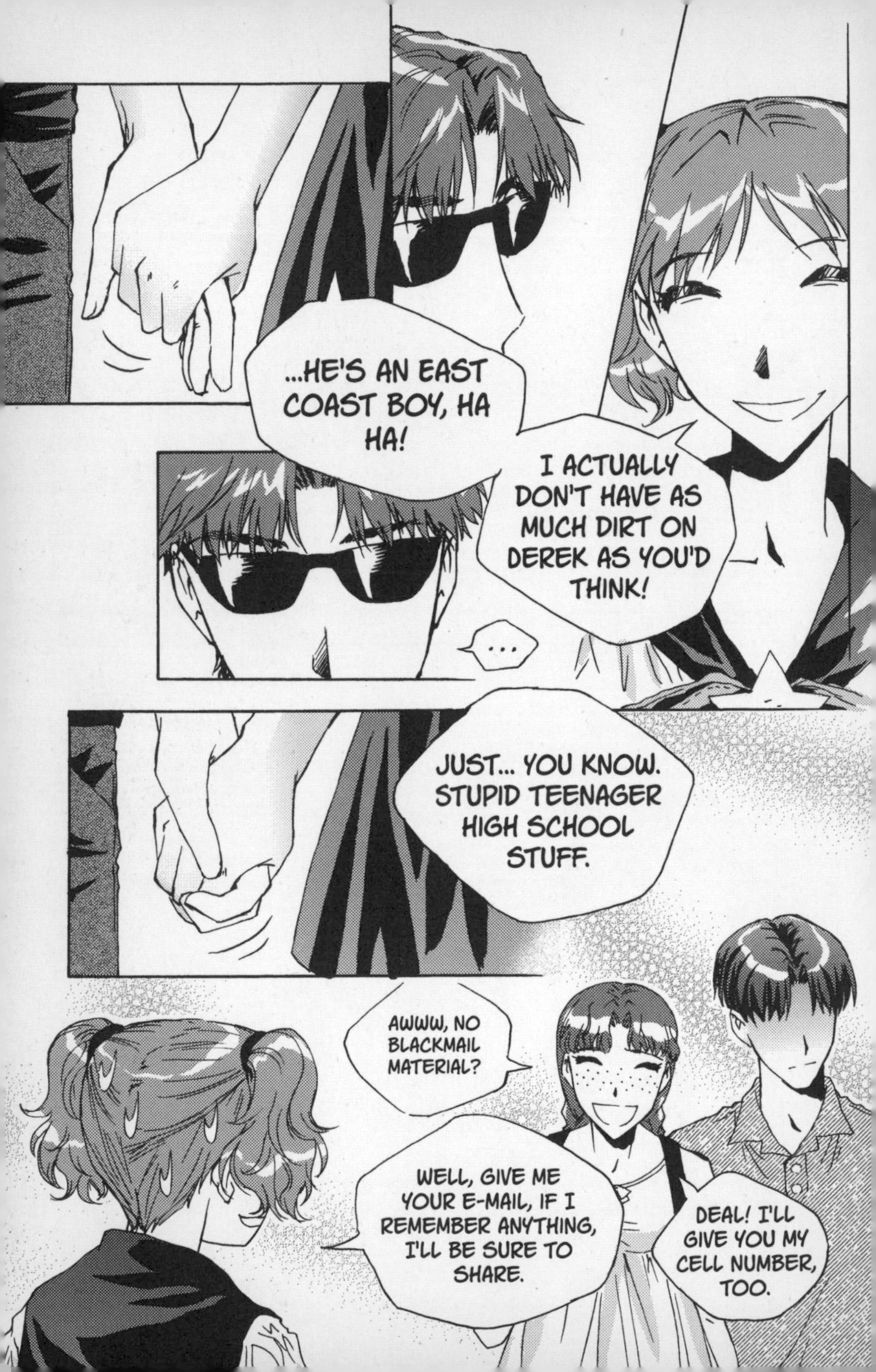
...HE'S AN EAST COAST BOY, HA HA!
I ACTUALLY DON'T HAVE AS MUCH DIRT ON DEREK AS YOU'D THINK!
...
JUST... YOU KNOW. STUPID TEENAGER HIGH SCHOOL STUFF.
AWWW, NO BLACKMAIL MATERIAL?
WELL, GIVE ME YOUR E-MAIL, IF I REMEMBER ANYTHING, I'LL BE SURE TO SHARE.
DEAL! I'LL GIVE YOU MY CELL NUMBER, TOO.

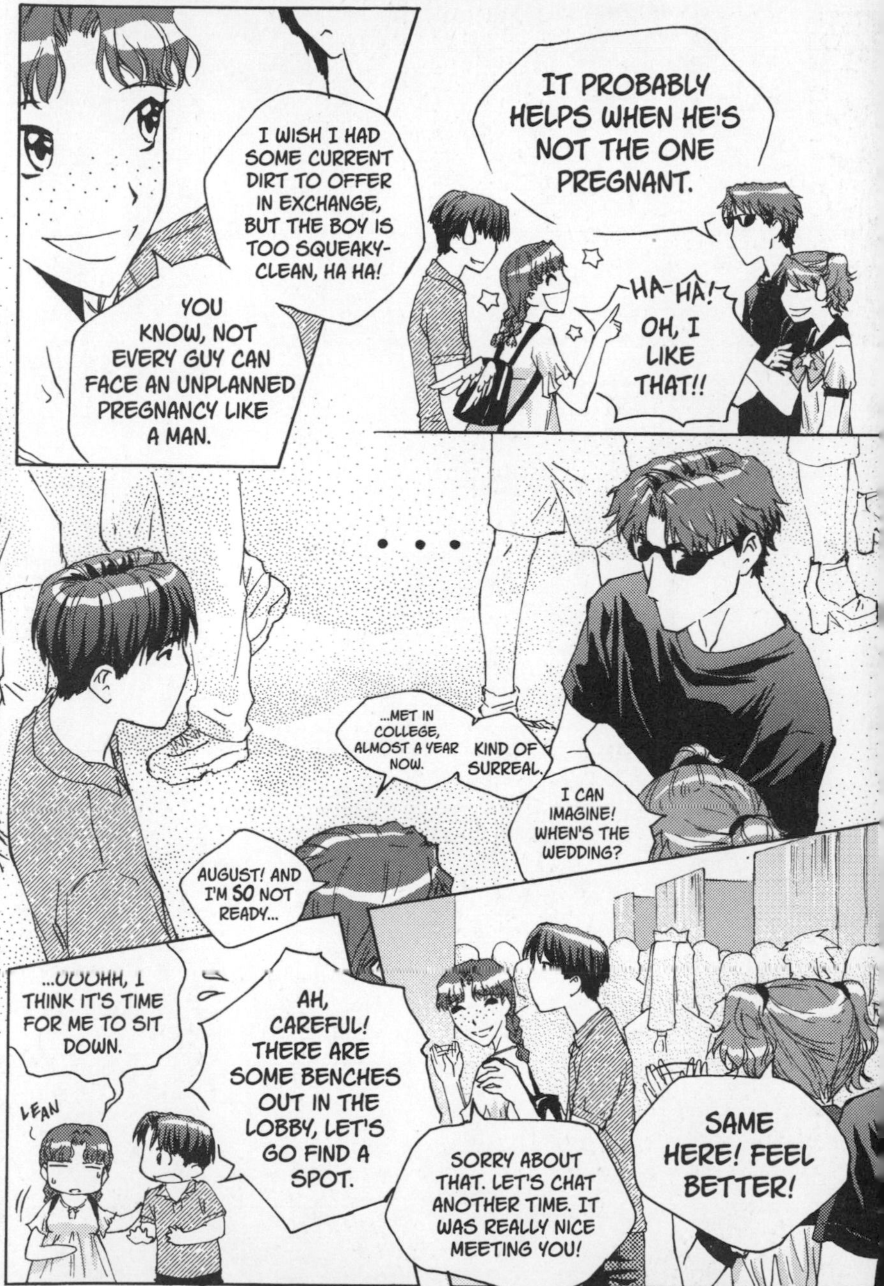
I WISH I HAD SOME CURRENT DIRT TO OFFER IN EXCHANGE, BUT THE BOY IS TOO SQUEAKY-CLEAN, HA HA!
YOU KNOW, NOT EVERY GUY CAN FACE AN UNPLANNED PREGNANCY LIKE A MAN.
IT PROBABLY HELPS WHEN HE'S NOT THE ONE PREGNANT.
HA-HA!
OH, I LIKE THAT!!
• • •
...MET IN COLLEGE, ALMOST A YEAR NOW.
KIND OF SURREAL.
I CAN IMAGINE! WHEN'S THE WEDDING?
AUGUST! AND I'M SO NOT READY...
...UUUHH, I THINK IT'S TIME FOR ME TO SIT DOWN.
AH, CAREFUL! THERE ARE SOME BENCHES OUT IN THE LOBBY, LET'S GO FIND A SPOT.
LEAN
SORRY ABOUT THAT. LET'S CHAT ANOTHER TIME. IT WAS REALLY NICE MEETING YOU!
SAME HERE! FEEL BETTER!

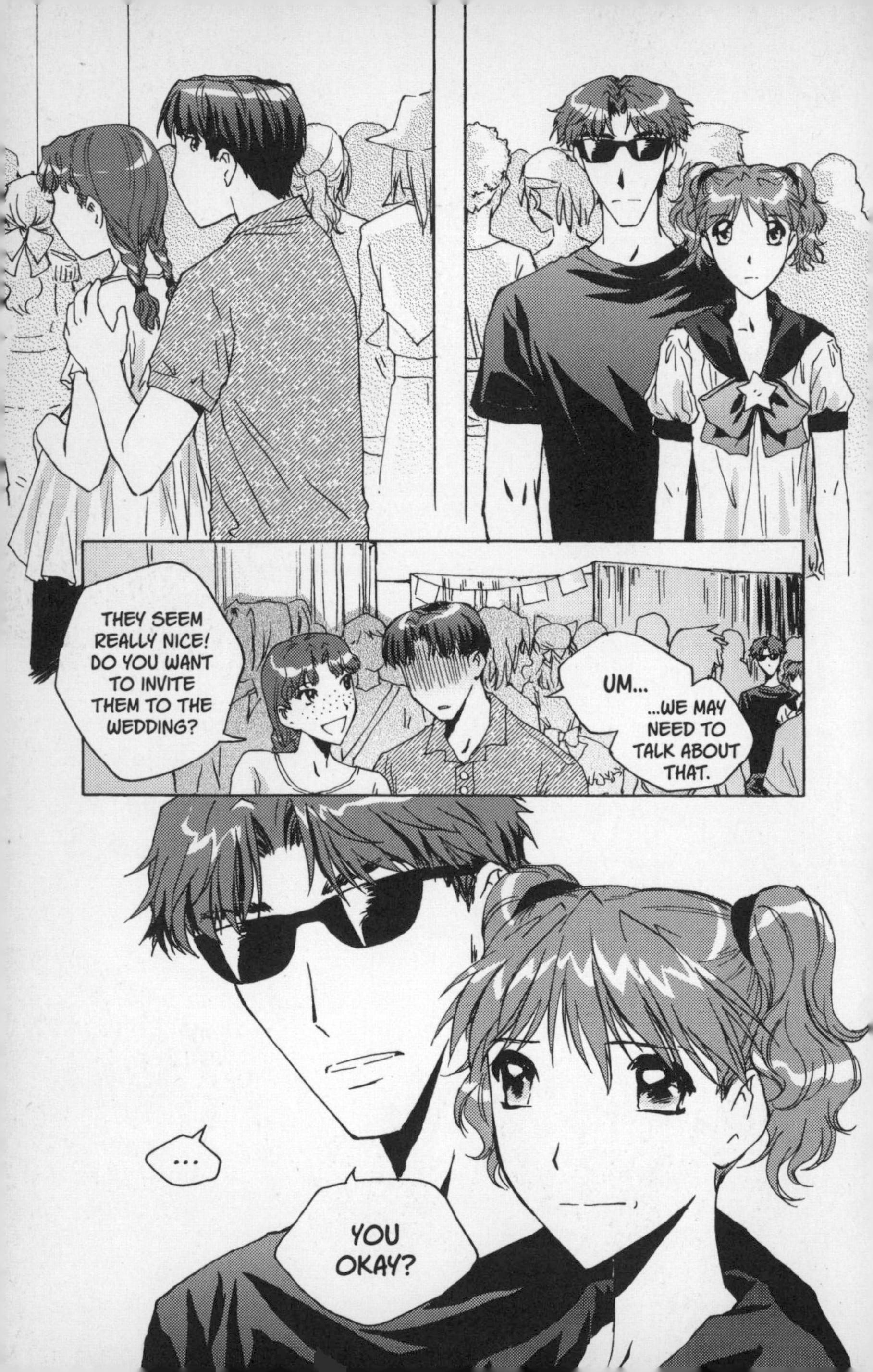
THEY SEEM REALLY NICE! DO YOU WANT TO INVITE THEM TO THE WEDDING?
UM...
...WE MAY NEED TO TALK ABOUT THAT.
...
YOU OKAY?

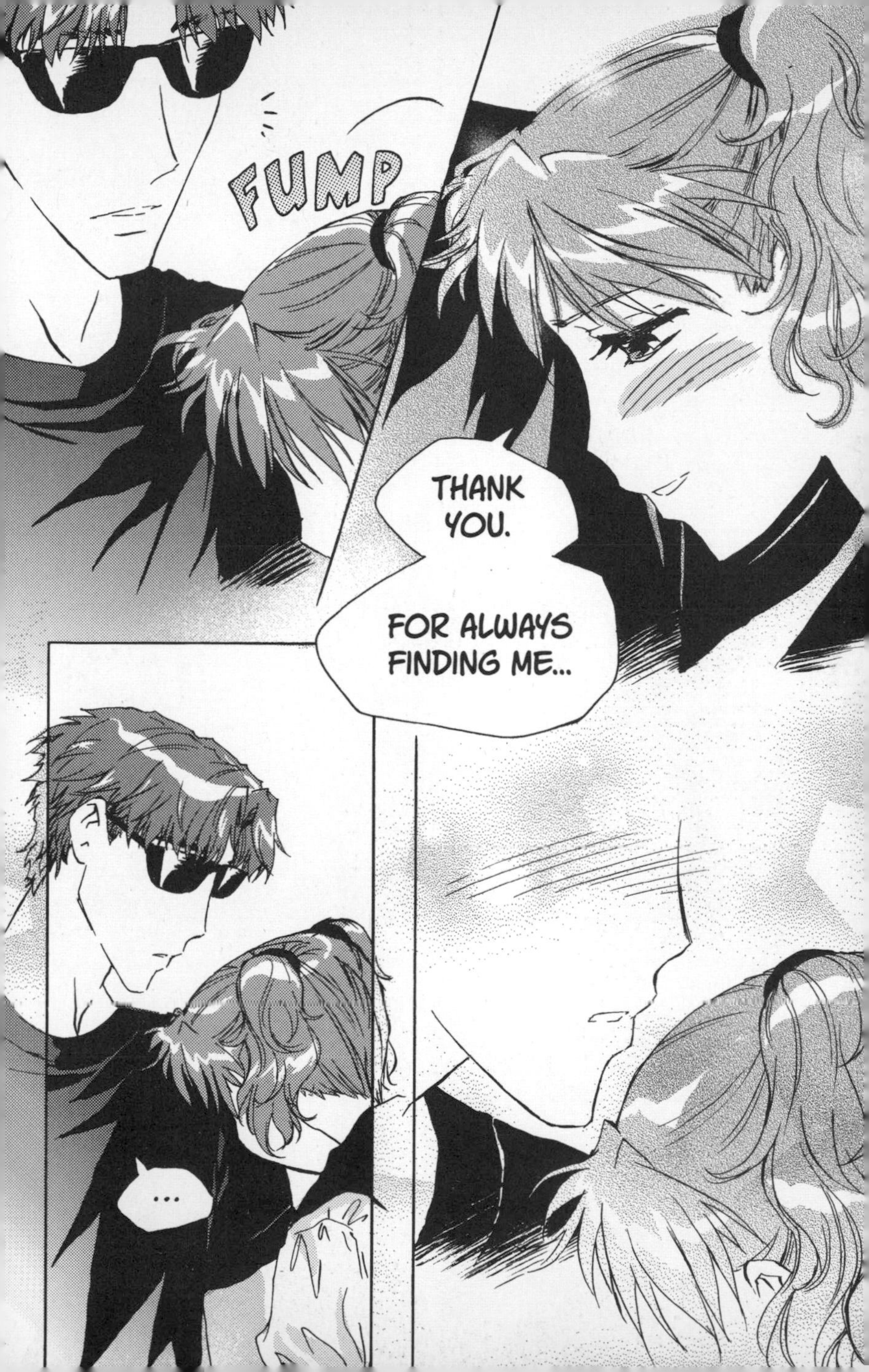
FUMP
THANK YOU.
FOR ALWAYS FINDING ME...
...

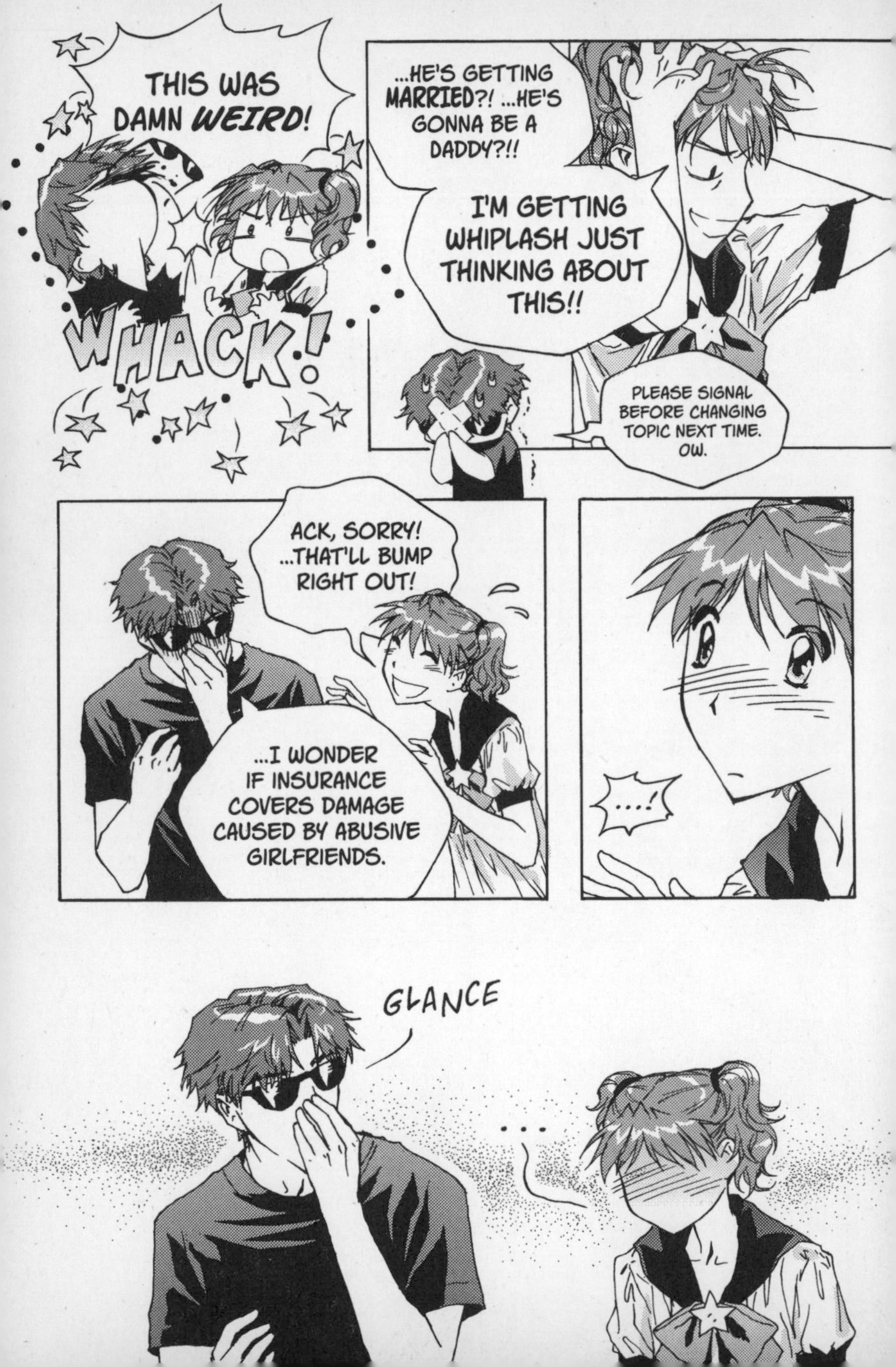

THIS WAS DAMN *WEIRD*!
WHACK!
...HE'S GETTING MARRIED?! ...HE'S GONNA BE A DADDY?!!
I'M GETTING WHIPLASH JUST THINKING ABOUT THIS!!
PLEASE SIGNAL BEFORE CHANGING TOPIC NEXT TIME. OW.
ACK, SORRY! ...THAT'LL BUMP RIGHT OUT!
...I WONDER IF INSURANCE COVERS DAMAGE CAUSED BY ABUSIVE GIRLFRIENDS.
...!
GLANCE
...

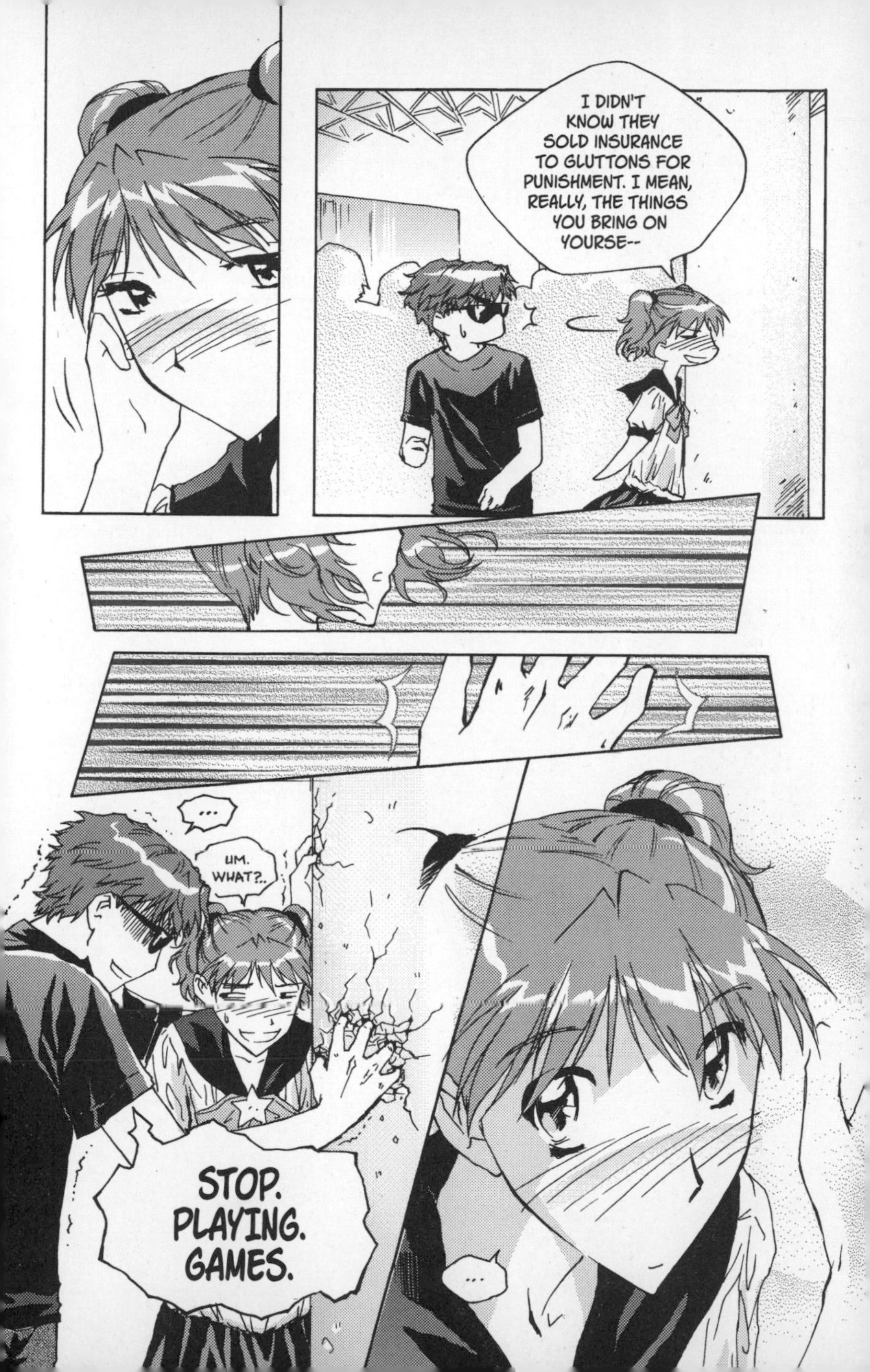
I DIDN'T KNOW THEY SOLD INSURANCE TO GLUTTONS FOR PUNISHMENT. I MEAN, REALLY, THE THINGS YOU BRING ON YOURSE--
...
UM. WHAT?..
STOP. PLAYING. GAMES.
...

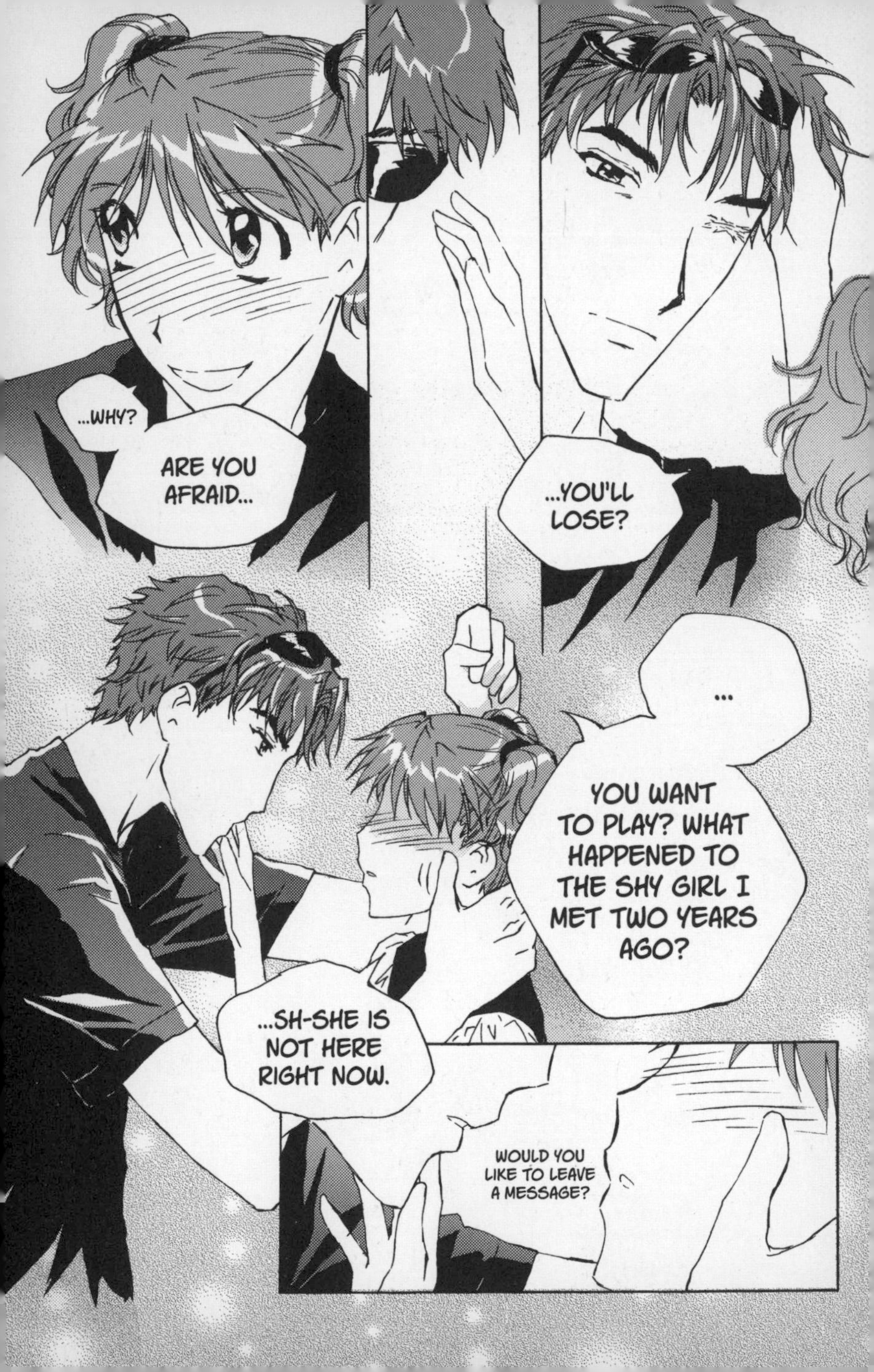
...WHY?
ARE YOU AFRAID...
...YOU'LL LOSE?
...
YOU WANT TO PLAY? WHAT HAPPENED TO THE SHY GIRL I MET TWO YEARS AGO?
...SH-SHE IS NOT HERE RIGHT NOW.
WOULD YOU LIKE TO LEAVE A MESSAGE?

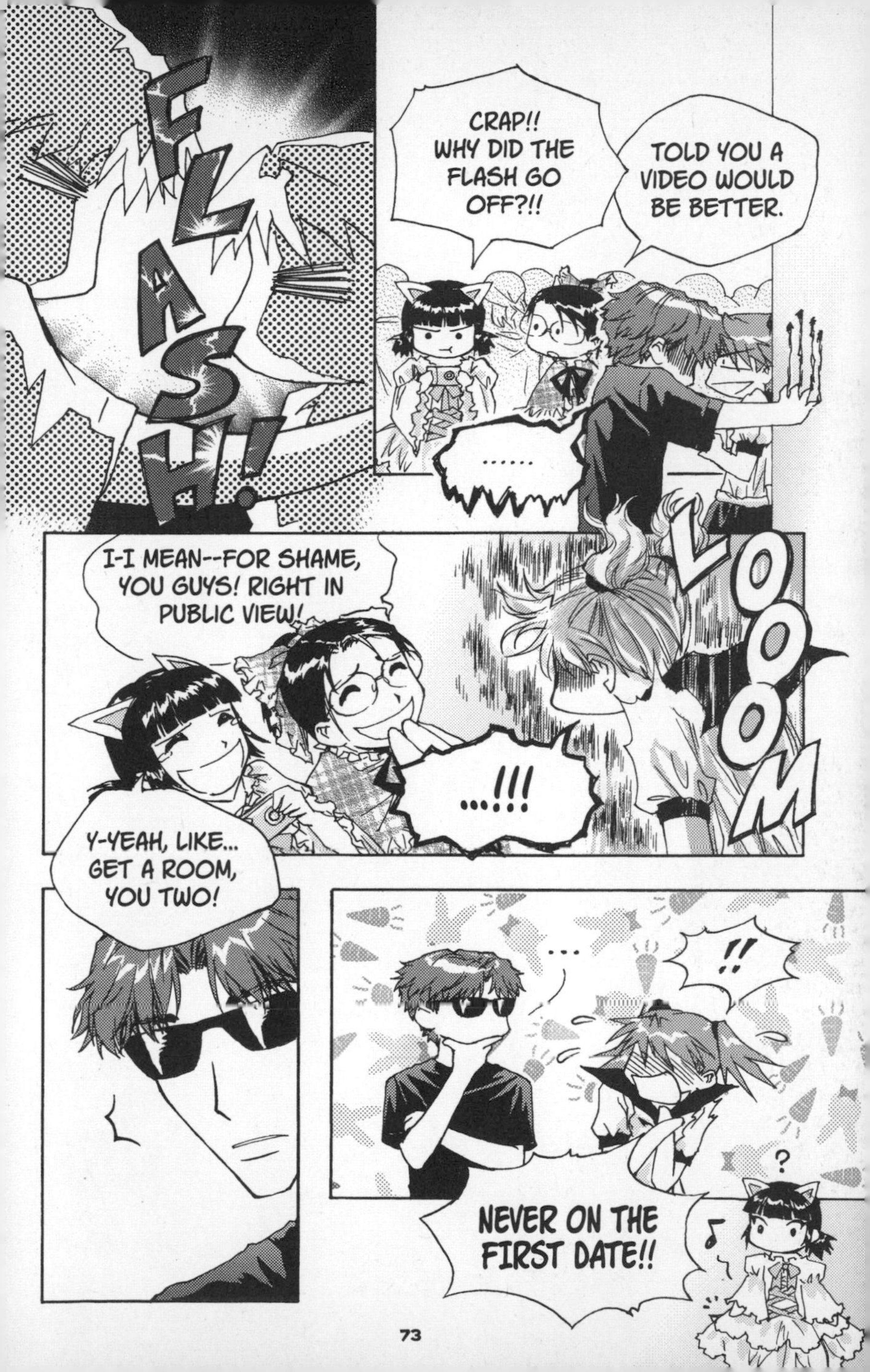
FLASH!
CRAP!! WHY DID THE FLASH GO OFF?!!
TOLD YOU A VIDEO WOULD BE BETTER.
......
I-I MEAN--FOR SHAME, YOU GUYS! RIGHT IN PUBLIC VIEW!
LOOOOM
...!!!
Y-YEAH, LIKE... GET A ROOM, YOU TWO!
...
!!
?
NEVER ON THE FIRST DATE!!

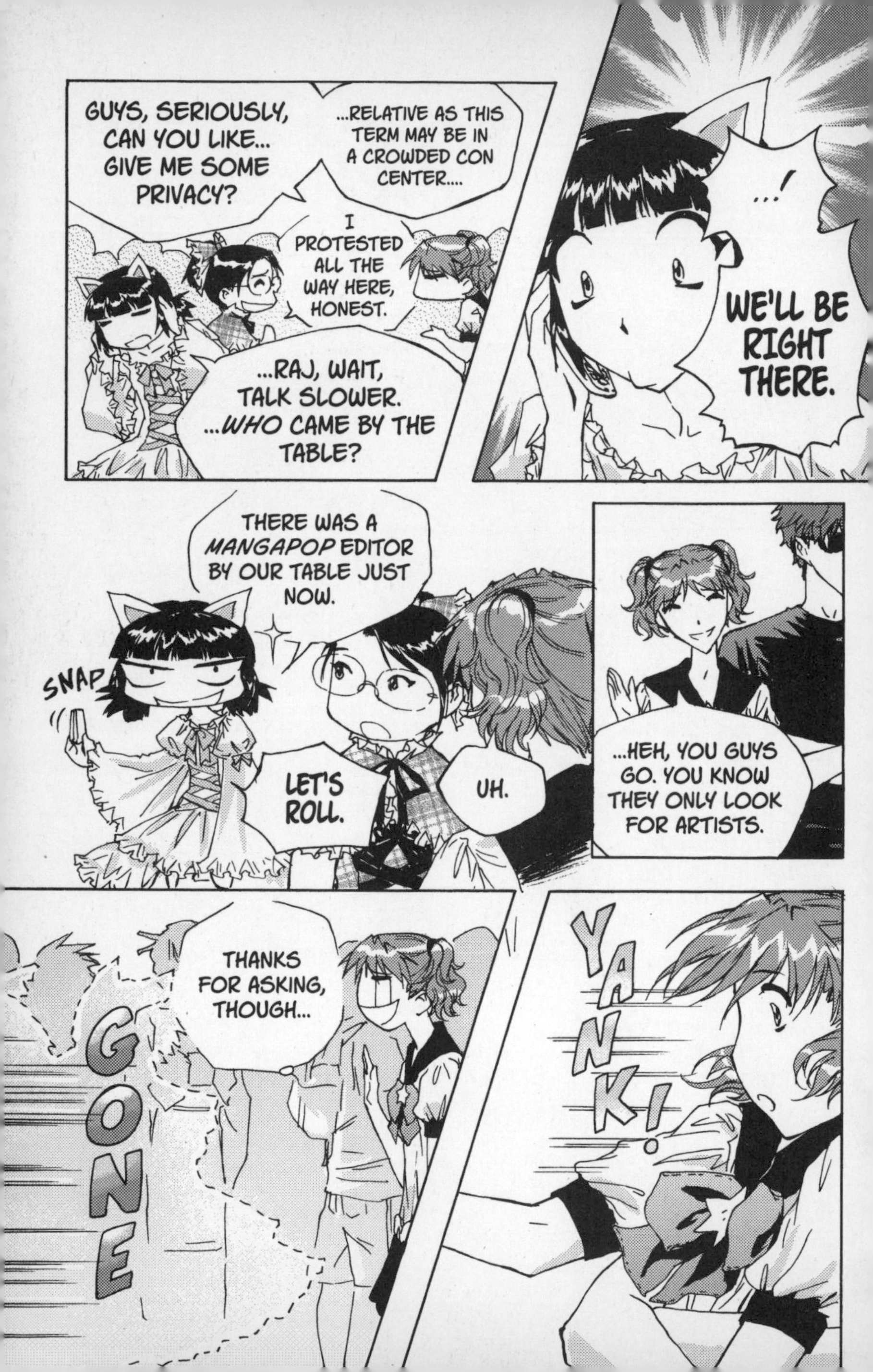
GUYS, SERIOUSLY, CAN YOU LIKE... GIVE ME SOME PRIVACY?
...RELATIVE AS THIS TERM MAY BE IN A CROWDED CON CENTER....
I PROTESTED ALL THE WAY HERE, HONEST.
...RAJ, WAIT, TALK SLOWER. ...*WHO* CAME BY THE TABLE?
...!
WE'LL BE RIGHT THERE.
THERE WAS A *MANGAPOP* EDITOR BY OUR TABLE JUST NOW.
SNAP
LET'S ROLL.
UH.
...HEH, YOU GUYS GO. YOU KNOW THEY ONLY LOOK FOR ARTISTS.
THANKS FOR ASKING, THOUGH...
GONE
YANK!

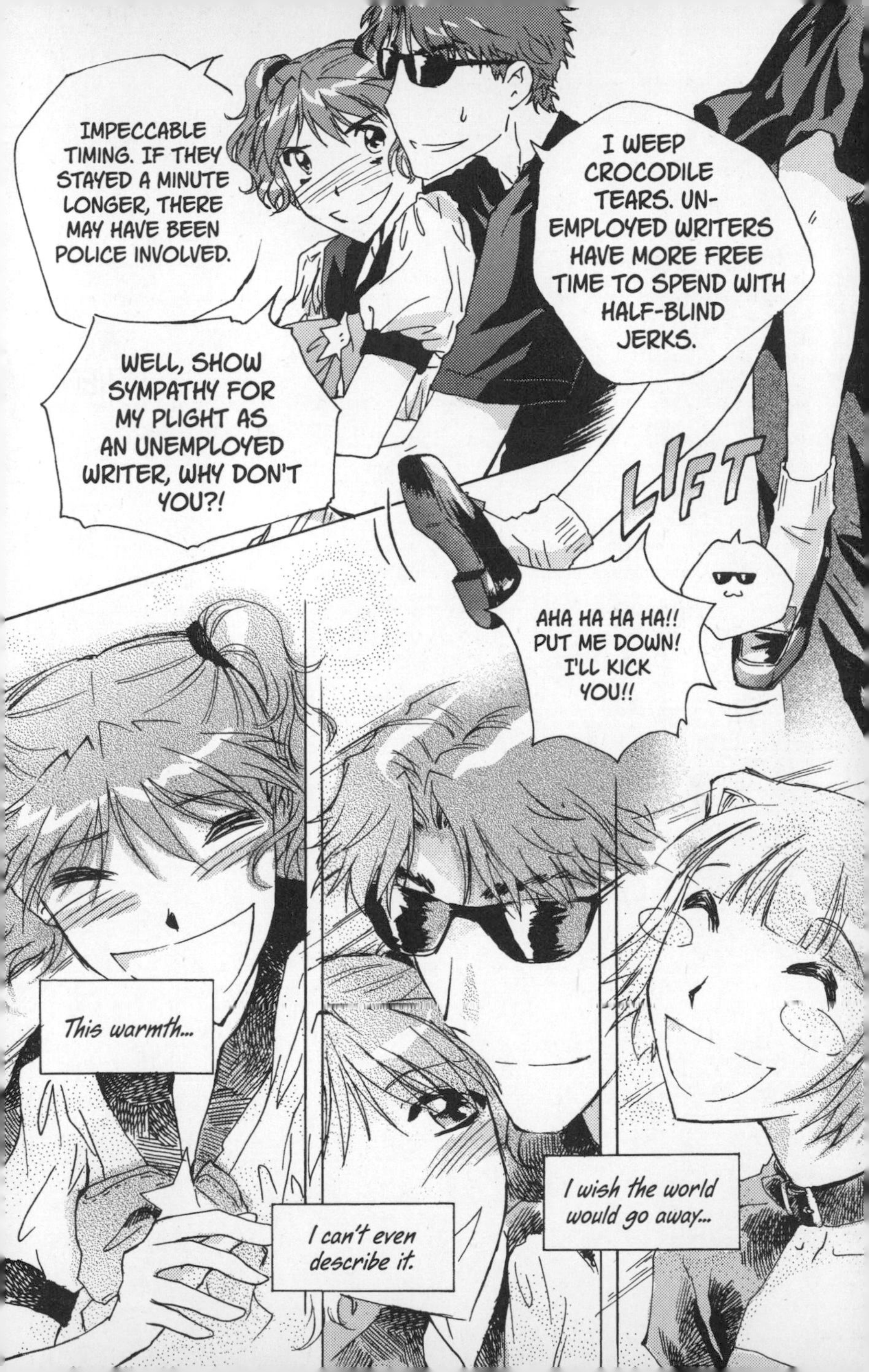
IMPECCABLE TIMING. IF THEY STAYED A MINUTE LONGER, THERE MAY HAVE BEEN POLICE INVOLVED.
WELL, SHOW SYMPATHY FOR MY PLIGHT AS AN UNEMPLOYED WRITER, WHY DON'T YOU?!
I WEEP CROCODILE TEARS. UN-EMPLOYED WRITERS HAVE MORE FREE TIME TO SPEND WITH HALF-BLIND JERKS.
LIFT
AHA HA HA HA!! PUT ME DOWN! I'LL KICK YOU!!
This warmth...
I can't even describe it.
I wish the world would go away...

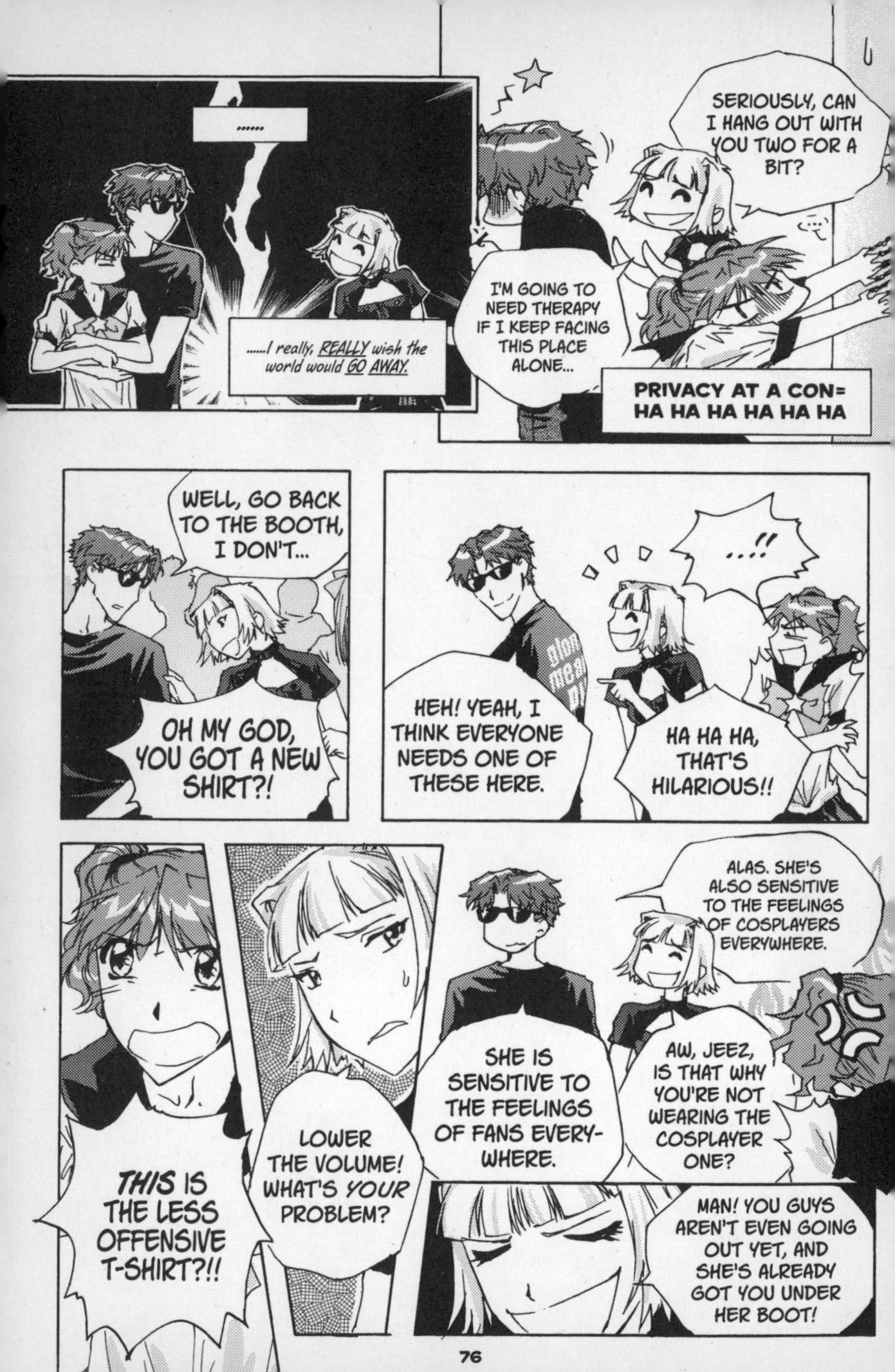
......
......I really, REALLY wish the world would GO AWAY.
SERIOUSLY, CAN I HANG OUT WITH YOU TWO FOR A BIT?
I'M GOING TO NEED THERAPY IF I KEEP FACING THIS PLACE ALONE...
PRIVACY AT A CON= HA HA HA HA HA HA
WELL, GO BACK TO THE BOOTH, I DON'T...
OH MY GOD, YOU GOT A NEW SHIRT?!
...!!
HEH! YEAH, I THINK EVERYONE NEEDS ONE OF THESE HERE.
HA HA HA, THAT'S HILARIOUS!!
THIS IS THE LESS OFFENSIVE T-SHIRT?!!
LOWER THE VOLUME! WHAT'S YOUR PROBLEM?
SHE IS SENSITIVE TO THE FEELINGS OF FANS EVERY-WHERE.
ALAS. SHE'S ALSO SENSITIVE TO THE FEELINGS OF COSPLAYERS EVERYWHERE.
AW, JEEZ, IS THAT WHY YOU'RE NOT WEARING THE COSPLAYER ONE?
MAN! YOU GUYS AREN'T EVEN GOING OUT YET, AND SHE'S ALREADY GOT YOU UNDER HER BOOT!

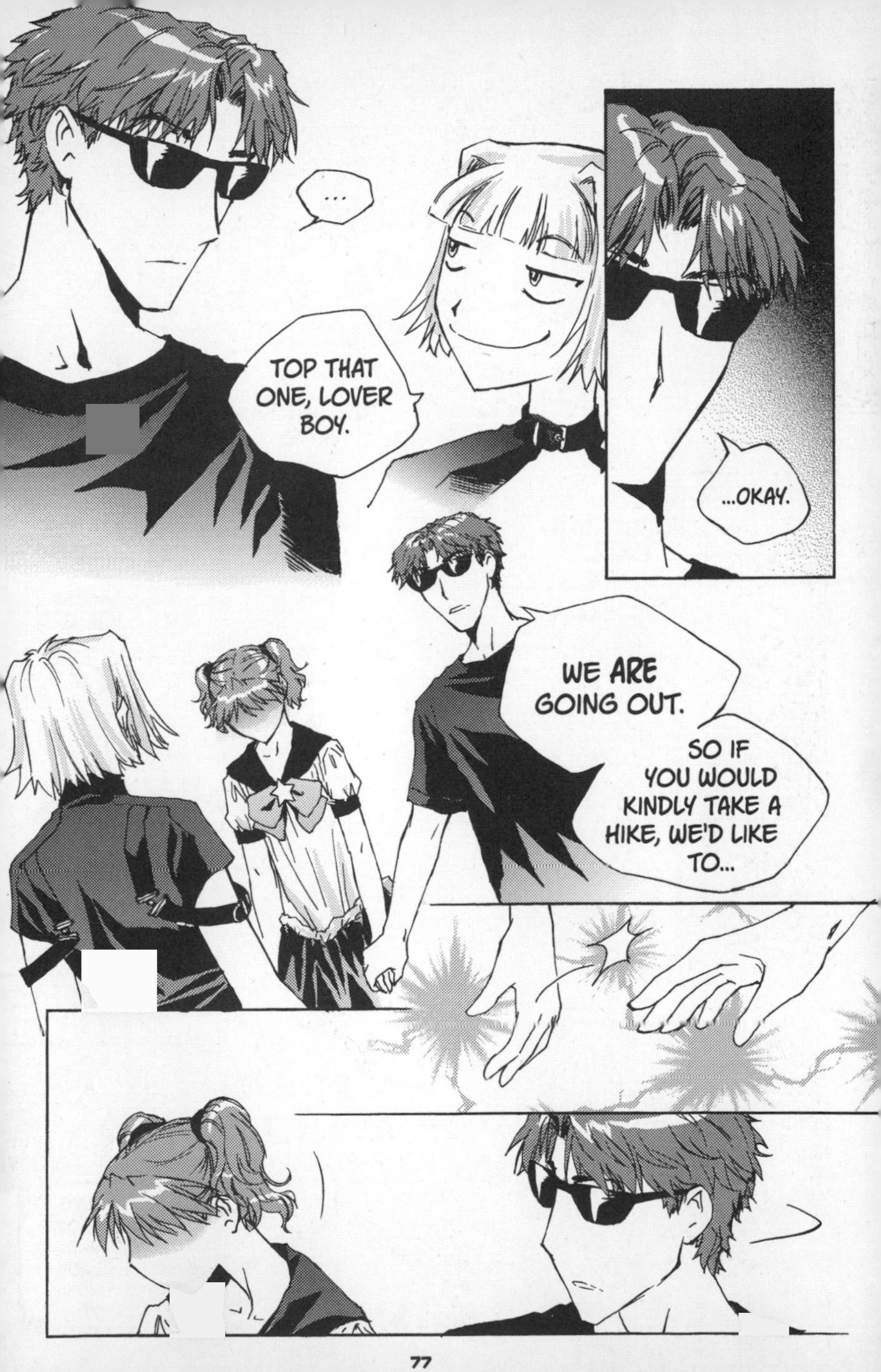
...
TOP THAT ONE, LOVER BOY.
...OKAY.
WE ARE GOING OUT.
SO IF YOU WOULD KINDLY TAKE A HIKE, WE'D LIKE TO...

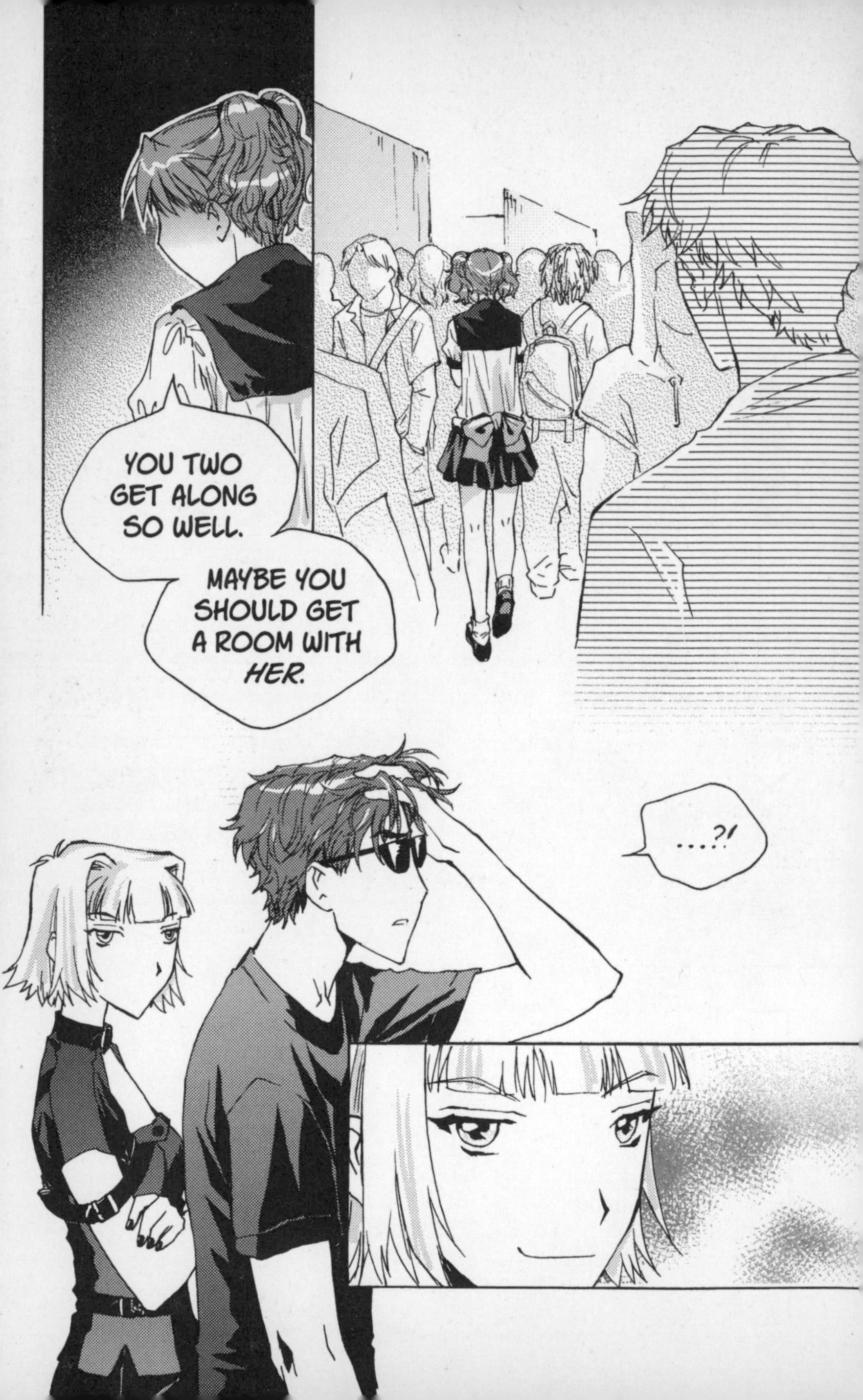
YOU TWO GET ALONG SO WELL.
MAYBE YOU SHOULD GET A ROOM WITH *HER*.
...?!

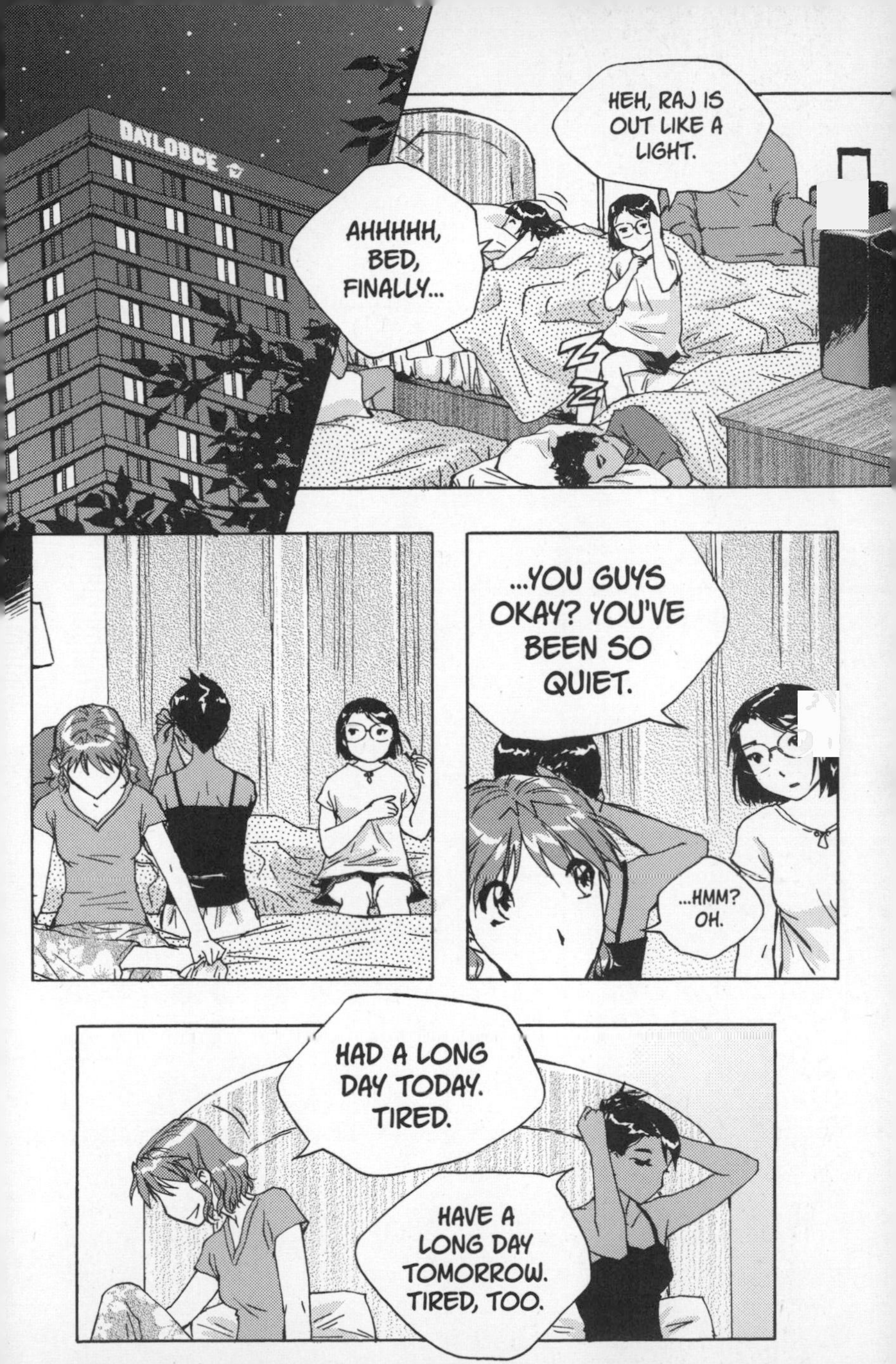
DAYLODGE
AHHHHH, BED, FINALLY...
HEH, RAJ IS OUT LIKE A LIGHT.
Z Z
...YOU GUYS OKAY? YOU'VE BEEN SO QUIET.
...HMM? OH.
HAD A LONG DAY TODAY. TIRED.
HAVE A LONG DAY TOMORROW. TIRED, TOO.

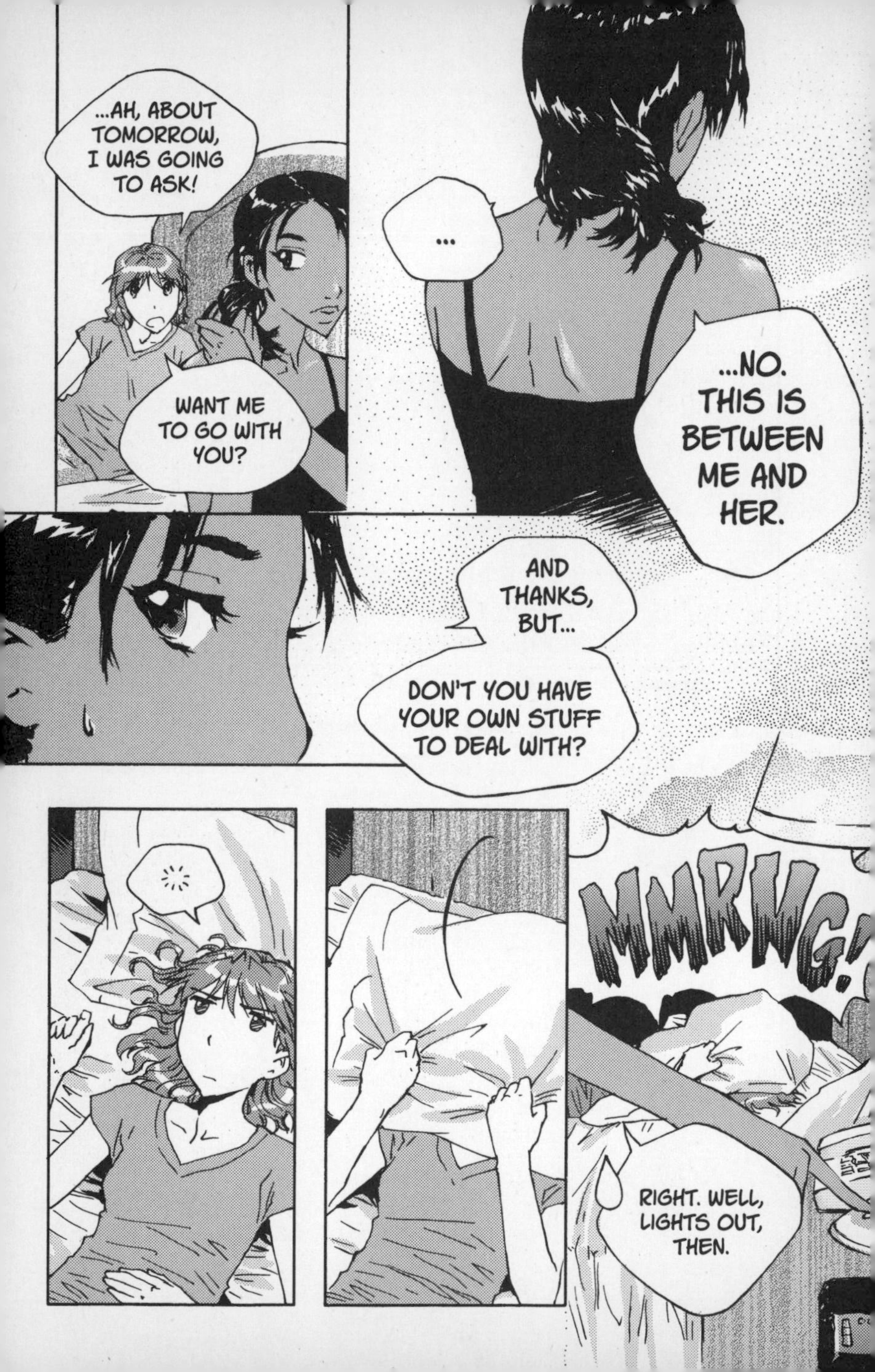
...AH, ABOUT TOMORROW, I WAS GOING TO ASK!
WANT ME TO GO WITH YOU?
...
...NO. THIS IS BETWEEN ME AND HER.
AND THANKS, BUT...
DON'T YOU HAVE YOUR OWN STUFF TO DEAL WITH?
MMRNG!
RIGHT. WELL, LIGHTS OUT, THEN.

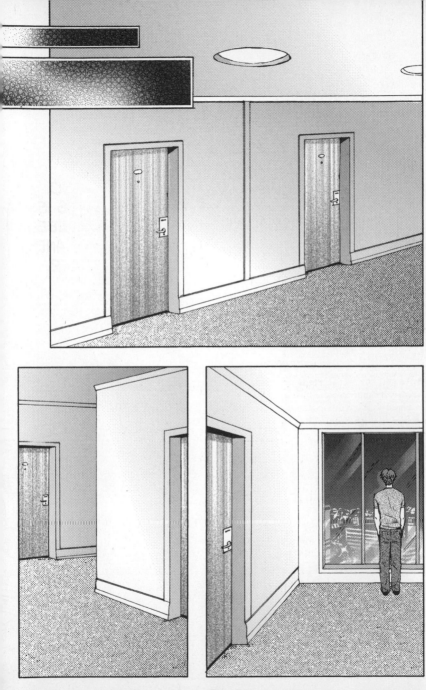

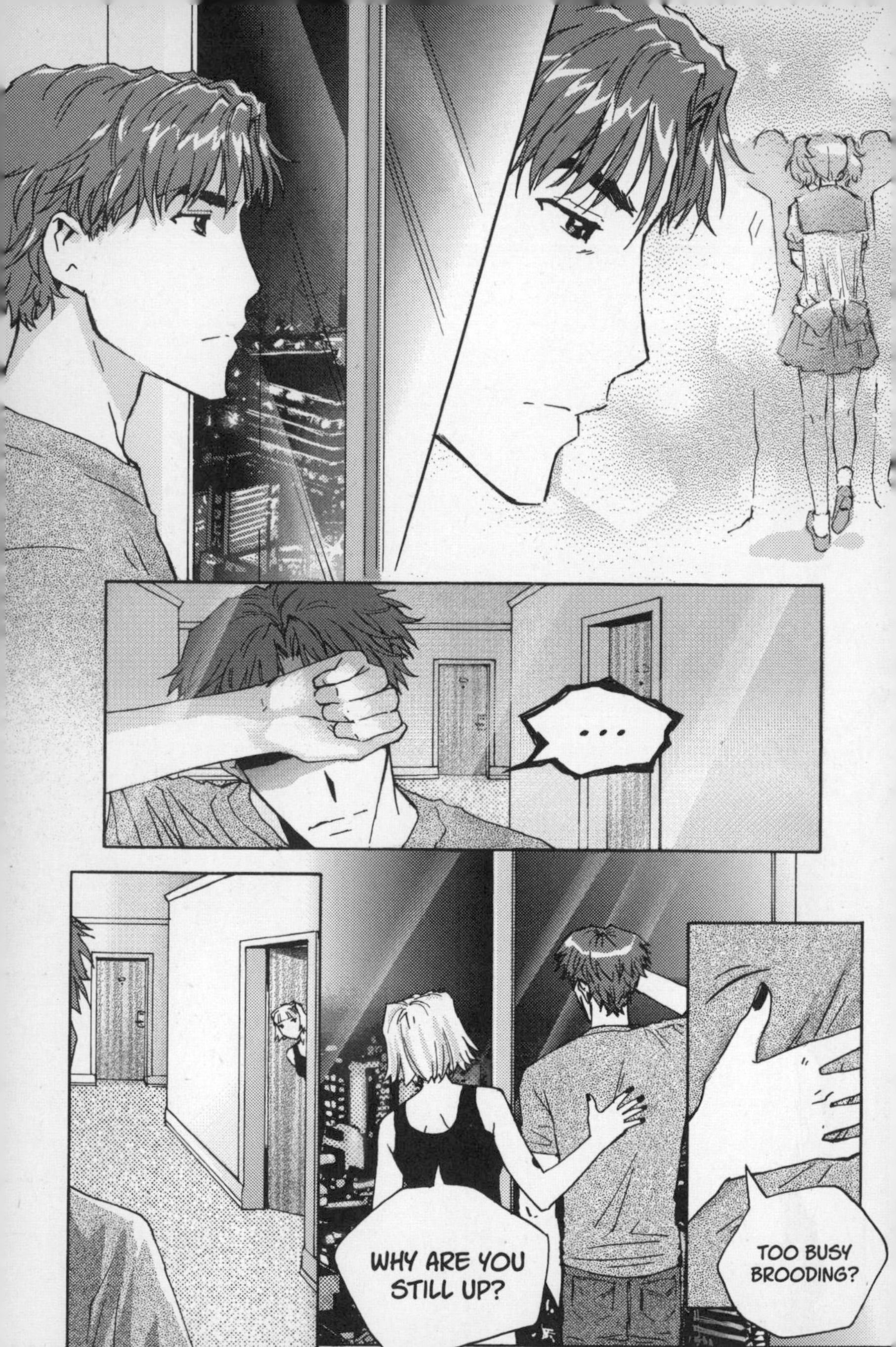
...
WHY ARE YOU STILL UP?
TOO BUSY BROODING?

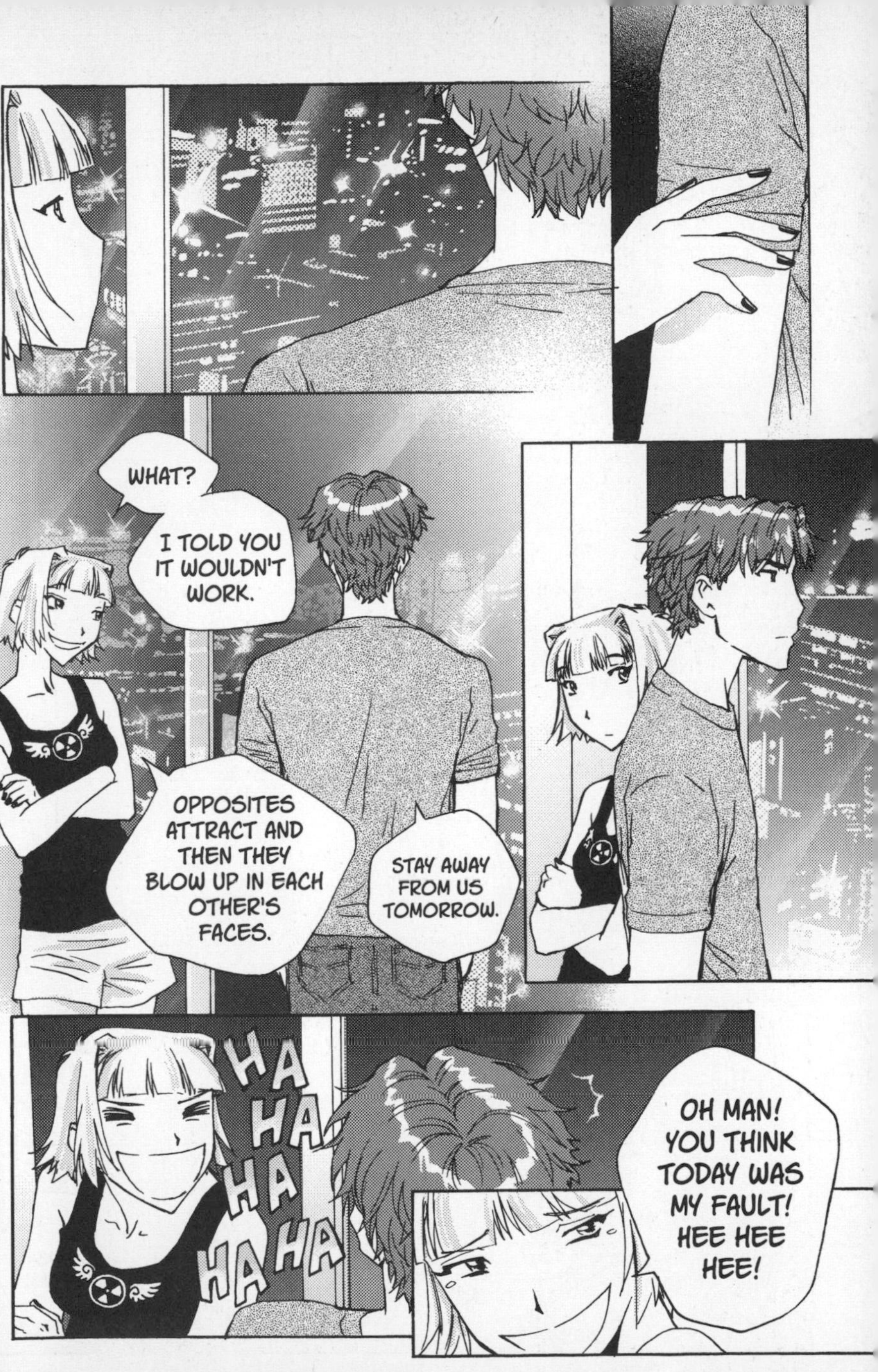
WHAT?
I TOLD YOU IT WOULDN'T WORK.
OPPOSITES ATTRACT AND THEN THEY BLOW UP IN EACH OTHER'S FACES.
STAY AWAY FROM US TOMORROW.
HA HA HA HA HA HA
OH MAN! YOU THINK TODAY WAS MY FAULT! HEE HEE HEE!

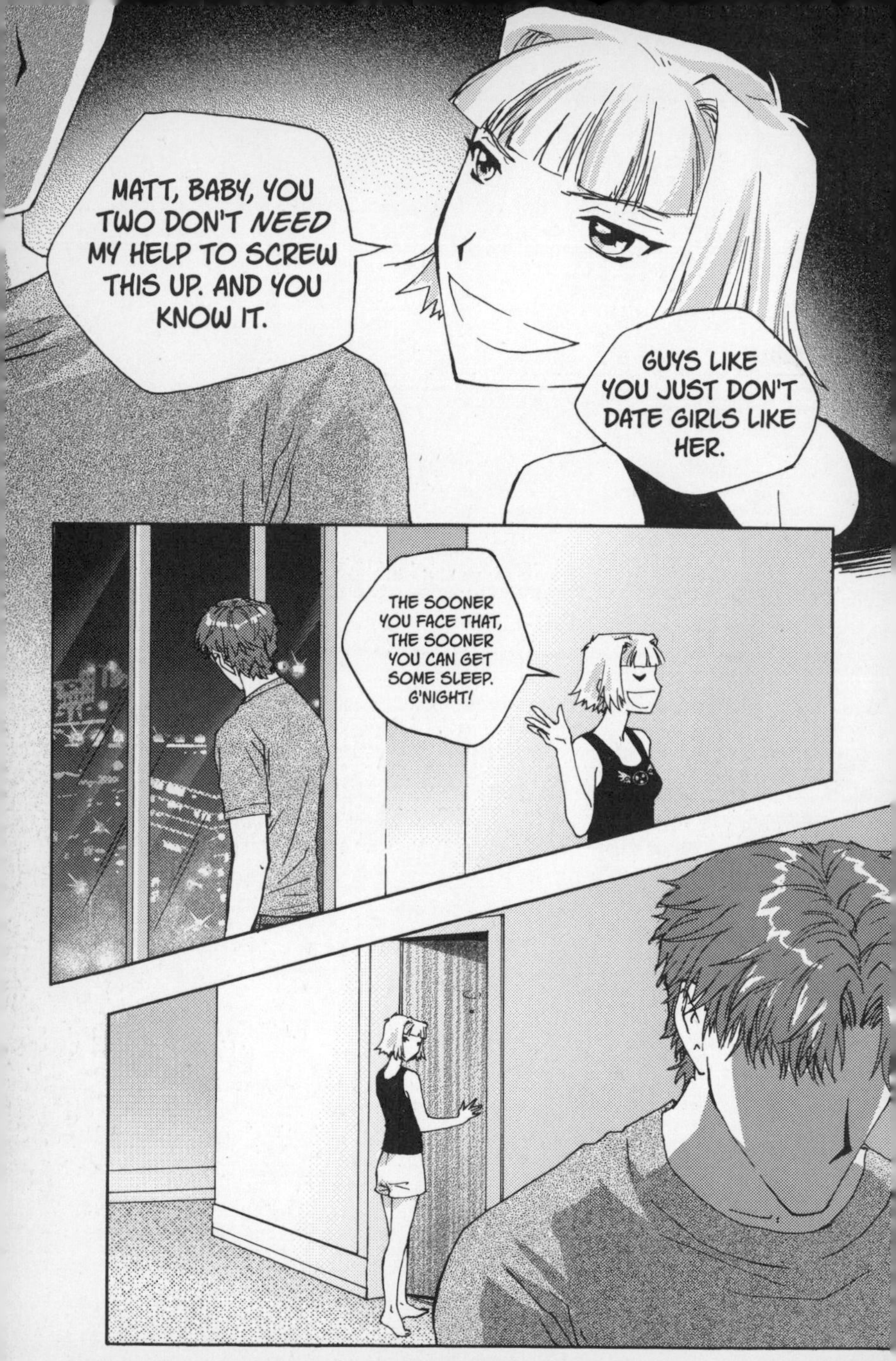
MATT, BABY, YOU TWO DON'T *NEED* MY HELP TO SCREW THIS UP. AND YOU KNOW IT.
GUYS LIKE YOU JUST DON'T DATE GIRLS LIKE HER.
THE SOONER YOU FACE THAT, THE SOONER YOU CAN GET SOME SLEEP. G'NIGHT!

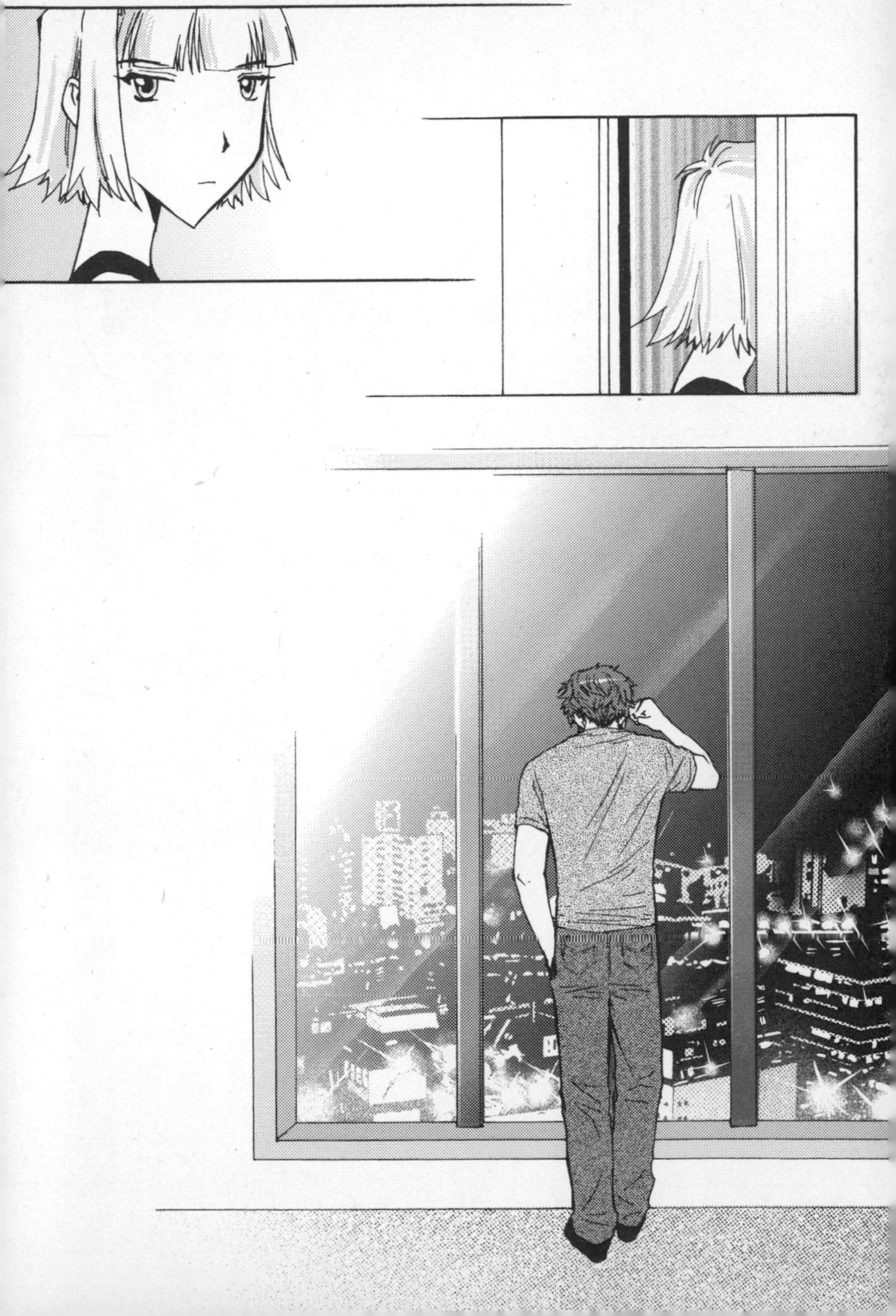

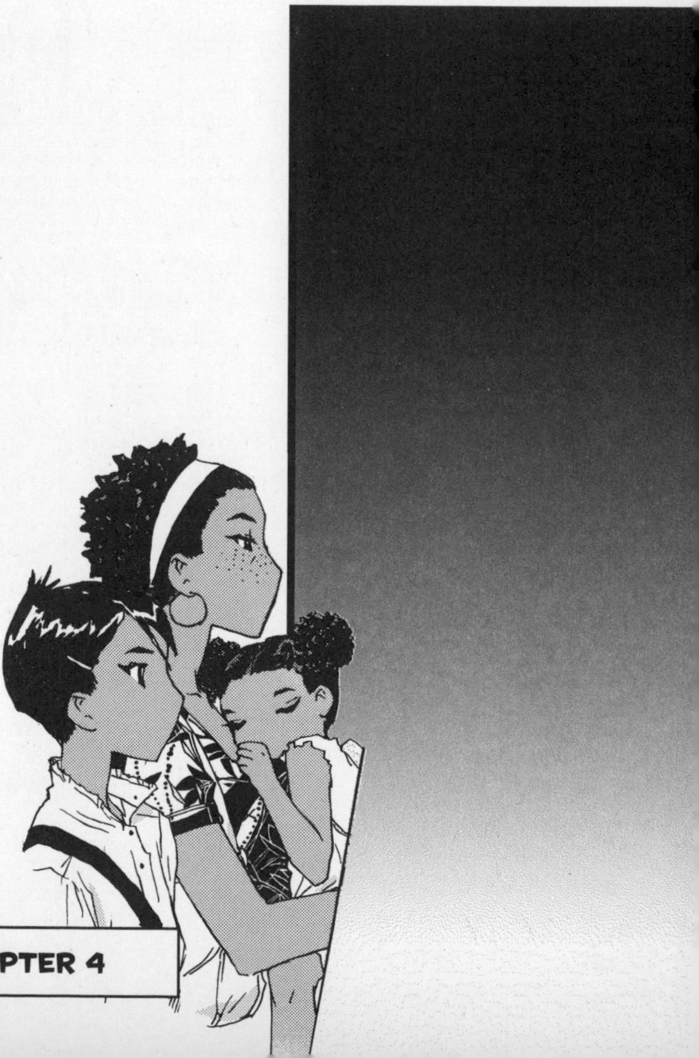

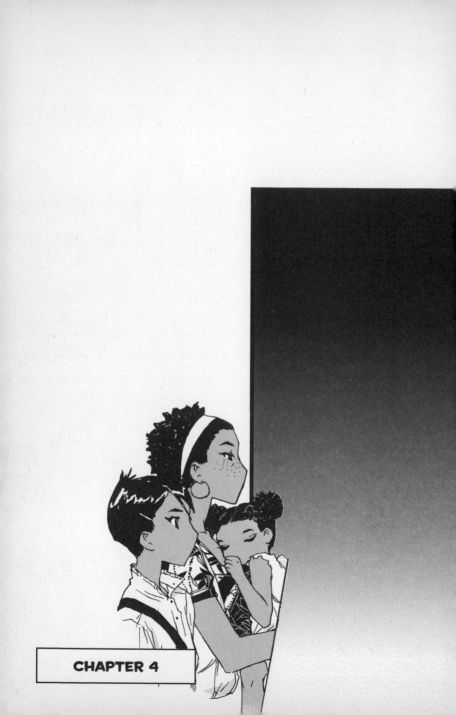

CHAPTER 4

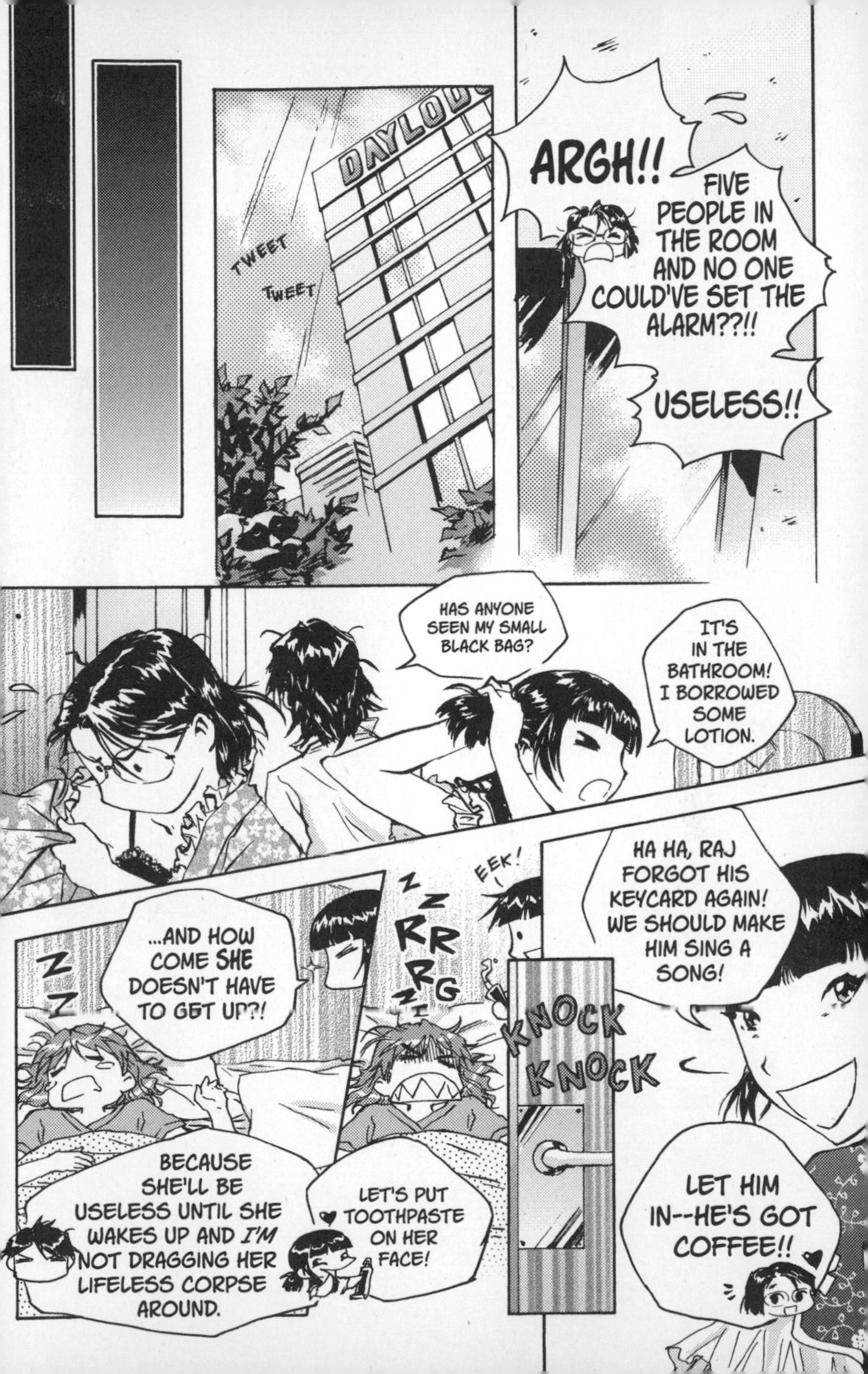
TWEET
TWEET
ARGH!!
FIVE PEOPLE IN THE ROOM AND NO ONE COULD'VE SET THE ALARM??!!
USELESS!!
HAS ANYONE SEEN MY SMALL BLACK BAG?
IT'S IN THE BATHROOM! I BORROWED SOME LOTION.
...AND HOW COME SHE DOESN'T HAVE TO GET UP?!
ZZ
BECAUSE SHE'LL BE USELESS UNTIL SHE WAKES UP AND I'M NOT DRAGGING HER LIFELESS CORPSE AROUND.
ZZRRRGZ
EEK!
LET'S PUT TOOTHPASTE ON HER FACE!
KNOCK KNOCK
HA HA, RAJ FORGOT HIS KEYCARD AGAIN! WE SHOULD MAKE HIM SING A SONG!
LET HIM IN--HE'S GOT COFFEE!!

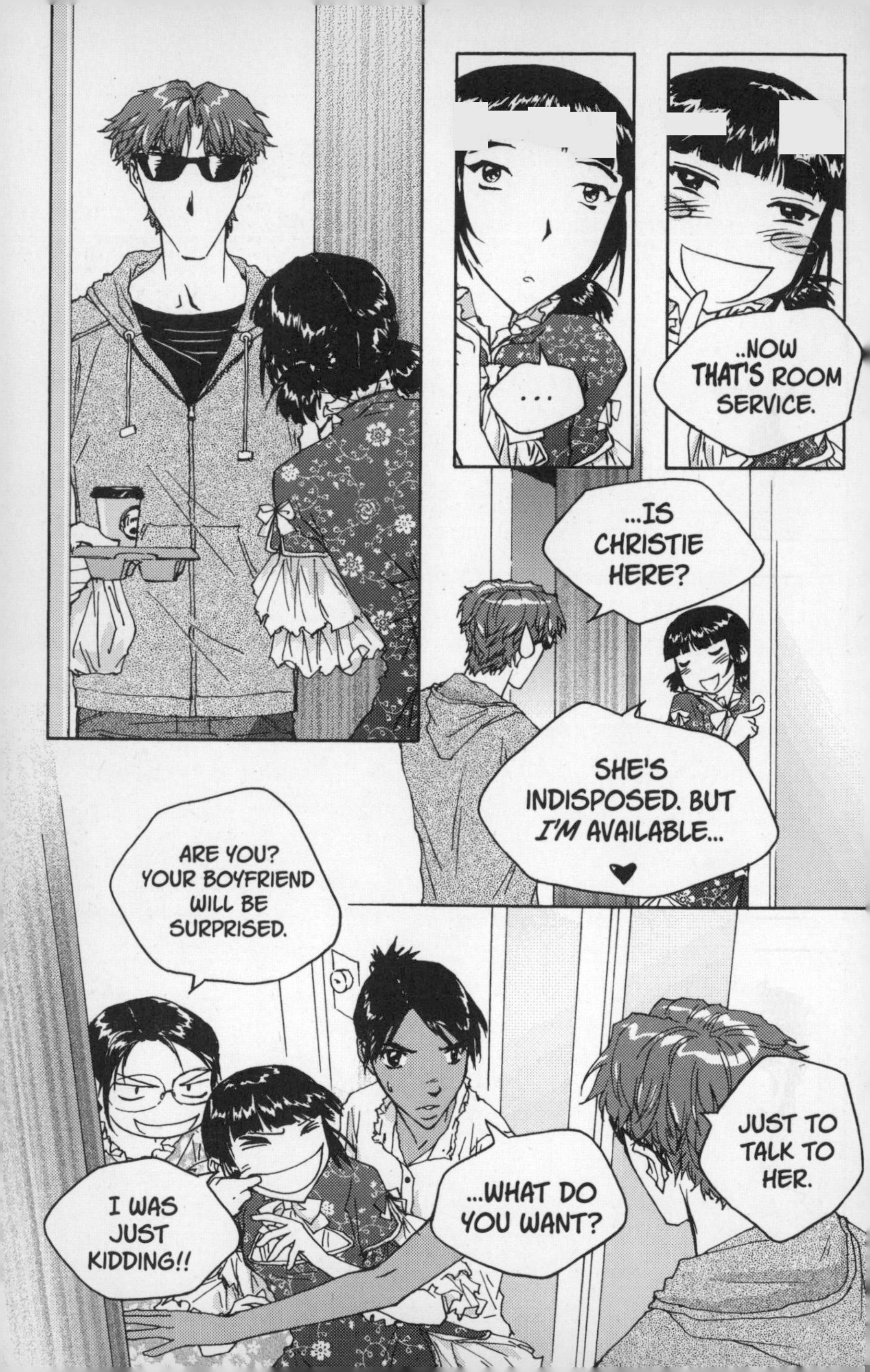
...
..NOW THAT'S ROOM SERVICE.
...IS CHRISTIE HERE?
SHE'S INDISPOSED. BUT *I'M* AVAILABLE... ♥
ARE YOU? YOUR BOYFRIEND WILL BE SURPRISED.
I WAS JUST KIDDING!!
...WHAT DO YOU WANT?
JUST TO TALK TO HER.

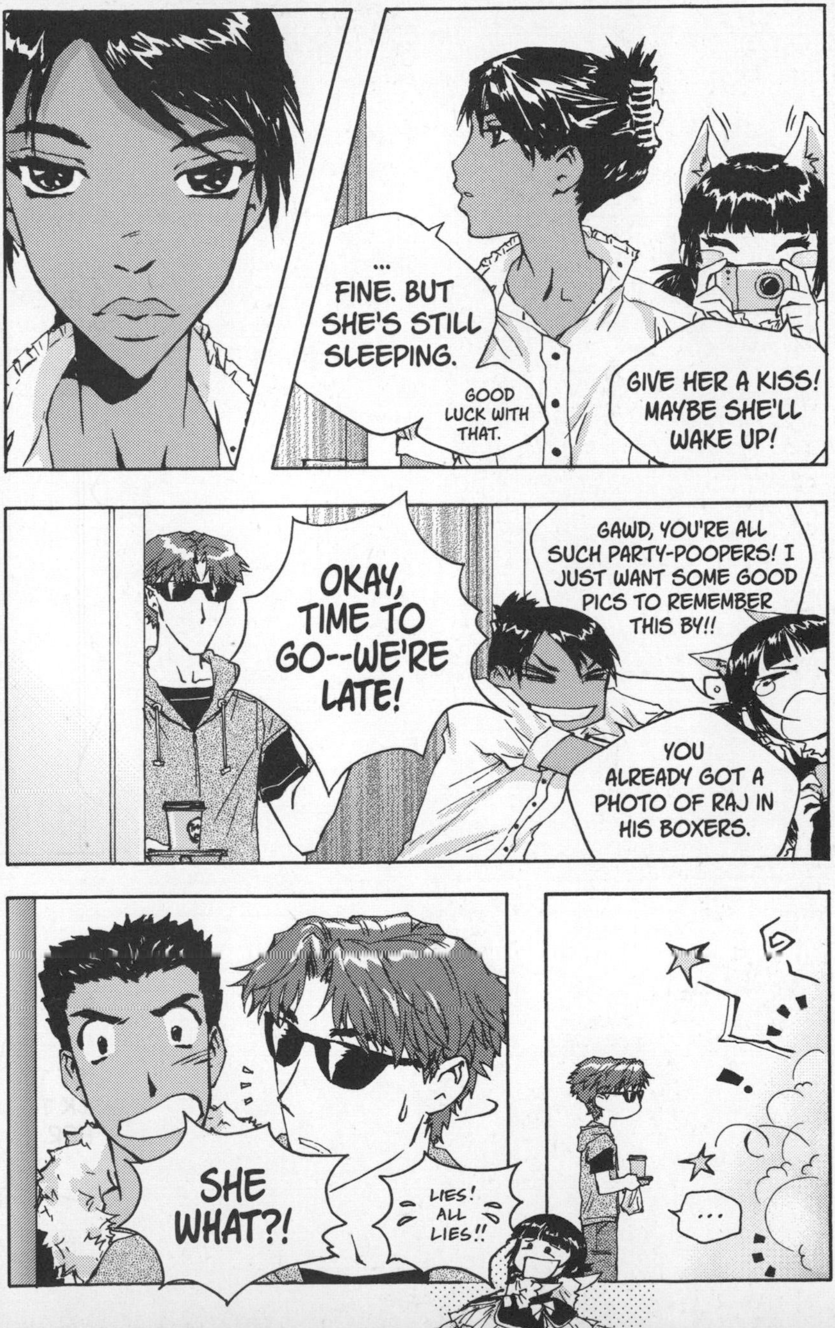

...
FINE. BUT SHE'S STILL SLEEPING.
GOOD LUCK WITH THAT.
GIVE HER A KISS! MAYBE SHE'LL WAKE UP!
OKAY, TIME TO GO--WE'RE LATE!
GAWD, YOU'RE ALL SUCH PARTY-POOPERS! I JUST WANT SOME GOOD PICS TO REMEMBER THIS BY!!
YOU ALREADY GOT A PHOTO OF RAJ IN HIS BOXERS.
SHE WHAT?!
LIES! ALL LIES!!
...

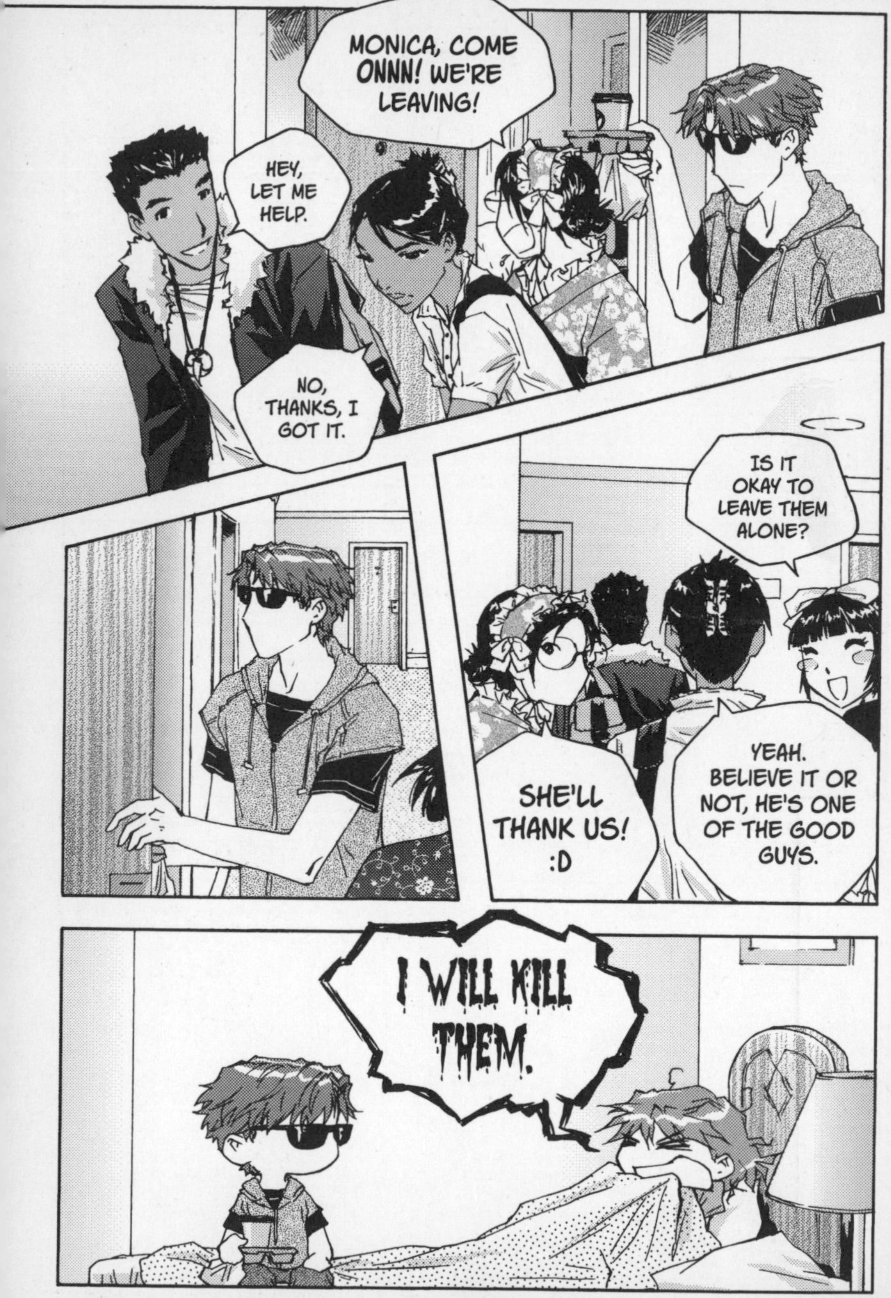
MONICA, COME ONNN! WE'RE LEAVING!
HEY, LET ME HELP.
NO, THANKS, I GOT IT.
IS IT OKAY TO LEAVE THEM ALONE?
SHE'LL THANK US! :D
YEAH. BELIEVE IT OR NOT, HE'S ONE OF THE GOOD GUYS.
I WILL KILL THEM.

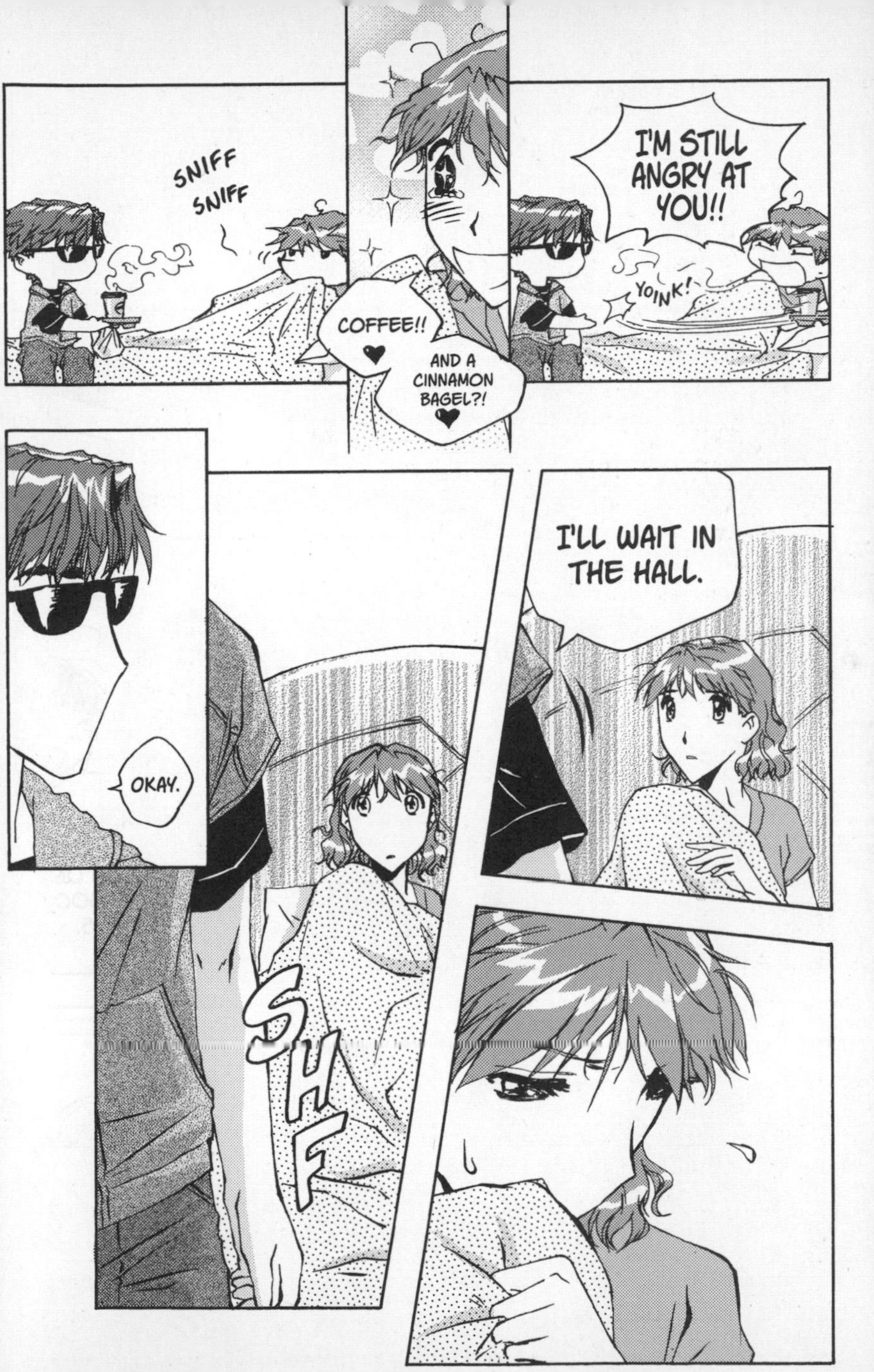
SNIFF
SNIFF
COFFEE!! ♥
AND A CINNAMON BAGEL?! ♥
I'M STILL ANGRY AT YOU!!
YOINK!
OKAY.
I'LL WAIT IN THE HALL.
SHF

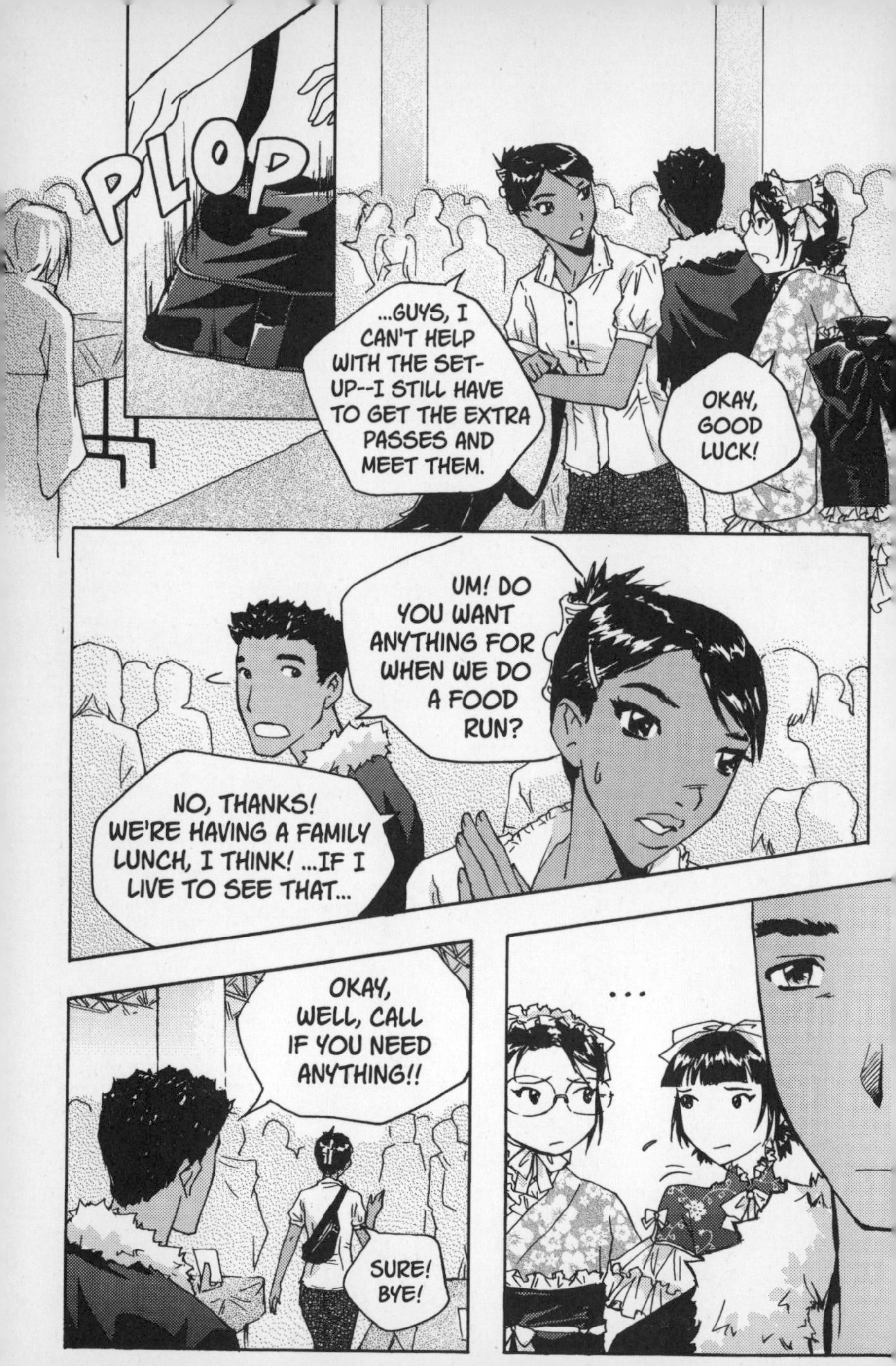
PLOP
...GUYS, I CAN'T HELP WITH THE SET-UP--I STILL HAVE TO GET THE EXTRA PASSES AND MEET THEM.
OKAY, GOOD LUCK!
UM! DO YOU WANT ANYTHING FOR WHEN WE DO A FOOD RUN?
NO, THANKS! WE'RE HAVING A FAMILY LUNCH, I THINK! ...IF I LIVE TO SEE THAT...
OKAY, WELL, CALL IF YOU NEED ANYTHING!!
SURE! BYE!
...

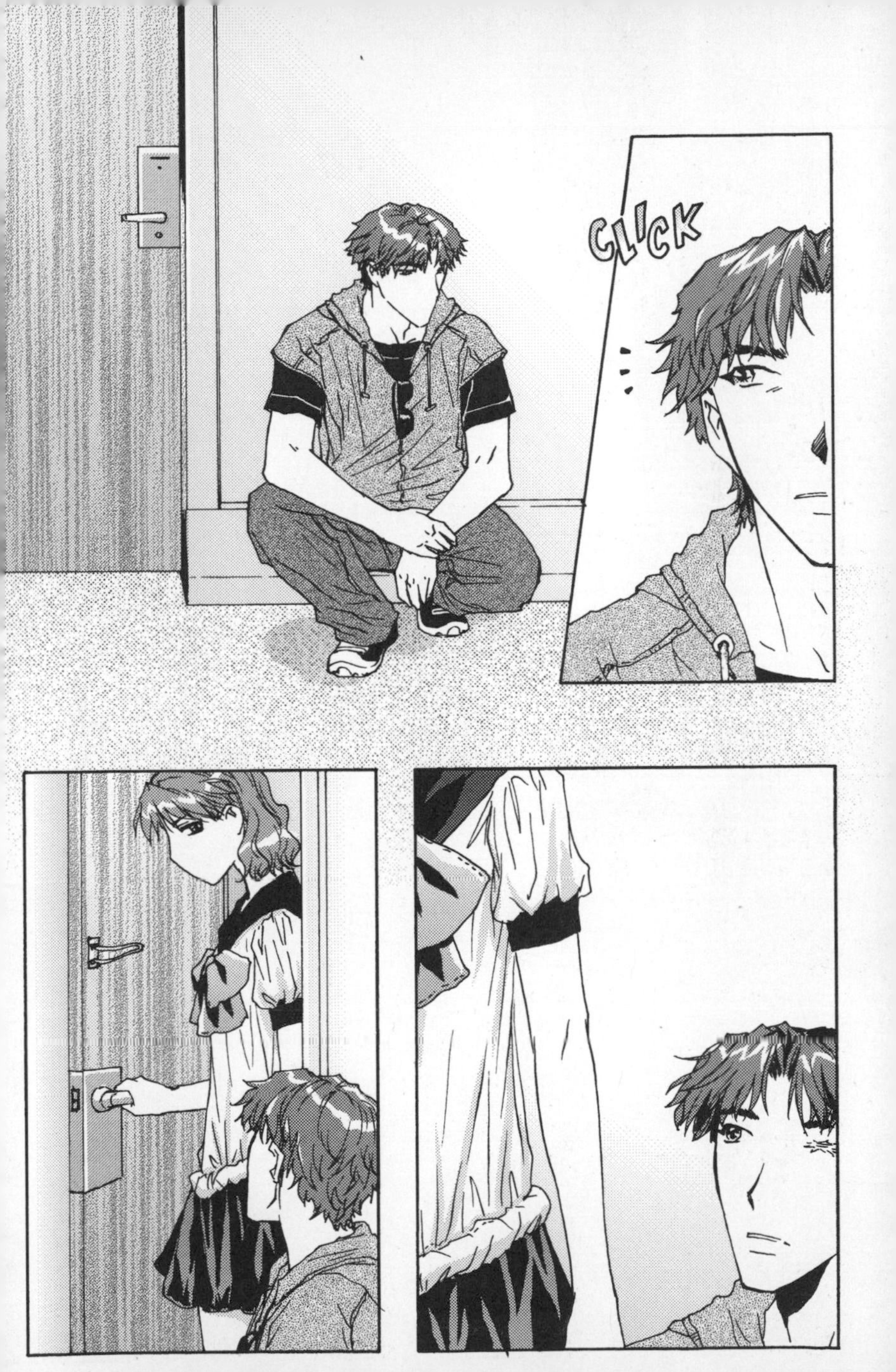
CLICK

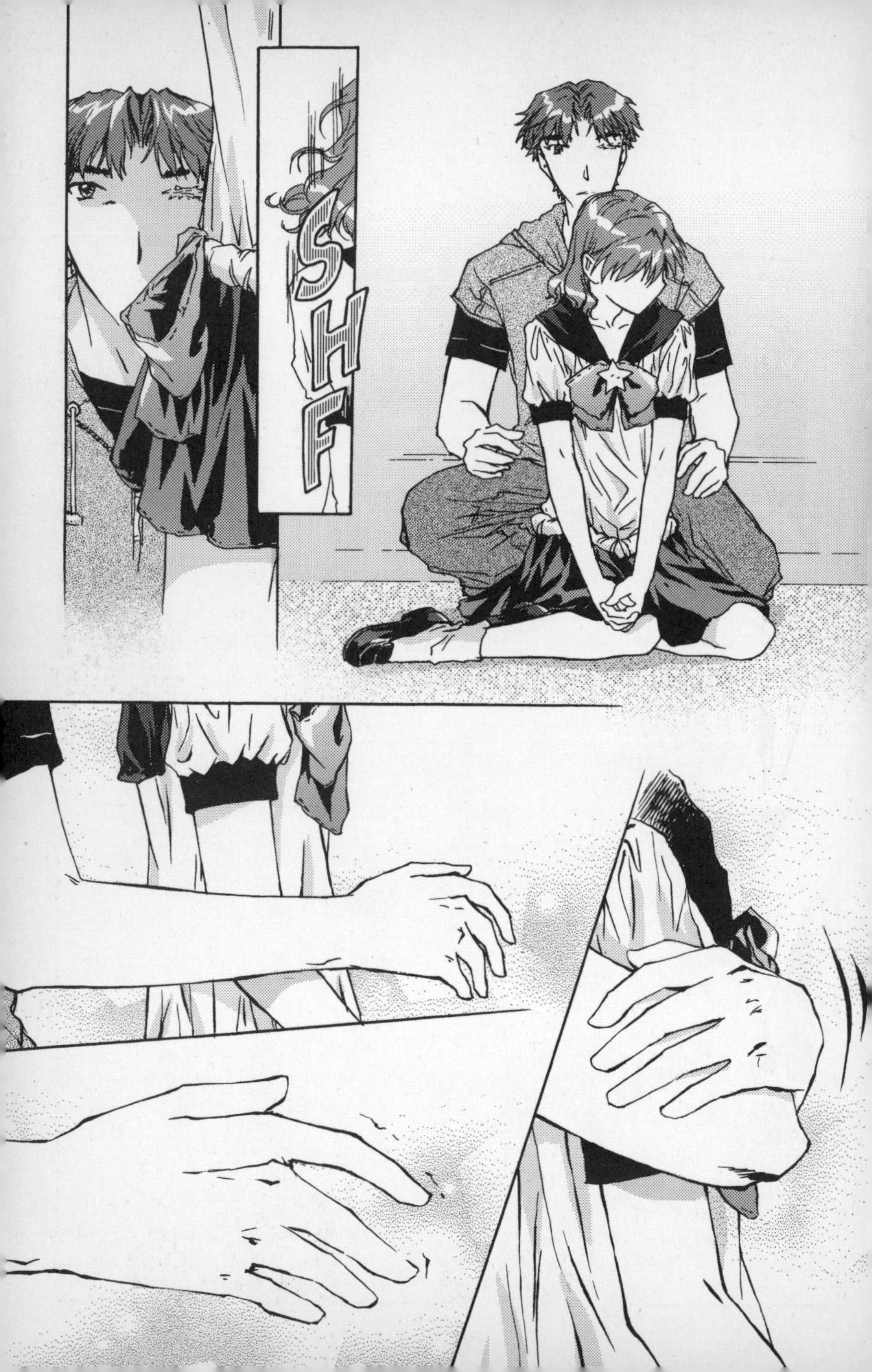
SHF

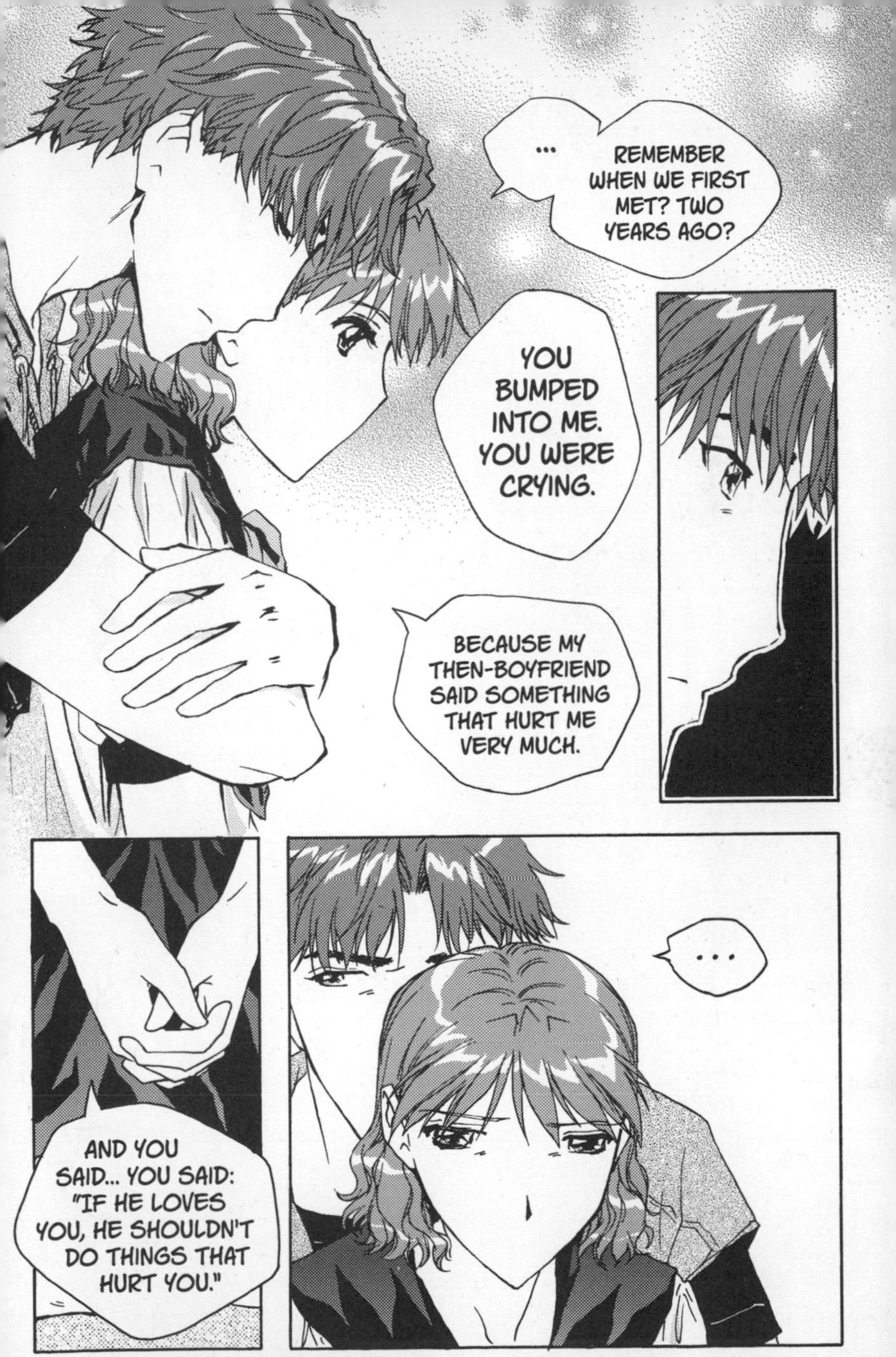

... REMEMBER WHEN WE FIRST MET? TWO YEARS AGO?
YOU BUMPED INTO ME. YOU WERE CRYING.
BECAUSE MY THEN-BOYFRIEND SAID SOMETHING THAT HURT ME VERY MUCH.
AND YOU SAID... YOU SAID: "IF HE LOVES YOU, HE SHOULDN'T DO THINGS THAT HURT YOU."
...

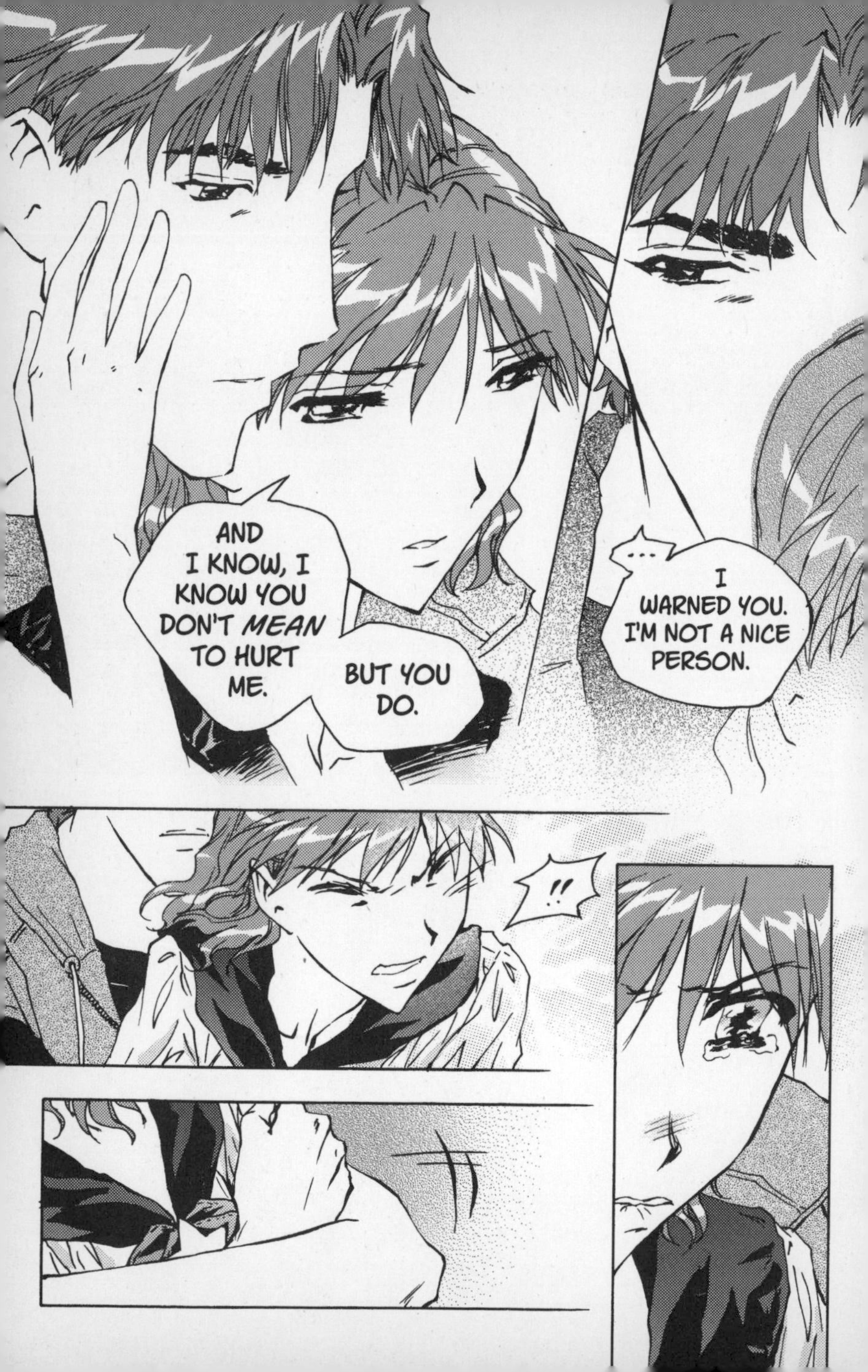
AND I KNOW, I KNOW YOU DON'T *MEAN* TO HURT ME.
BUT YOU DO.
...
I WARNED YOU. I'M NOT A NICE PERSON.
!!

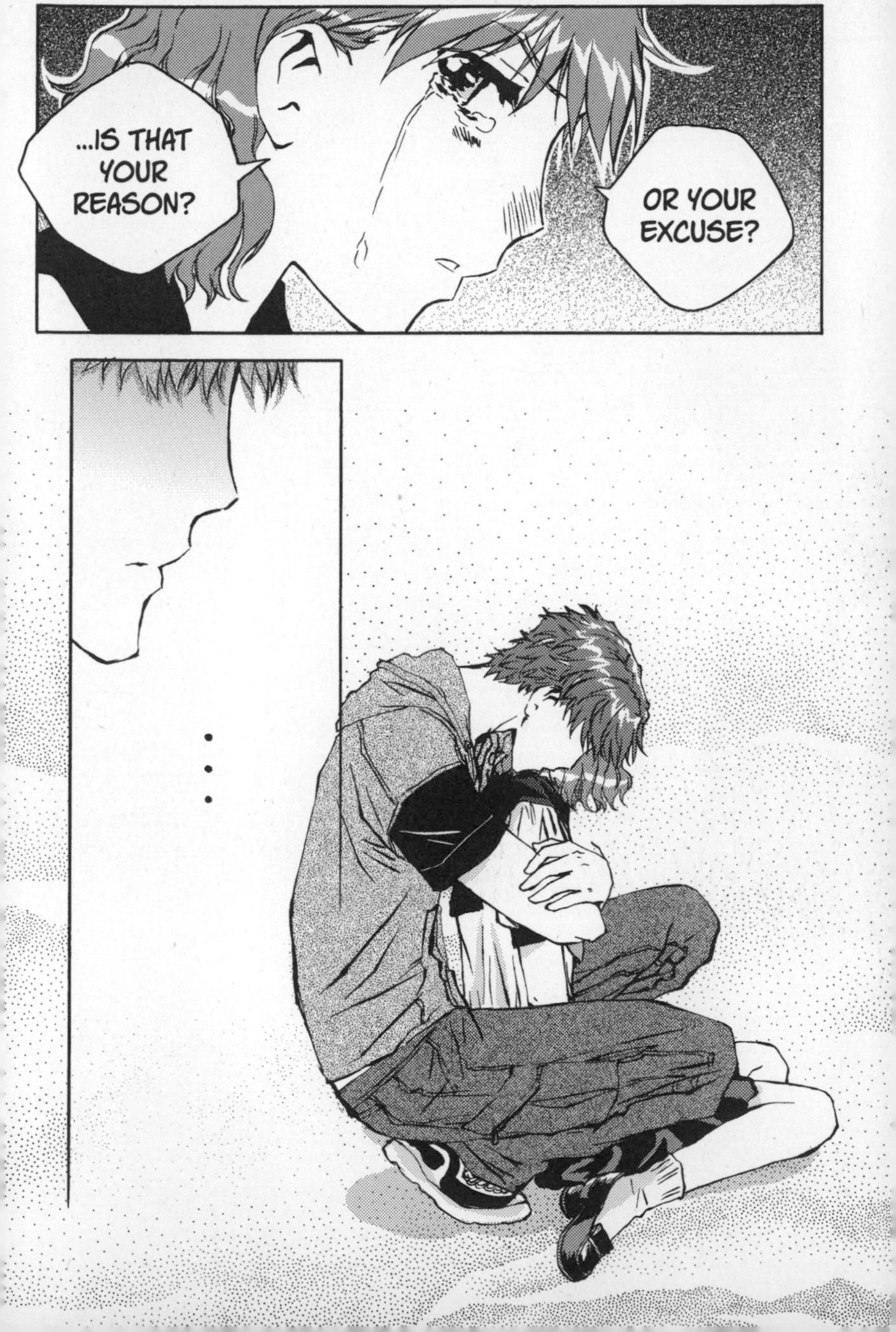
...IS THAT YOUR REASON?
OR YOUR EXCUSE?
...

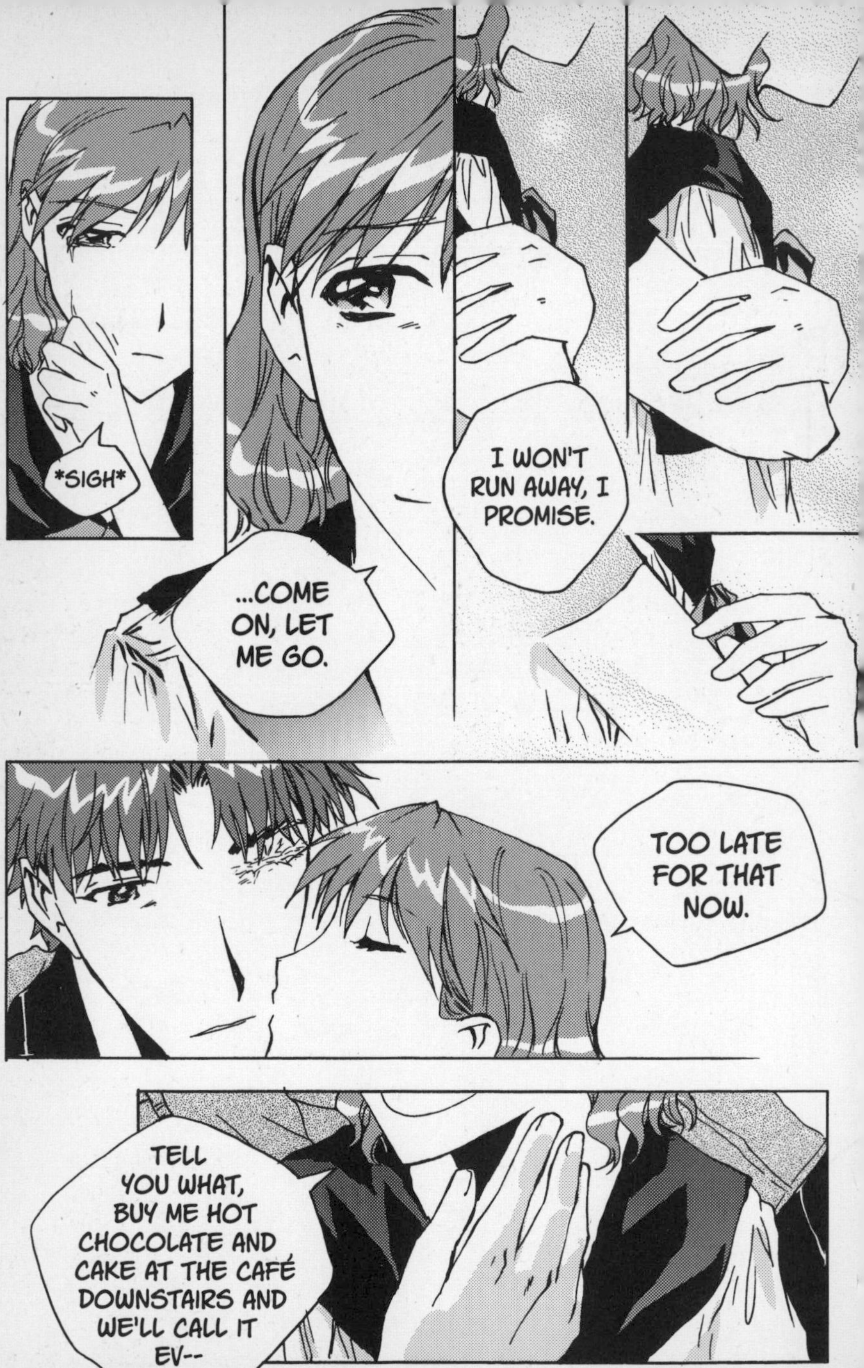
SIGH
...COME ON, LET ME GO.
I WON'T RUN AWAY, I PROMISE.
TOO LATE FOR THAT NOW.
TELL YOU WHAT, BUY ME HOT CHOCOLATE AND CAKE AT THE CAFÉ DOWNSTAIRS AND WE'LL CALL IT EV--

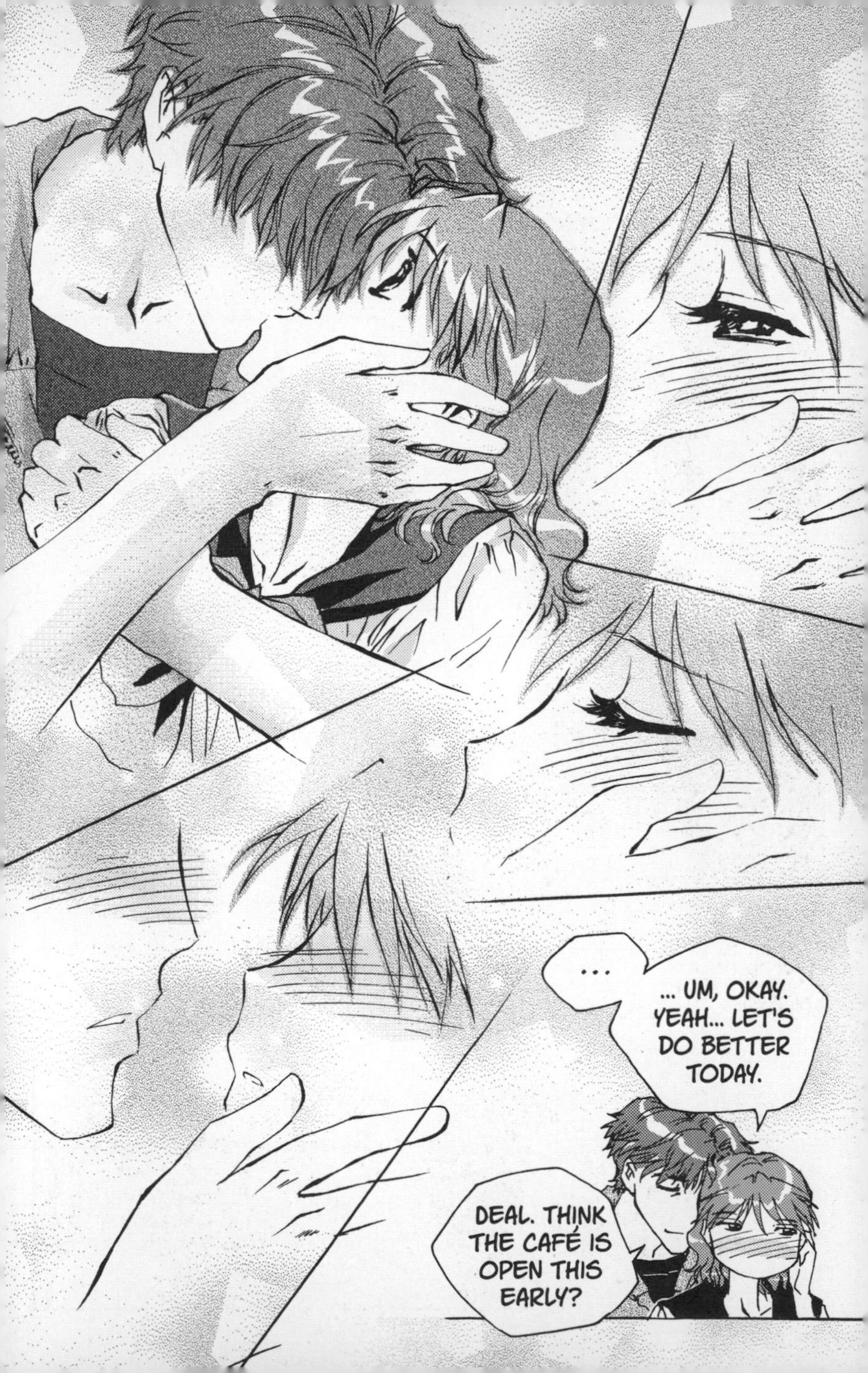
...
... UM, OKAY. YEAH... LET'S DO BETTER TODAY.
DEAL. THINK THE CAFÉ IS OPEN THIS EARLY?

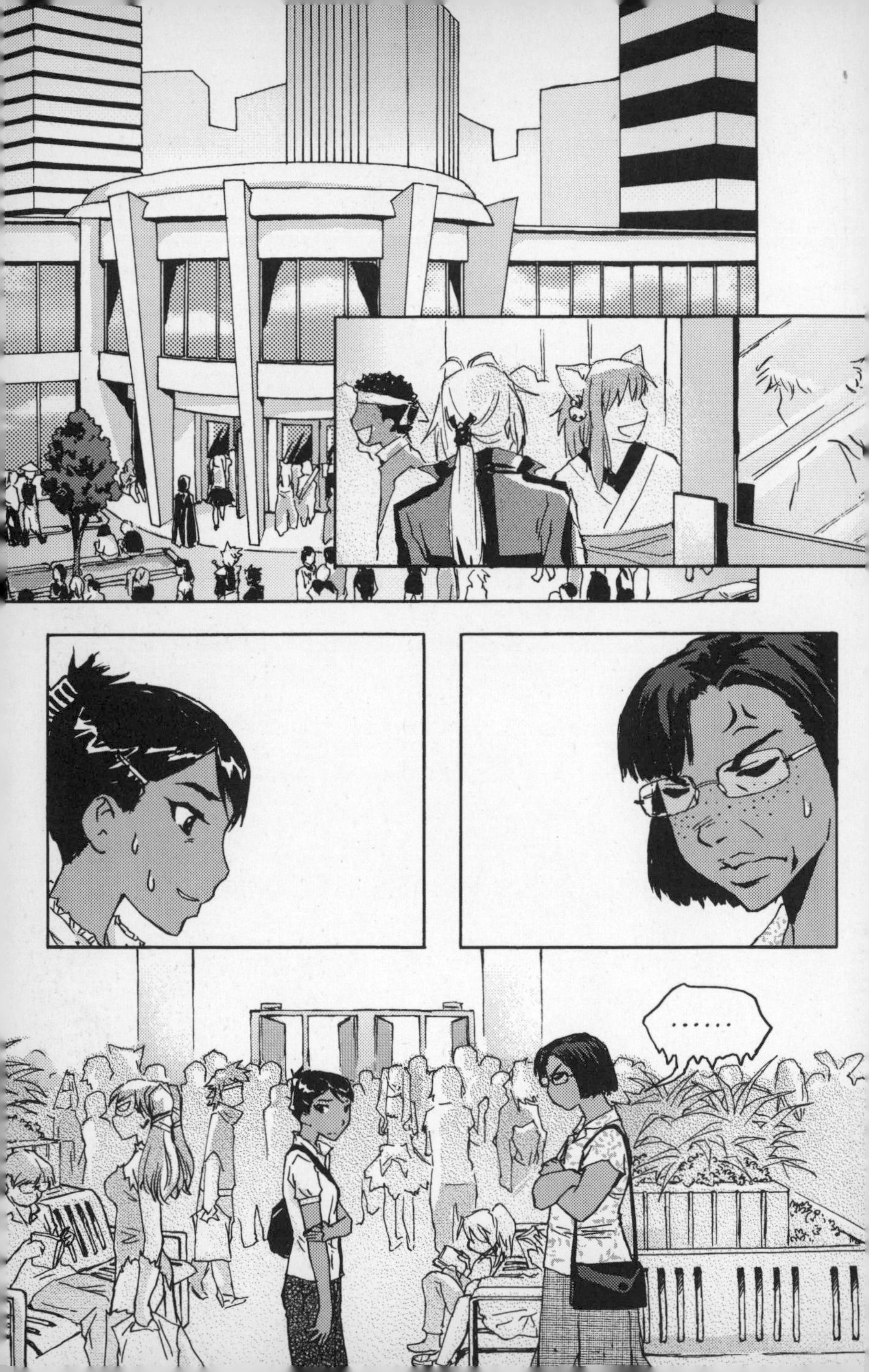
......

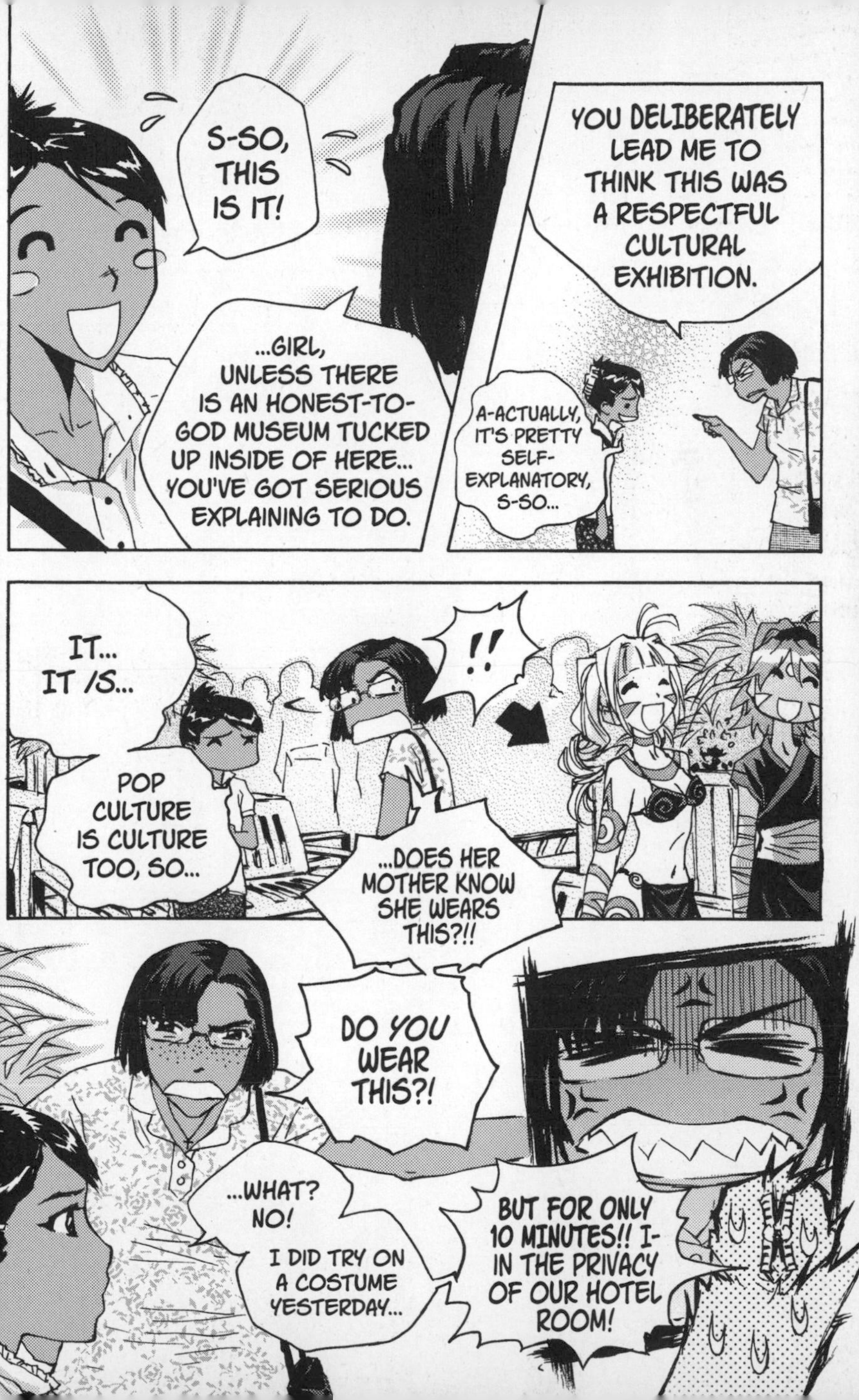
S-SO, THIS IS IT!
...GIRL, UNLESS THERE IS AN HONEST-TO-GOD MUSEUM TUCKED UP INSIDE OF HERE... YOU'VE GOT SERIOUS EXPLAINING TO DO.
YOU DELIBERATELY LEAD ME TO THINK THIS WAS A RESPECTFUL CULTURAL EXHIBITION.
A-ACTUALLY, IT'S PRETTY SELF-EXPLANATORY, S-SO...
IT... IT IS...
POP CULTURE IS CULTURE TOO, SO...
!!
...DOES HER MOTHER KNOW SHE WEARS THIS?!!
DO YOU WEAR THIS?!
...WHAT? NO!
I DID TRY ON A COSTUME YESTERDAY...
BUT FOR ONLY 10 MINUTES!! I-IN THE PRIVACY OF OUR HOTEL ROOM!

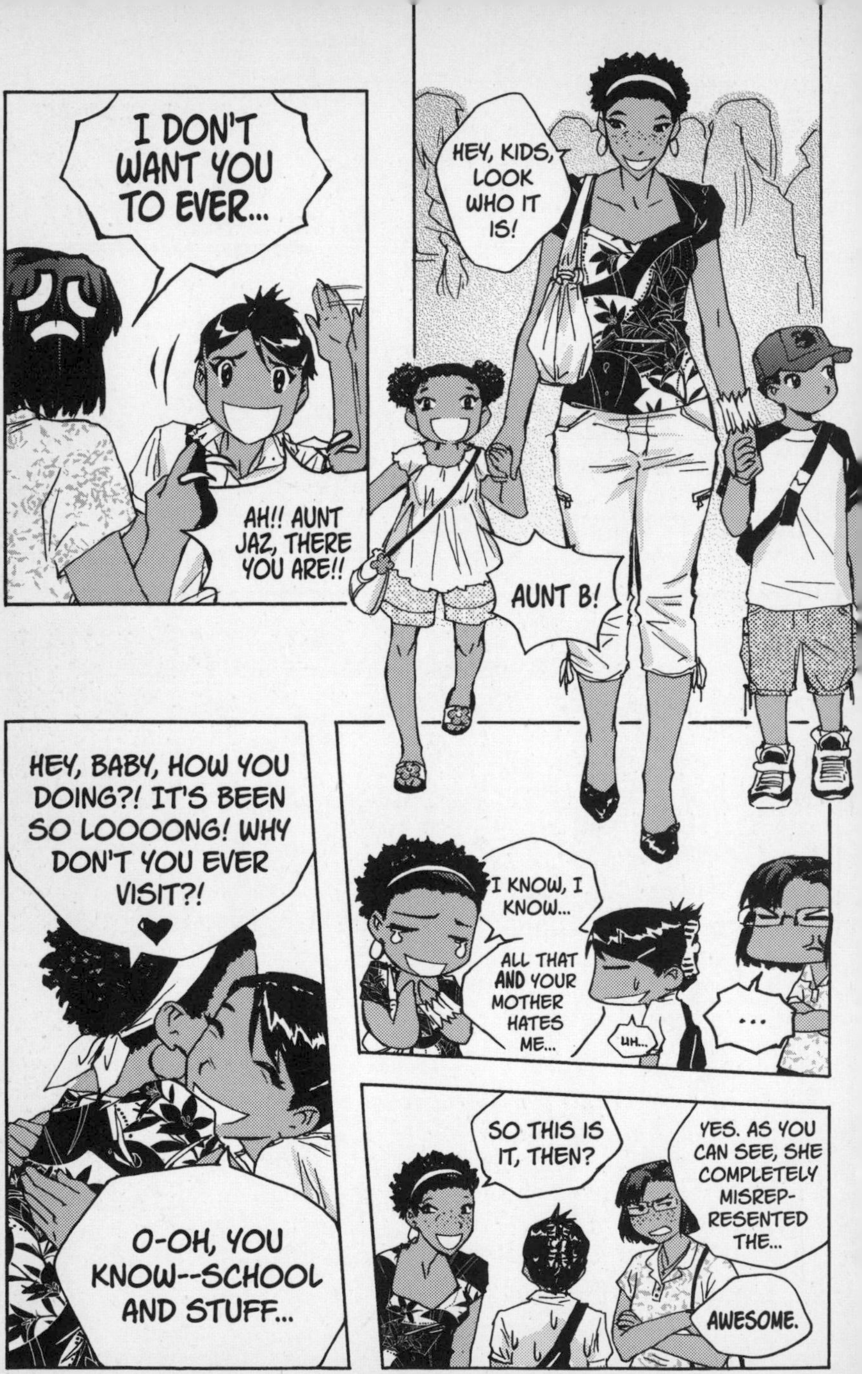
I DON'T WANT YOU TO EVER...
AH!! AUNT JAZ, THERE YOU ARE!!
HEY, KIDS, LOOK WHO IT IS!
AUNT B!
HEY, BABY, HOW YOU DOING?! IT'S BEEN SO LOOOONG! WHY DON'T YOU EVER VISIT?!
O-OH, YOU KNOW--SCHOOL AND STUFF...
I KNOW, I KNOW...
ALL THAT AND YOUR MOTHER HATES ME...
UH...
...
SO THIS IS IT, THEN?
YES. AS YOU CAN SEE, SHE COMPLETELY MISREP-RESENTED THE...
AWESOME.

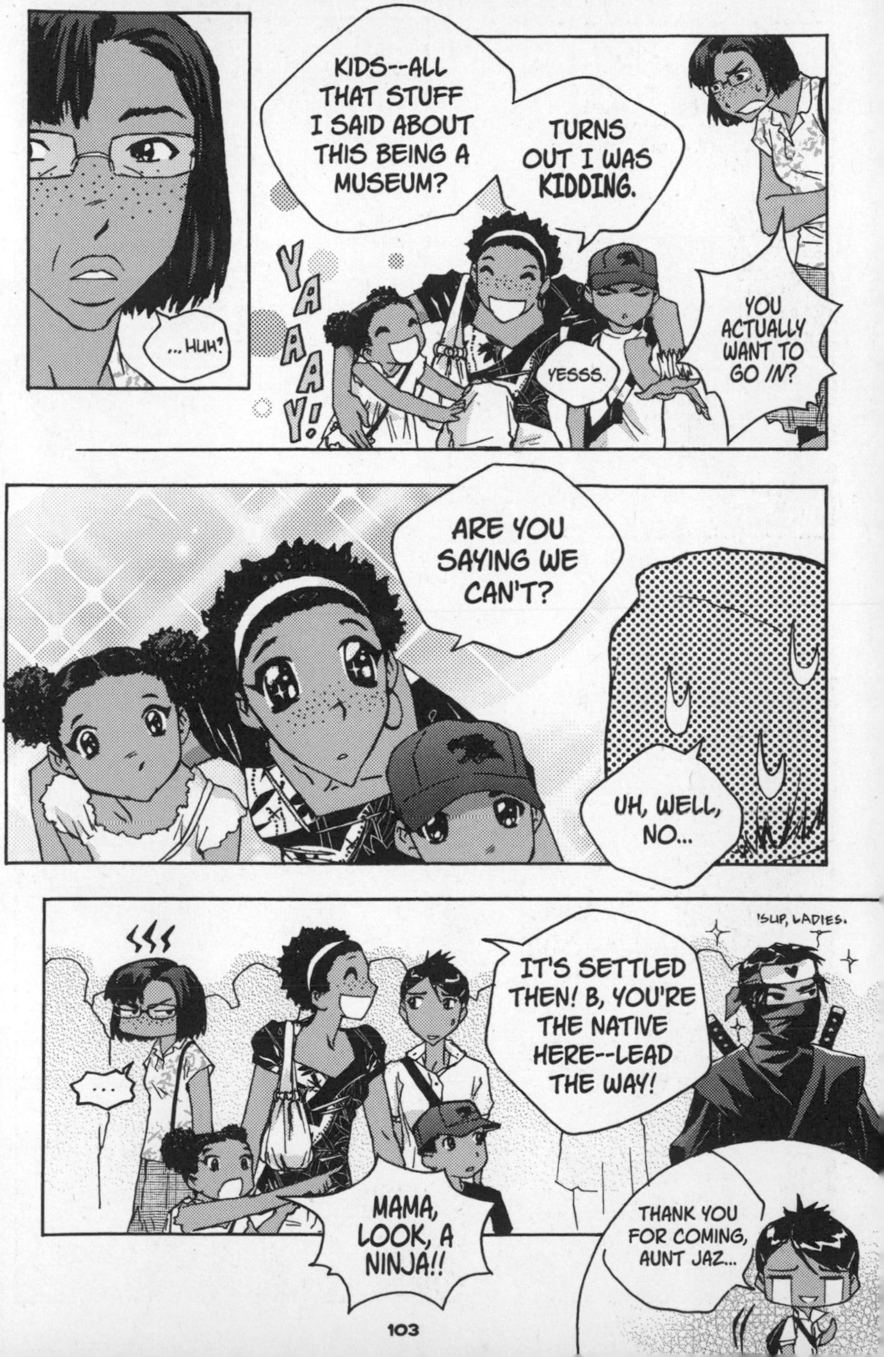
...HUH?
KIDS--ALL THAT STUFF I SAID ABOUT THIS BEING A MUSEUM?
TURNS OUT I WAS KIDDING.
YAAAAY!
YESSS.
YOU ACTUALLY WANT TO GO IN?
ARE YOU SAYING WE CAN'T?
UH, WELL, NO...
...
IT'S SETTLED THEN! B, YOU'RE THE NATIVE HERE--LEAD THE WAY!
'SUP, LADIES.
MAMA, LOOK, A NINJA!!
THANK YOU FOR COMING, AUNT JAZ...

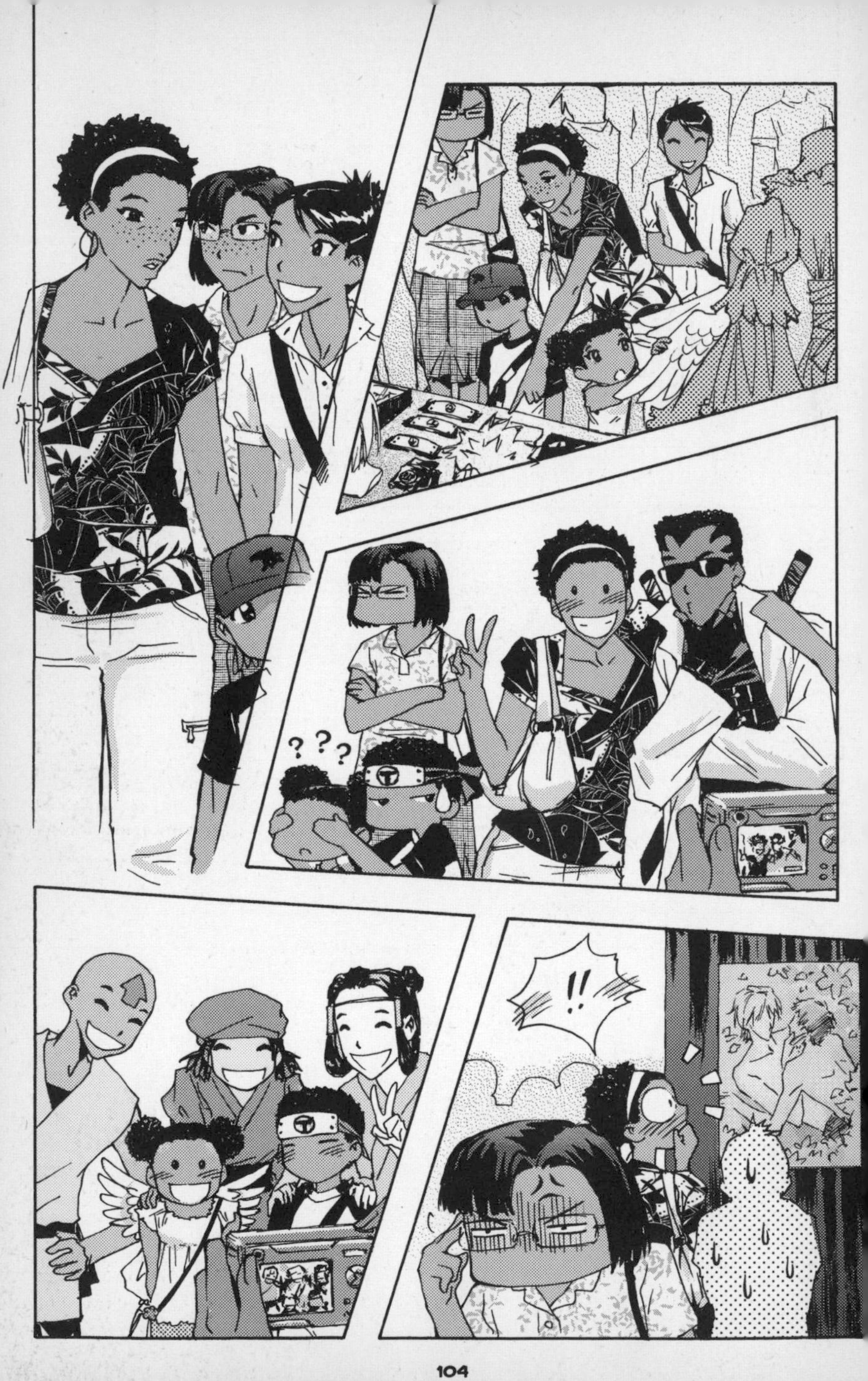

? ? ?
!!

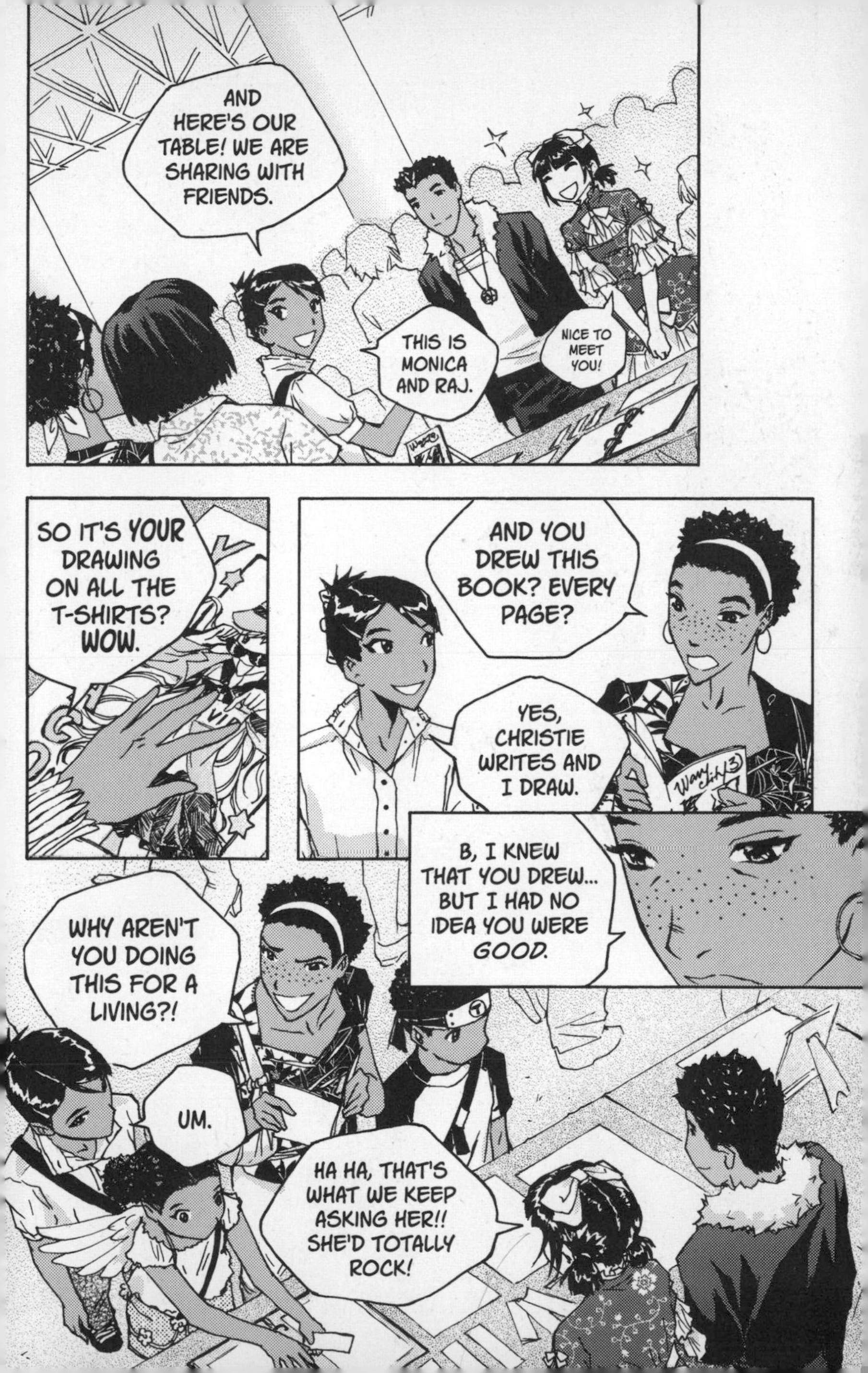
AND HERE'S OUR TABLE! WE ARE SHARING WITH FRIENDS.
THIS IS MONICA AND RAJ.
NICE TO MEET YOU!
SO IT'S YOUR DRAWING ON ALL THE T-SHIRTS? WOW.
AND YOU DREW THIS BOOK? EVERY PAGE?
YES, CHRISTIE WRITES AND I DRAW.
B, I KNEW THAT YOU DREW... BUT I HAD NO IDEA YOU WERE GOOD.
WHY AREN'T YOU DOING THIS FOR A LIVING?!
UM.
HA HA, THAT'S WHAT WE KEEP ASKING HER!! SHE'D TOTALLY ROCK!

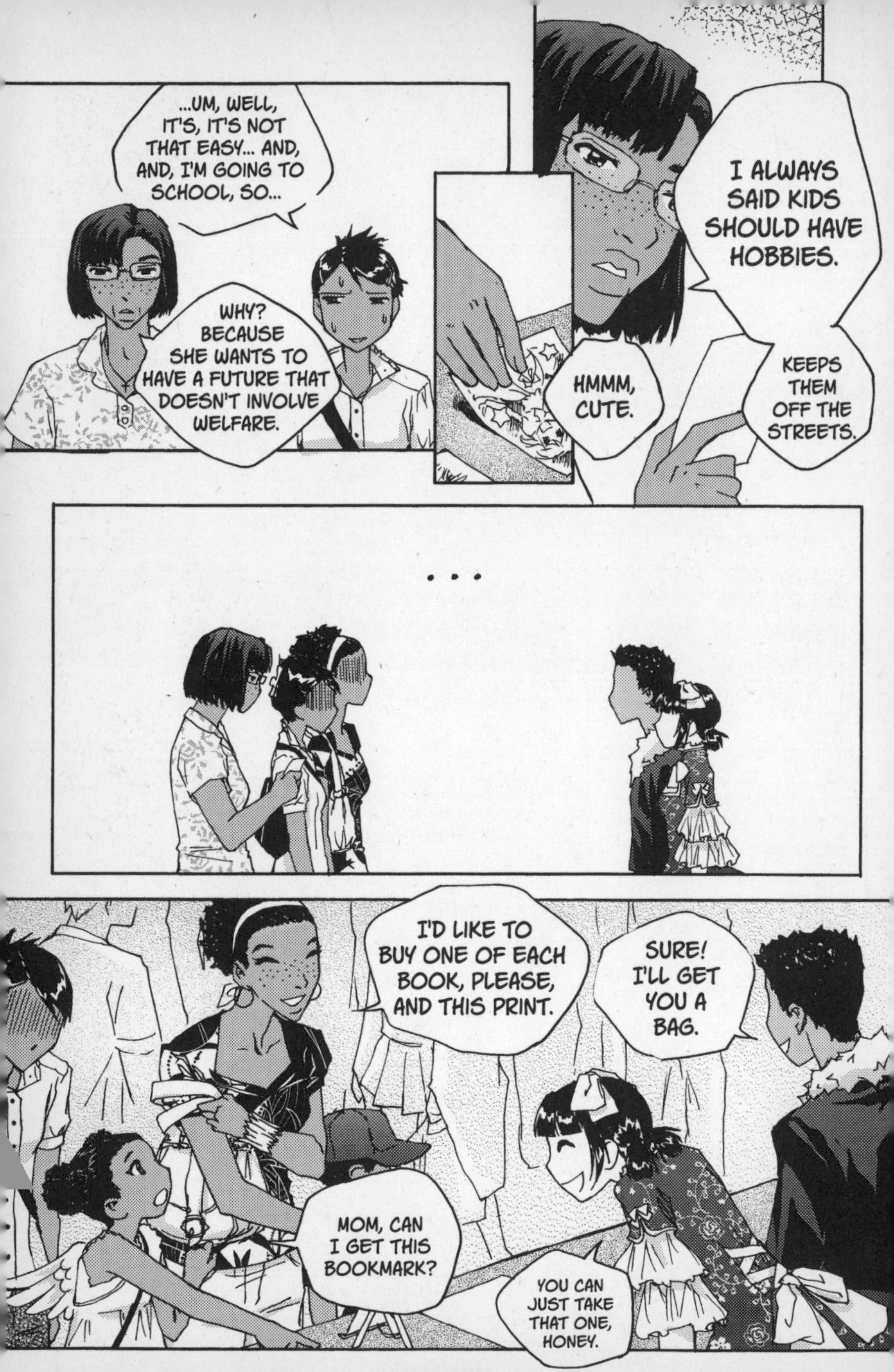
...UM, WELL, IT'S, IT'S NOT THAT EASY... AND, AND, I'M GOING TO SCHOOL, SO...
WHY? BECAUSE SHE WANTS TO HAVE A FUTURE THAT DOESN'T INVOLVE WELFARE.
I ALWAYS SAID KIDS SHOULD HAVE HOBBIES.
HMMM, CUTE.
KEEPS THEM OFF THE STREETS.
• • •
I'D LIKE TO BUY ONE OF EACH BOOK, PLEASE, AND THIS PRINT.
SURE! I'LL GET YOU A BAG.
MOM, CAN I GET THIS BOOKMARK?
YOU CAN JUST TAKE THAT ONE, HONEY.

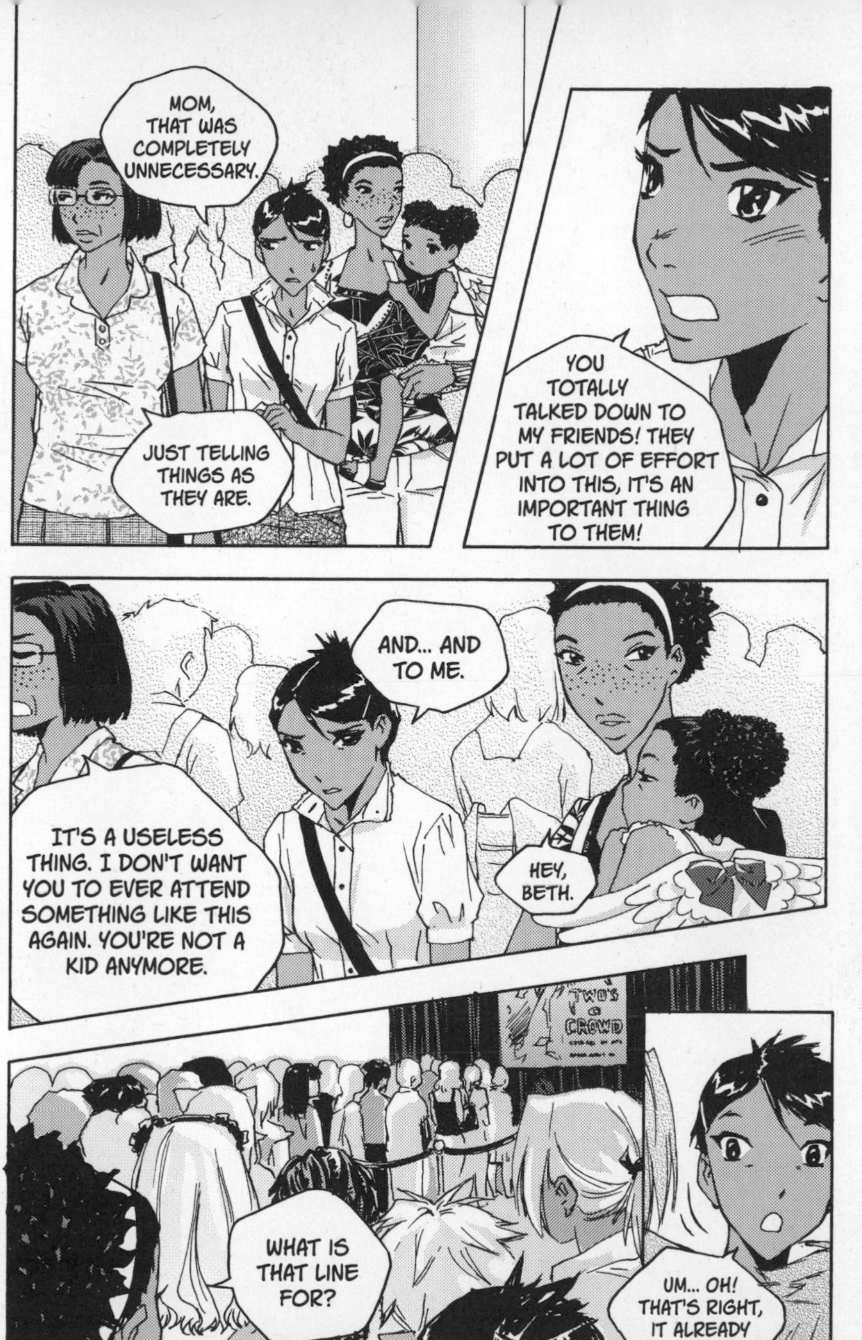
MOM, THAT WAS COMPLETELY UNNECESSARY.
JUST TELLING THINGS AS THEY ARE.
YOU TOTALLY TALKED DOWN TO MY FRIENDS! THEY PUT A LOT OF EFFORT INTO THIS, IT'S AN IMPORTANT THING TO THEM!
AND... AND TO ME.
IT'S A USELESS THING. I DON'T WANT YOU TO EVER ATTEND SOMETHING LIKE THIS AGAIN. YOU'RE NOT A KID ANYMORE.
HEY, BETH.
WHAT IS THAT LINE FOR?
UM... OH! THAT'S RIGHT, IT ALREADY STARTED!

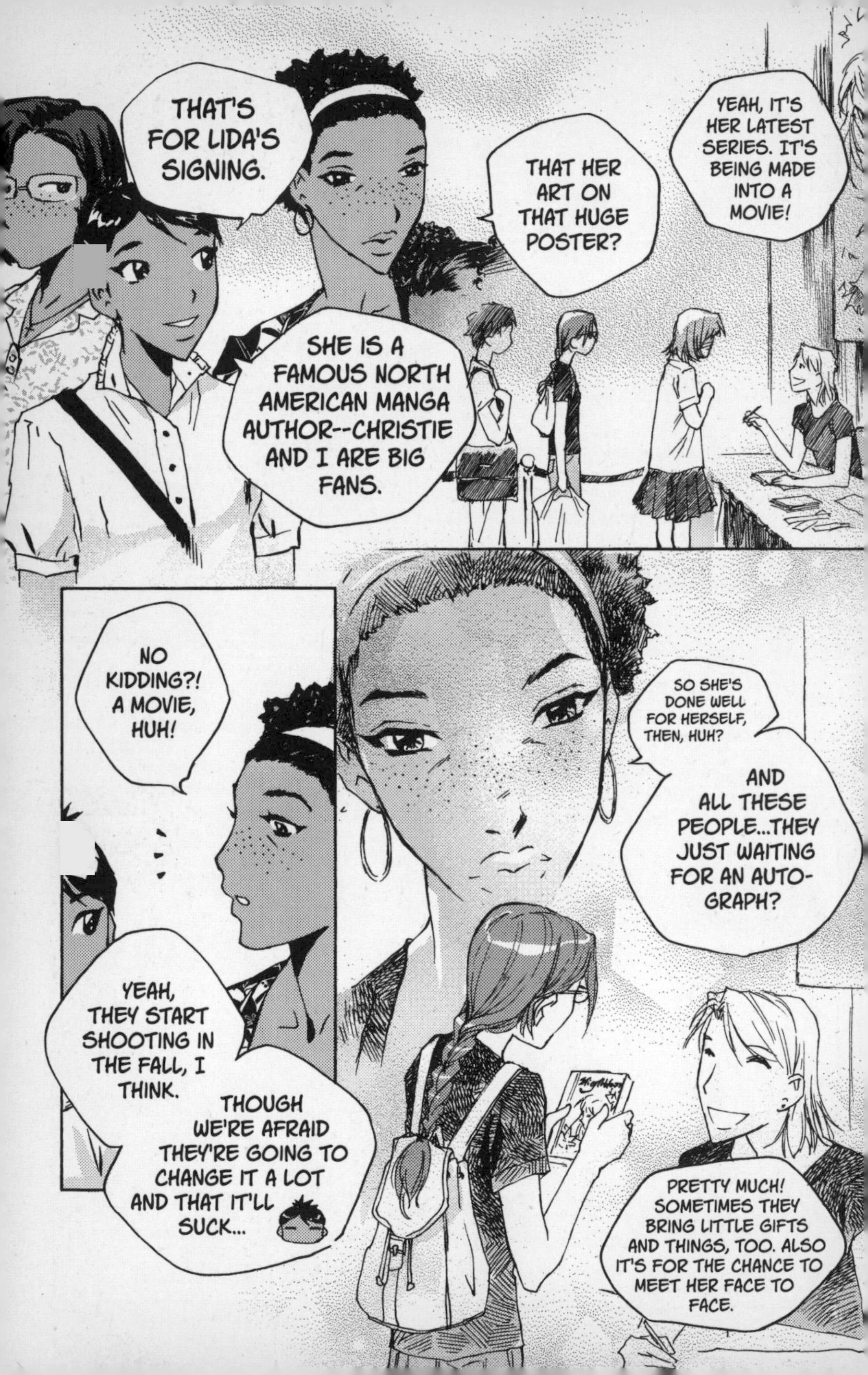
THAT'S FOR LIDA'S SIGNING.
SHE IS A FAMOUS NORTH AMERICAN MANGA AUTHOR--CHRISTIE AND I ARE BIG FANS.
THAT HER ART ON THAT HUGE POSTER?
YEAH, IT'S HER LATEST SERIES. IT'S BEING MADE INTO A MOVIE!
NO KIDDING?! A MOVIE, HUH!
YEAH, THEY START SHOOTING IN THE FALL, I THINK.
THOUGH WE'RE AFRAID THEY'RE GOING TO CHANGE IT A LOT AND THAT IT'LL SUCK...
SO SHE'S DONE WELL FOR HERSELF, THEN, HUH?
AND ALL THESE PEOPLE...THEY JUST WAITING FOR AN AUTO-GRAPH?
PRETTY MUCH! SOMETIMES THEY BRING LITTLE GIFTS AND THINGS, TOO. ALSO IT'S FOR THE CHANCE TO MEET HER FACE TO FACE.

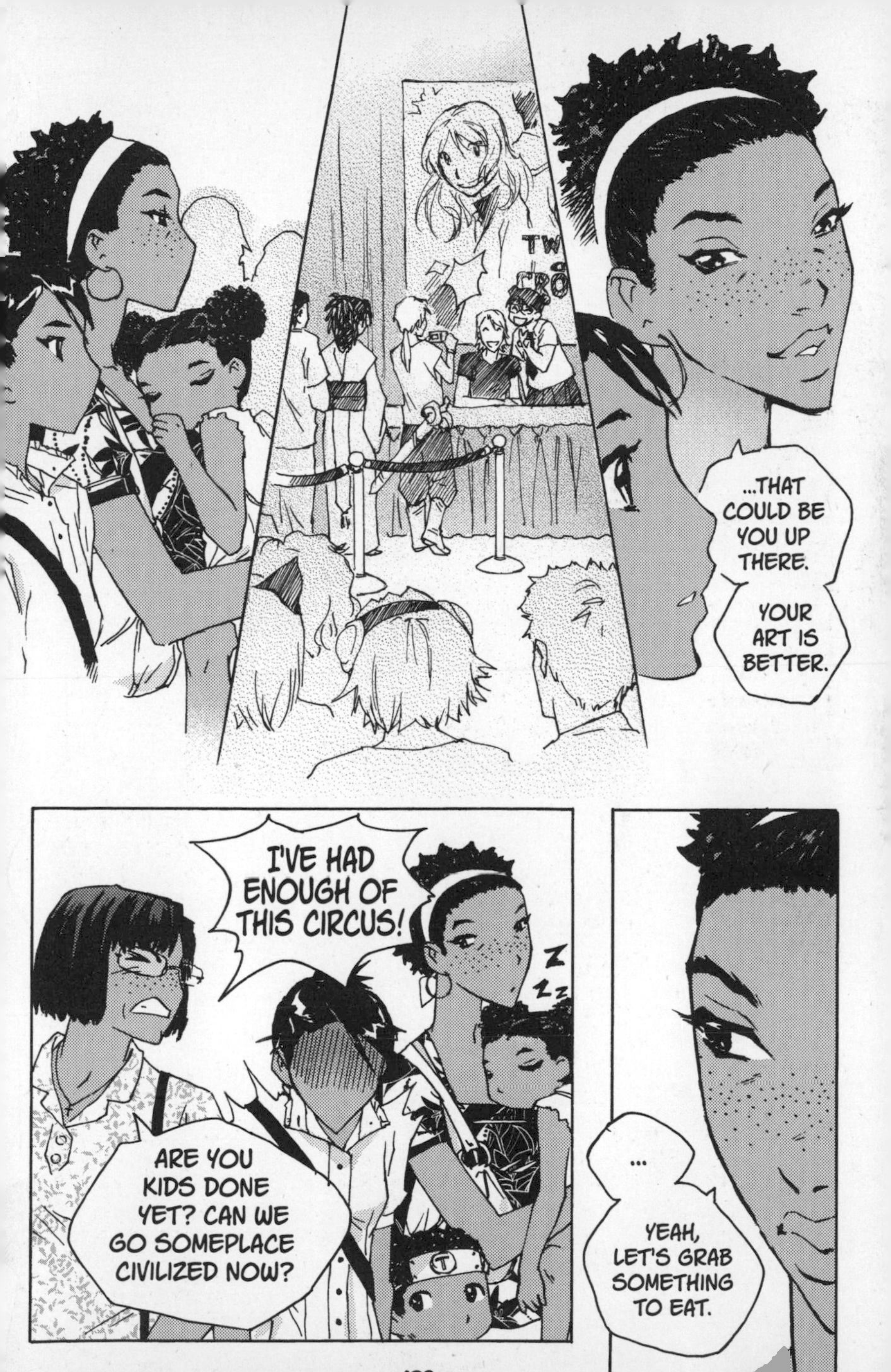
...THAT COULD BE YOU UP THERE.
YOUR ART IS BETTER.
I'VE HAD ENOUGH OF THIS CIRCUS!
ZZZ
ARE YOU KIDS DONE YET? CAN WE GO SOMEPLACE CIVILIZED NOW?
...
YEAH, LET'S GRAB SOMETHING TO EAT.

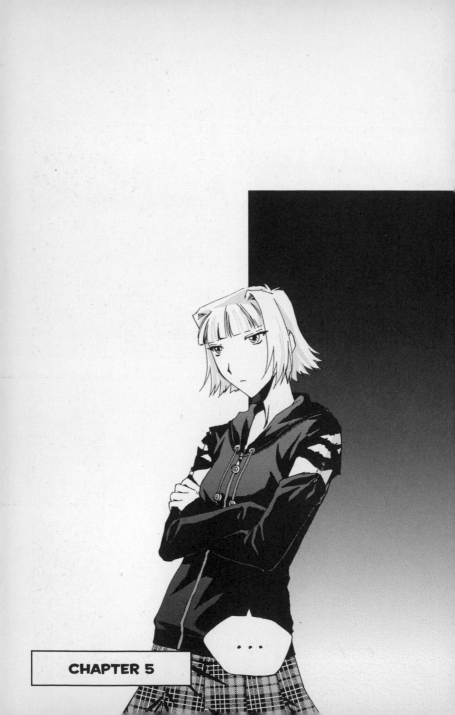

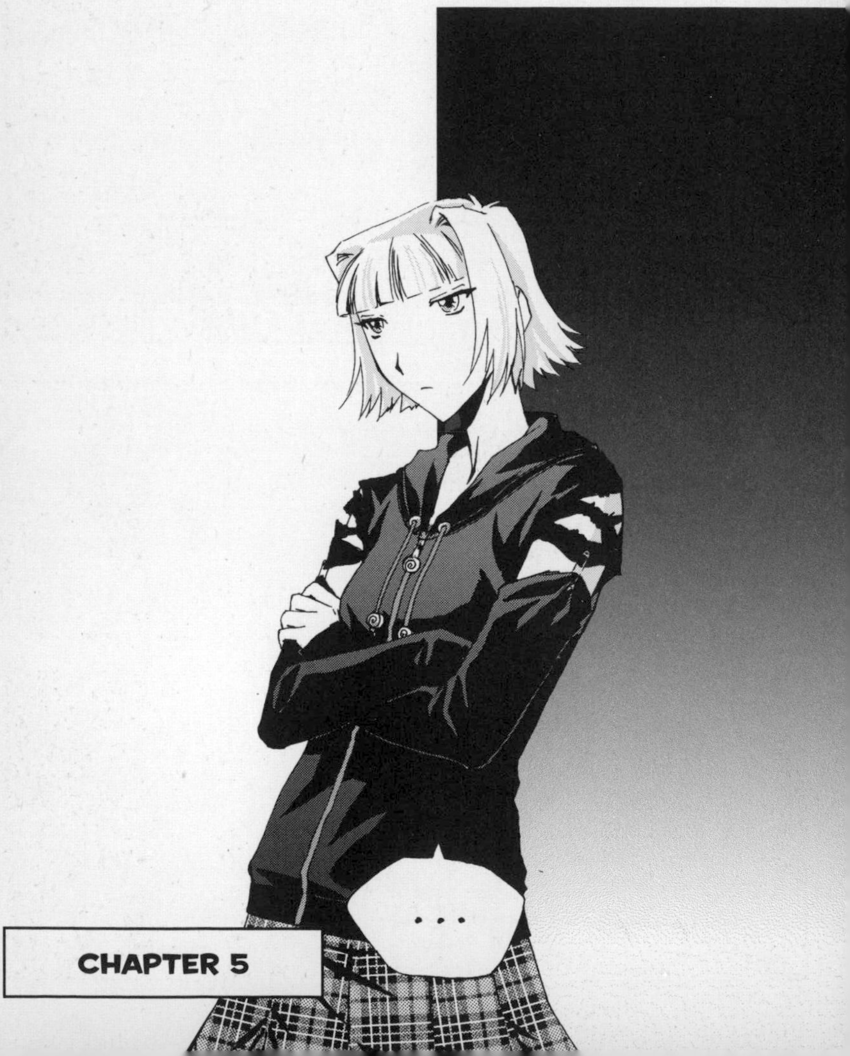
...
CHAPTER 5

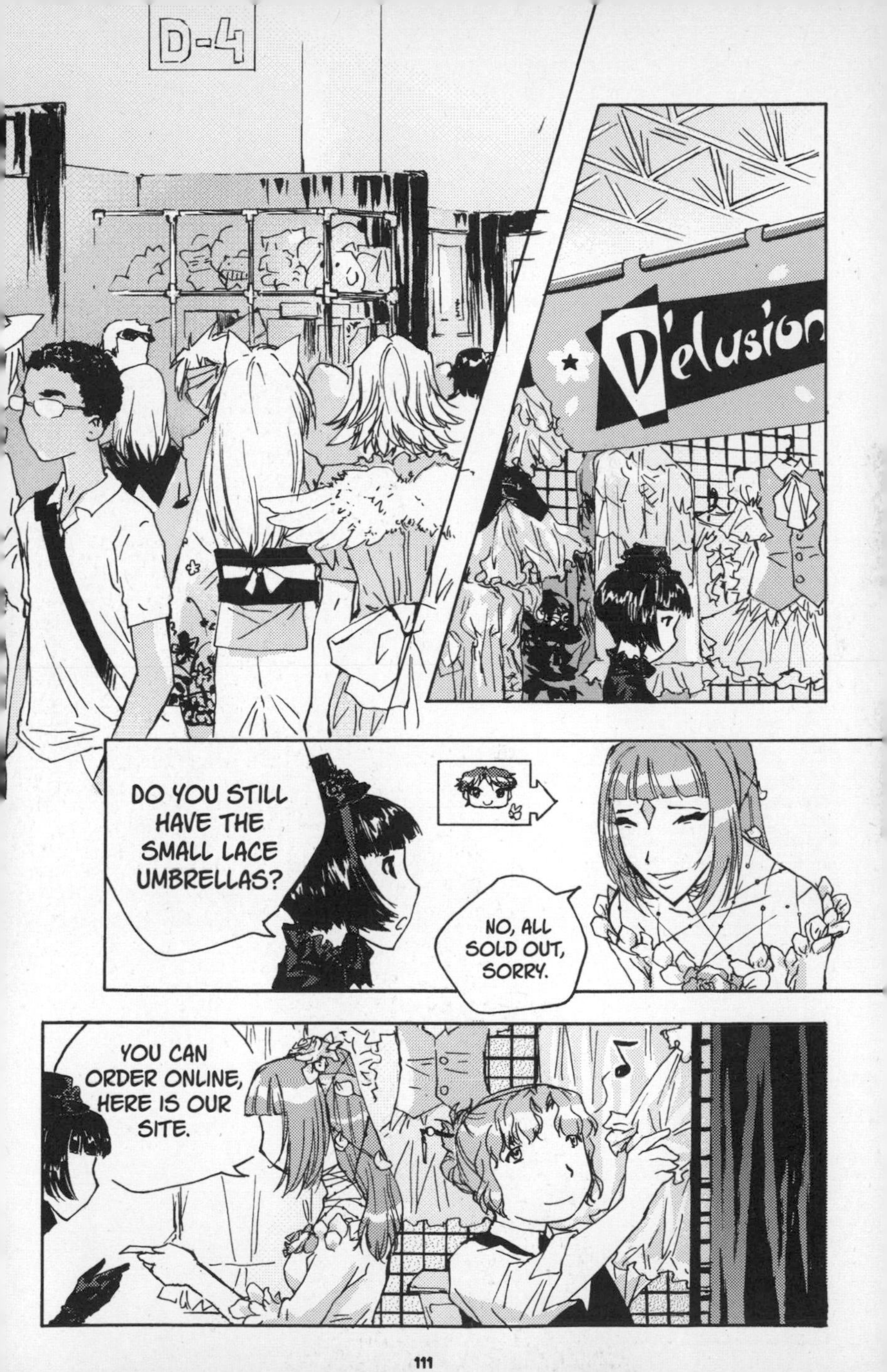
D-4
D'elusion
DO YOU STILL HAVE THE SMALL LACE UMBRELLAS?
NO, ALL SOLD OUT, SORRY.
YOU CAN ORDER ONLINE, HERE IS OUR SITE.

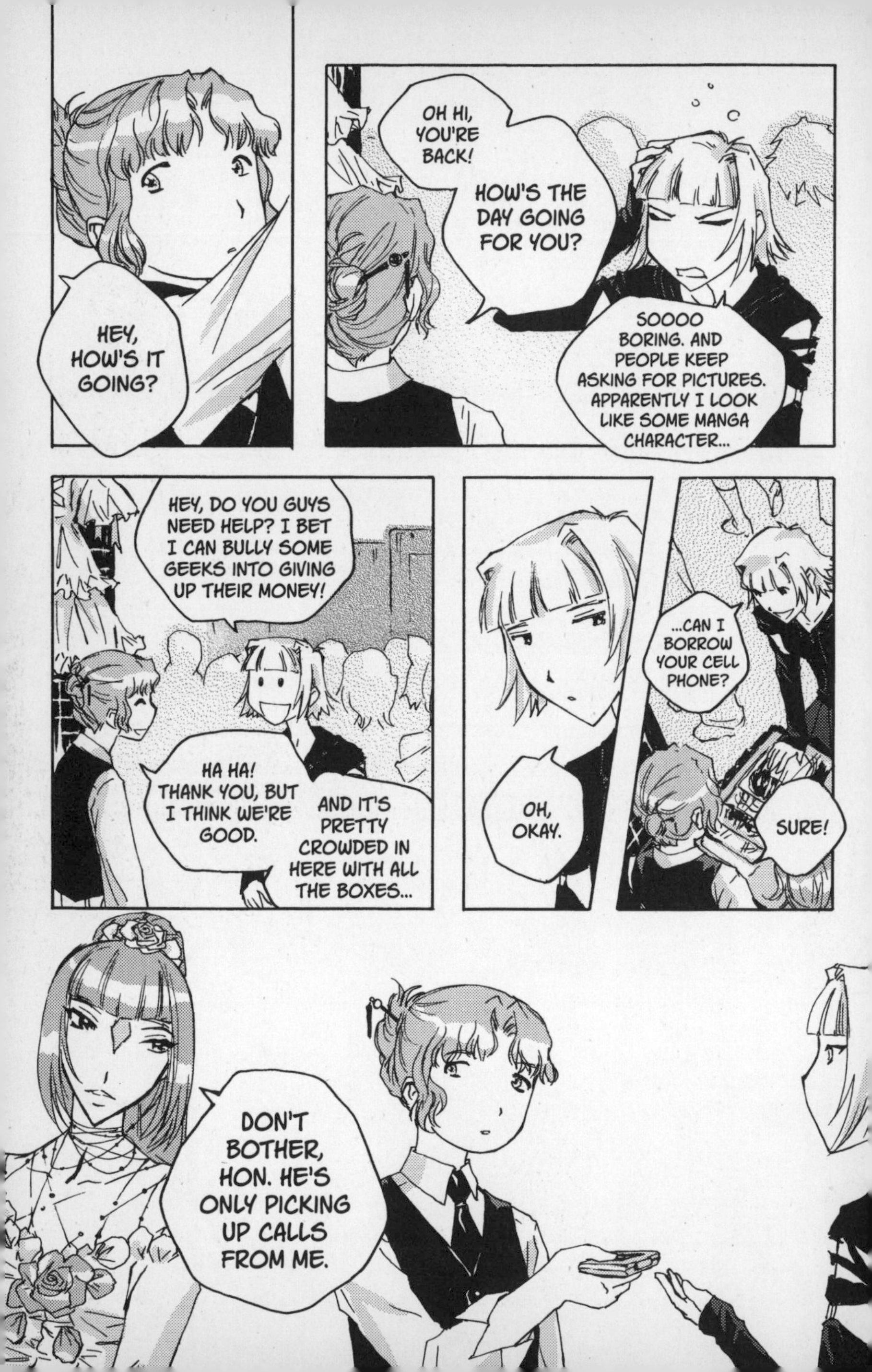
HEY, HOW'S IT GOING?
OH HI, YOU'RE BACK!
HOW'S THE DAY GOING FOR YOU?
SOOOO BORING. AND PEOPLE KEEP ASKING FOR PICTURES. APPARENTLY I LOOK LIKE SOME MANGA CHARACTER...
HEY, DO YOU GUYS NEED HELP? I BET I CAN BULLY SOME GEEKS INTO GIVING UP THEIR MONEY!
HA HA! THANK YOU, BUT I THINK WE'RE GOOD.
AND IT'S PRETTY CROWDED IN HERE WITH ALL THE BOXES...
OH, OKAY.
...CAN I BORROW YOUR CELL PHONE?
SURE!
DON'T BOTHER, HON. HE'S ONLY PICKING UP CALLS FROM ME.

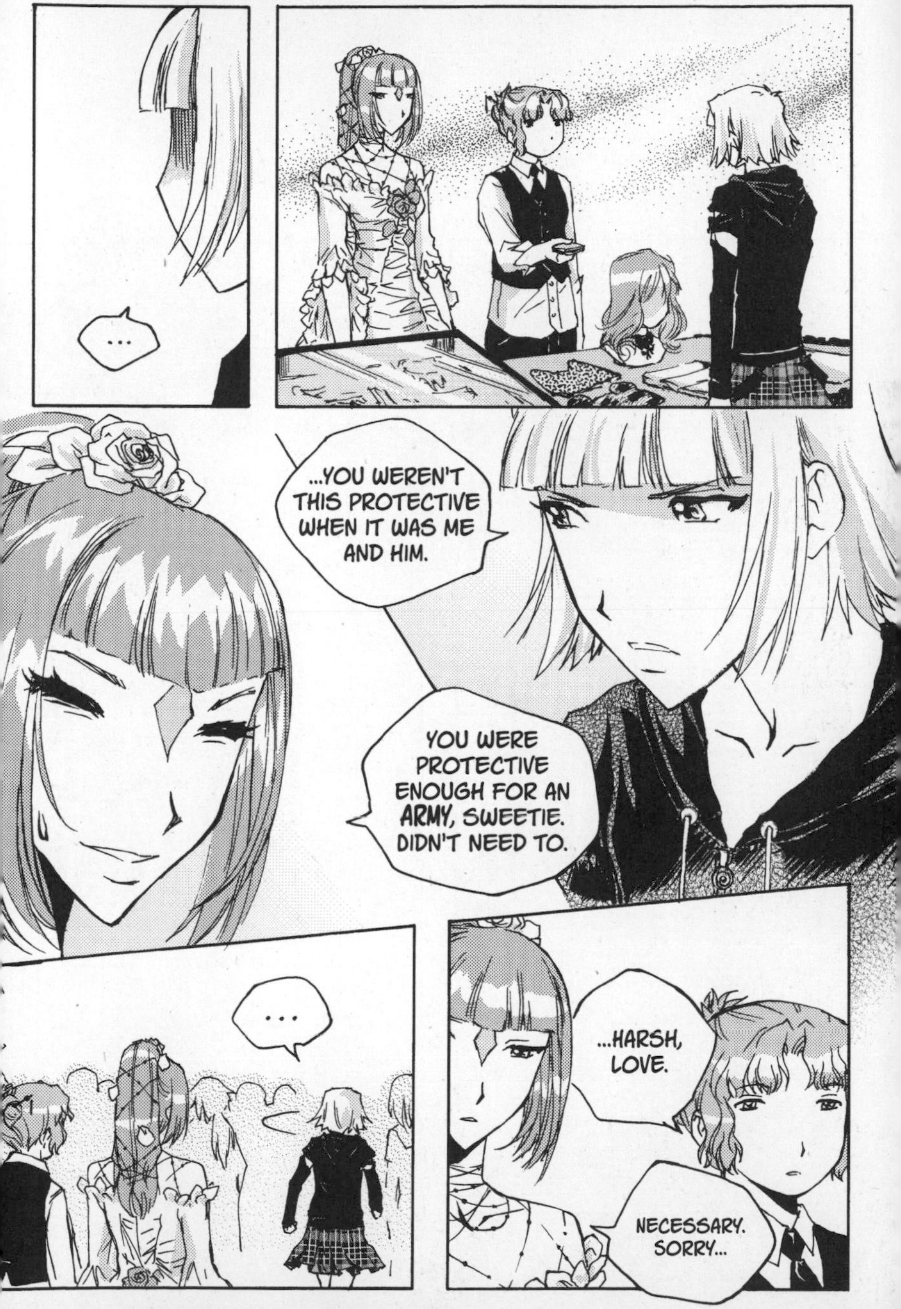
...
...YOU WEREN'T THIS PROTECTIVE WHEN IT WAS ME AND HIM.
YOU WERE PROTECTIVE ENOUGH FOR AN ARMY, SWEETIE. DIDN'T NEED TO.
...
...HARSH, LOVE.
NECESSARY. SORRY...

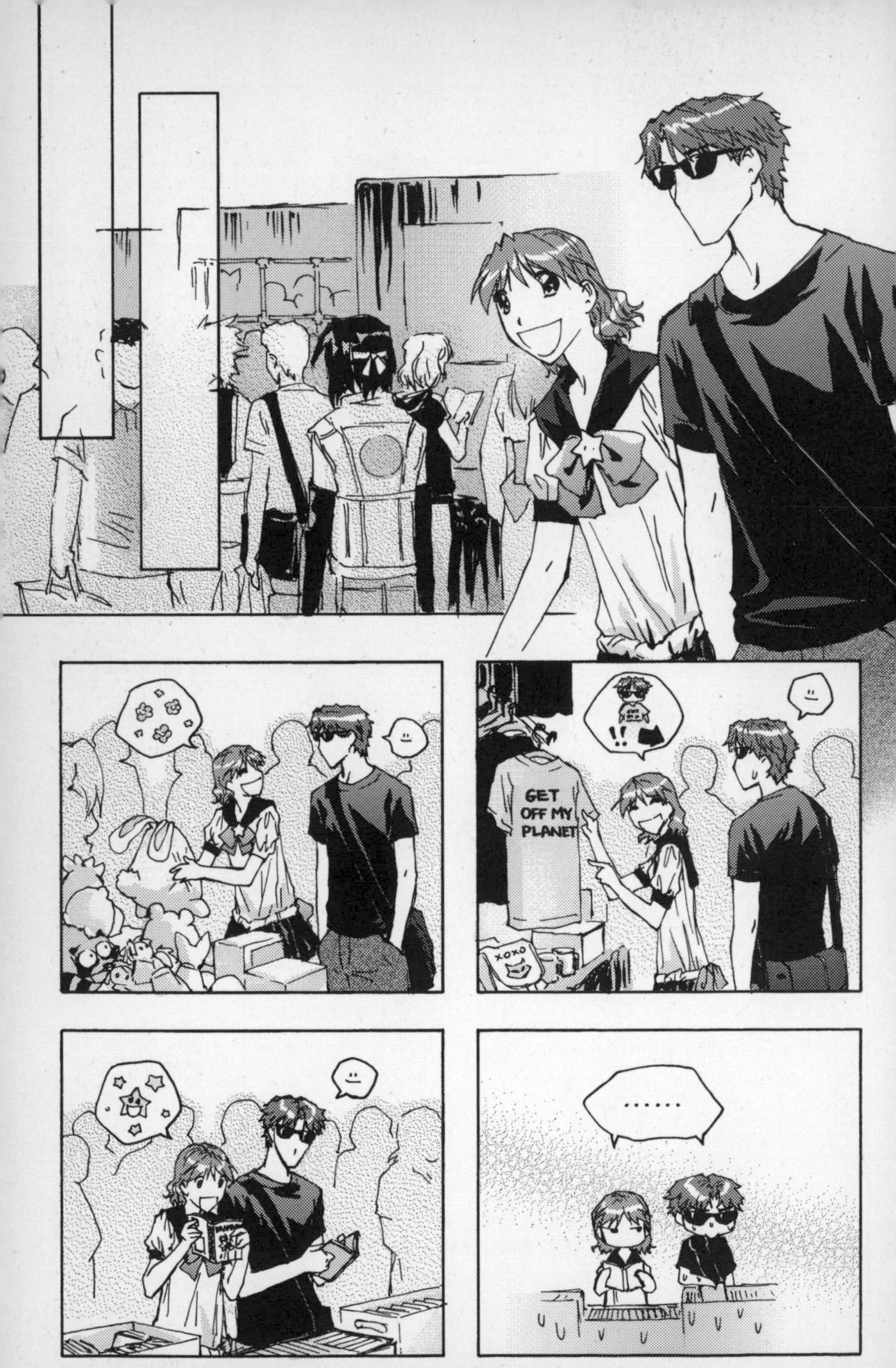
!!
GET OFF MY PLANET
XOXO
......

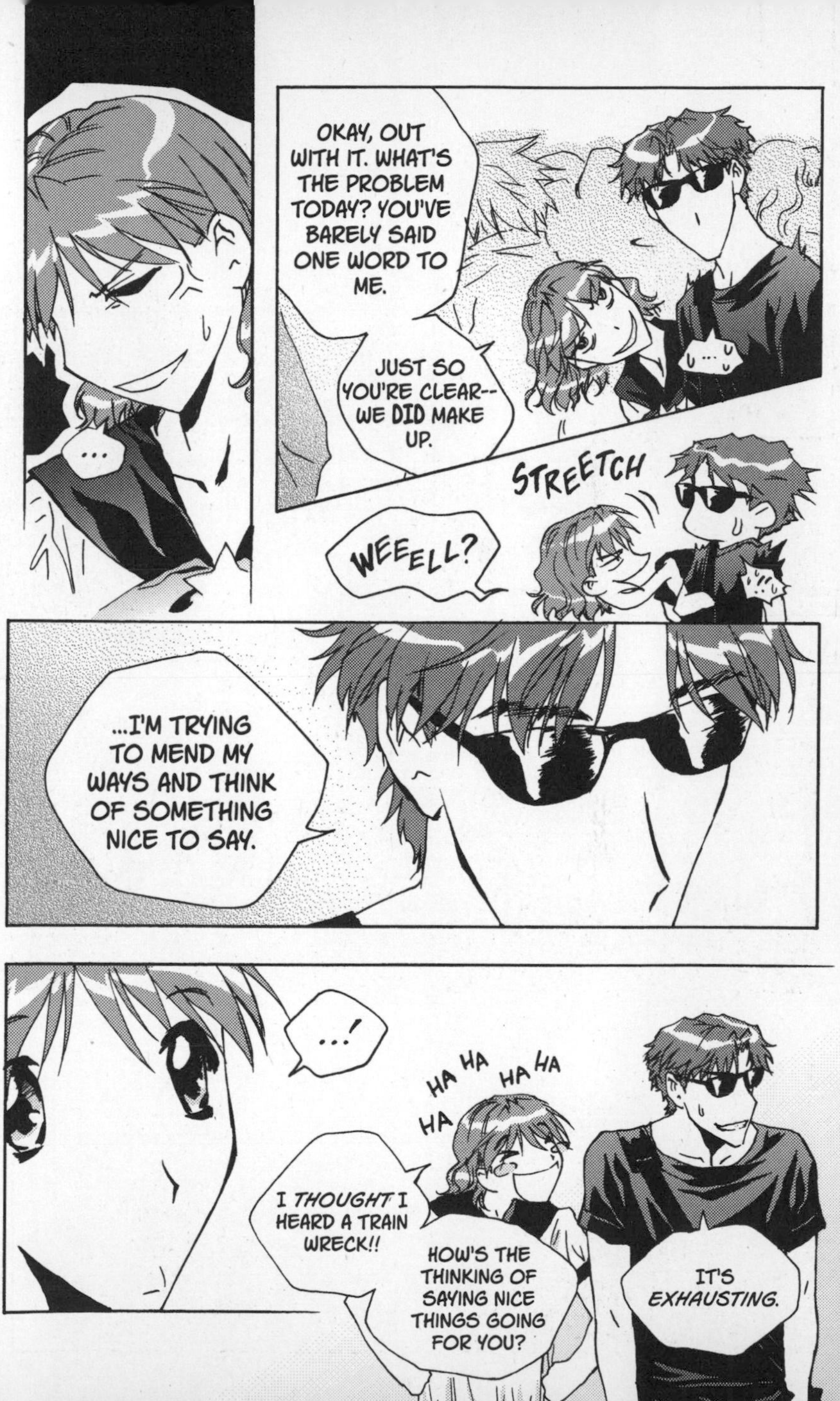
...
OKAY, OUT WITH IT. WHAT'S THE PROBLEM TODAY? YOU'VE BARELY SAID ONE WORD TO ME.
JUST SO YOU'RE CLEAR-- WE DID MAKE UP.
...
STREETCH
WEEELL?
...I'M TRYING TO MEND MY WAYS AND THINK OF SOMETHING NICE TO SAY.
...!
HA HA HA HA HA
I THOUGHT I HEARD A TRAIN WRECK!!
HOW'S THE THINKING OF SAYING NICE THINGS GOING FOR YOU?
IT'S EXHAUSTING.

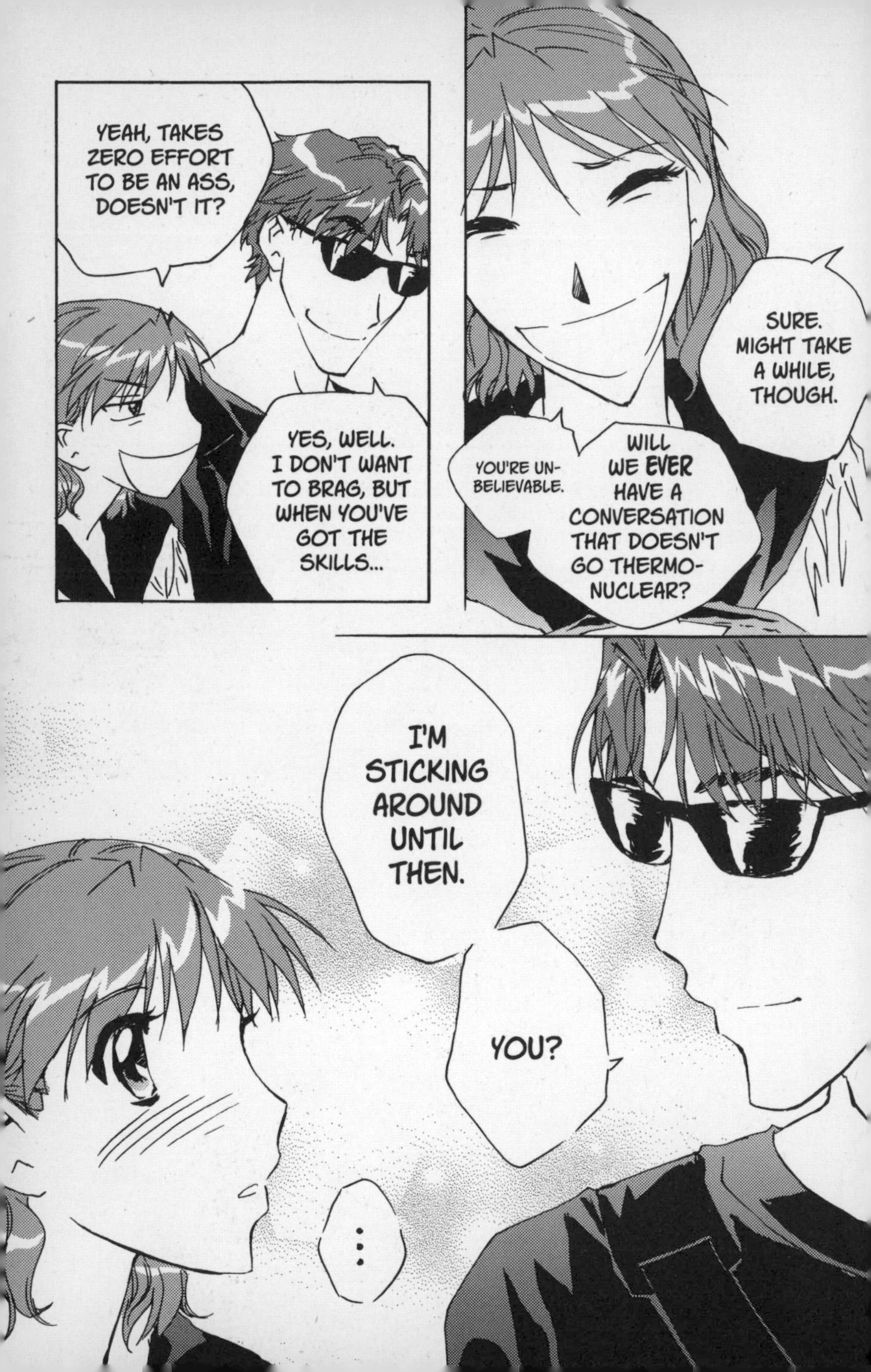
YEAH, TAKES ZERO EFFORT TO BE AN ASS, DOESN'T IT?
YES, WELL. I DON'T WANT TO BRAG, BUT WHEN YOU'VE GOT THE SKILLS...
YOU'RE UN-BELIEVABLE.
WILL WE EVER HAVE A CONVERSATION THAT DOESN'T GO THERMO-NUCLEAR?
SURE. MIGHT TAKE A WHILE, THOUGH.
I'M STICKING AROUND UNTIL THEN.
YOU?
...

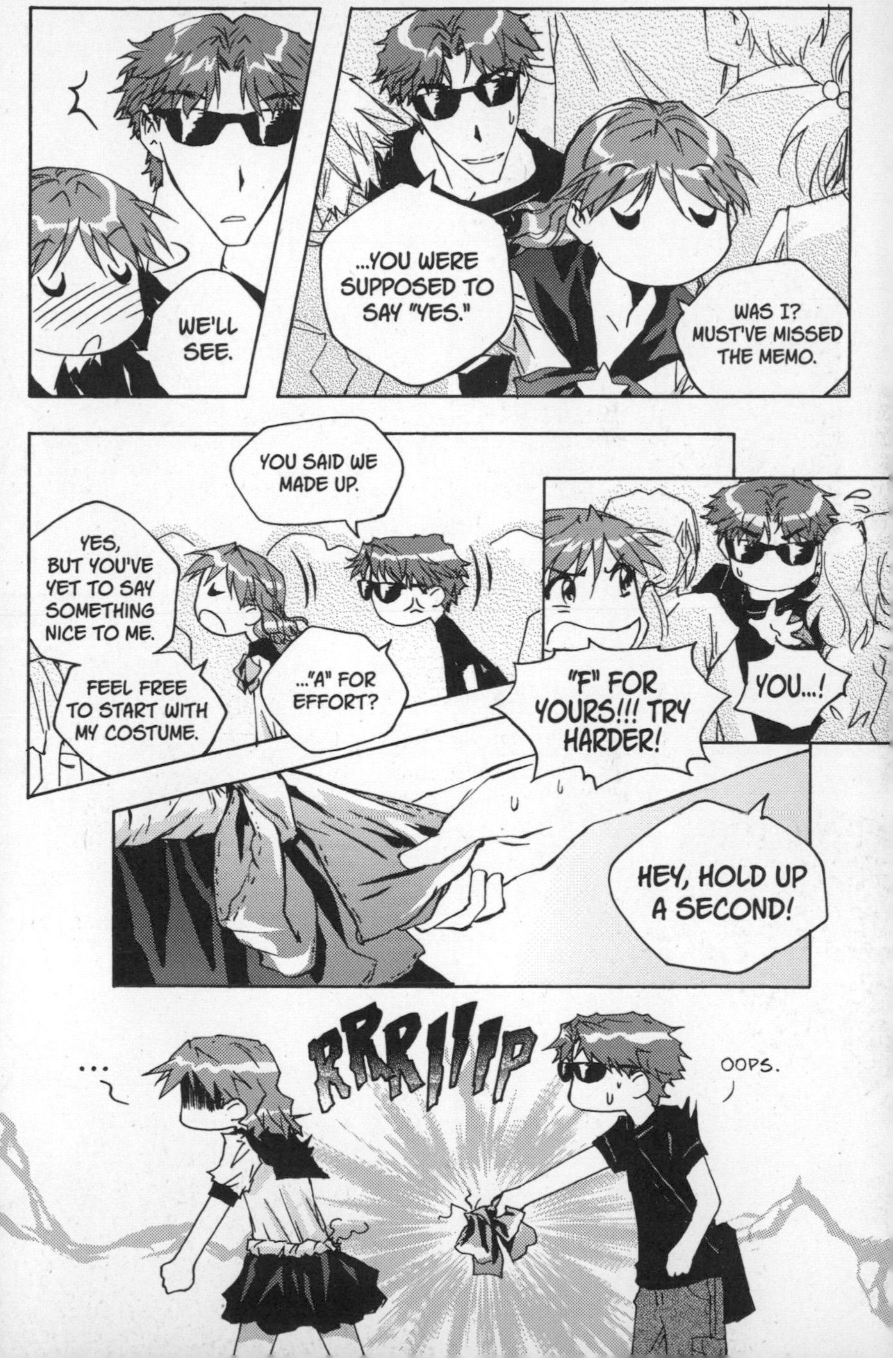
WE'LL SEE.
...YOU WERE SUPPOSED TO SAY "YES."
WAS I? MUST'VE MISSED THE MEMO.
YOU SAID WE MADE UP.
YES, BUT YOU'VE YET TO SAY SOMETHING NICE TO ME.
FEEL FREE TO START WITH MY COSTUME.
..."A" FOR EFFORT?
"F" FOR YOURS!!! TRY HARDER!
YOU...!
HEY, HOLD UP A SECOND!
...
RRRIIIP
OOPS.

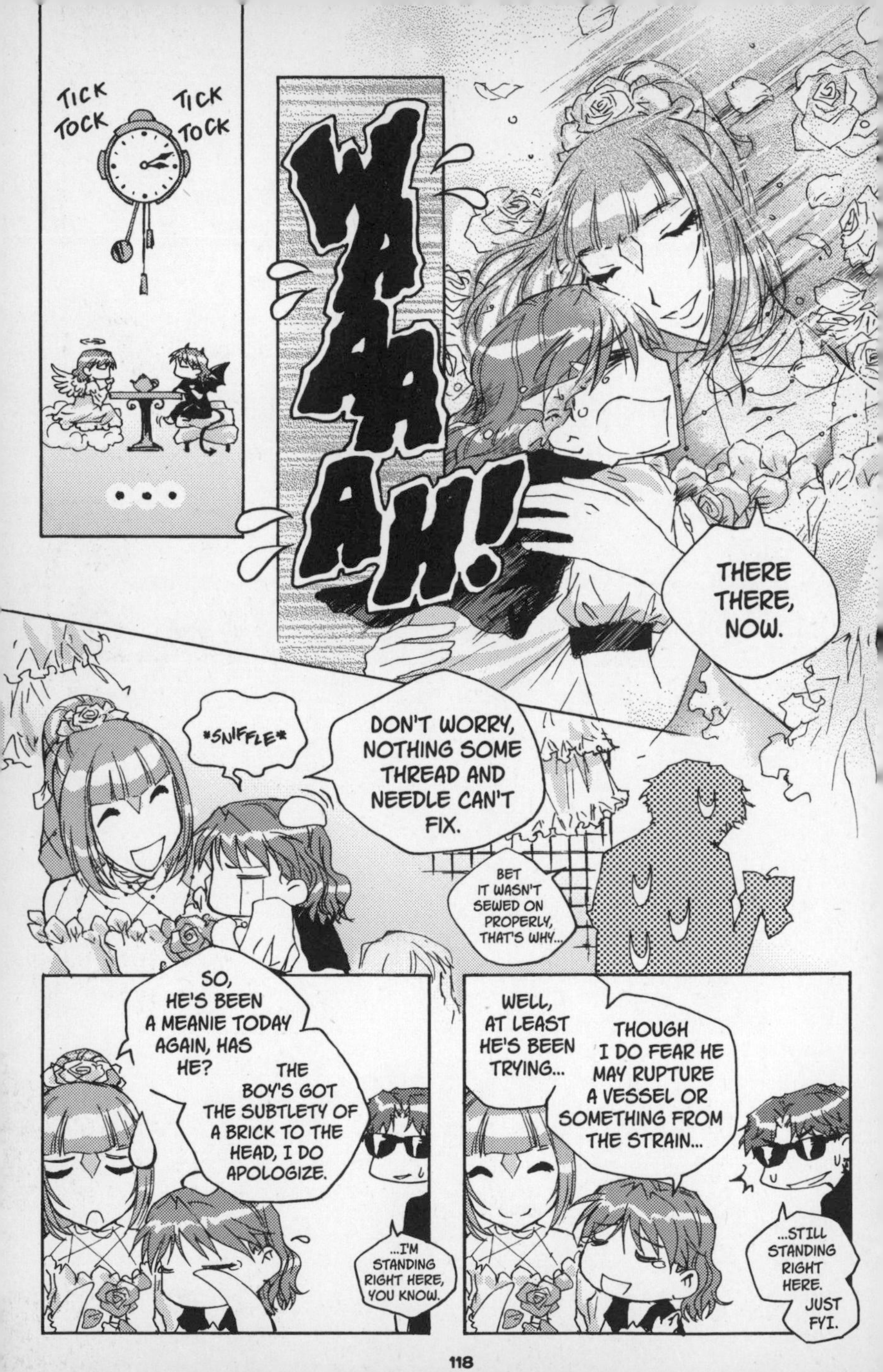
TICK TOCK
TICK TOCK
• • •
WAAAH!
THERE THERE, NOW.
SNIFFLE
DON'T WORRY, NOTHING SOME THREAD AND NEEDLE CAN'T FIX.
BET IT WASN'T SEWED ON PROPERLY, THAT'S WHY...
SO, HE'S BEEN A MEANIE TODAY AGAIN, HAS HE?
THE BOY'S GOT THE SUBTLETY OF A BRICK TO THE HEAD, I DO APOLOGIZE.
...I'M STANDING RIGHT HERE, YOU KNOW.
WELL, AT LEAST HE'S BEEN TRYING...
THOUGH I DO FEAR HE MAY RUPTURE A VESSEL OR SOMETHING FROM THE STRAIN...
...STILL STANDING RIGHT HERE. JUST FYI.

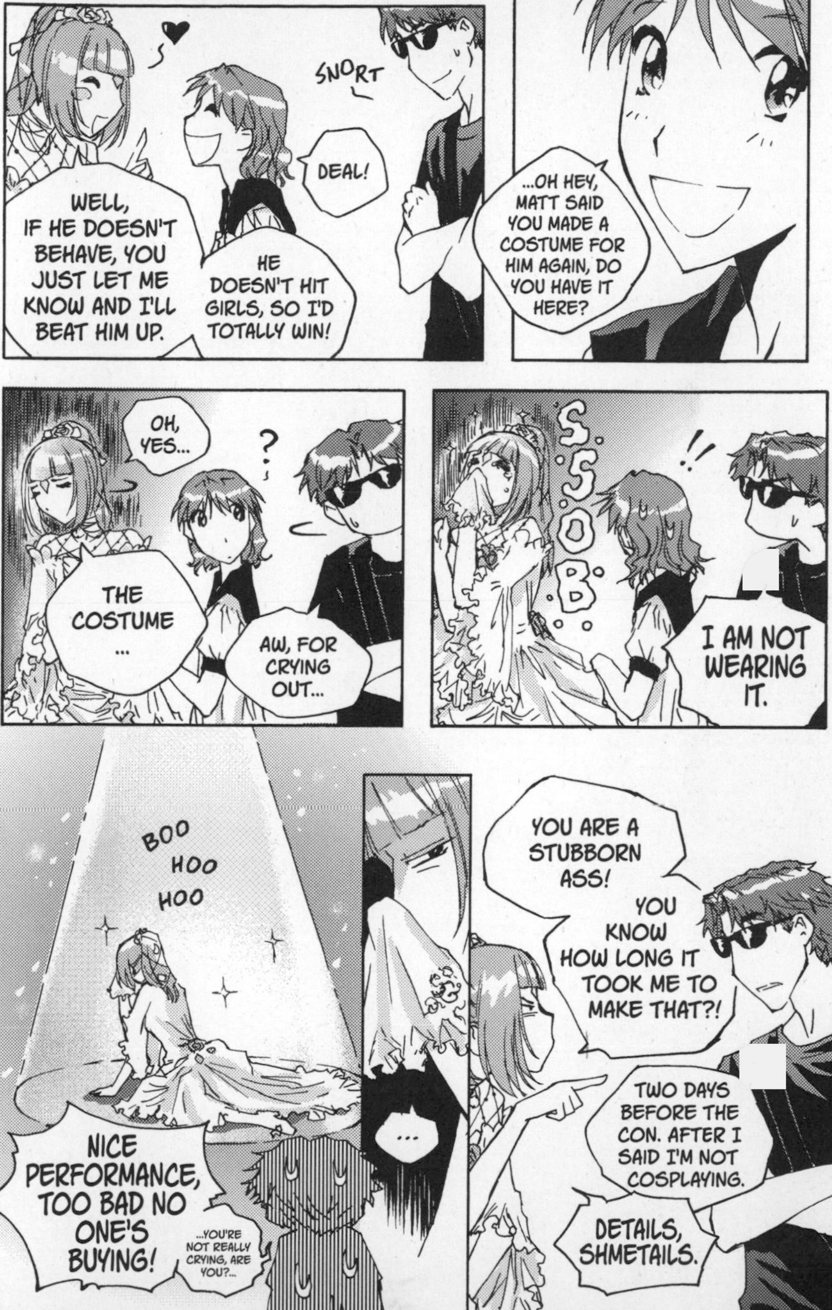
WELL, IF HE DOESN'T BEHAVE, YOU JUST LET ME KNOW AND I'LL BEAT HIM UP.
DEAL!
SNORT
HE DOESN'T HIT GIRLS, SO I'D TOTALLY WIN!
...OH HEY, MATT SAID YOU MADE A COSTUME FOR HIM AGAIN, DO YOU HAVE IT HERE?
OH, YES...
?
THE COSTUME ...
AW, FOR CRYING OUT...
SOB
!!
I AM NOT WEARING IT.
BOO HOO HOO
NICE PERFORMANCE, TOO BAD NO ONE'S BUYING!
...YOU'RE NOT REALLY CRYING, ARE YOU?...
...
YOU ARE A STUBBORN ASS!
YOU KNOW HOW LONG IT TOOK ME TO MAKE THAT?!
TWO DAYS BEFORE THE CON. AFTER I SAID I'M NOT COSPLAYING.
DETAILS, SHMETAILS.

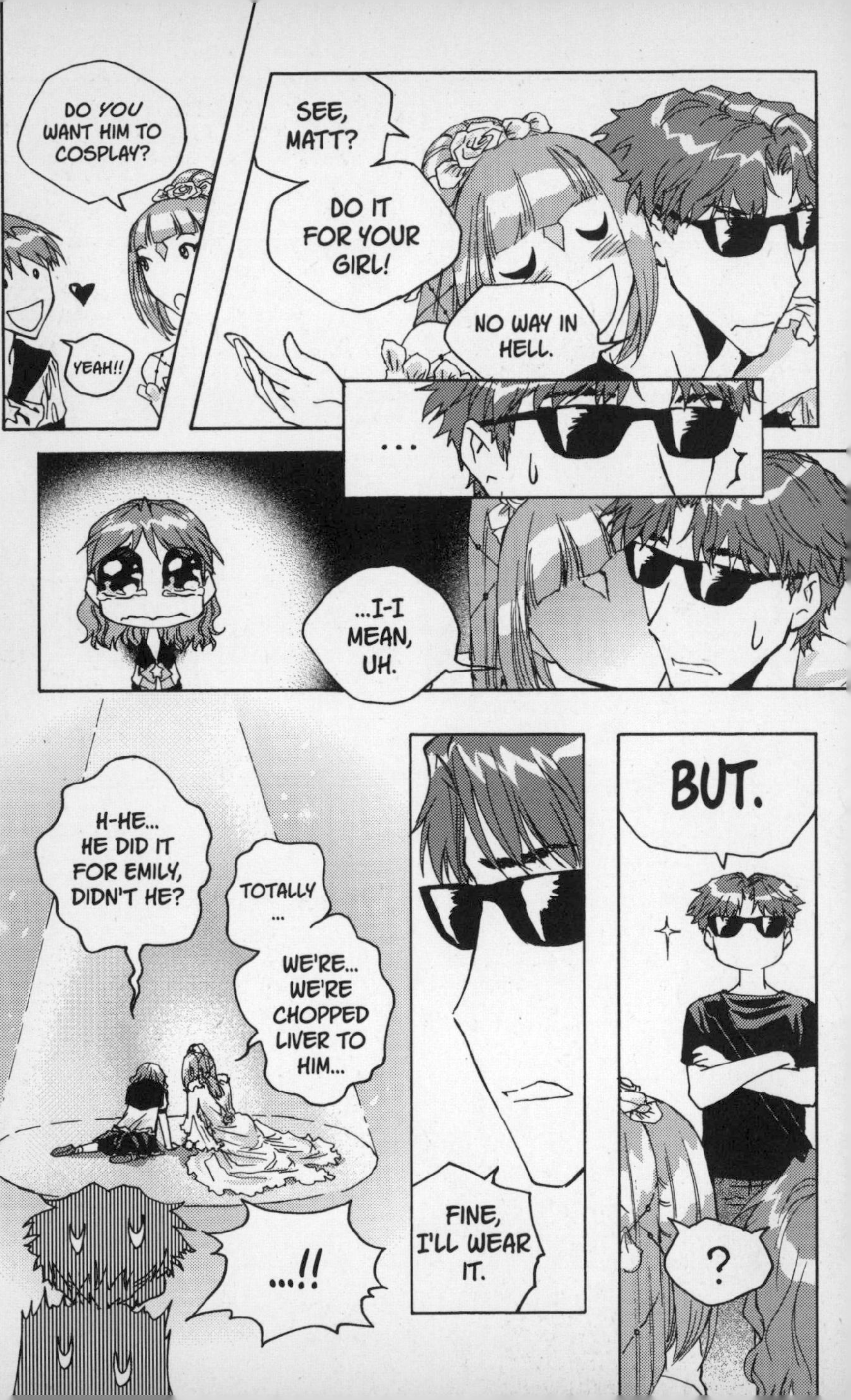
DO YOU WANT HIM TO COSPLAY?
YEAH!!
SEE, MATT?
DO IT FOR YOUR GIRL!
NO WAY IN HELL.
...
...I-I MEAN, UH.
H-HE... HE DID IT FOR EMILY, DIDN'T HE?
TOTALLY ...
WE'RE... WE'RE CHOPPED LIVER TO HIM...
...!!
FINE, I'LL WEAR IT.
BUT.
?

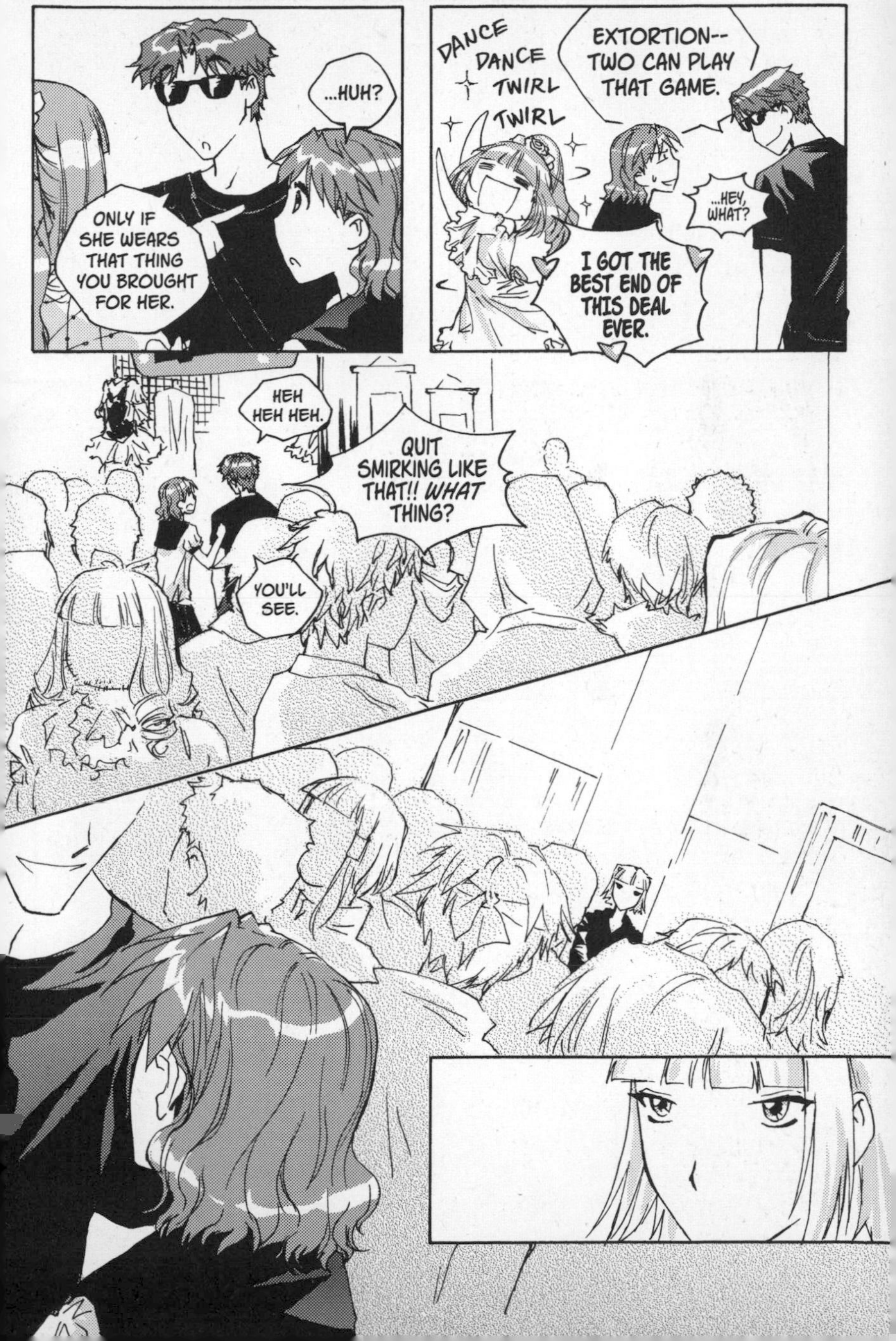
...HUH?
ONLY IF SHE WEARS THAT THING YOU BROUGHT FOR HER.
DANCE DANCE TWIRL TWIRL
EXTORTION-- TWO CAN PLAY THAT GAME.
...HEY, WHAT?
I GOT THE BEST END OF THIS DEAL EVER.
HEH HEH HEH.
QUIT SMIRKING LIKE THAT!! *WHAT* THING?
YOU'LL SEE.

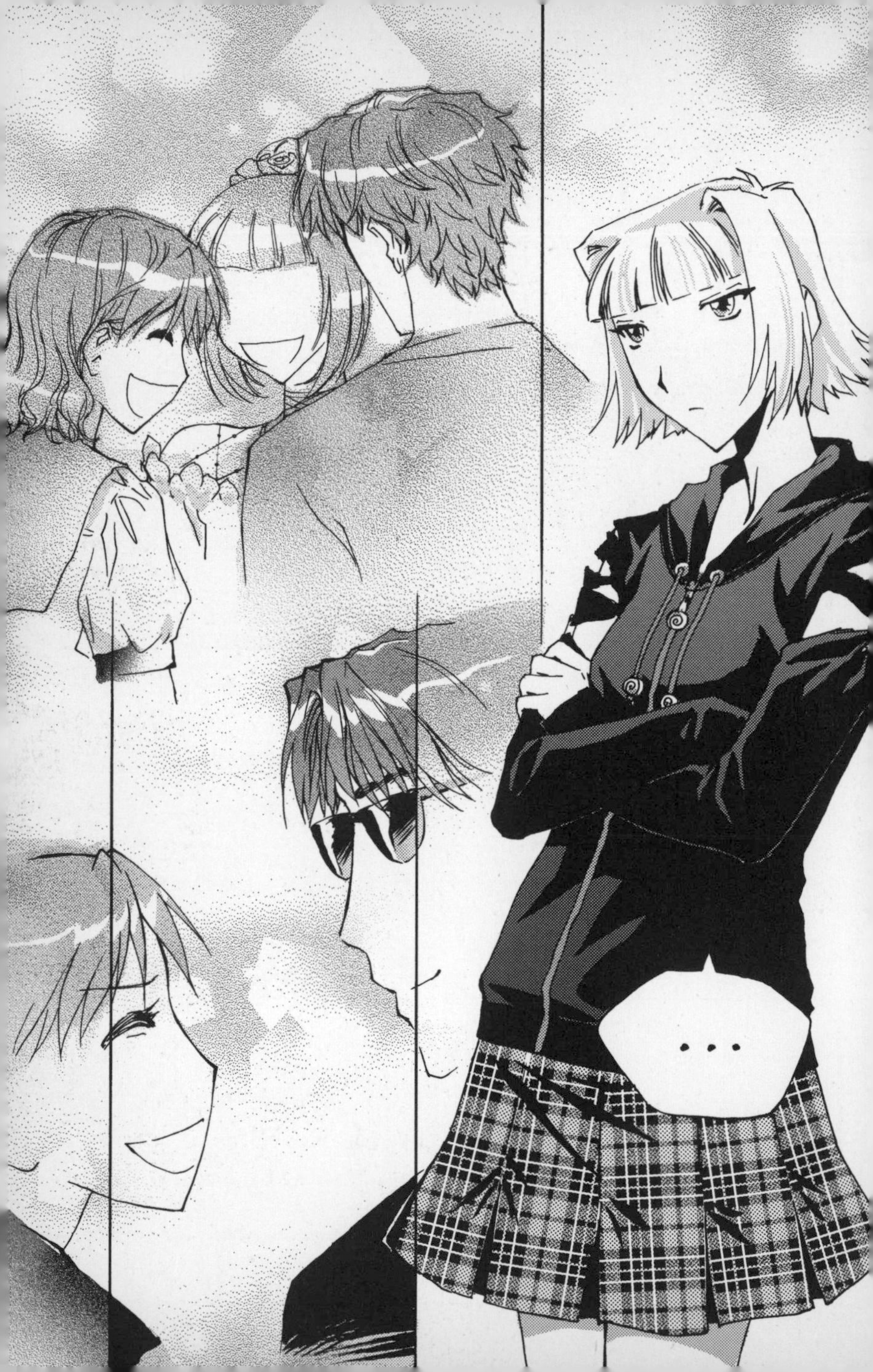
...

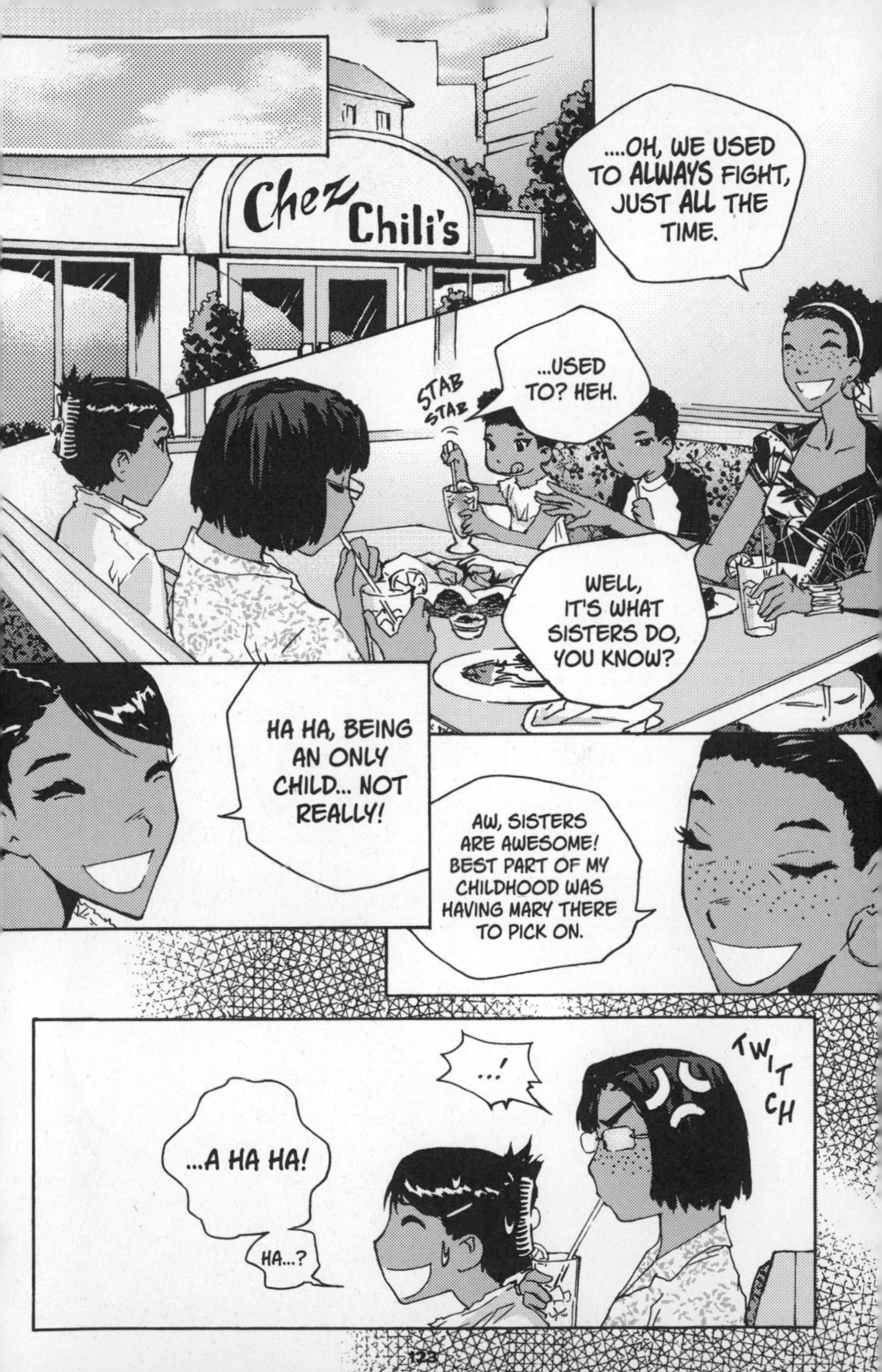
Chez Chili's
....OH, WE USED TO ALWAYS FIGHT, JUST ALL THE TIME.
STAB STAB
...USED TO? HEH.
WELL, IT'S WHAT SISTERS DO, YOU KNOW?
HA HA, BEING AN ONLY CHILD... NOT REALLY!
AW, SISTERS ARE AWESOME! BEST PART OF MY CHILDHOOD WAS HAVING MARY THERE TO PICK ON.
...A HA HA!
HA...?
...!
TWITCH

I ALWAYS WON, AS YOU'LL RECALL.

HA HA, IT'S TRUE, YOU DID. WHICH USUALLY INVOLVED CHASING ME INTO THE BATHROOM UNTIL MOM CAME HOME.

YOU SHOULD'VE SEEN YOUR GRANDMA, SHE WAS ALL...

"YOU TWO ARE GOING TO GET ALONG IF IT KILLS YOU!"

SO NOW HERE WE ARE. GETTING ALONG IF IT KILLS US, HA HA! RIGHT, MARY?

WHERE DID THAT GIRL GO WITH THE CHECK...?

DAMN LAZY WAITERS ...

MAYBE YOU SCARED HER OFF. WOULDN'T BE A FIRST.

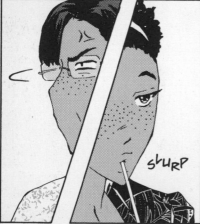

SLURP

S-SO!!

S-SO, HOW IS SCHOOL GOING FOR YOU GUYS?

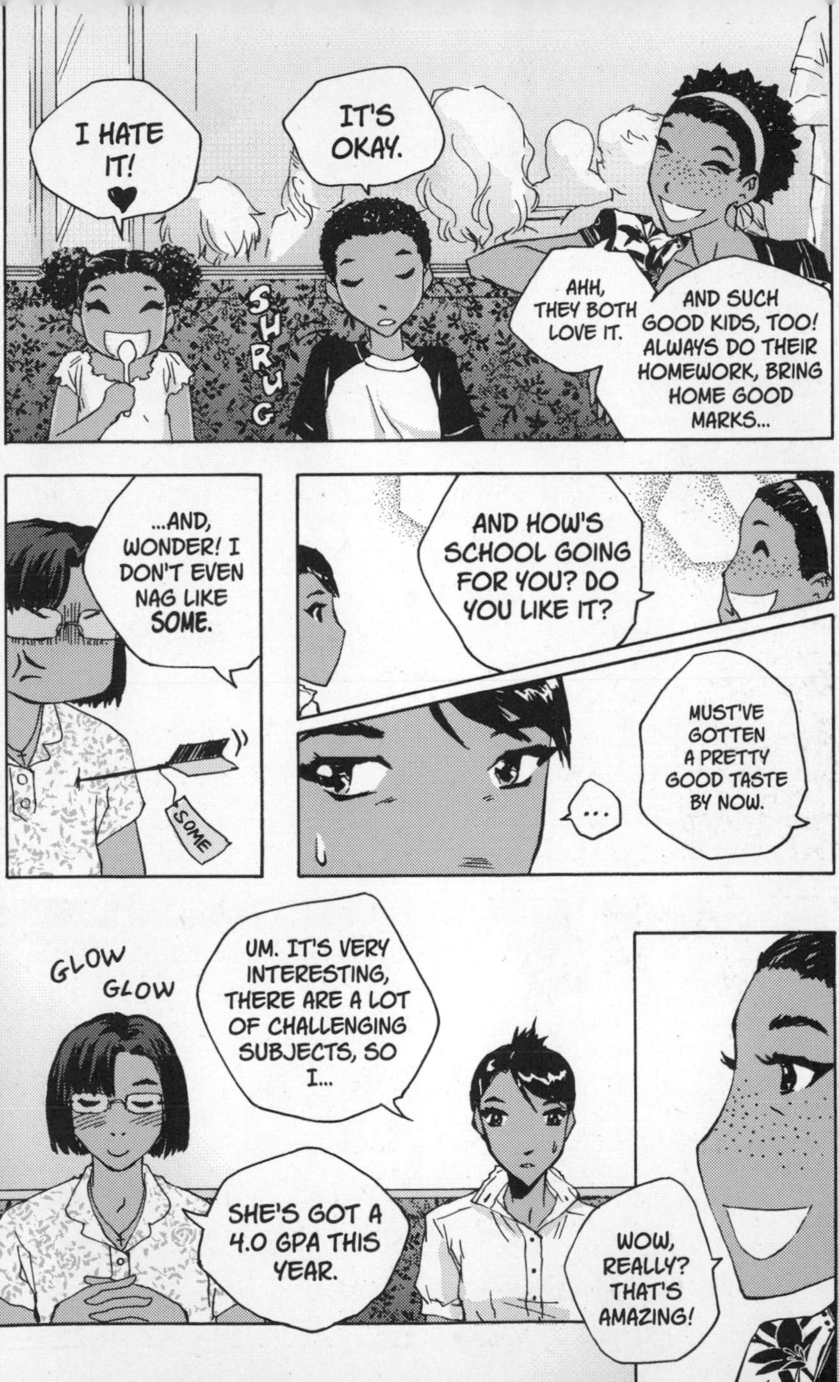
I HATE IT!
IT'S OKAY.
SHRUG
AHH, THEY BOTH LOVE IT.
AND SUCH GOOD KIDS, TOO! ALWAYS DO THEIR HOMEWORK, BRING HOME GOOD MARKS...
...AND, WONDER! I DON'T EVEN NAG LIKE SOME.
SOME
AND HOW'S SCHOOL GOING FOR YOU? DO YOU LIKE IT?
...
MUST'VE GOTTEN A PRETTY GOOD TASTE BY NOW.
GLOW GLOW
UM. IT'S VERY INTERESTING, THERE ARE A LOT OF CHALLENGING SUBJECTS, SO I...
SHE'S GOT A 4.0 GPA THIS YEAR.
WOW, REALLY? THAT'S AMAZING!

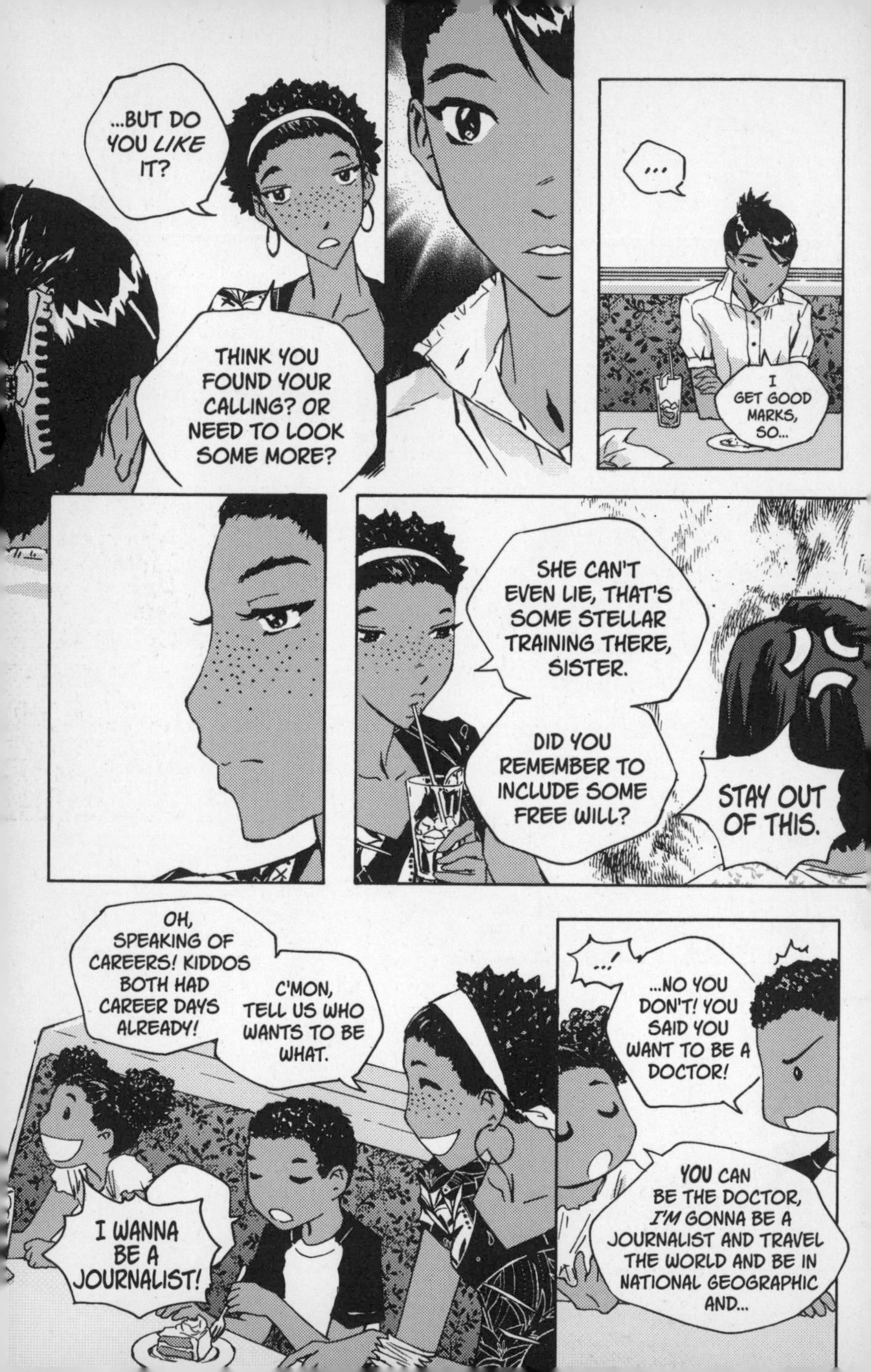
...BUT DO YOU *LIKE* IT?
THINK YOU FOUND YOUR CALLING? OR NEED TO LOOK SOME MORE?
...
I GET GOOD MARKS, SO...
SHE CAN'T EVEN LIE, THAT'S SOME STELLAR TRAINING THERE, SISTER.
DID YOU REMEMBER TO INCLUDE SOME FREE WILL?
STAY OUT OF THIS.
OH, SPEAKING OF CAREERS! KIDDOS BOTH HAD CAREER DAYS ALREADY!
C'MON, TELL US WHO WANTS TO BE WHAT.
I WANNA BE A JOURNALIST!
...!
...NO YOU DON'T! YOU SAID YOU WANT TO BE A DOCTOR!
YOU CAN BE THE DOCTOR, *I'M* GONNA BE A JOURNALIST AND TRAVEL THE WORLD AND BE IN NATIONAL GEOGRAPHIC AND...

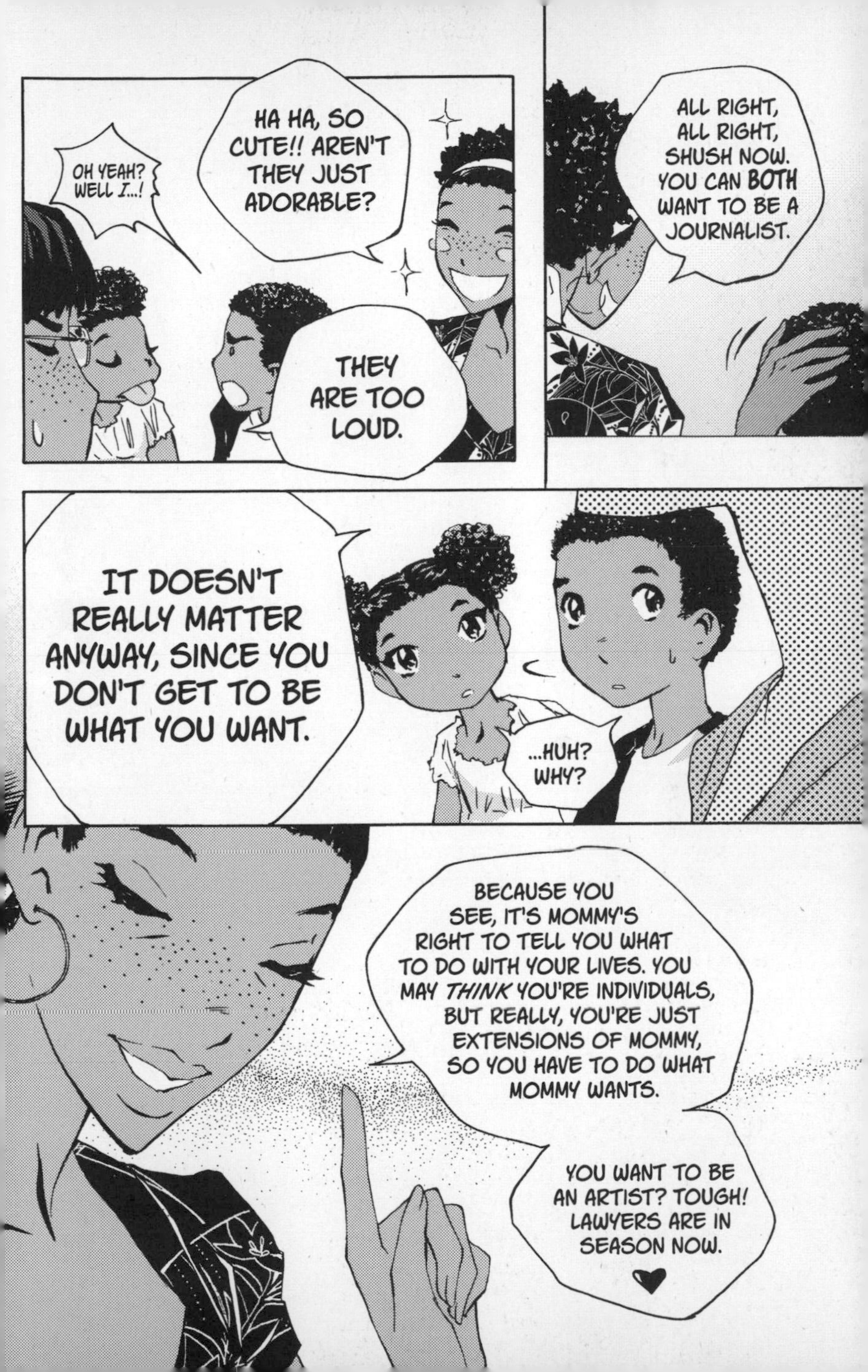
OH YEAH? WELL I...!
HA HA, SO CUTE!! AREN'T THEY JUST ADORABLE?
THEY ARE TOO LOUD.
ALL RIGHT, ALL RIGHT, SHUSH NOW. YOU CAN BOTH WANT TO BE A JOURNALIST.
IT DOESN'T REALLY MATTER ANYWAY, SINCE YOU DON'T GET TO BE WHAT YOU WANT.
...HUH? WHY?
BECAUSE YOU SEE, IT'S MOMMY'S RIGHT TO TELL YOU WHAT TO DO WITH YOUR LIVES. YOU MAY THINK YOU'RE INDIVIDUALS, BUT REALLY, YOU'RE JUST EXTENSIONS OF MOMMY, SO YOU HAVE TO DO WHAT MOMMY WANTS.
YOU WANT TO BE AN ARTIST? TOUGH! LAWYERS ARE IN SEASON NOW.

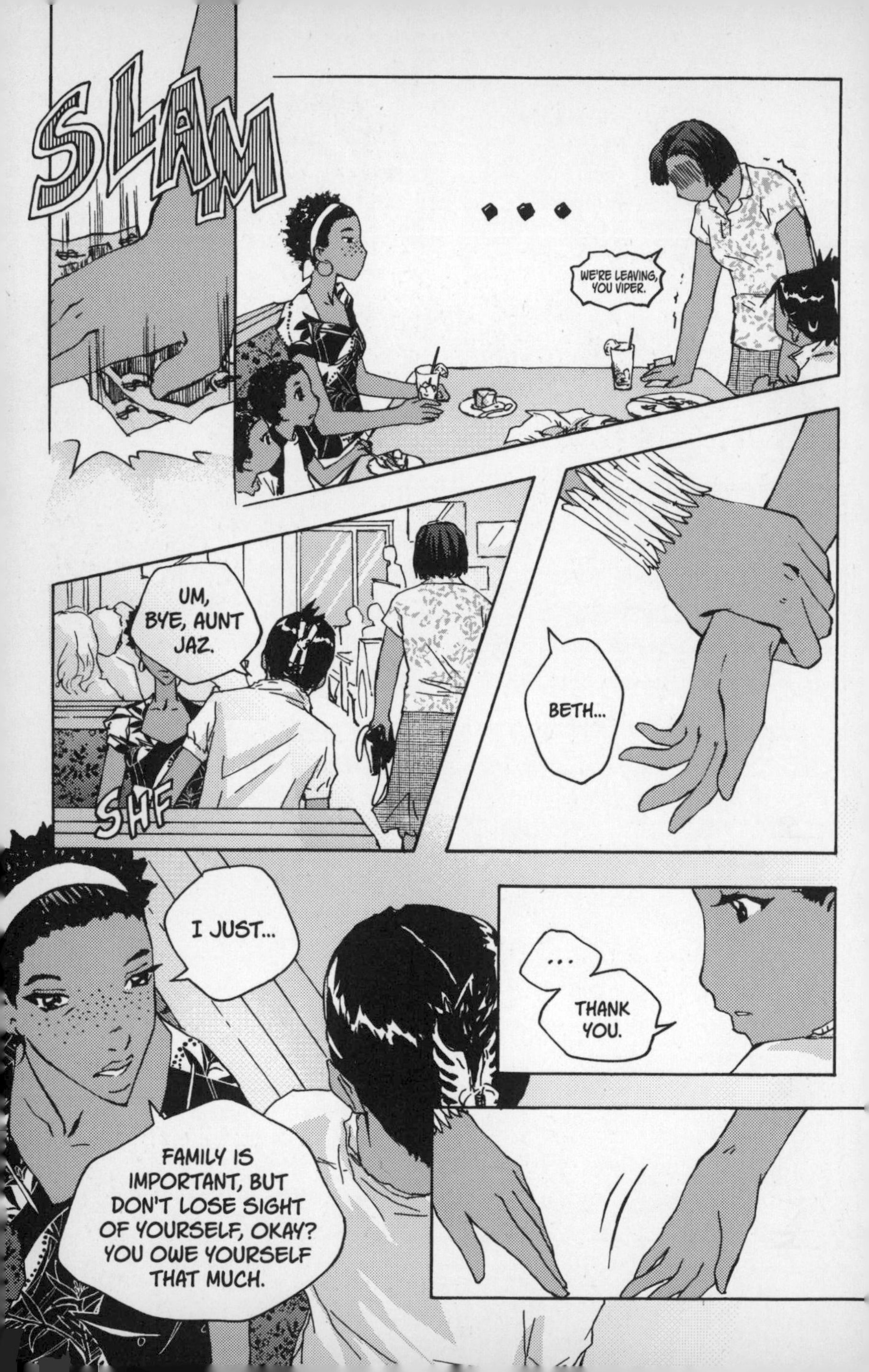
SLAM
...
WE'RE LEAVING, YOU VIPER.
UM, BYE, AUNT JAZ.
SHF
BETH...
I JUST...
FAMILY IS IMPORTANT, BUT DON'T LOSE SIGHT OF YOURSELF, OKAY? YOU OWE YOURSELF THAT MUCH.
...
THANK YOU.

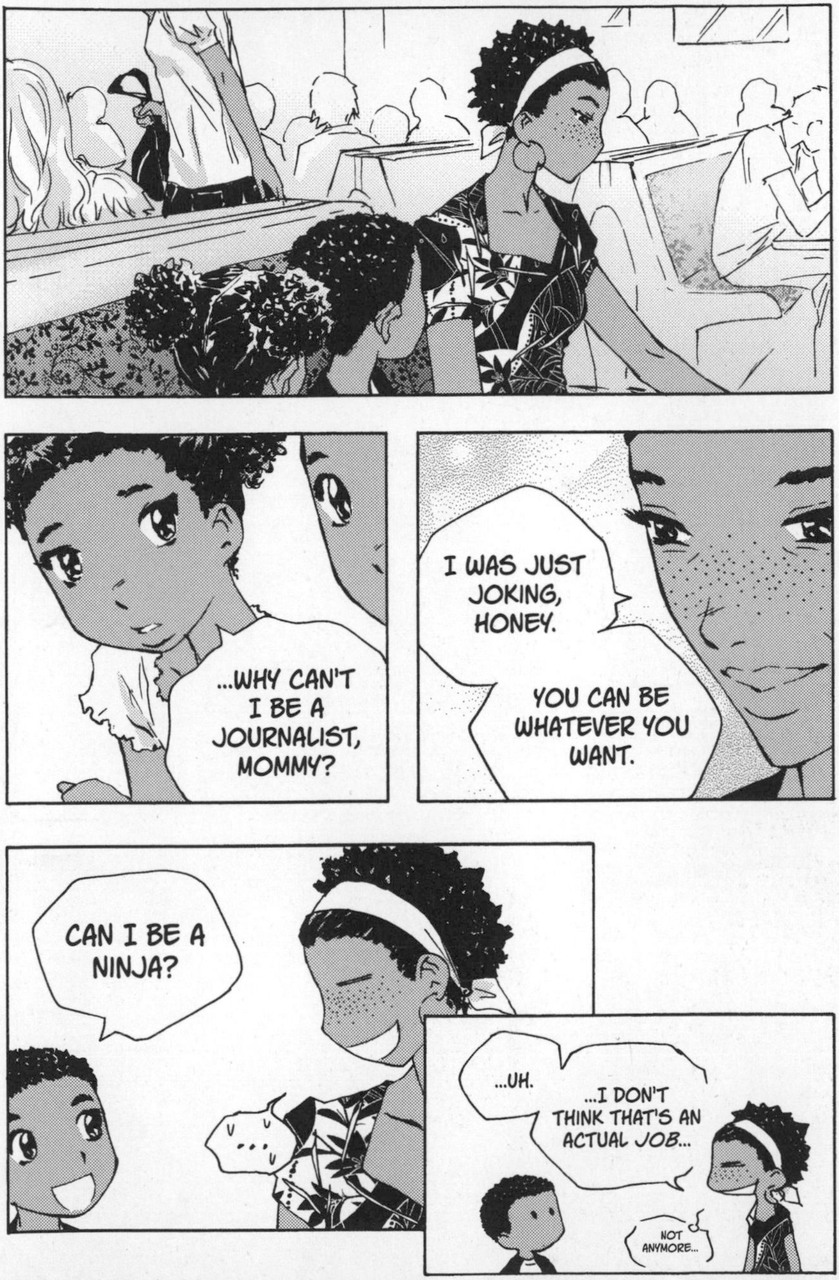
...WHY CAN'T I BE A JOURNALIST, MOMMY?
I WAS JUST JOKING, HONEY.
YOU CAN BE WHATEVER YOU WANT.
CAN I BE A NINJA?
...
...UH.
...I DON'T THINK THAT'S AN ACTUAL JOB...
NOT ANYMORE...

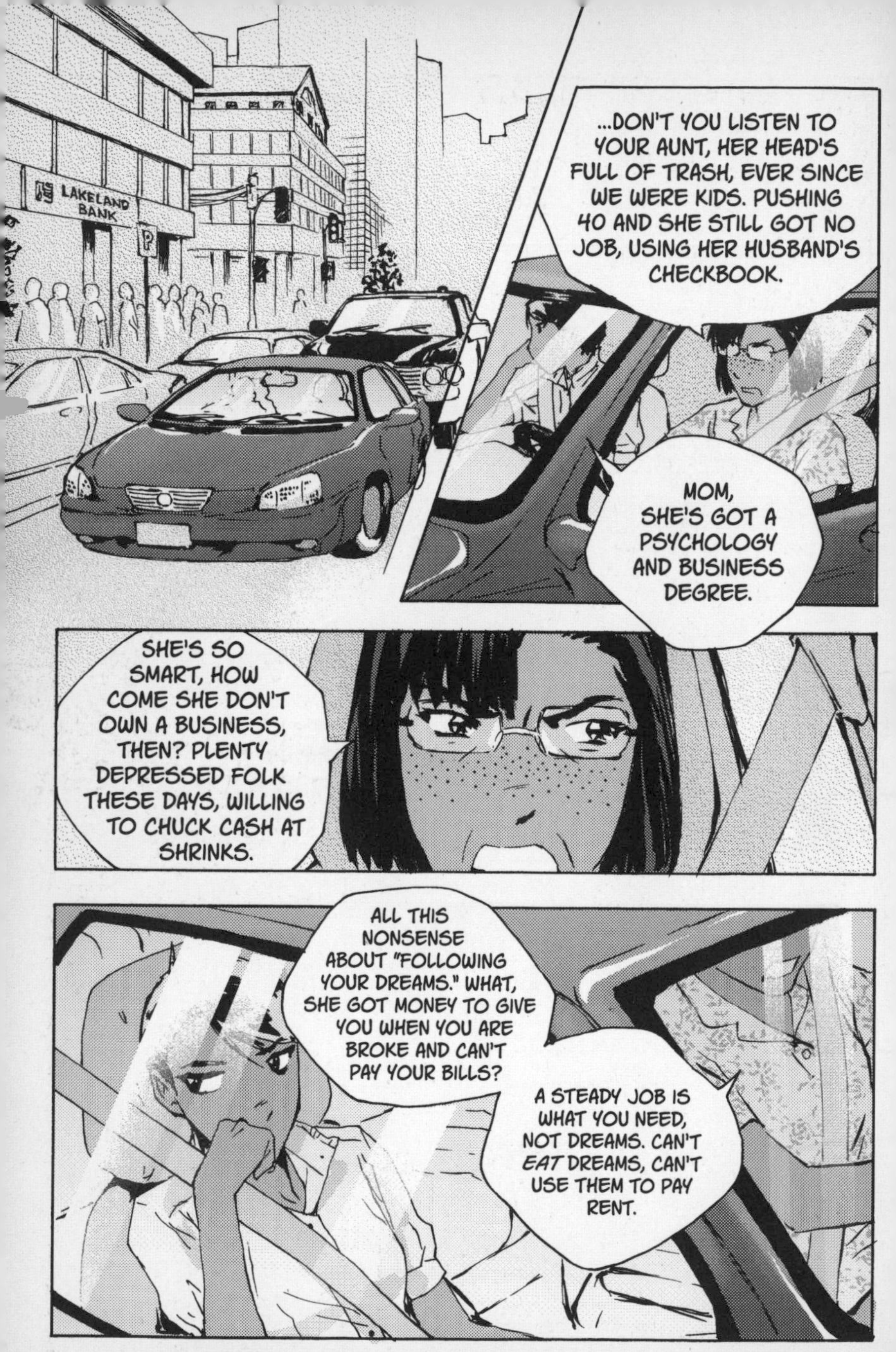
LAKELAND BANK
...DON'T YOU LISTEN TO YOUR AUNT, HER HEAD'S FULL OF TRASH, EVER SINCE WE WERE KIDS. PUSHING 40 AND SHE STILL GOT NO JOB, USING HER HUSBAND'S CHECKBOOK.
MOM, SHE'S GOT A PSYCHOLOGY AND BUSINESS DEGREE.
SHE'S SO SMART, HOW COME SHE DON'T OWN A BUSINESS, THEN? PLENTY DEPRESSED FOLK THESE DAYS, WILLING TO CHUCK CASH AT SHRINKS.
ALL THIS NONSENSE ABOUT "FOLLOWING YOUR DREAMS." WHAT, SHE GOT MONEY TO GIVE YOU WHEN YOU ARE BROKE AND CAN'T PAY YOUR BILLS?
A STEADY JOB IS WHAT YOU NEED, NOT DREAMS. CAN'T *EAT* DREAMS, CAN'T USE THEM TO PAY RENT.

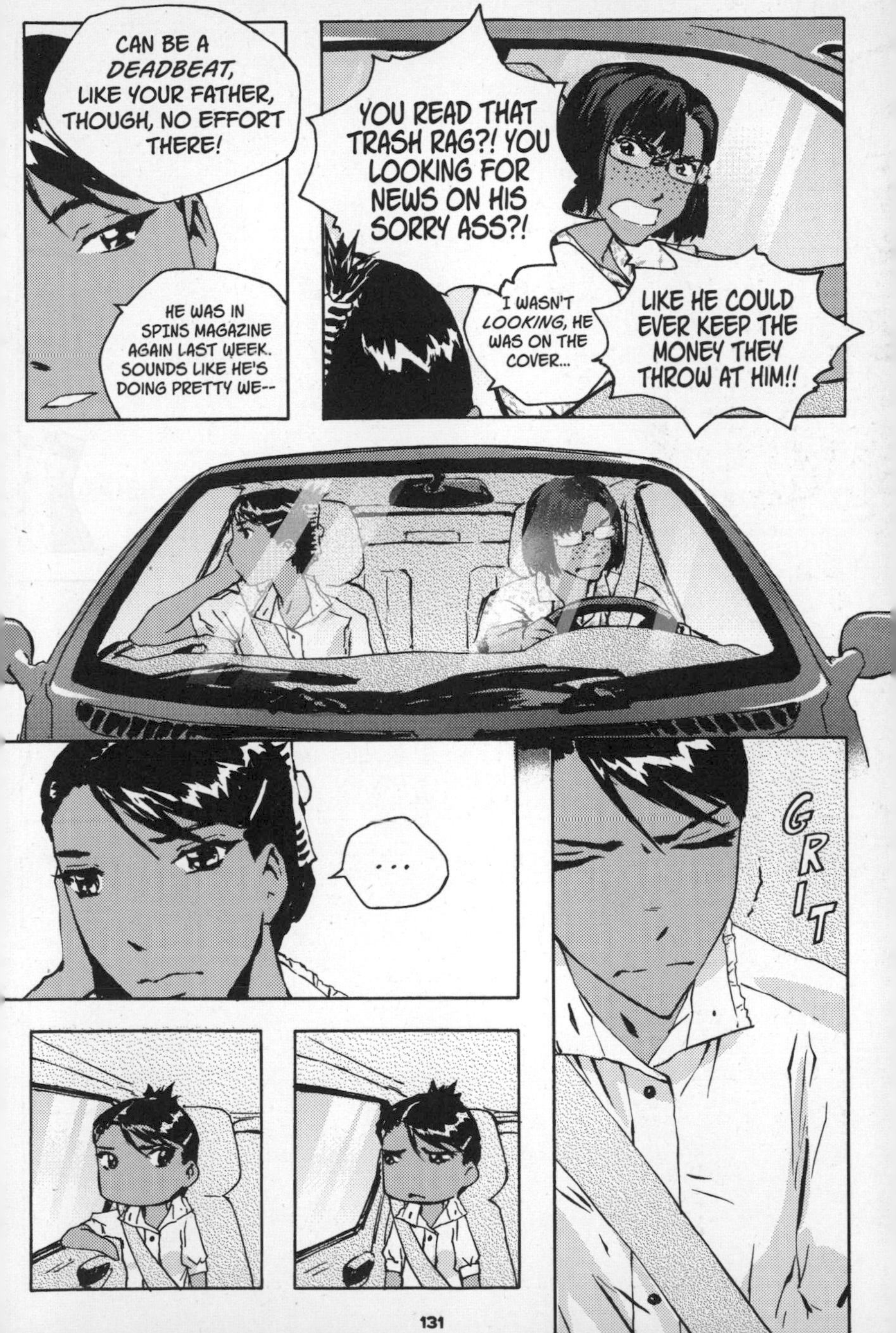
CAN BE A *DEADBEAT*, LIKE YOUR FATHER, THOUGH, NO EFFORT THERE!
HE WAS IN SPINS MAGAZINE AGAIN LAST WEEK. SOUNDS LIKE HE'S DOING PRETTY WE--
YOU READ THAT TRASH RAG?! YOU LOOKING FOR NEWS ON HIS SORRY ASS?!
I WASN'T *LOOKING*, HE WAS ON THE COVER...
LIKE HE COULD EVER KEEP THE MONEY THEY THROW AT HIM!!
...
GRIT

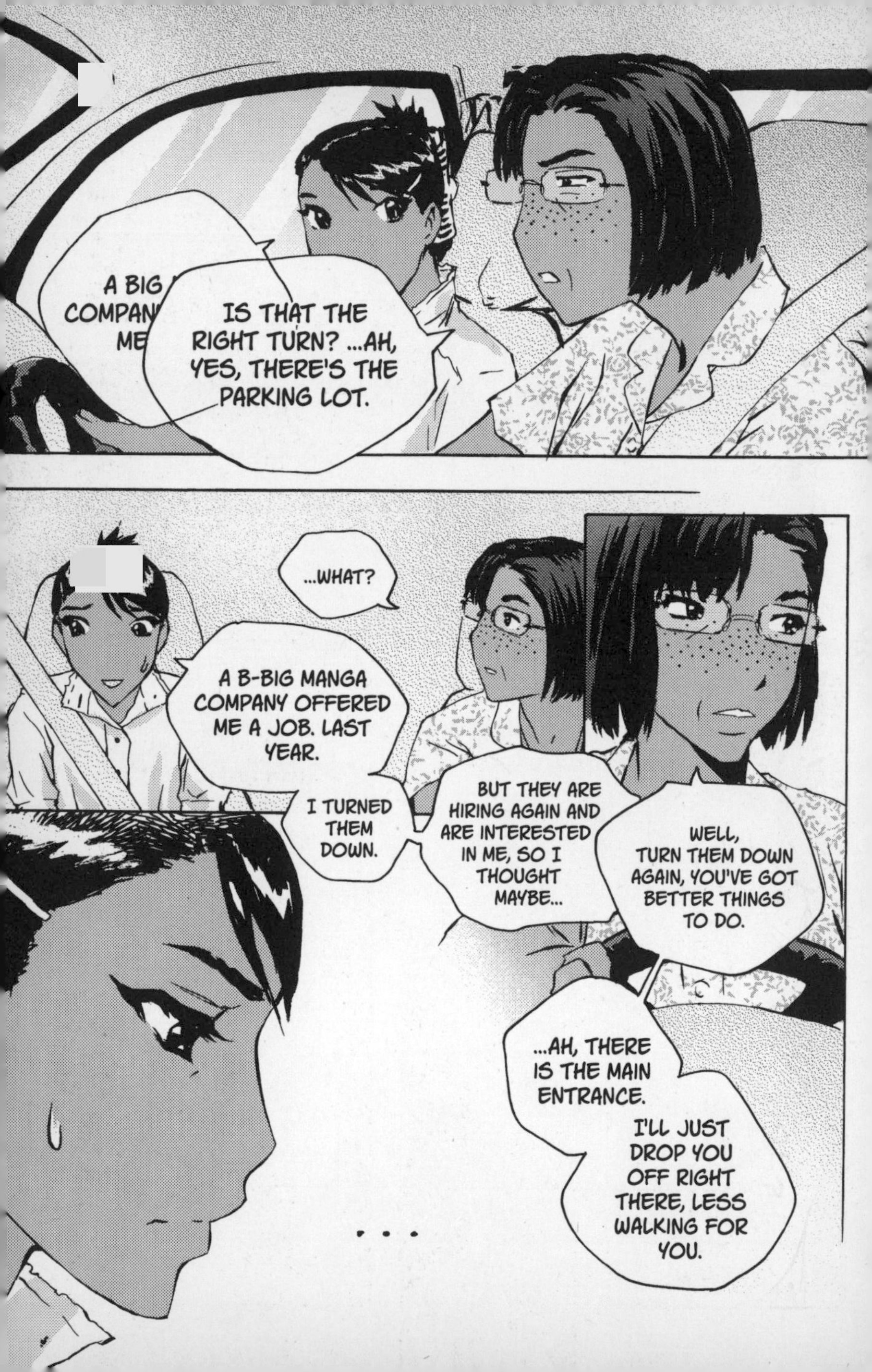
A BIG COMPAN ME
IS THAT THE RIGHT TURN? ...AH, YES, THERE'S THE PARKING LOT.
...WHAT?
A B-BIG MANGA COMPANY OFFERED ME A JOB. LAST YEAR.
I TURNED THEM DOWN.
BUT THEY ARE HIRING AGAIN AND ARE INTERESTED IN ME, SO I THOUGHT MAYBE...
WELL, TURN THEM DOWN AGAIN, YOU'VE GOT BETTER THINGS TO DO.
• • •
...AH, THERE IS THE MAIN ENTRANCE.
I'LL JUST DROP YOU OFF RIGHT THERE, LESS WALKING FOR YOU.

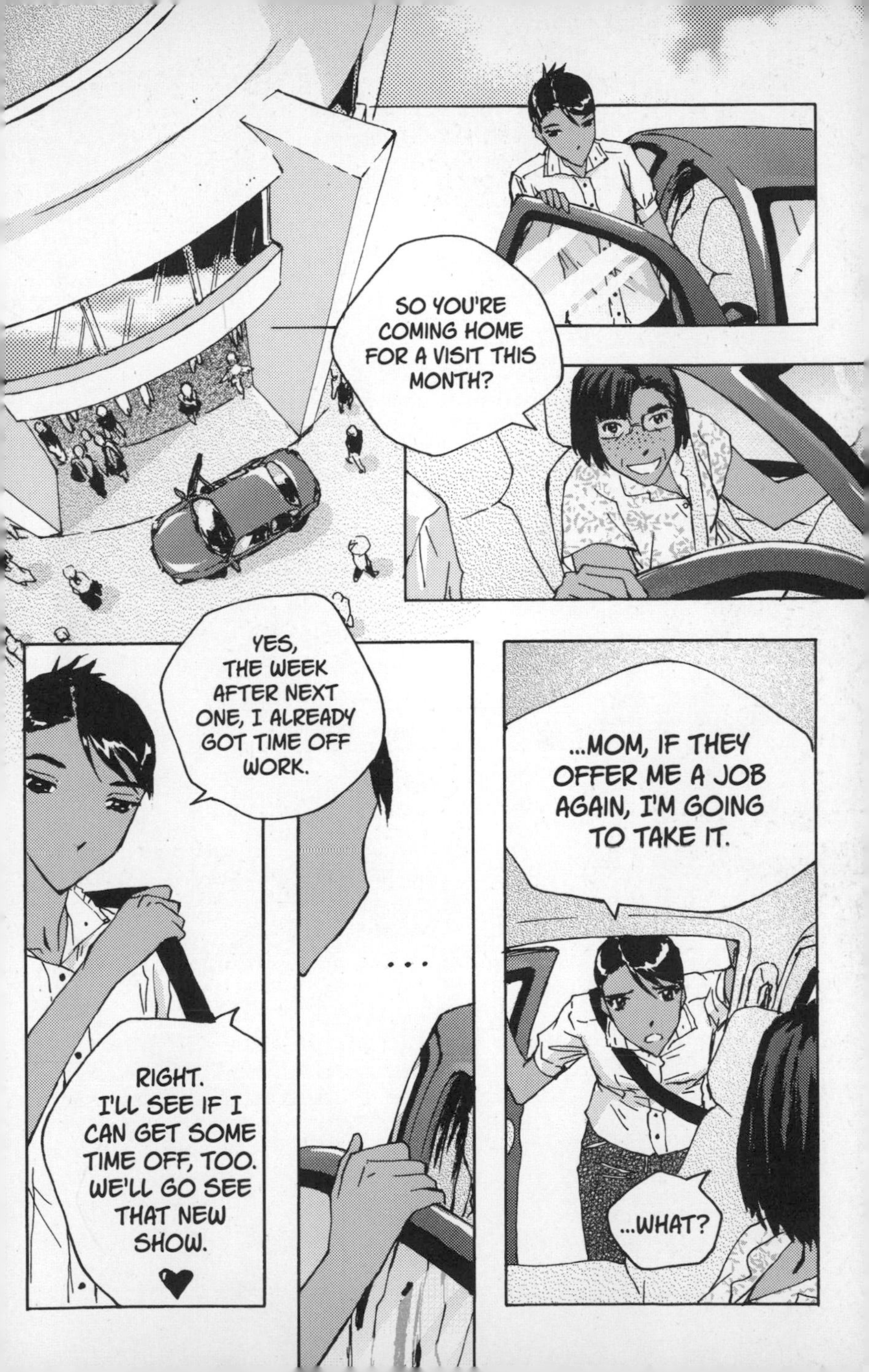
SO YOU'RE COMING HOME FOR A VISIT THIS MONTH?
YES, THE WEEK AFTER NEXT ONE, I ALREADY GOT TIME OFF WORK.
RIGHT. I'LL SEE IF I CAN GET SOME TIME OFF, TOO. WE'LL GO SEE THAT NEW SHOW. ♥
...
...MOM, IF THEY OFFER ME A JOB AGAIN, I'M GOING TO TAKE IT.
...WHAT?

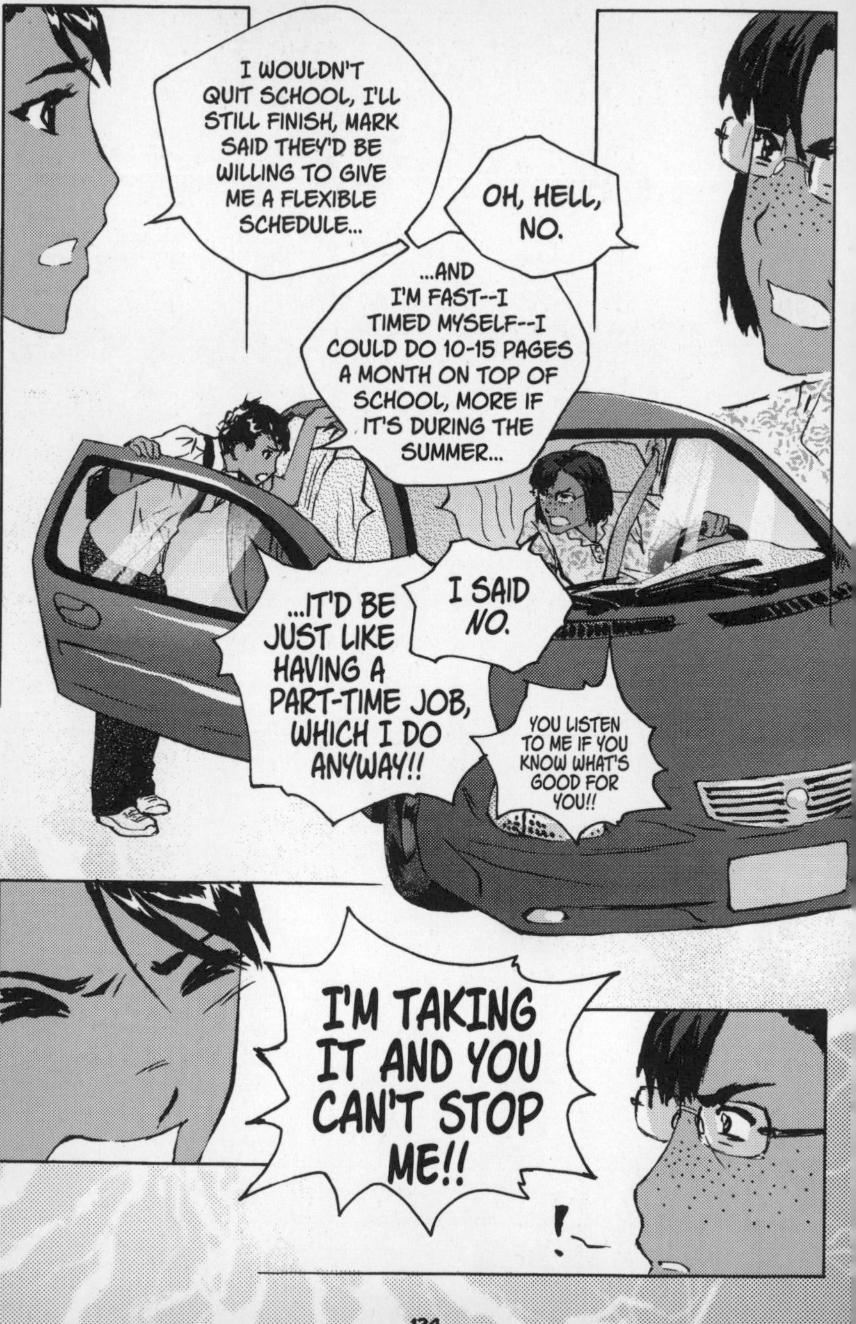
I WOULDN'T QUIT SCHOOL, I'LL STILL FINISH, MARK SAID THEY'D BE WILLING TO GIVE ME A FLEXIBLE SCHEDULE...
OH, HELL, NO.
...AND I'M FAST--I TIMED MYSELF--I COULD DO 10-15 PAGES A MONTH ON TOP OF SCHOOL, MORE IF IT'S DURING THE SUMMER...
...IT'D BE JUST LIKE HAVING A PART-TIME JOB, WHICH I DO ANYWAY!!
I SAID NO.
YOU LISTEN TO ME IF YOU KNOW WHAT'S GOOD FOR YOU!!
I'M TAKING IT AND YOU CAN'T STOP ME!!
!

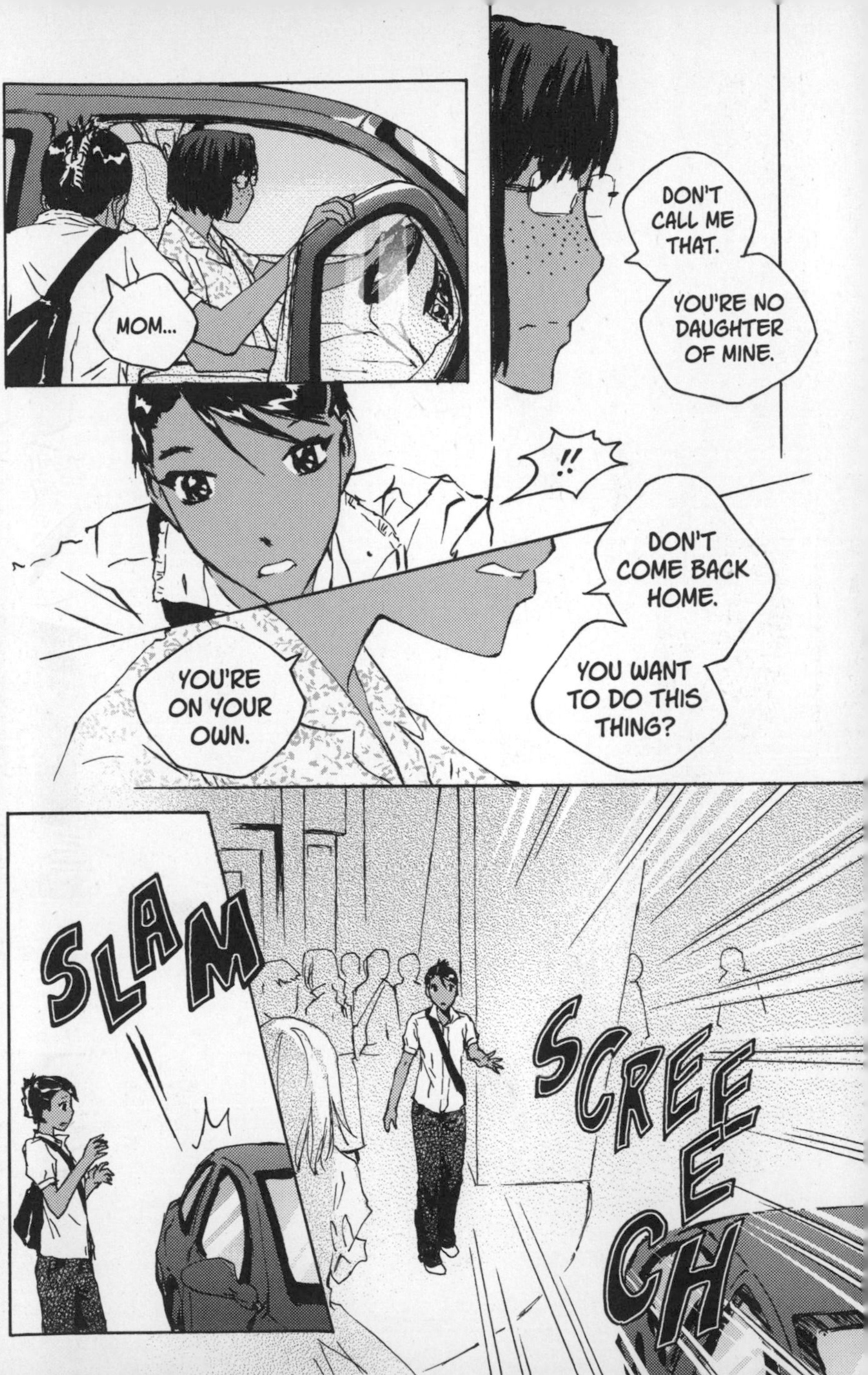
MOM...
DON'T CALL ME THAT.
YOU'RE NO DAUGHTER OF MINE.
!!
DON'T COME BACK HOME.
YOU WANT TO DO THIS THING?
YOU'RE ON YOUR OWN.
SLAM
SCREEECH

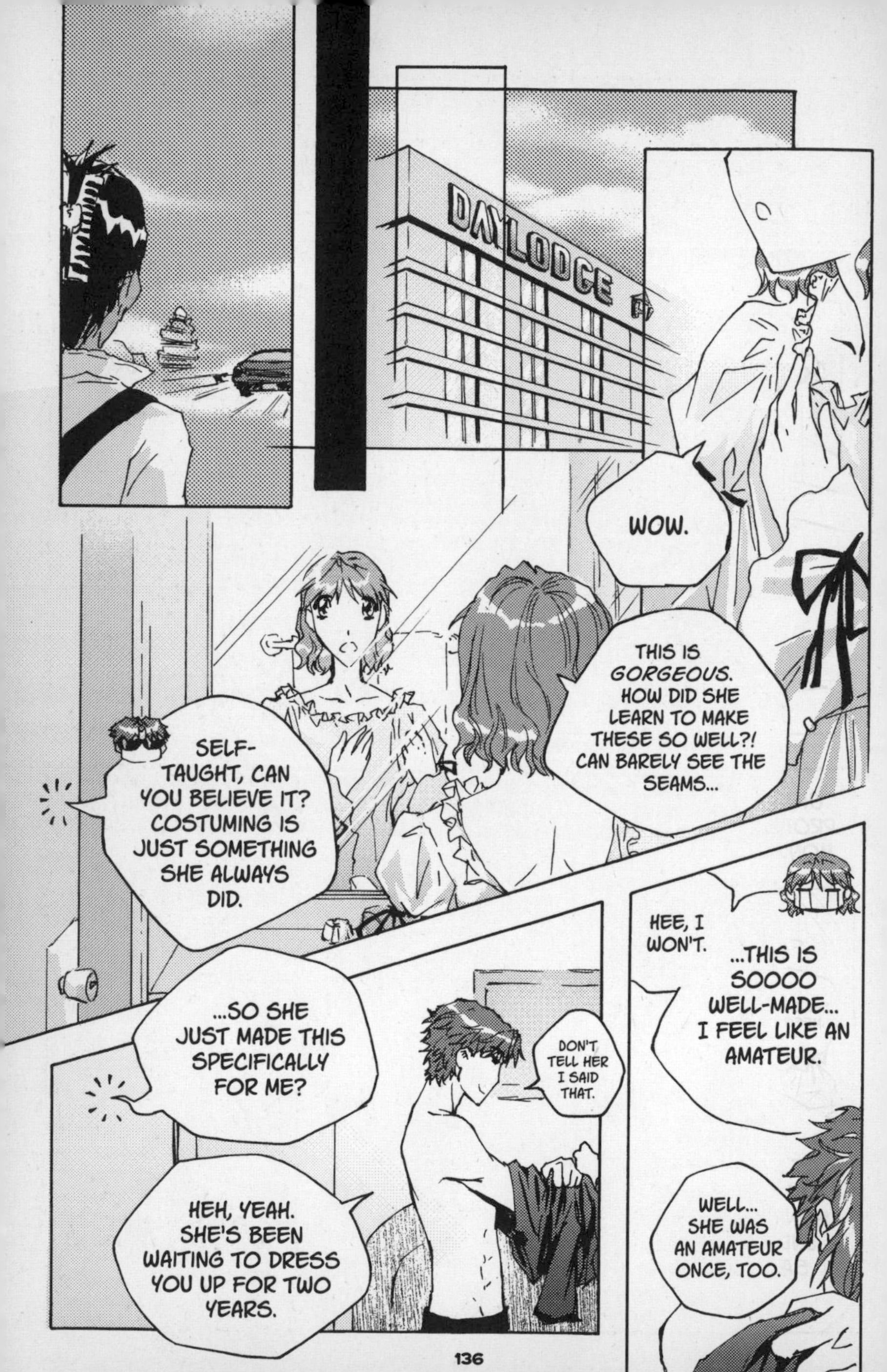
DAYLODGE
WOW.
THIS IS GORGEOUS. HOW DID SHE LEARN TO MAKE THESE SO WELL?! CAN BARELY SEE THE SEAMS...
SELF-TAUGHT, CAN YOU BELIEVE IT? COSTUMING IS JUST SOMETHING SHE ALWAYS DID.
...SO SHE JUST MADE THIS SPECIFICALLY FOR ME?
HEH, YEAH. SHE'S BEEN WAITING TO DRESS YOU UP FOR TWO YEARS.
DON'T TELL HER I SAID THAT.
HEE, I WON'T.
...THIS IS SOOOO WELL-MADE... I FEEL LIKE AN AMATEUR.
WELL... SHE WAS AN AMATEUR ONCE, TOO.

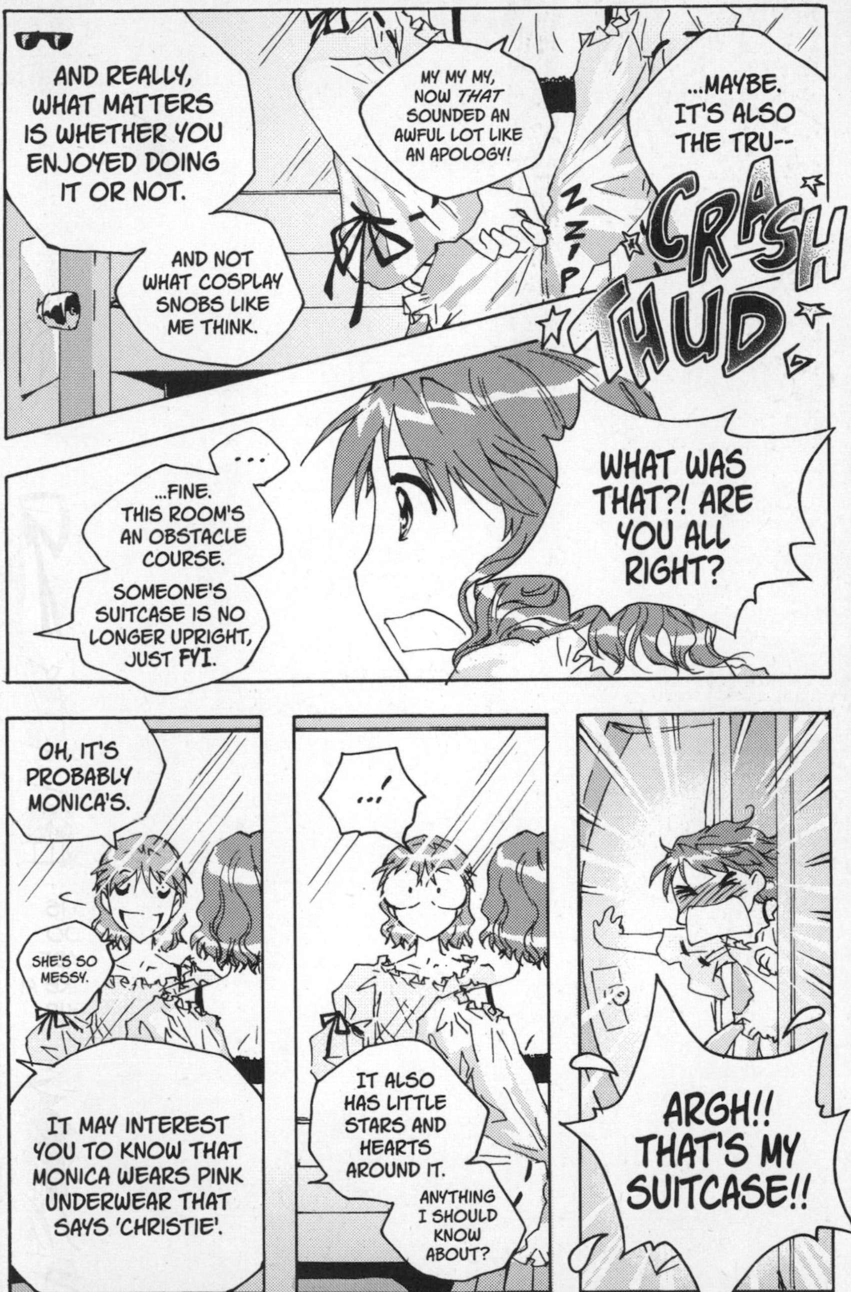
AND REALLY, WHAT MATTERS IS WHETHER YOU ENJOYED DOING IT OR NOT.
MY MY MY, NOW THAT SOUNDED AN AWFUL LOT LIKE AN APOLOGY!
...MAYBE. IT'S ALSO THE TRU--
AND NOT WHAT COSPLAY SNOBS LIKE ME THINK.
ZZIP
CRASH
THUD
...
...FINE. THIS ROOM'S AN OBSTACLE COURSE.
SOMEONE'S SUITCASE IS NO LONGER UPRIGHT, JUST FYI.
WHAT WAS THAT?! ARE YOU ALL RIGHT?
OH, IT'S PROBABLY MONICA'S.
SHE'S SO MESSY.
IT MAY INTEREST YOU TO KNOW THAT MONICA WEARS PINK UNDERWEAR THAT SAYS 'CHRISTIE'.
...!
IT ALSO HAS LITTLE STARS AND HEARTS AROUND IT.
ANYTHING I SHOULD KNOW ABOUT?
ARGH!! THAT'S MY SUITCASE!!

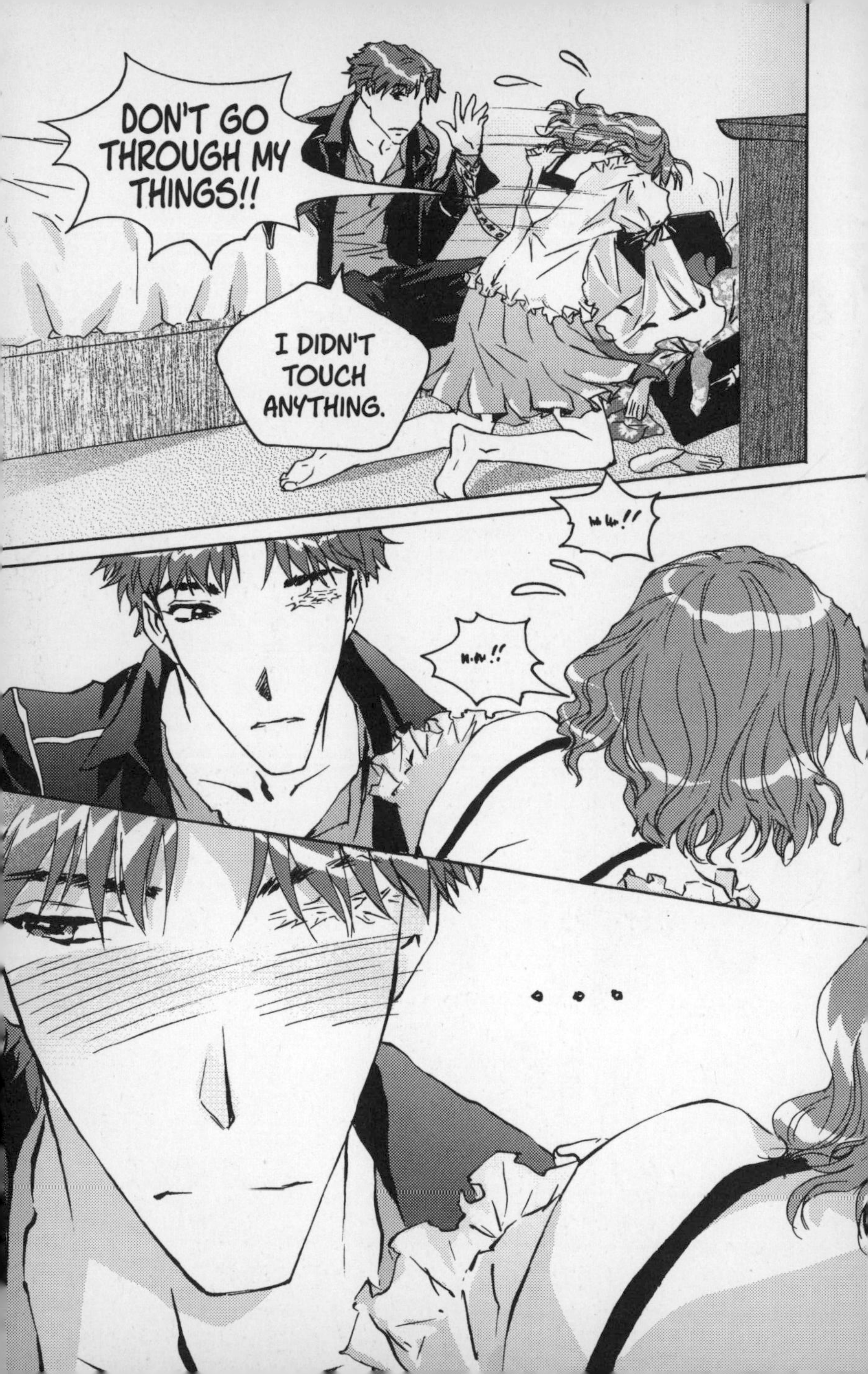
DON'T GO THROUGH MY THINGS!!
I DIDN'T TOUCH ANYTHING.
...

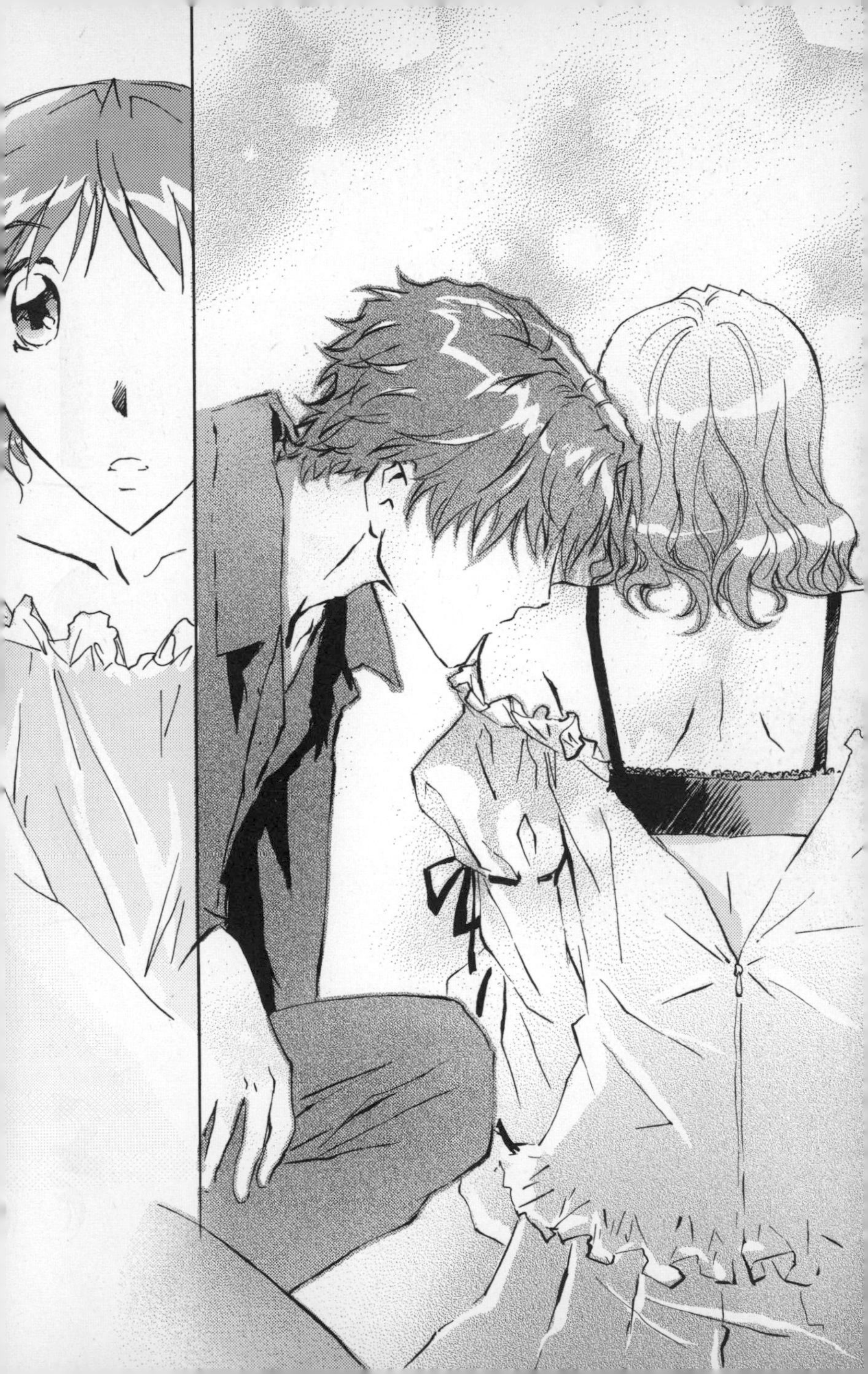

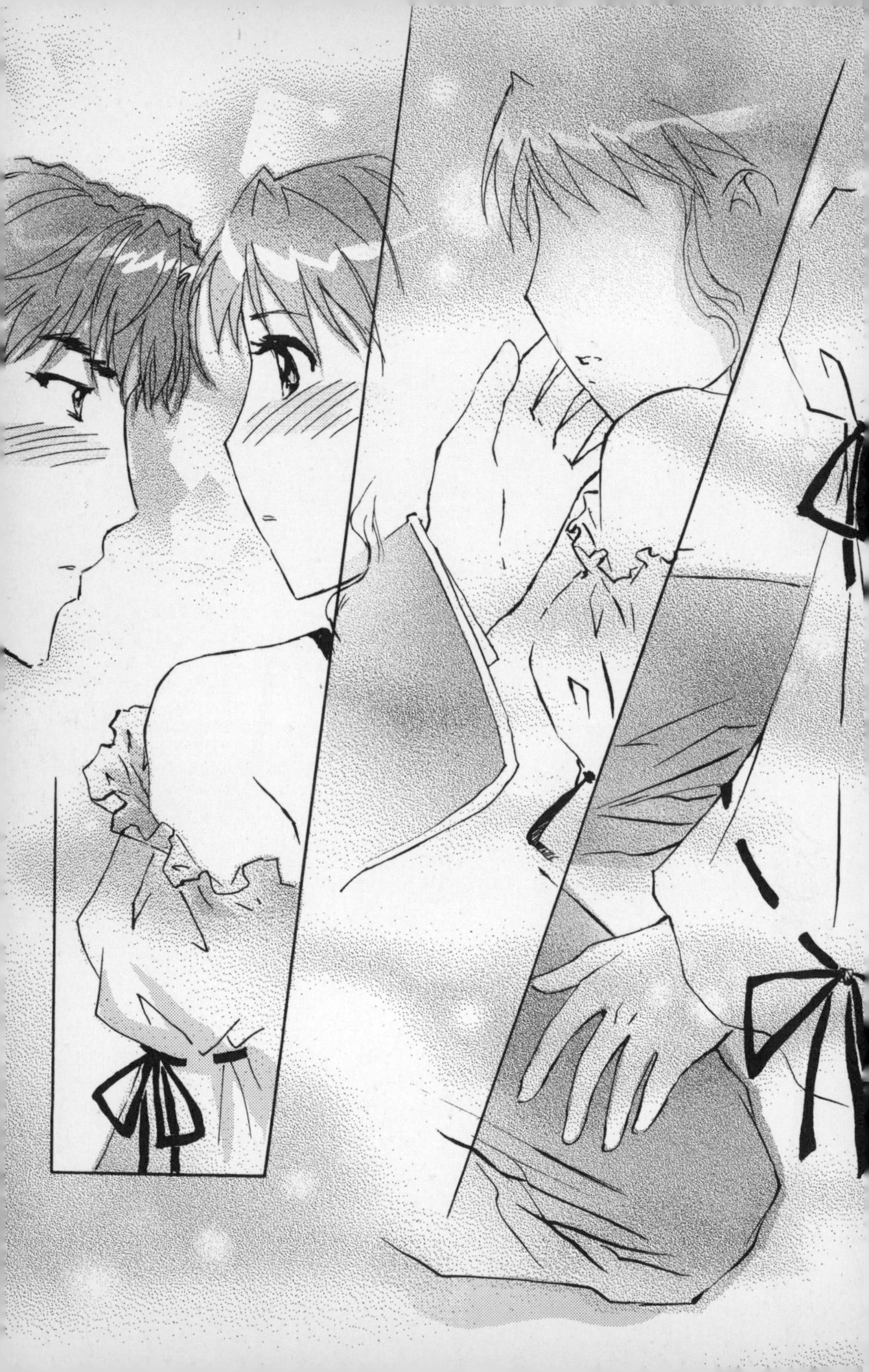

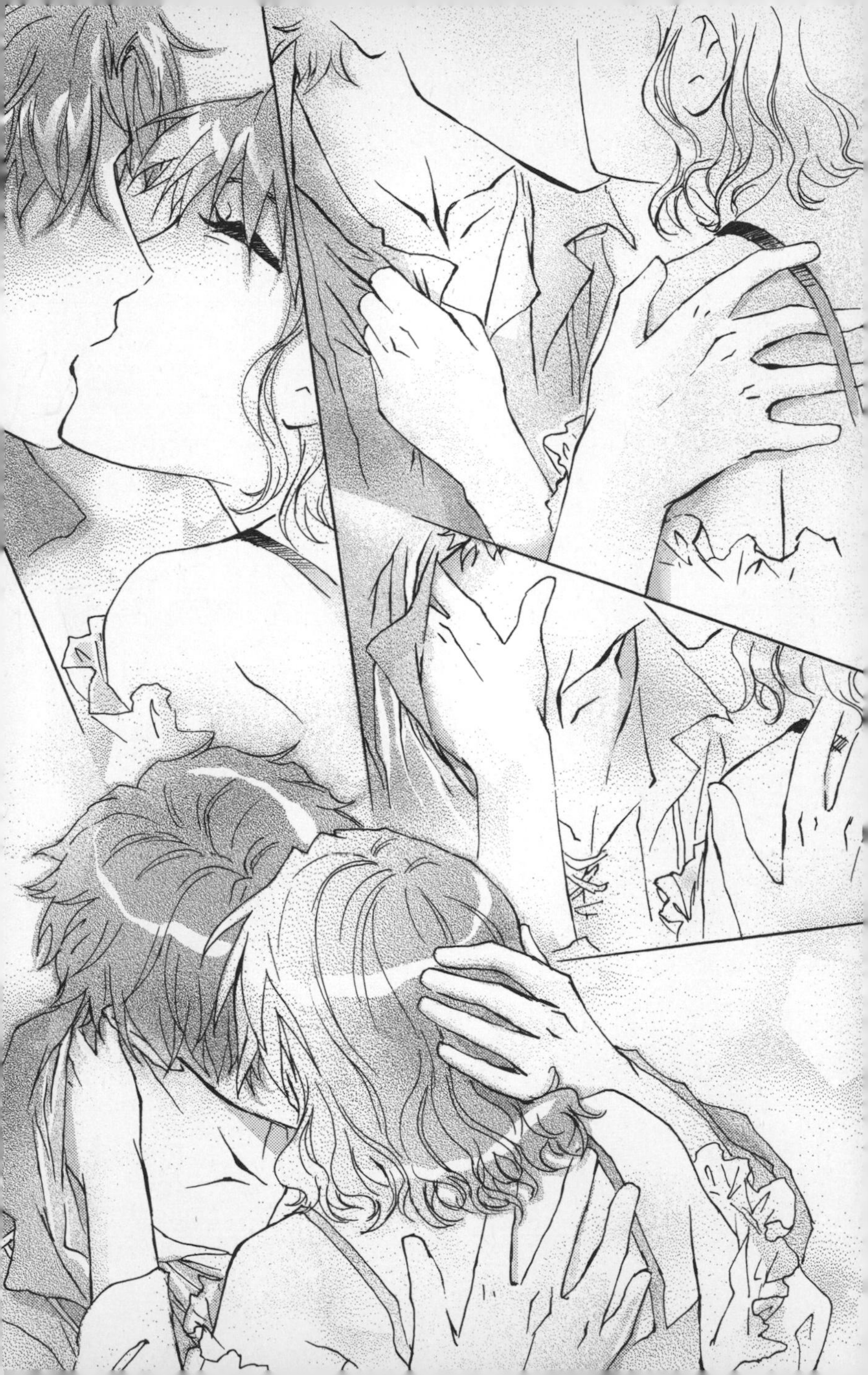

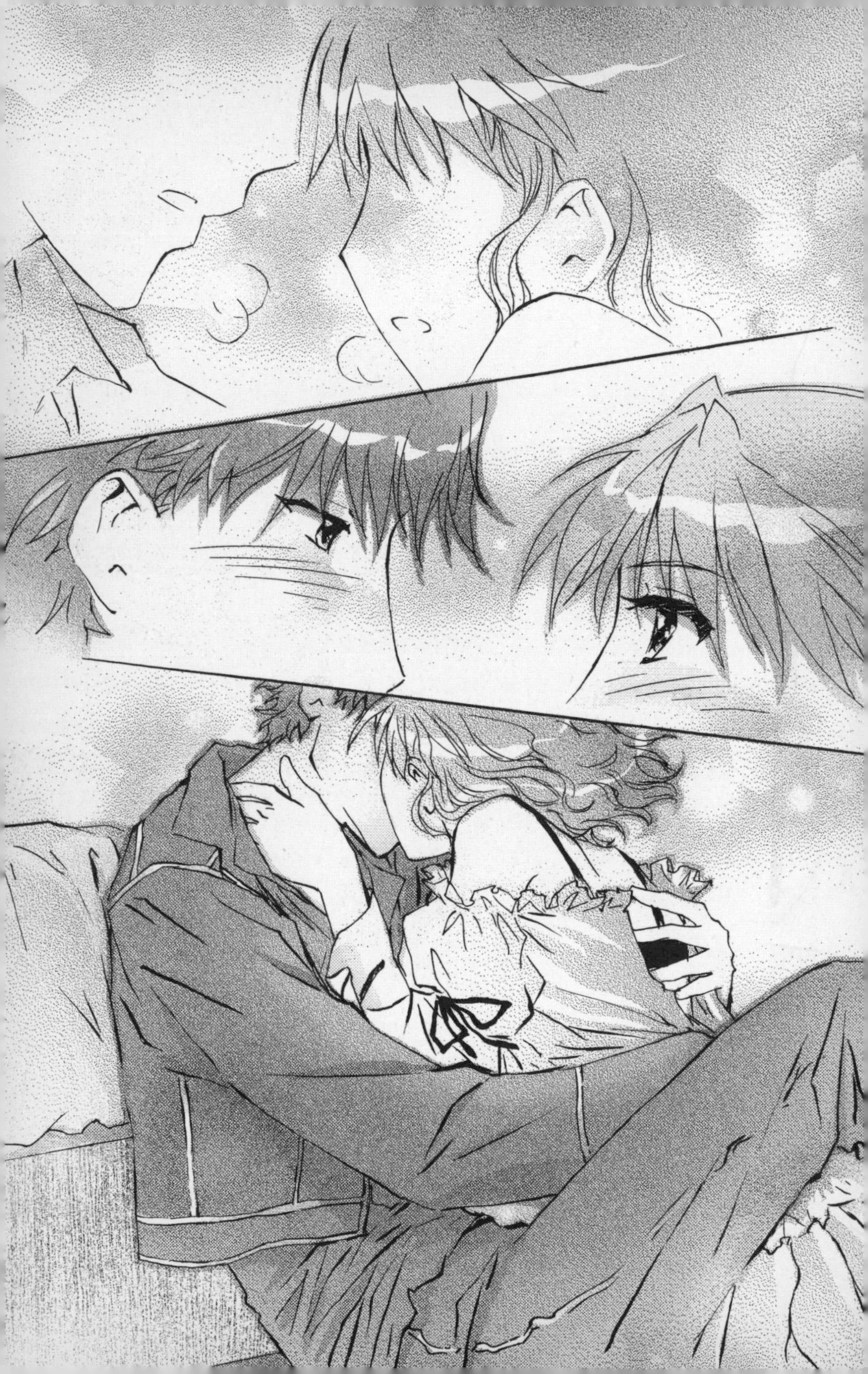

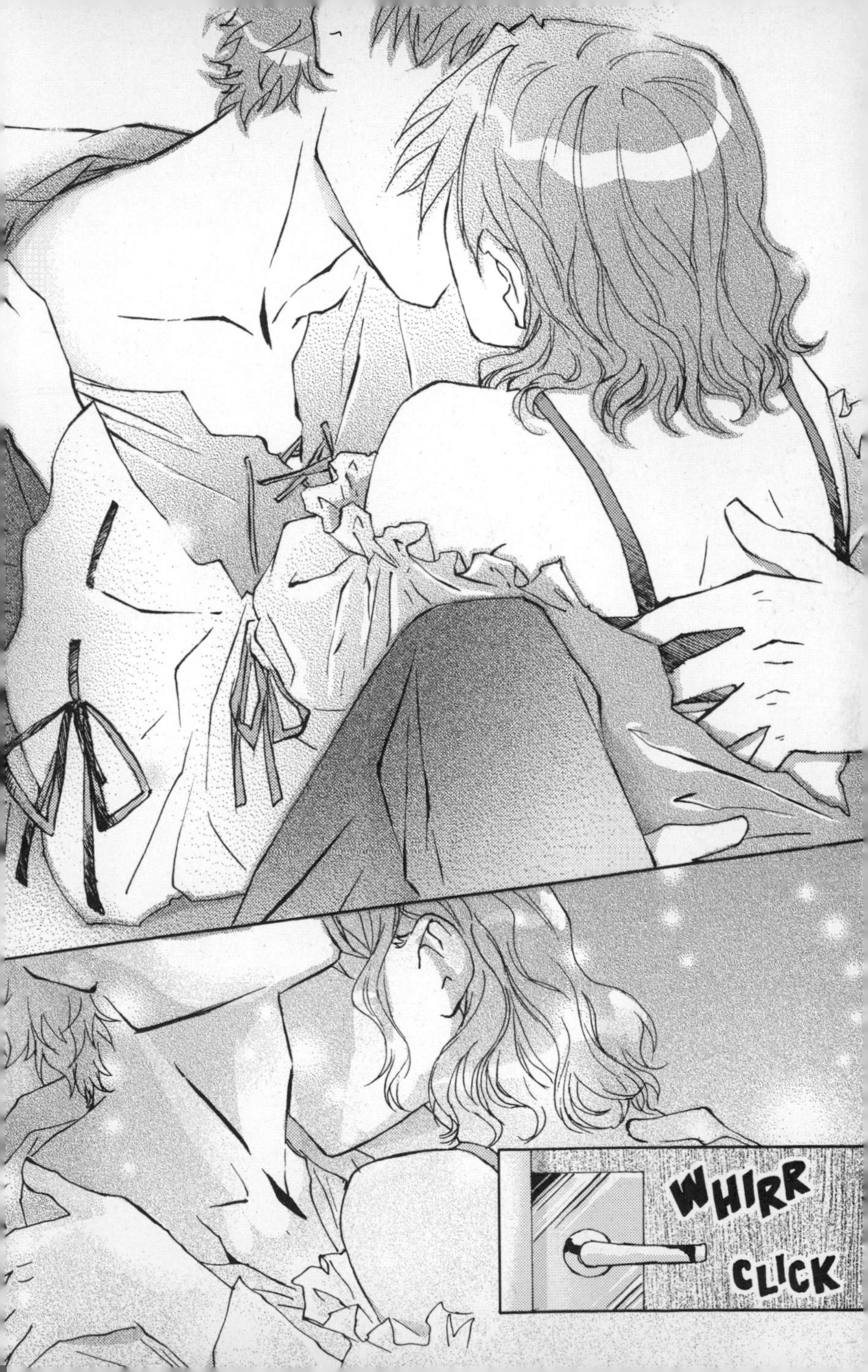
WHIRR
CLICK

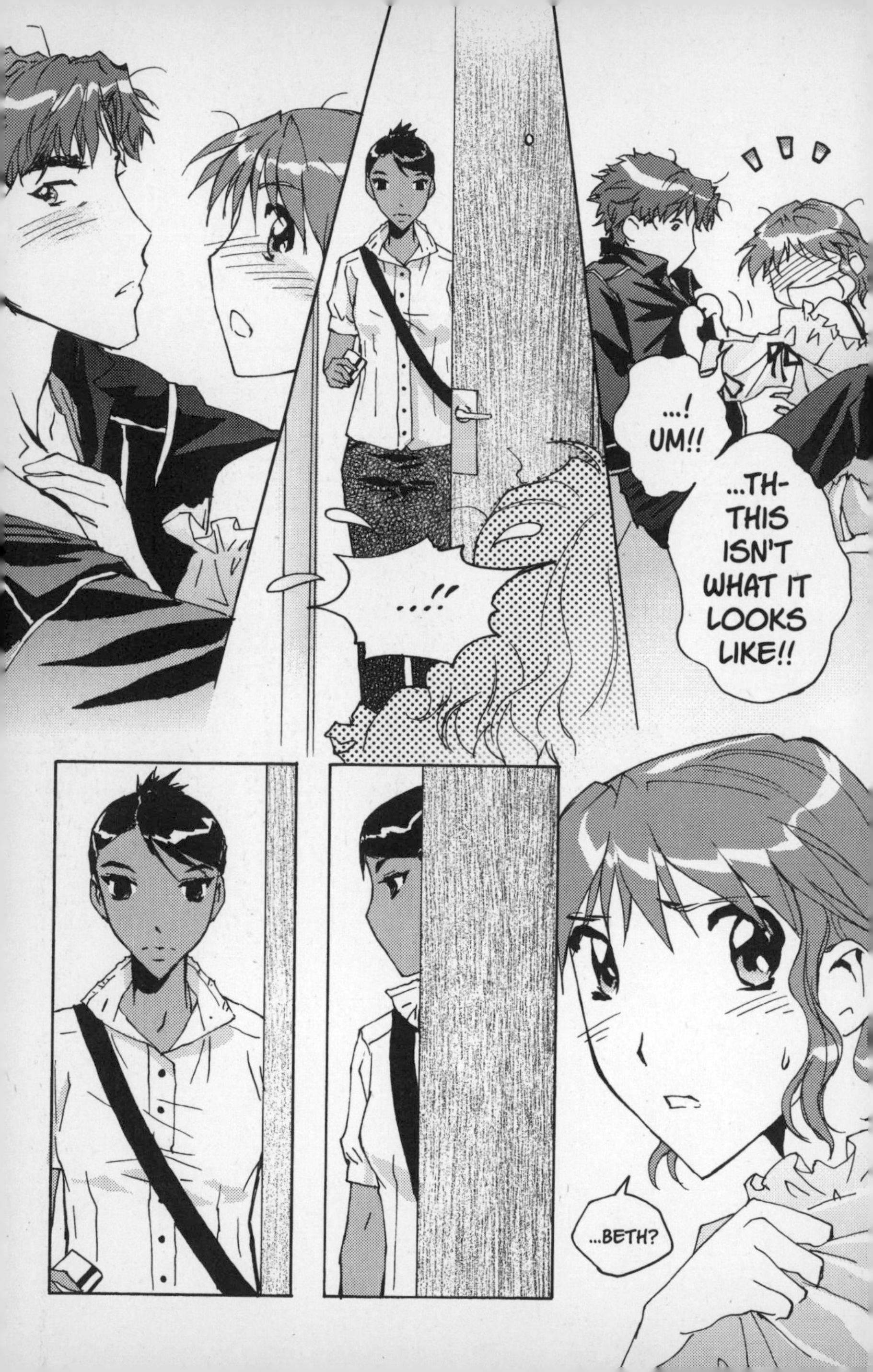
...!!
...! UM!!
...TH-THIS ISN'T WHAT IT LOOKS LIKE!!
...BETH?

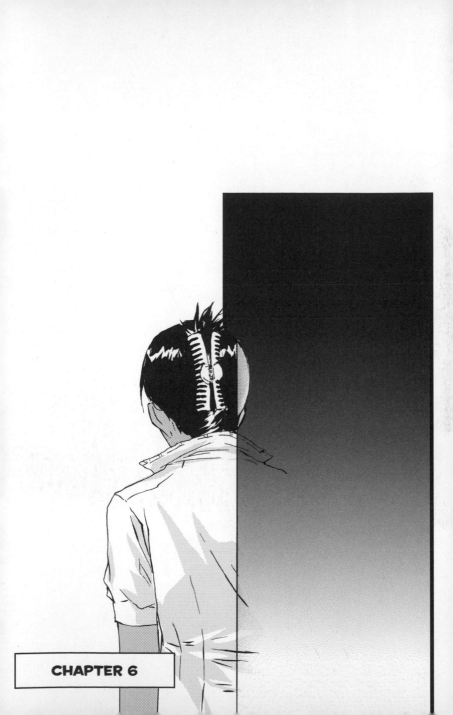

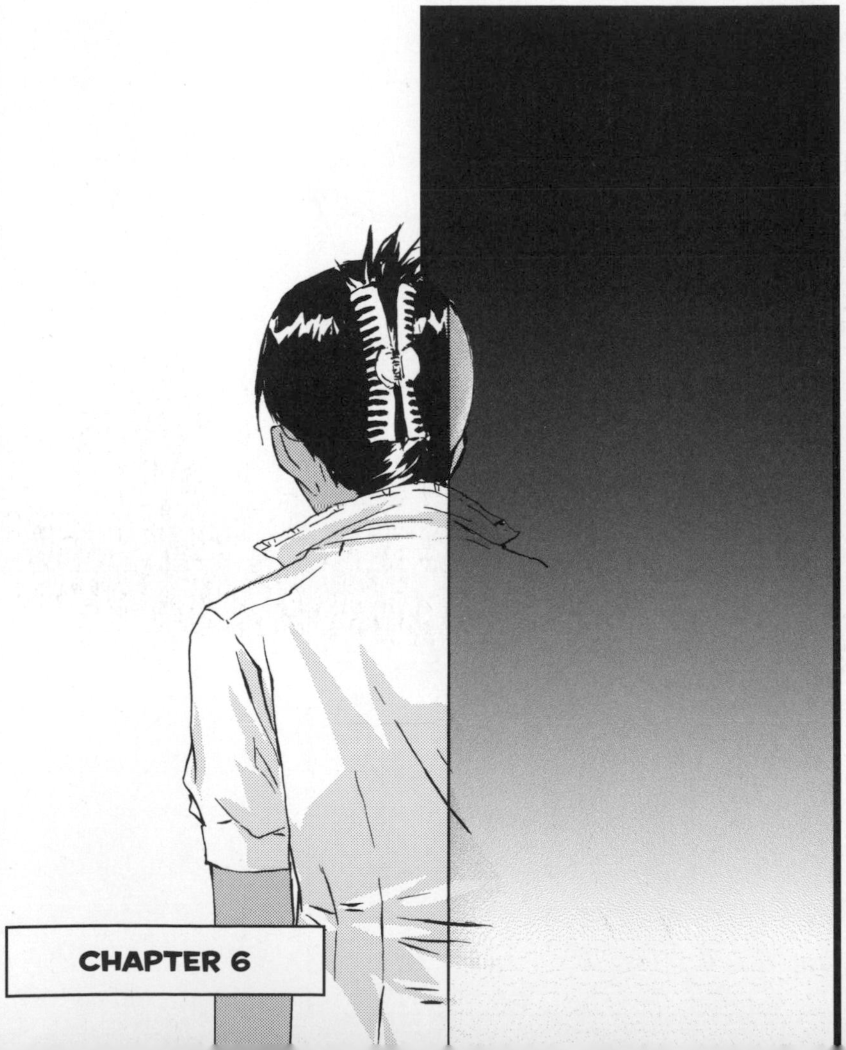
CHAPTER 6

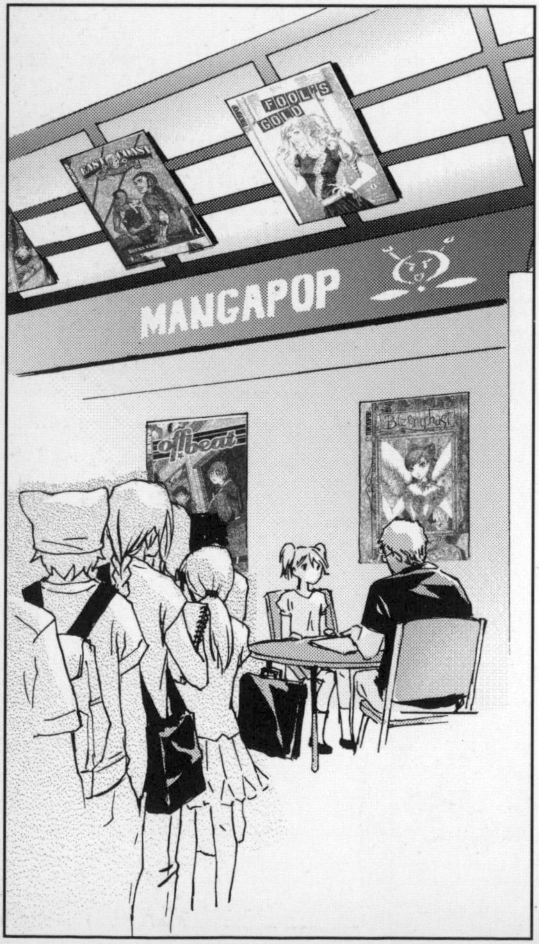
FOOL'S GOLD
MANGAPOP
offbeat
Bizenghast

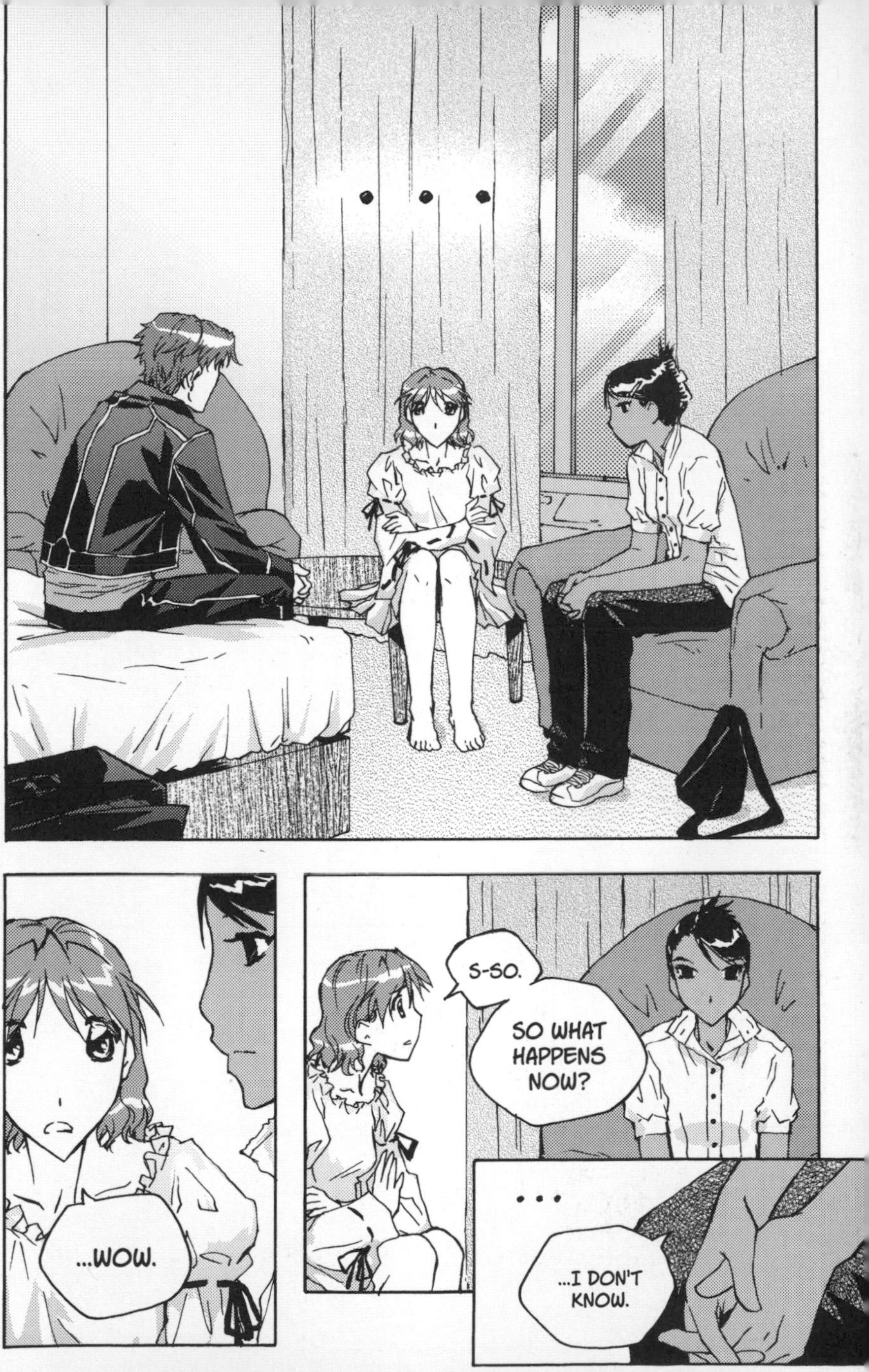
...
...WOW.
S-SO.
SO WHAT HAPPENS NOW?
...
...I DON'T KNOW.

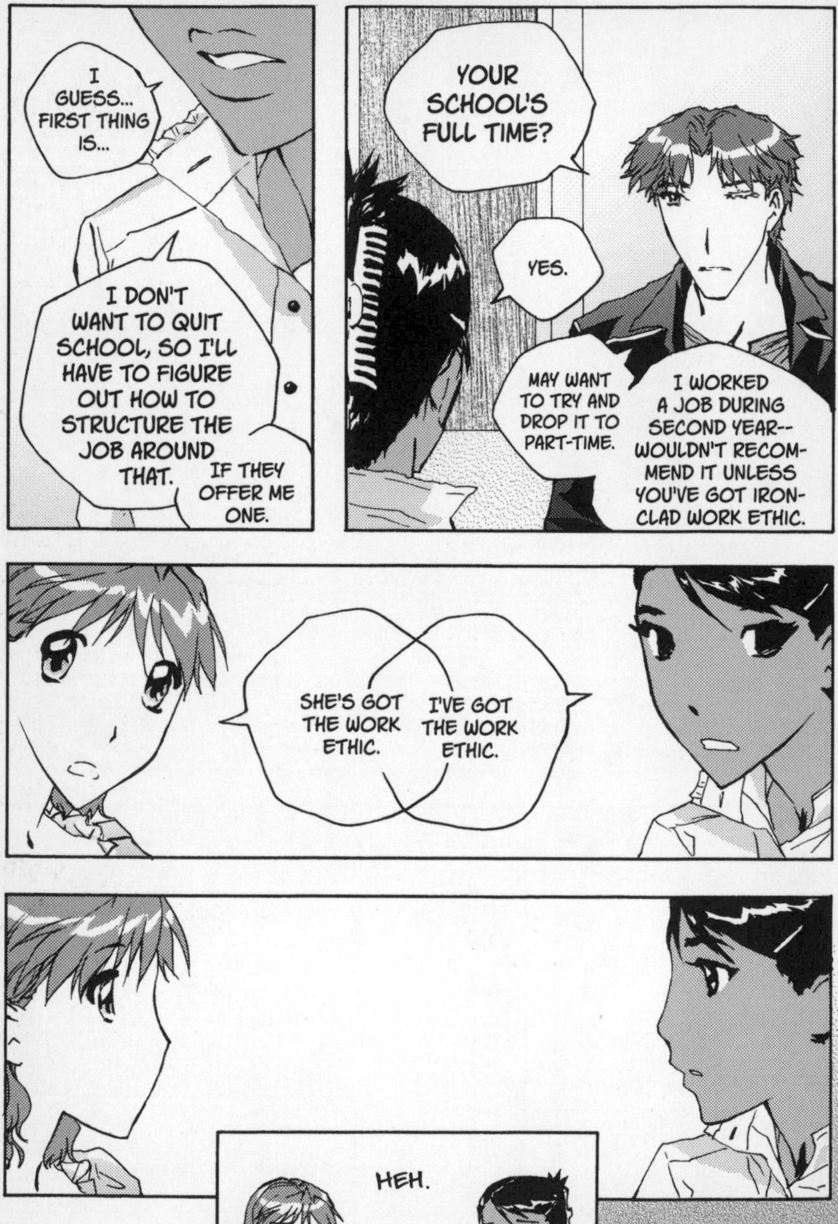
I GUESS... FIRST THING IS...
I DON'T WANT TO QUIT SCHOOL, SO I'LL HAVE TO FIGURE OUT HOW TO STRUCTURE THE JOB AROUND THAT.
IF THEY OFFER ME ONE.
YOUR SCHOOL'S FULL TIME?
YES.
MAY WANT TO TRY AND DROP IT TO PART-TIME.
I WORKED A JOB DURING SECOND YEAR--WOULDN'T RECOMMEND IT UNLESS YOU'VE GOT IRON-CLAD WORK ETHIC.
SHE'S GOT THE WORK ETHIC.
I'VE GOT THE WORK ETHIC.
HEH.

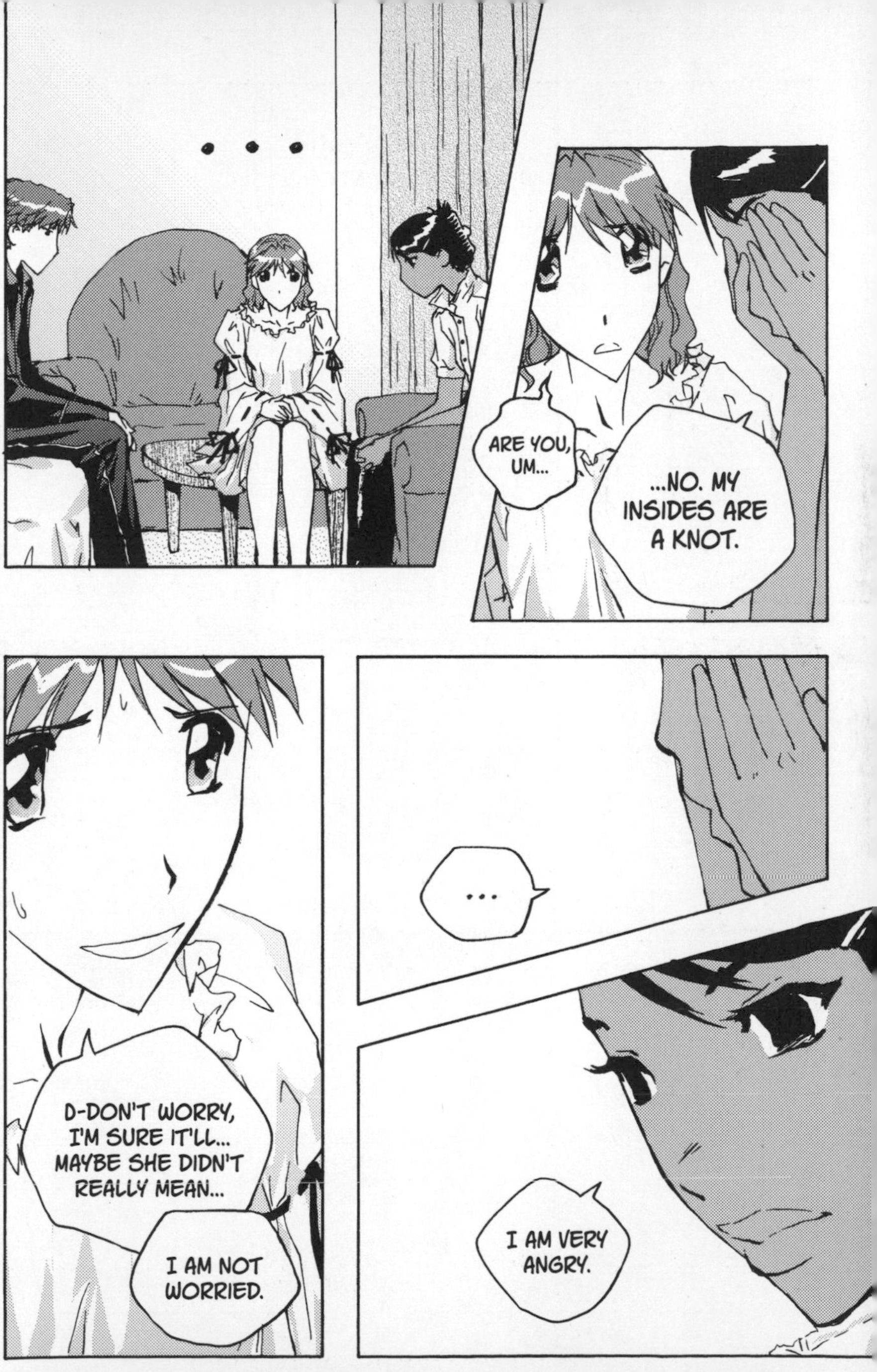
• • •
ARE YOU, UM...
...NO. MY INSIDES ARE A KNOT.
D-DON'T WORRY, I'M SURE IT'LL... MAYBE SHE DIDN'T REALLY MEAN...
I AM NOT WORRIED.
...
I AM VERY ANGRY.

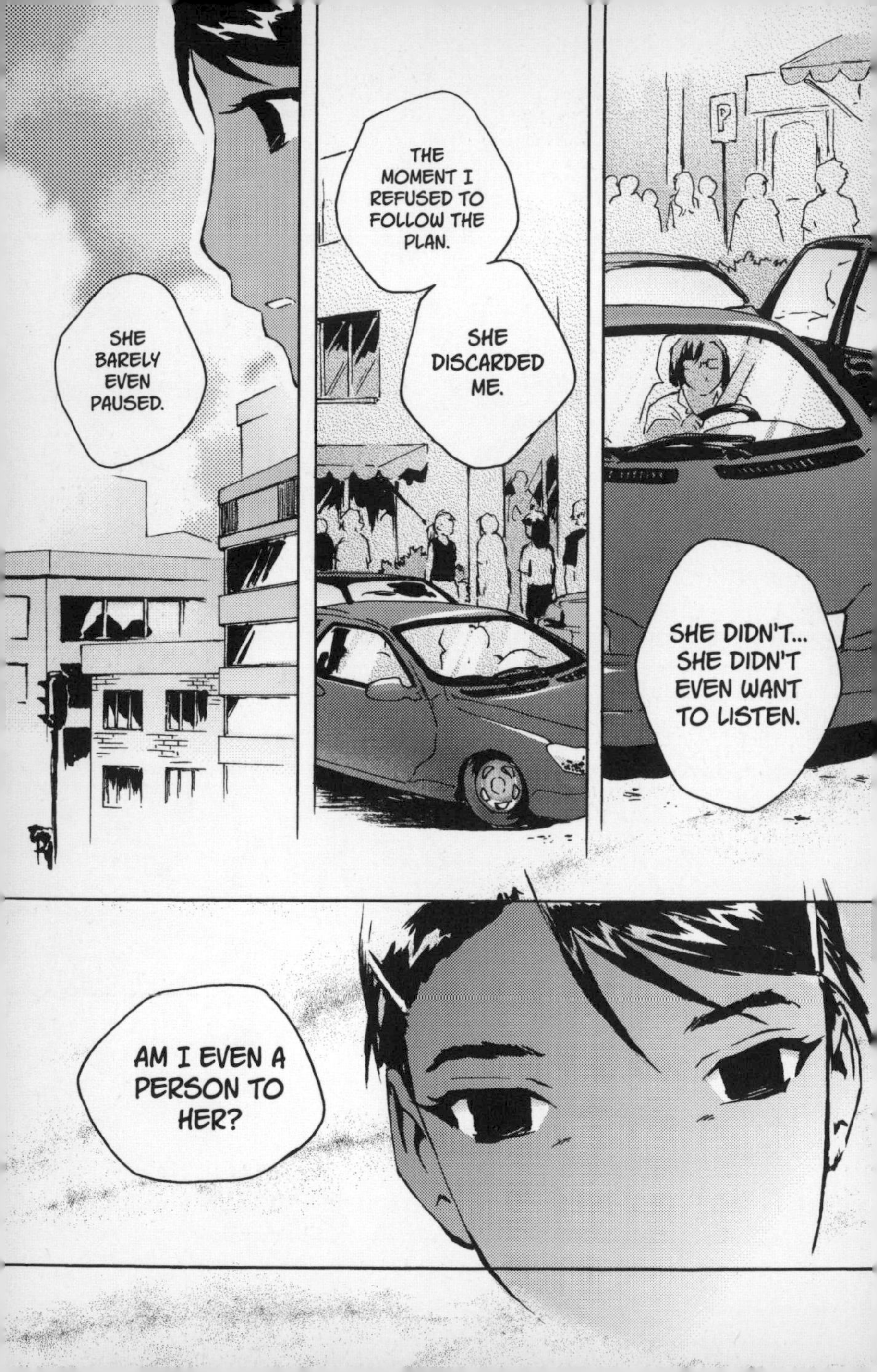
SHE BARELY EVEN PAUSED.
THE MOMENT I REFUSED TO FOLLOW THE PLAN.
SHE DISCARDED ME.
SHE DIDN'T... SHE DIDN'T EVEN WANT TO LISTEN.
AM I EVEN A PERSON TO HER?

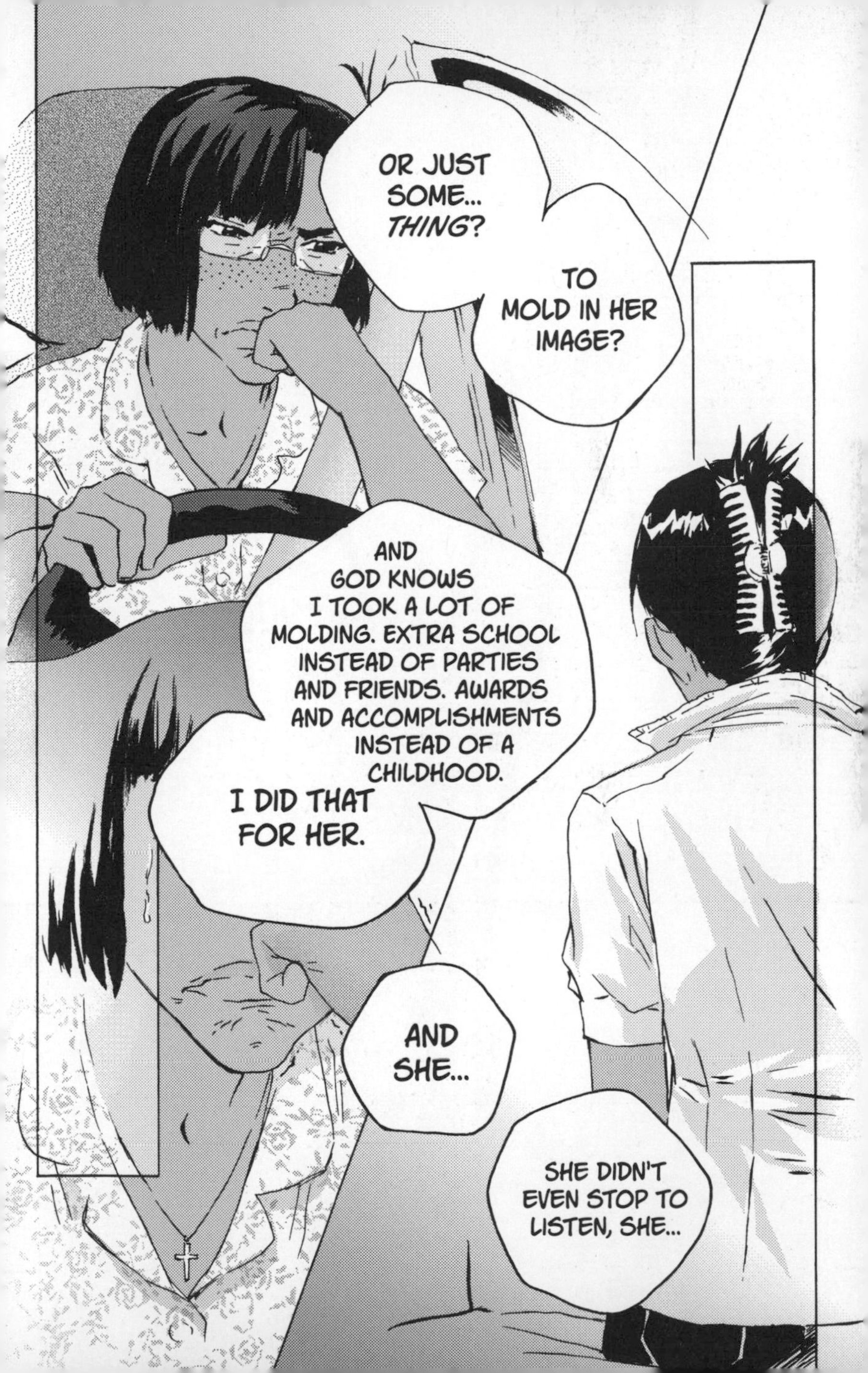
OR JUST SOME... *THING*?
TO MOLD IN HER IMAGE?
AND GOD KNOWS I TOOK A LOT OF MOLDING. EXTRA SCHOOL INSTEAD OF PARTIES AND FRIENDS. AWARDS AND ACCOMPLISHMENTS INSTEAD OF A CHILDHOOD.
I DID THAT FOR HER.
AND SHE...
SHE DIDN'T EVEN STOP TO LISTEN, SHE...

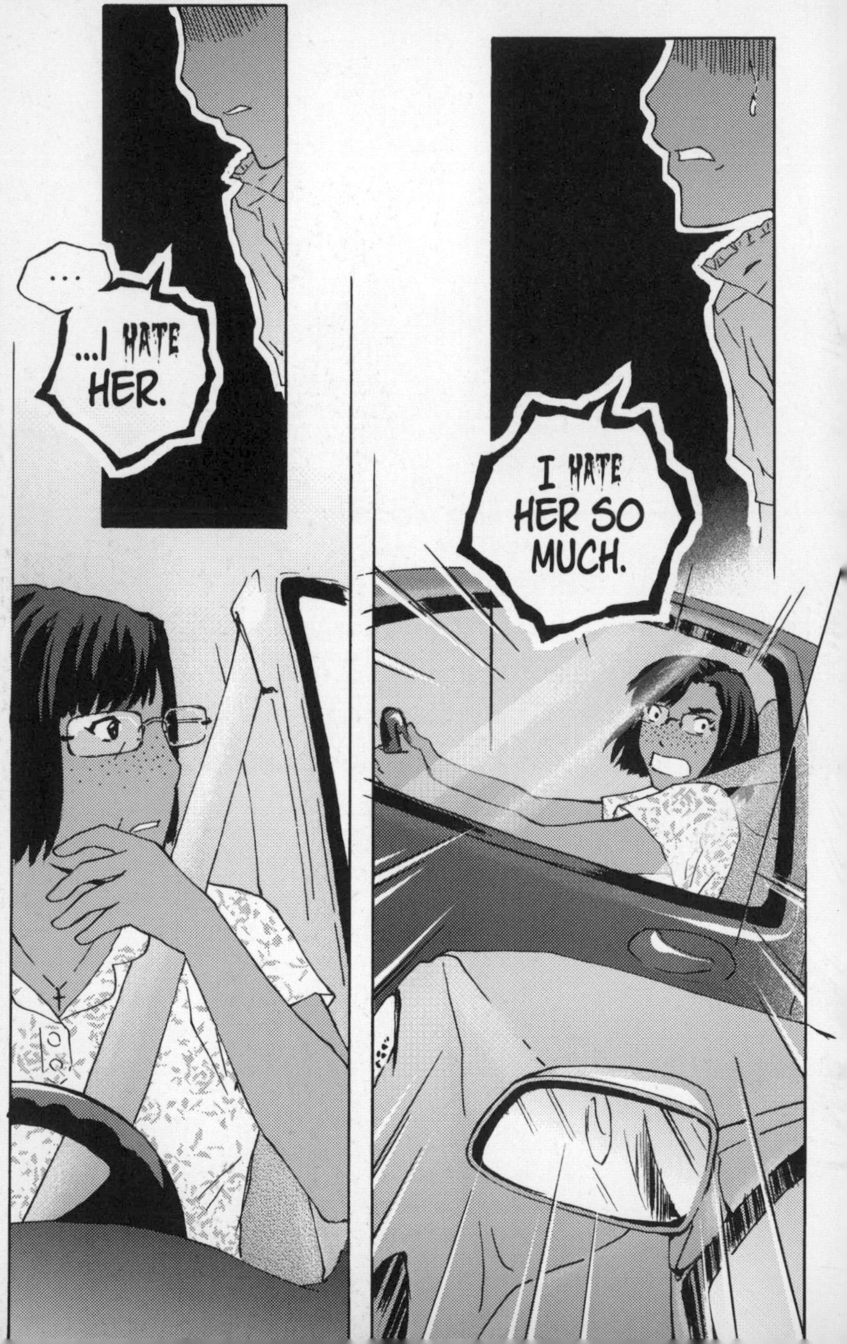
...
...I HATE HER.
I HATE HER SO MUCH.

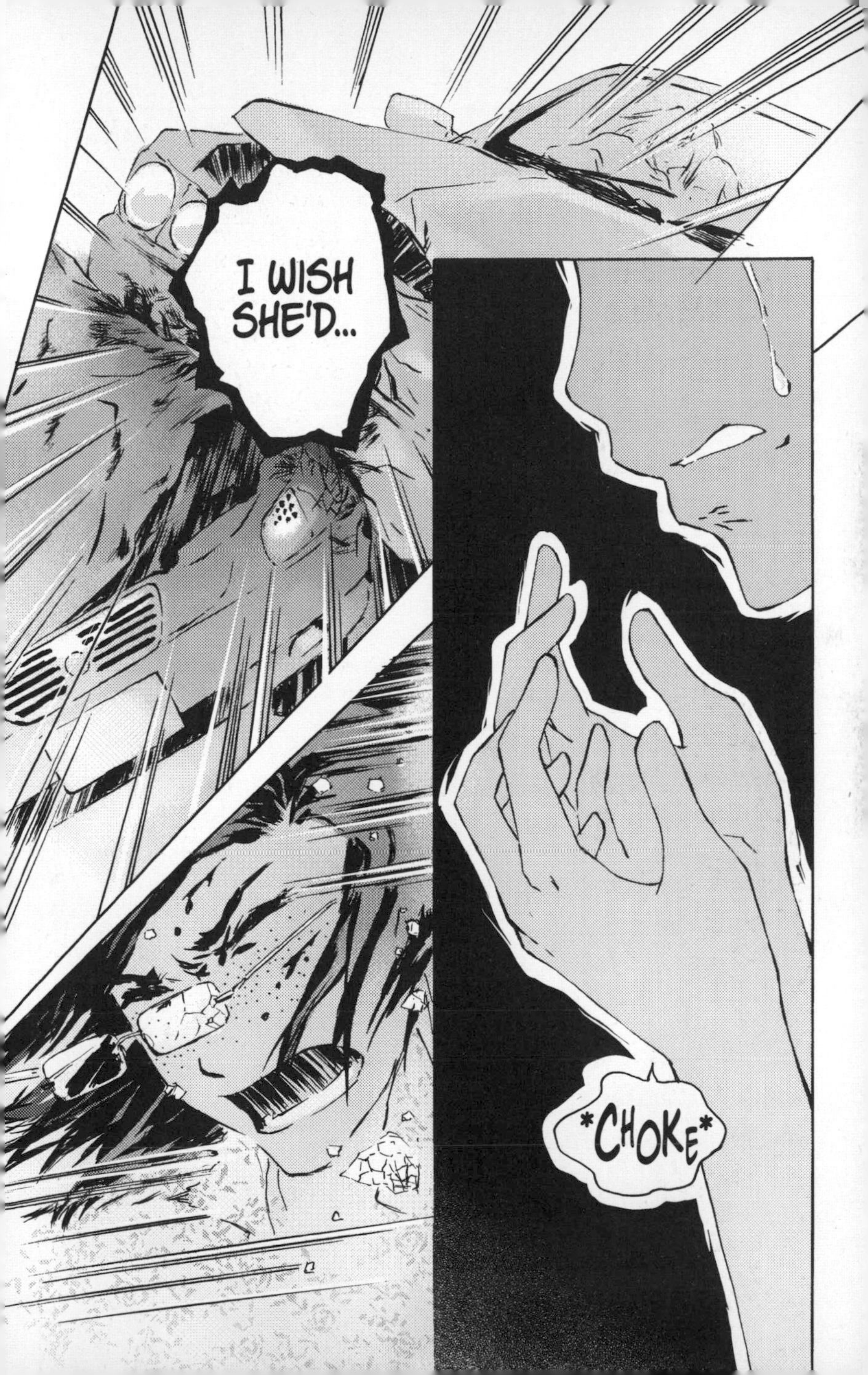
I WISH SHE'D...
CHOKE

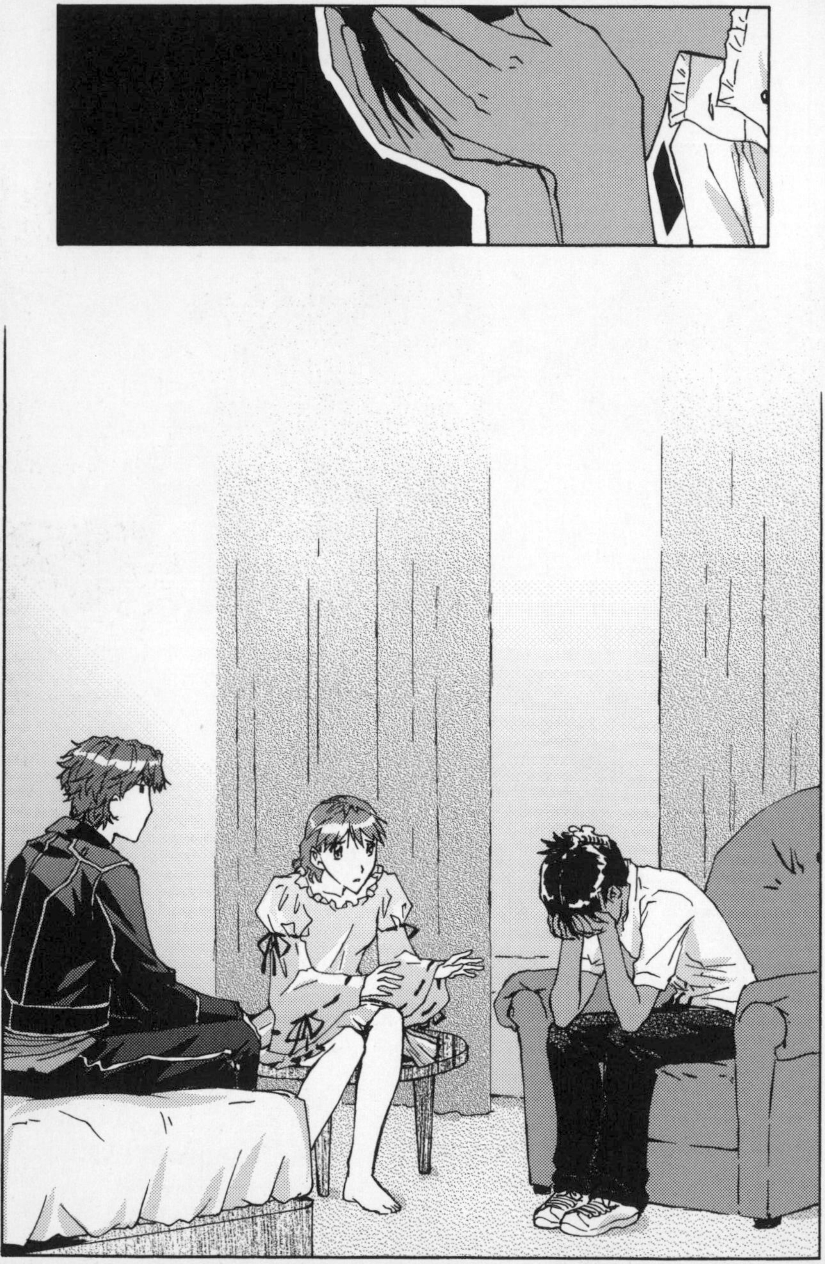

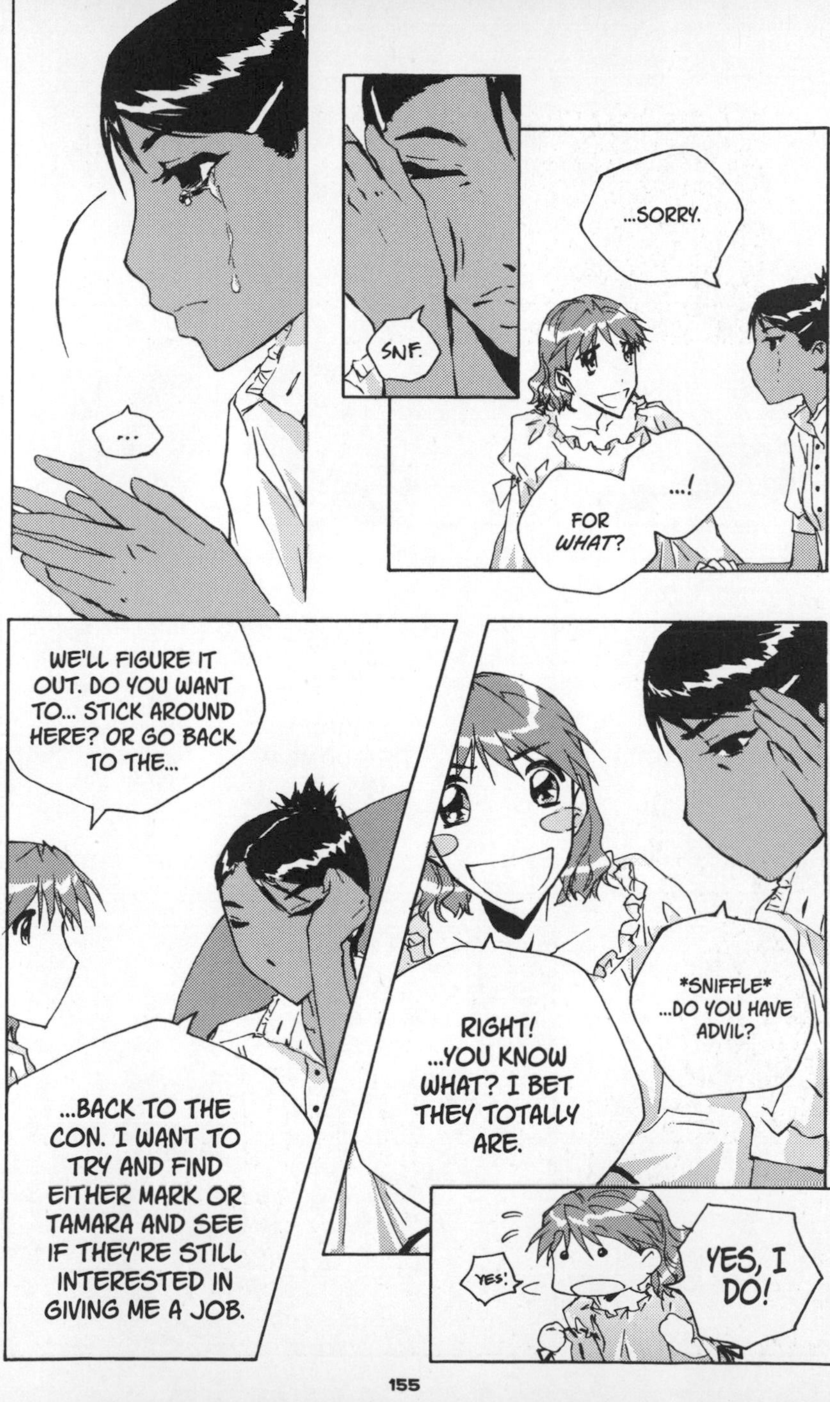
...
SNF.
...SORRY.
...!
FOR WHAT?
WE'LL FIGURE IT OUT. DO YOU WANT TO... STICK AROUND HERE? OR GO BACK TO THE...
...BACK TO THE CON. I WANT TO TRY AND FIND EITHER MARK OR TAMARA AND SEE IF THEY'RE STILL INTERESTED IN GIVING ME A JOB.
RIGHT! ...YOU KNOW WHAT? I BET THEY TOTALLY ARE.
SNIFFLE ...DO YOU HAVE ADVIL?
YES!
YES, I DO!

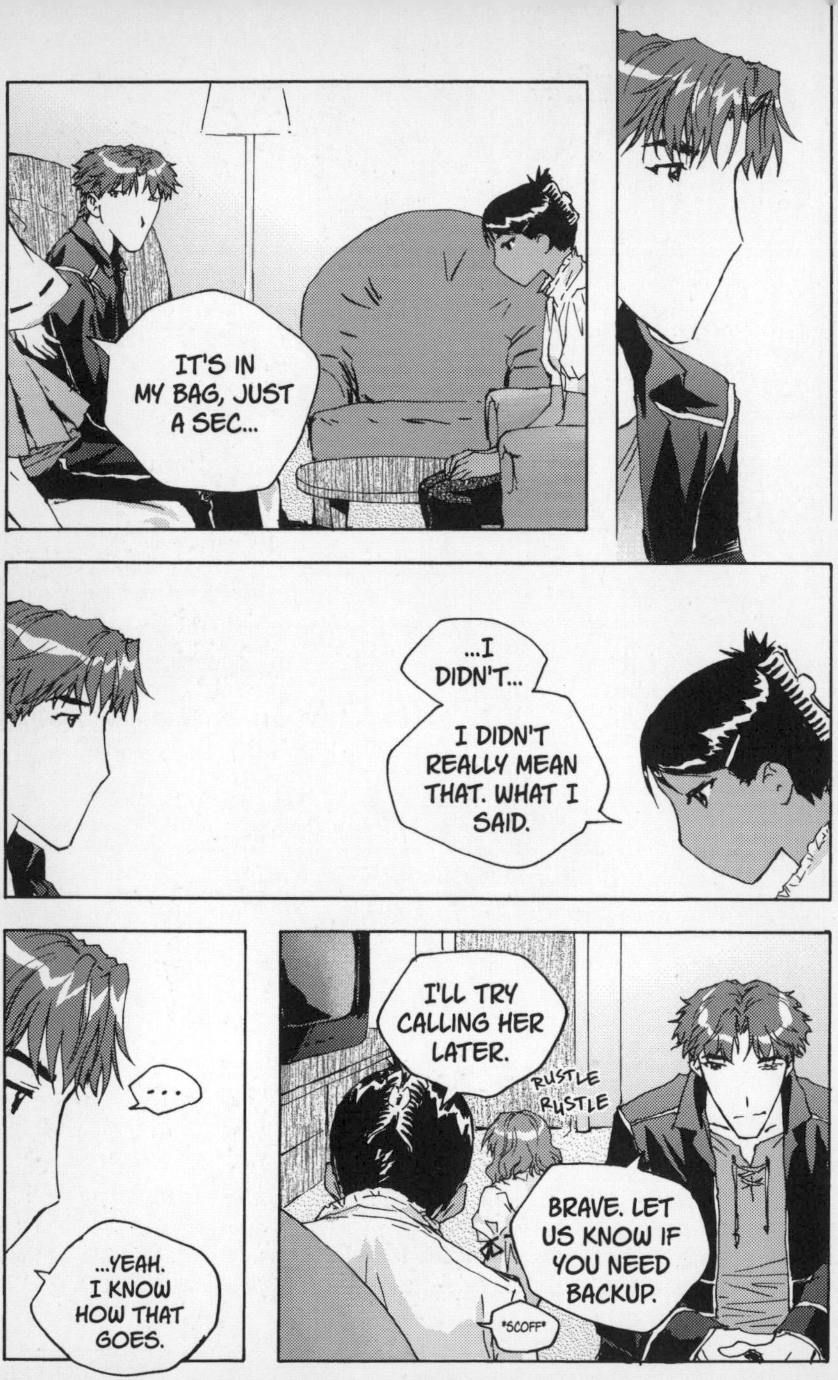
IT'S IN MY BAG, JUST A SEC...
...I DIDN'T...
I DIDN'T REALLY MEAN THAT. WHAT I SAID.
...
...YEAH. I KNOW HOW THAT GOES.
I'LL TRY CALLING HER LATER.
RUSTLE RUSTLE
BRAVE. LET US KNOW IF YOU NEED BACKUP.
SCOFF

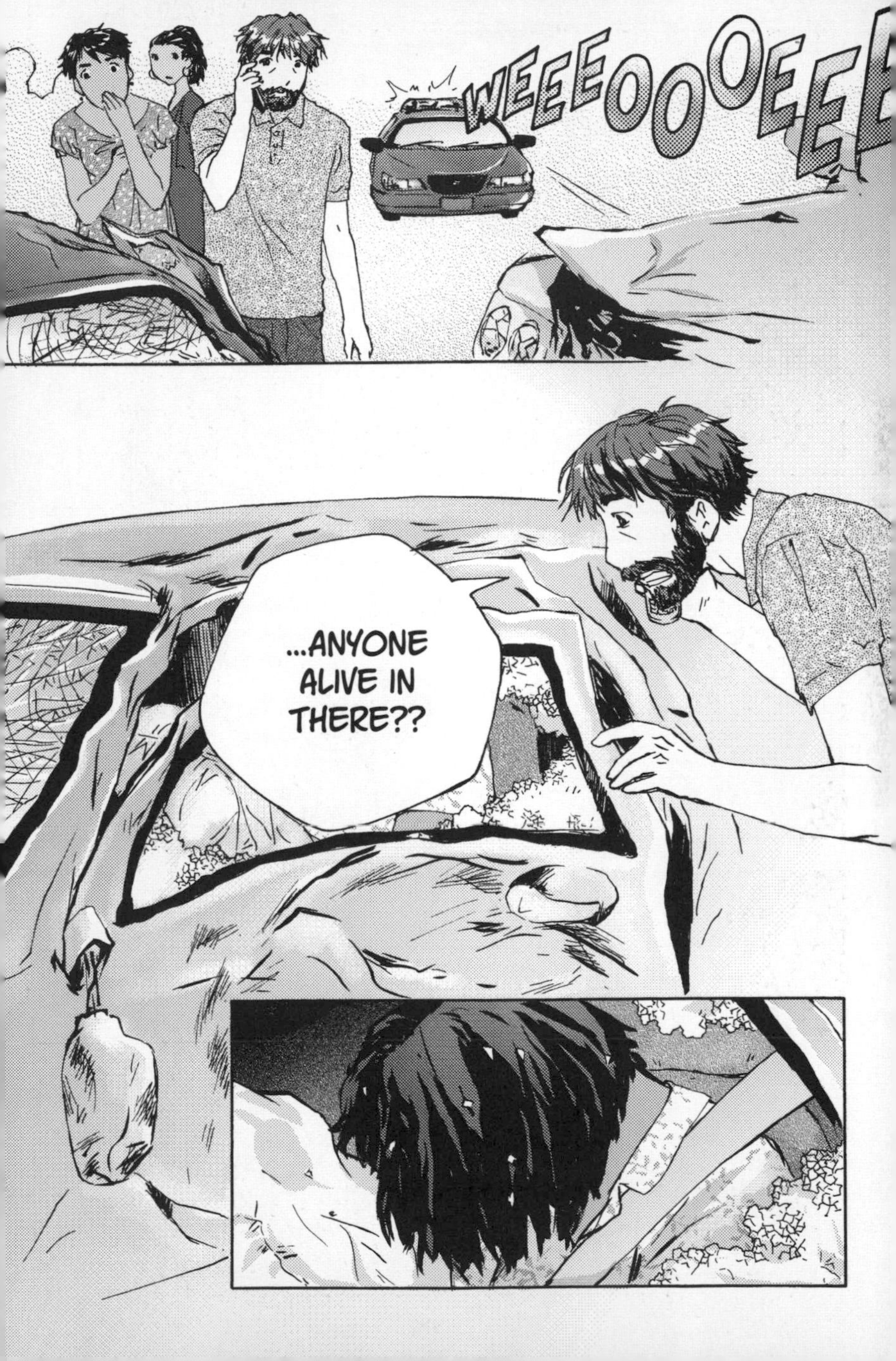
WEEEOOOOEEE
...ANYONE ALIVE IN THERE??

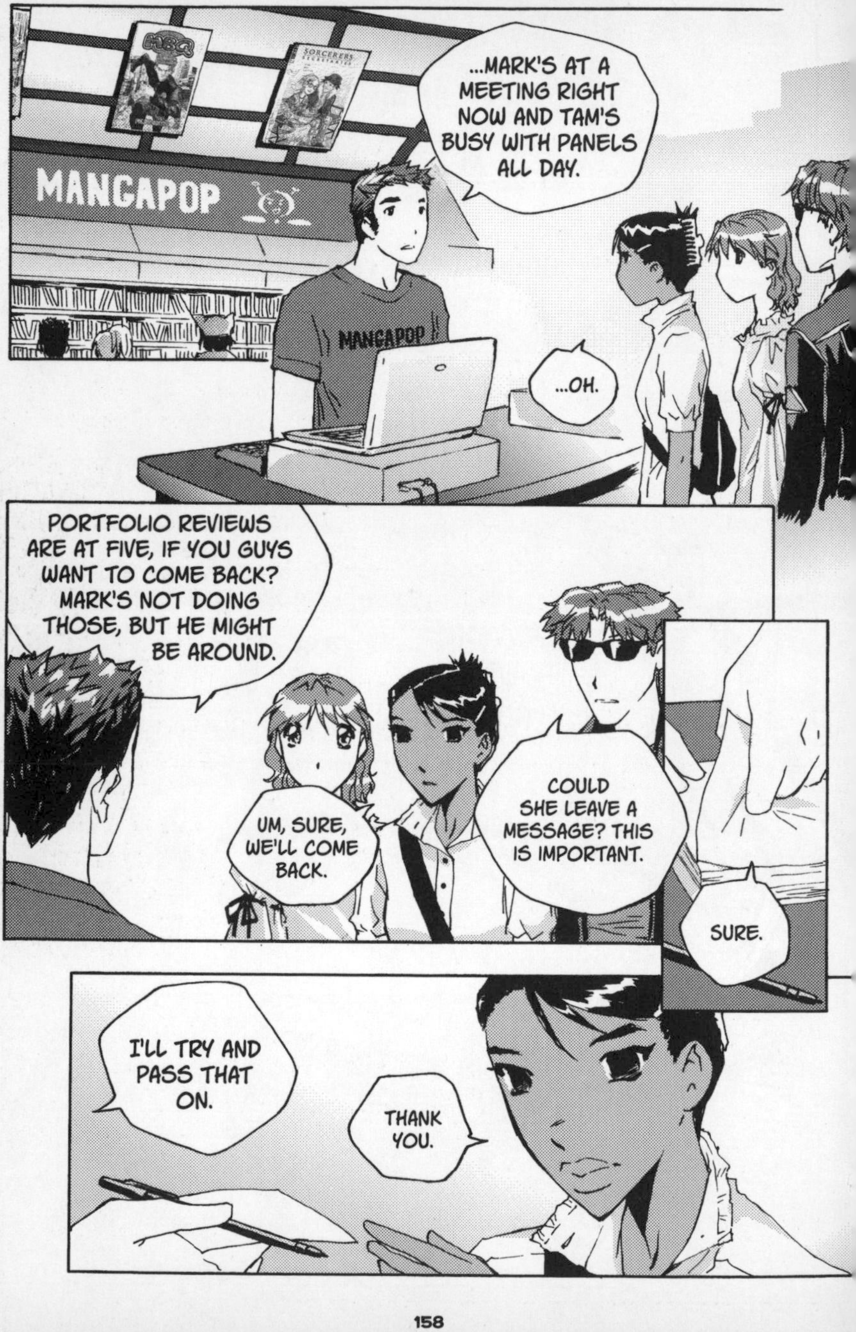
MANGAPOP
...MARK'S AT A MEETING RIGHT NOW AND TAM'S BUSY WITH PANELS ALL DAY.
MANGAPOP
...OH.
PORTFOLIO REVIEWS ARE AT FIVE, IF YOU GUYS WANT TO COME BACK? MARK'S NOT DOING THOSE, BUT HE MIGHT BE AROUND.
UM, SURE, WE'LL COME BACK.
COULD SHE LEAVE A MESSAGE? THIS IS IMPORTANT.
SURE.
I'LL TRY AND PASS THAT ON.
THANK YOU.

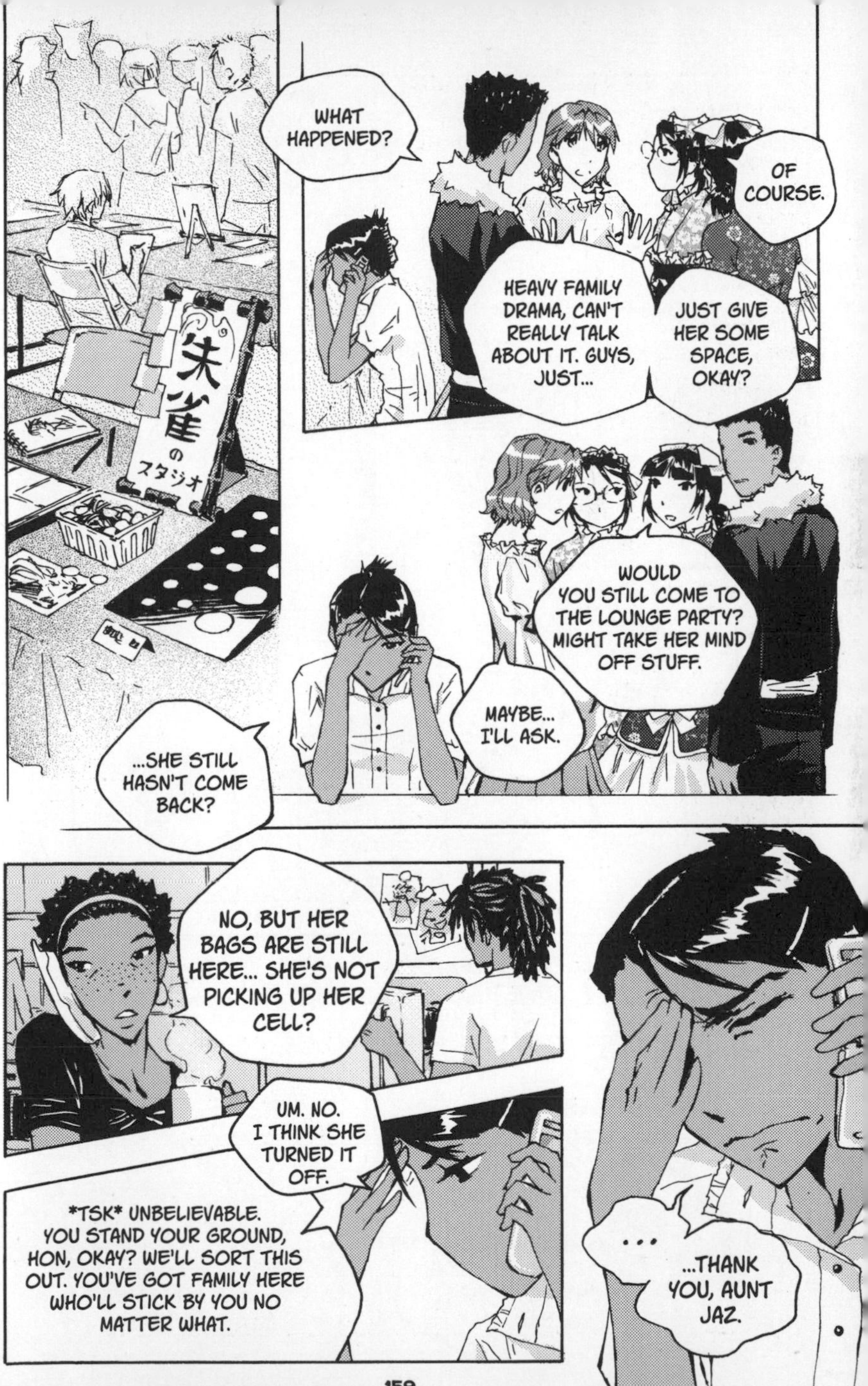
朱雀のスタジオ
WHAT HAPPENED?
HEAVY FAMILY DRAMA, CAN'T REALLY TALK ABOUT IT. GUYS, JUST...
JUST GIVE HER SOME SPACE, OKAY?
OF COURSE.
WOULD YOU STILL COME TO THE LOUNGE PARTY? MIGHT TAKE HER MIND OFF STUFF.
MAYBE... I'LL ASK.
...SHE STILL HASN'T COME BACK?
NO, BUT HER BAGS ARE STILL HERE... SHE'S NOT PICKING UP HER CELL?
UM. NO. I THINK SHE TURNED IT OFF.
TSK UNBELIEVABLE. YOU STAND YOUR GROUND, HON, OKAY? WE'LL SORT THIS OUT. YOU'VE GOT FAMILY HERE WHO'LL STICK BY YOU NO MATTER WHAT.
...
...THANK YOU, AUNT JAZ.

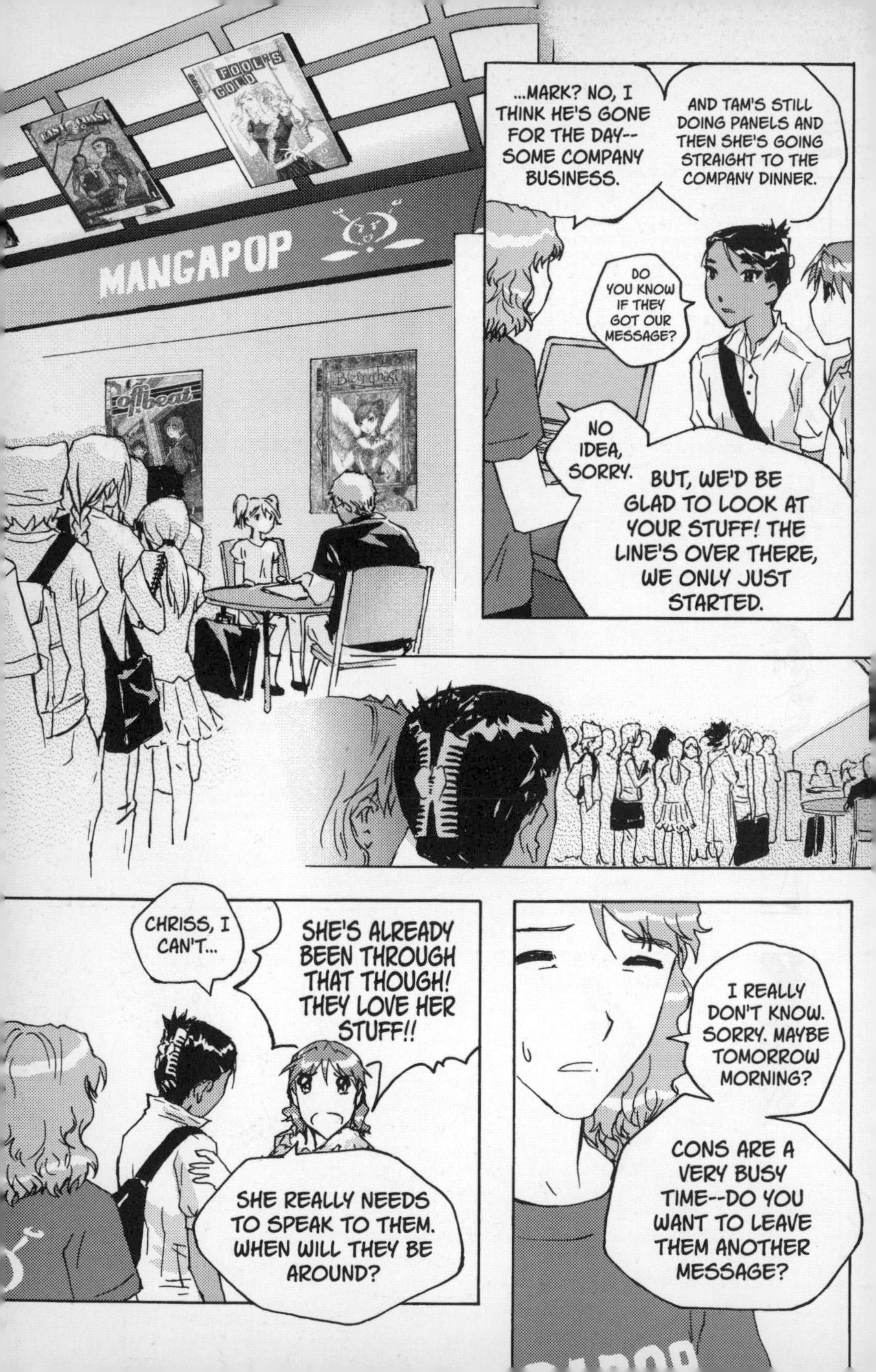
FOOL'S GOLD
MANGAPOP
offbeat
...MARK? NO, I THINK HE'S GONE FOR THE DAY-- SOME COMPANY BUSINESS.
AND TAM'S STILL DOING PANELS AND THEN SHE'S GOING STRAIGHT TO THE COMPANY DINNER.
DO YOU KNOW IF THEY GOT OUR MESSAGE?
NO IDEA, SORRY.
BUT, WE'D BE GLAD TO LOOK AT YOUR STUFF! THE LINE'S OVER THERE, WE ONLY JUST STARTED.
CHRISS, I CAN'T...
SHE'S ALREADY BEEN THROUGH THAT THOUGH! THEY LOVE HER STUFF!!
SHE REALLY NEEDS TO SPEAK TO THEM. WHEN WILL THEY BE AROUND?
I REALLY DON'T KNOW. SORRY. MAYBE TOMORROW MORNING?
CONS ARE A VERY BUSY TIME--DO YOU WANT TO LEAVE THEM ANOTHER MESSAGE?

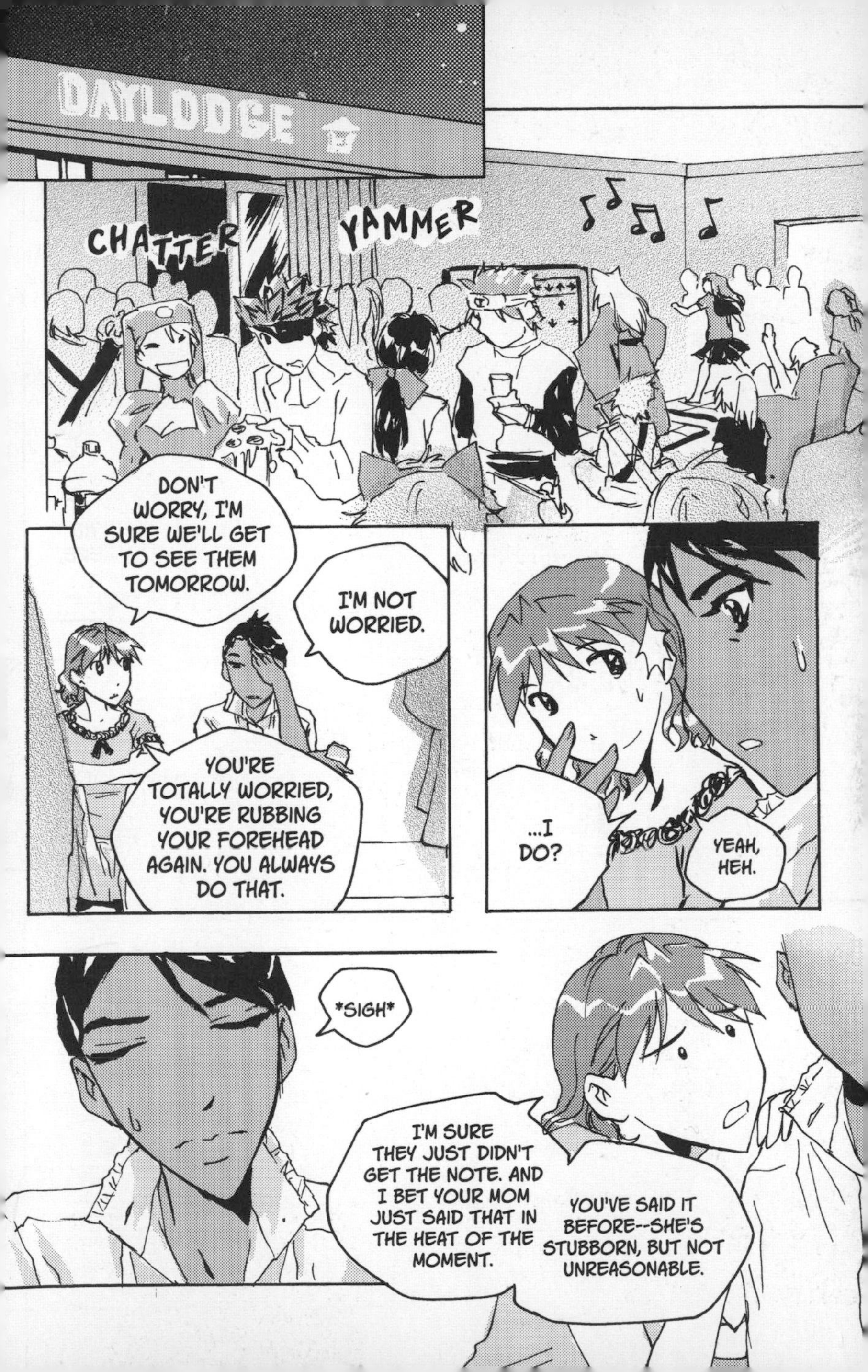
DAYLODGE
CHATTER
YAMMER
DON'T WORRY, I'M SURE WE'LL GET TO SEE THEM TOMORROW.
I'M NOT WORRIED.
YOU'RE TOTALLY WORRIED, YOU'RE RUBBING YOUR FOREHEAD AGAIN. YOU ALWAYS DO THAT.
...I DO?
YEAH, HEH.
SIGH
I'M SURE THEY JUST DIDN'T GET THE NOTE. AND I BET YOUR MOM JUST SAID THAT IN THE HEAT OF THE MOMENT.
YOU'VE SAID IT BEFORE--SHE'S STUBBORN, BUT NOT UNREASONABLE.

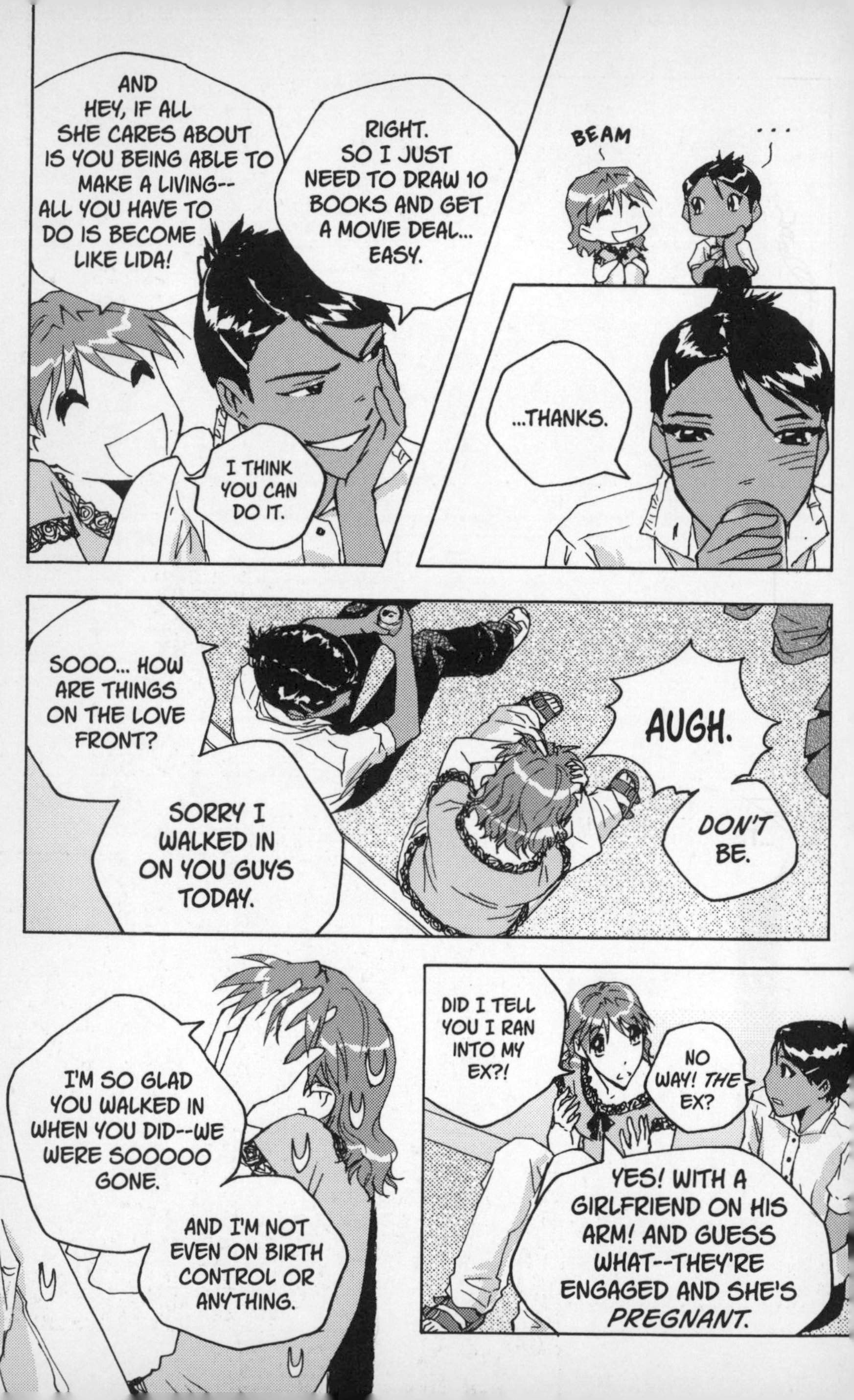
AND HEY, IF ALL SHE CARES ABOUT IS YOU BEING ABLE TO MAKE A LIVING--ALL YOU HAVE TO DO IS BECOME LIKE LIDA!
RIGHT. SO I JUST NEED TO DRAW 10 BOOKS AND GET A MOVIE DEAL... EASY.
I THINK YOU CAN DO IT.
BEAM
...
...THANKS.
SOOO... HOW ARE THINGS ON THE LOVE FRONT?
SORRY I WALKED IN ON YOU GUYS TODAY.
AUGH.
DON'T BE.
I'M SO GLAD YOU WALKED IN WHEN YOU DID--WE WERE SOOOOO GONE.
AND I'M NOT EVEN ON BIRTH CONTROL OR ANYTHING.
DID I TELL YOU I RAN INTO MY EX?!
NO WAY! THE EX?
YES! WITH A GIRLFRIEND ON HIS ARM! AND GUESS WHAT--THEY'RE ENGAGED AND SHE'S PREGNANT.

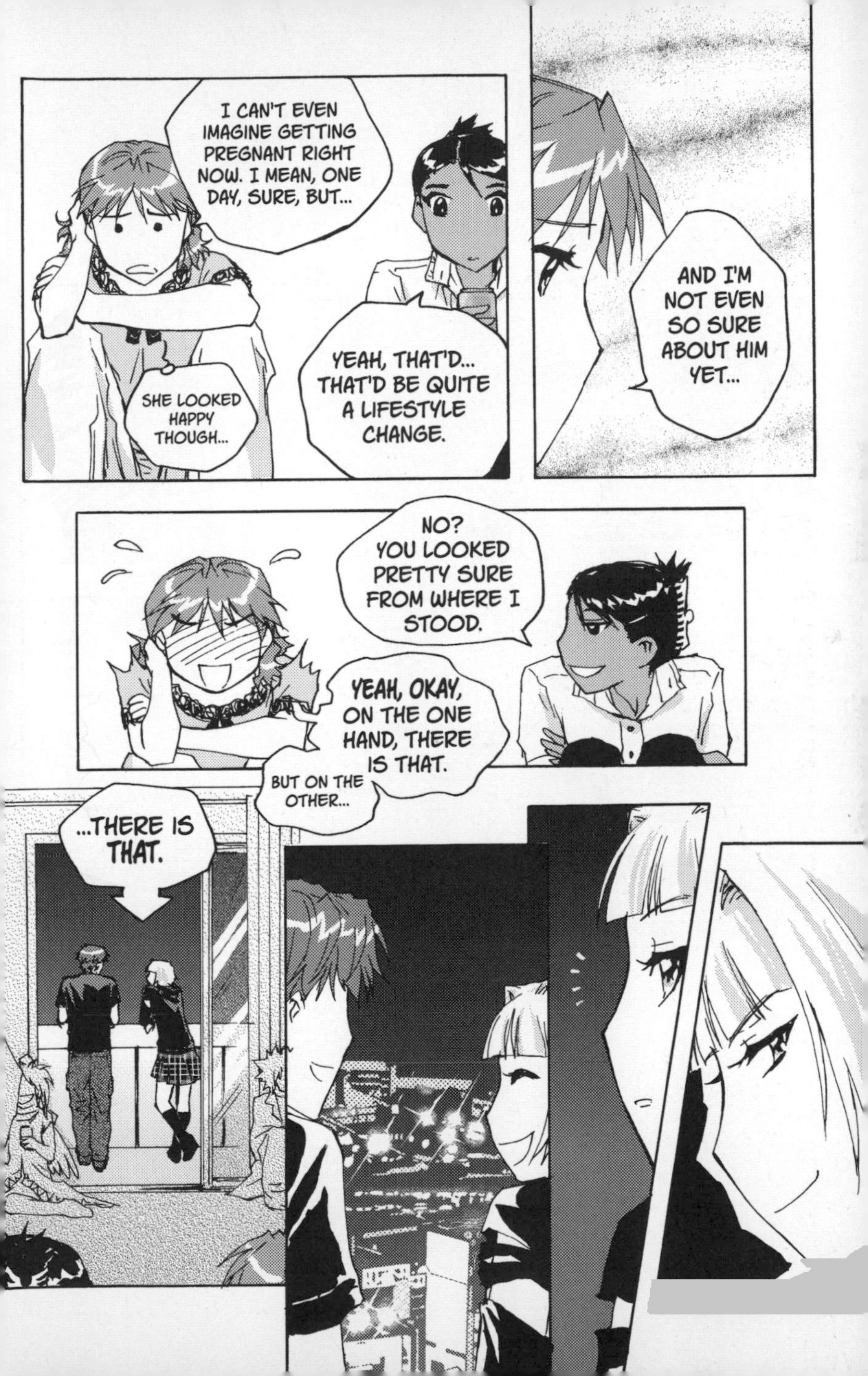
I CAN'T EVEN IMAGINE GETTING PREGNANT RIGHT NOW. I MEAN, ONE DAY, SURE, BUT...
SHE LOOKED HAPPY THOUGH...
YEAH, THAT'D... THAT'D BE QUITE A LIFESTYLE CHANGE.
AND I'M NOT EVEN SO SURE ABOUT HIM YET...
NO? YOU LOOKED PRETTY SURE FROM WHERE I STOOD.
YEAH, OKAY, ON THE ONE HAND, THERE IS THAT.
BUT ON THE OTHER...
...THERE IS THAT.

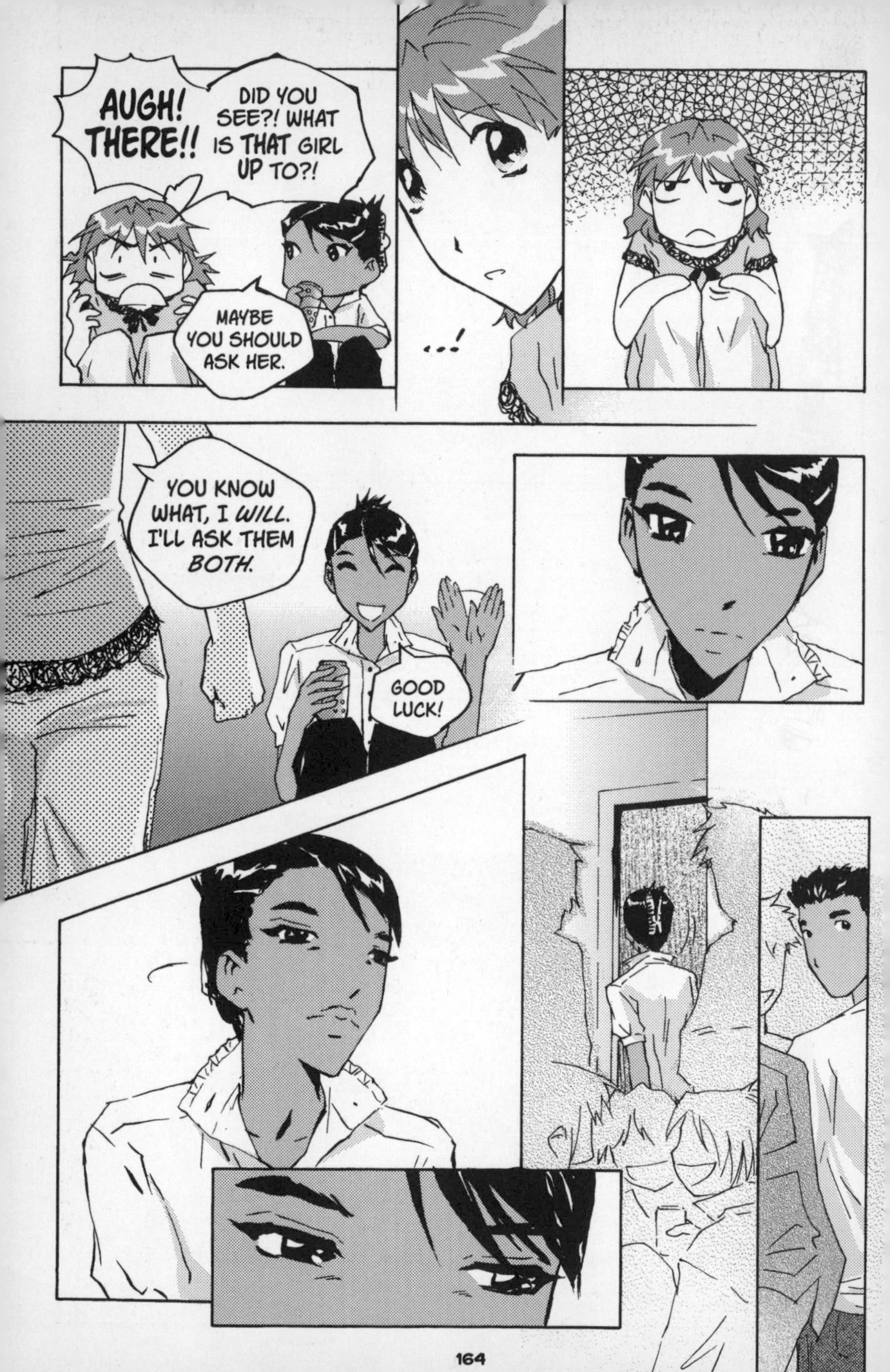
AUGH! THERE!!
DID YOU SEE?! WHAT IS THAT GIRL UP TO?!
MAYBE YOU SHOULD ASK HER.
...!
YOU KNOW WHAT, I *WILL*. I'LL ASK THEM *BOTH*.
GOOD LUCK!

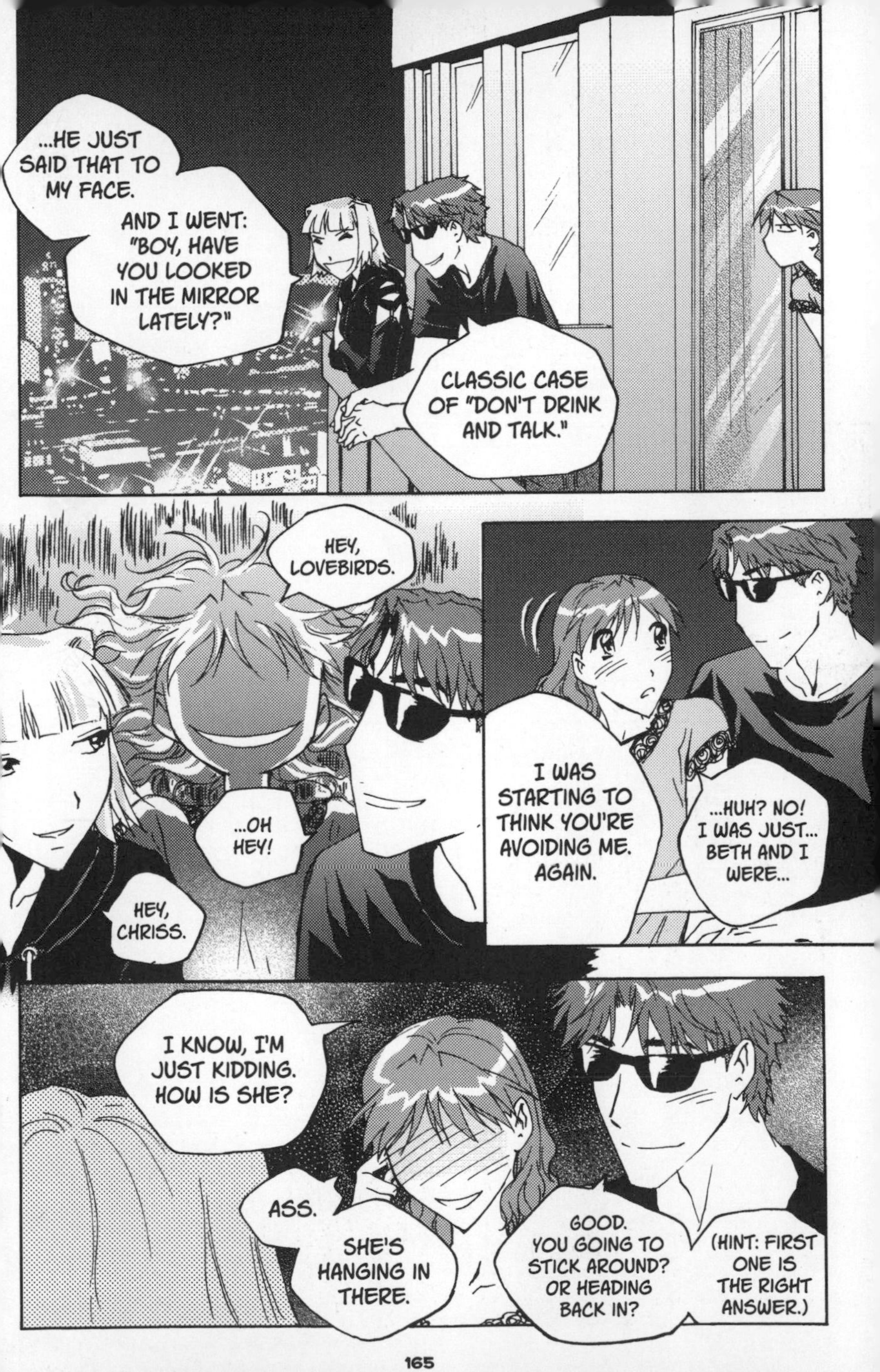
...HE JUST SAID THAT TO MY FACE.
AND I WENT: "BOY, HAVE YOU LOOKED IN THE MIRROR LATELY?"
CLASSIC CASE OF "DON'T DRINK AND TALK."
HEY, LOVEBIRDS.
...OH HEY!
HEY, CHRISS.
I WAS STARTING TO THINK YOU'RE AVOIDING ME. AGAIN.
...HUH? NO! I WAS JUST... BETH AND I WERE...
I KNOW, I'M JUST KIDDING. HOW IS SHE?
ASS.
SHE'S HANGING IN THERE.
GOOD. YOU GOING TO STICK AROUND? OR HEADING BACK IN?
(HINT: FIRST ONE IS THE RIGHT ANSWER.)

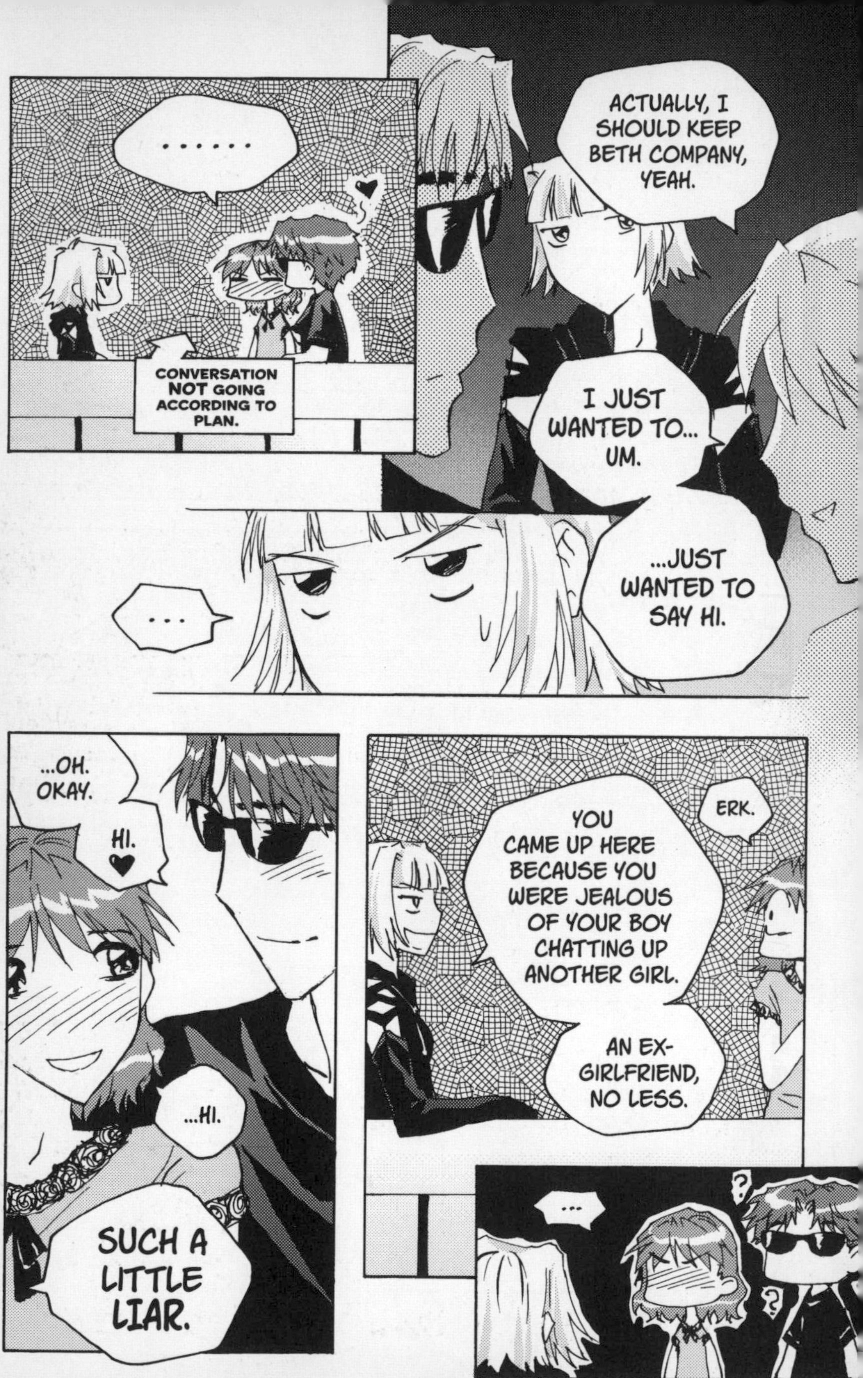

......
CONVERSATION NOT GOING ACCORDING TO PLAN.
ACTUALLY, I SHOULD KEEP BETH COMPANY, YEAH.
I JUST WANTED TO... UM.
...
...JUST WANTED TO SAY HI.
...OH. OKAY.
HI. ♥
...HI.
SUCH A LITTLE LIAR.
YOU CAME UP HERE BECAUSE YOU WERE JEALOUS OF YOUR BOY CHATTING UP ANOTHER GIRL.
ERK.
AN EX-GIRLFRIEND, NO LESS.
...
?
?

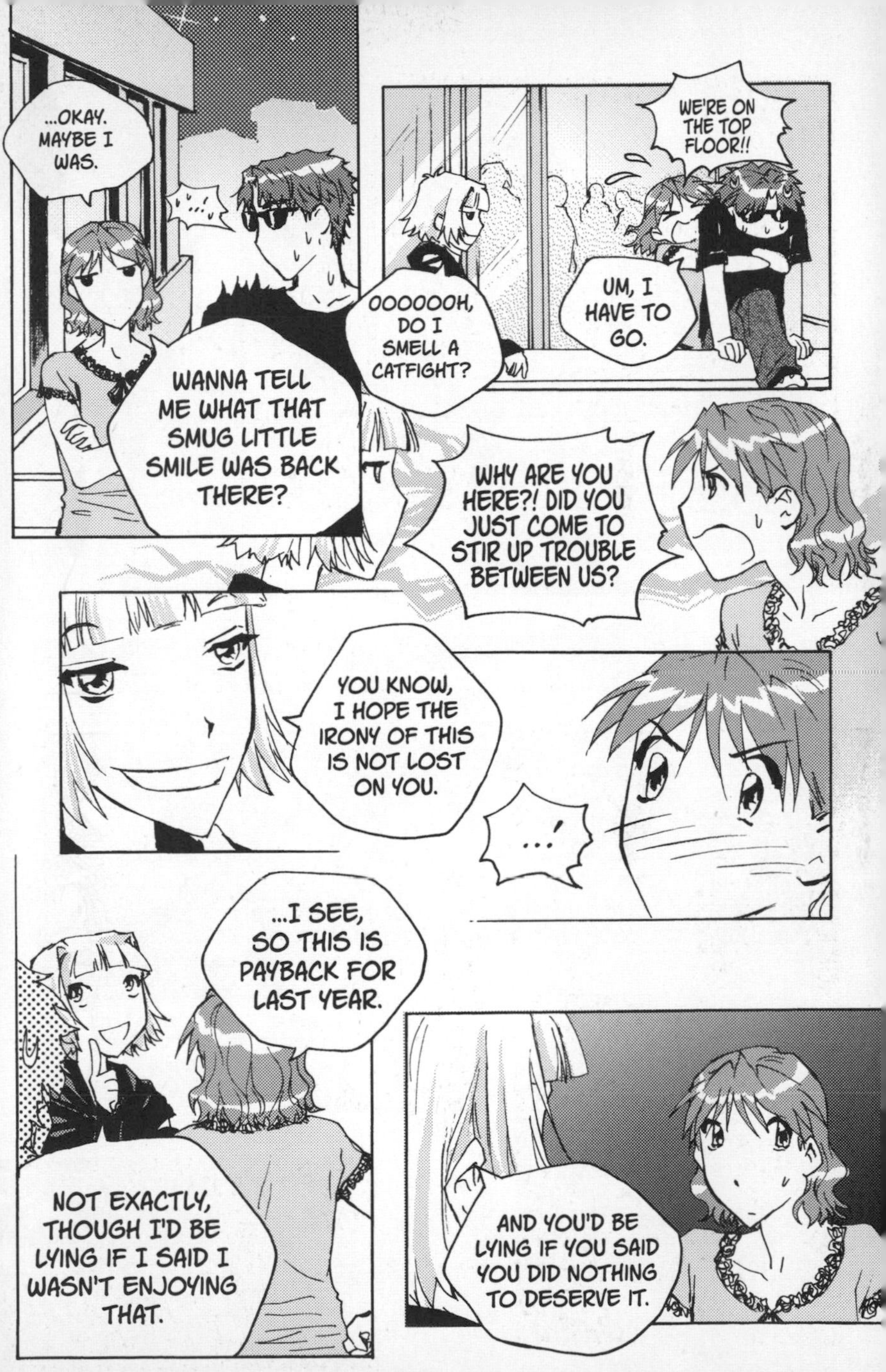
...OKAY. MAYBE I WAS.
...!
WANNA TELL ME WHAT THAT SMUG LITTLE SMILE WAS BACK THERE?
WE'RE ON THE TOP FLOOR!!
OOOOOOH, DO I SMELL A CATFIGHT?
UM, I HAVE TO GO.
WHY ARE YOU HERE?! DID YOU JUST COME TO STIR UP TROUBLE BETWEEN US?
YOU KNOW, I HOPE THE IRONY OF THIS IS NOT LOST ON YOU.
...!
...I SEE, SO THIS IS PAYBACK FOR LAST YEAR.
NOT EXACTLY, THOUGH I'D BE LYING IF I SAID I WASN'T ENJOYING THAT.
AND YOU'D BE LYING IF YOU SAID YOU DID NOTHING TO DESERVE IT.

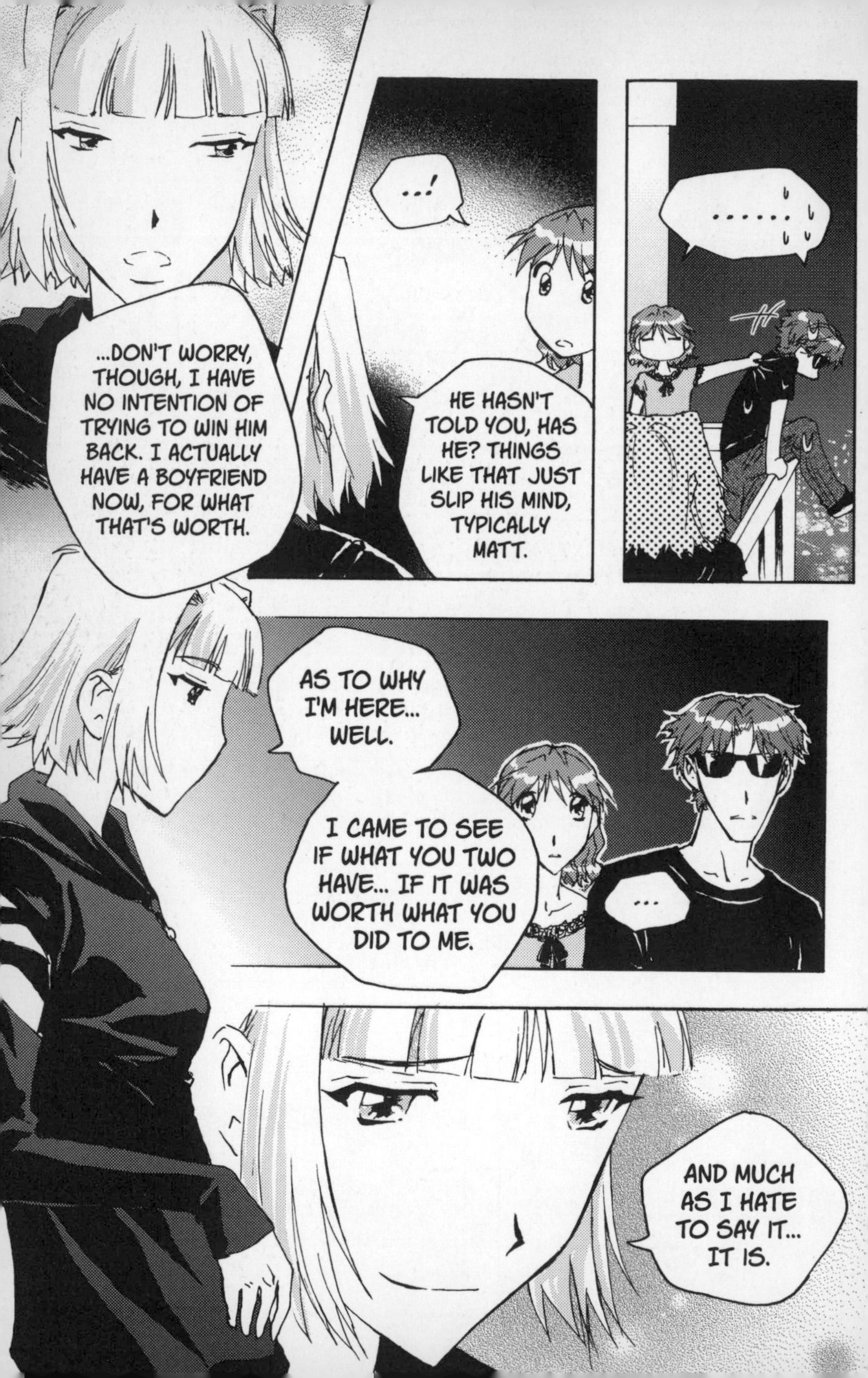
...DON'T WORRY, THOUGH, I HAVE NO INTENTION OF TRYING TO WIN HIM BACK. I ACTUALLY HAVE A BOYFRIEND NOW, FOR WHAT THAT'S WORTH.
...!
HE HASN'T TOLD YOU, HAS HE? THINGS LIKE THAT JUST SLIP HIS MIND, TYPICALLY MATT.
......
AS TO WHY I'M HERE... WELL.
I CAME TO SEE IF WHAT YOU TWO HAVE... IF IT WAS WORTH WHAT YOU DID TO ME.
...
AND MUCH AS I HATE TO SAY IT... IT IS.

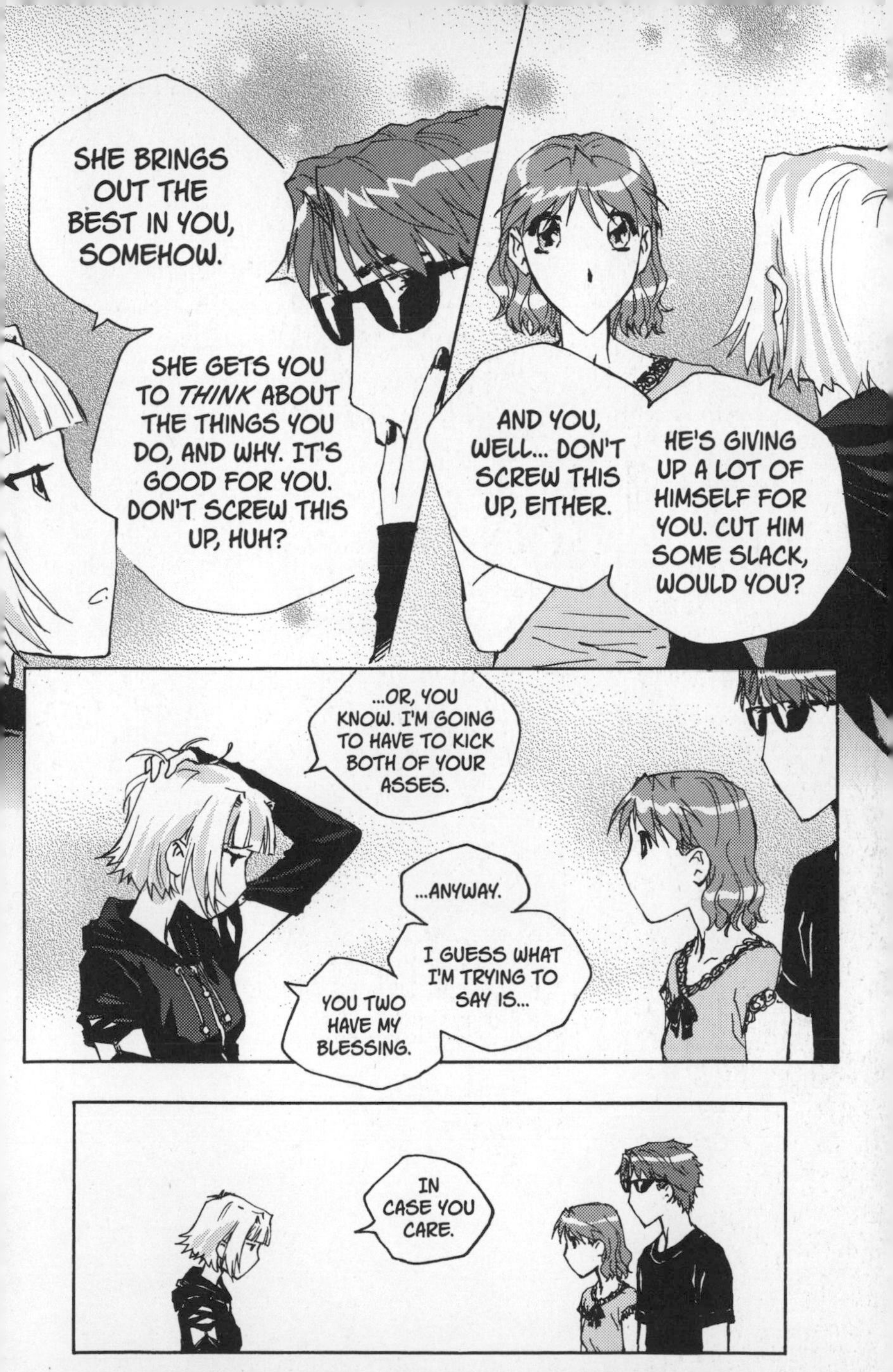
SHE BRINGS OUT THE BEST IN YOU, SOMEHOW.
SHE GETS YOU TO *THINK* ABOUT THE THINGS YOU DO, AND WHY. IT'S GOOD FOR YOU. DON'T SCREW THIS UP, HUH?
AND YOU, WELL... DON'T SCREW THIS UP, EITHER.
HE'S GIVING UP A LOT OF HIMSELF FOR YOU. CUT HIM SOME SLACK, WOULD YOU?
...OR, YOU KNOW. I'M GOING TO HAVE TO KICK BOTH OF YOUR ASSES.
...ANYWAY.
I GUESS WHAT I'M TRYING TO SAY IS...
YOU TWO HAVE MY BLESSING.
IN CASE YOU CARE.

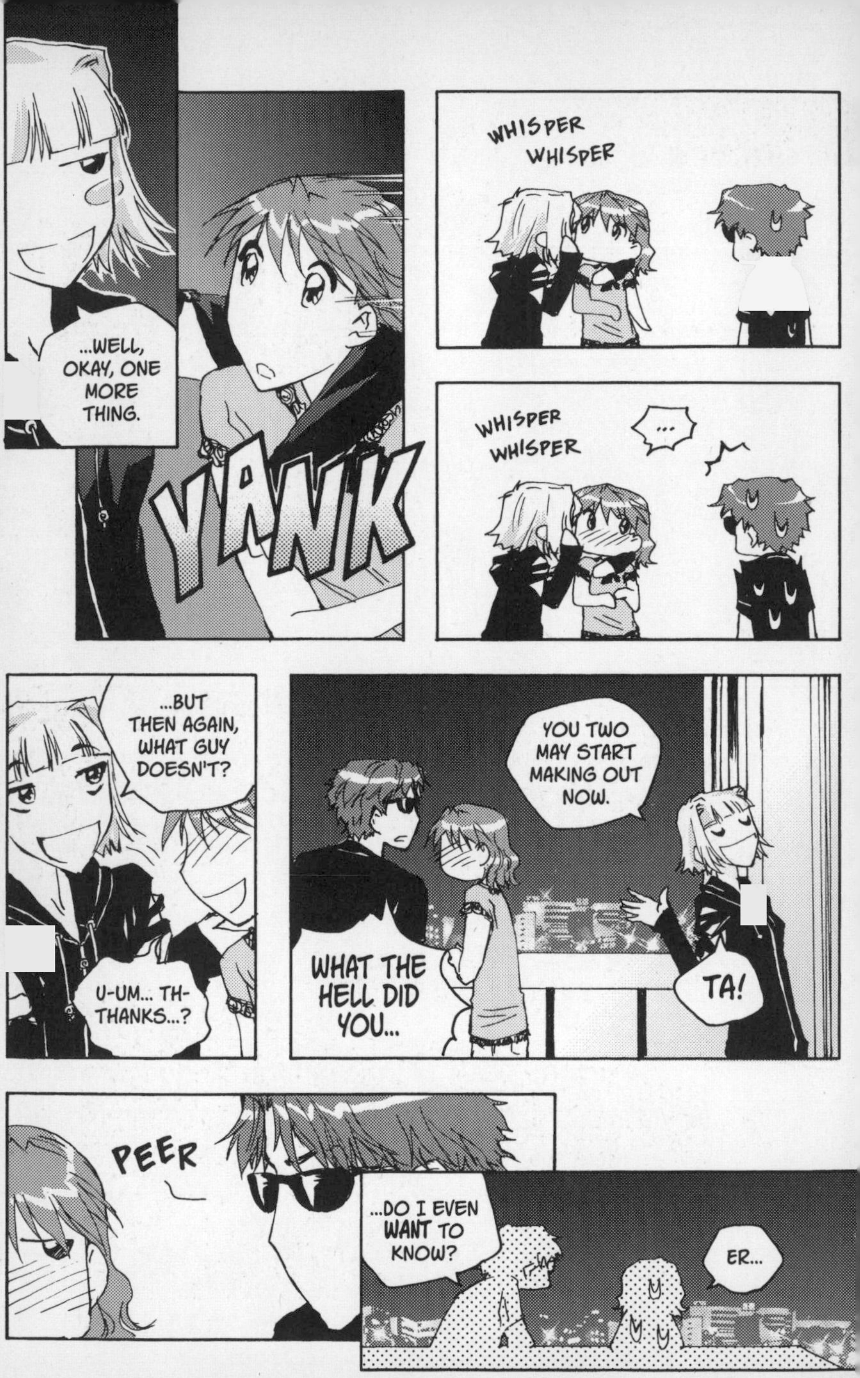
...WELL, OKAY, ONE MORE THING.
YANK
WHISPER WHISPER
WHISPER WHISPER
...
...BUT THEN AGAIN, WHAT GUY DOESN'T?
U-UM... TH-THANKS...?
YOU TWO MAY START MAKING OUT NOW.
WHAT THE HELL DID YOU...
TA!
PEER
...DO I EVEN WANT TO KNOW?
ER...

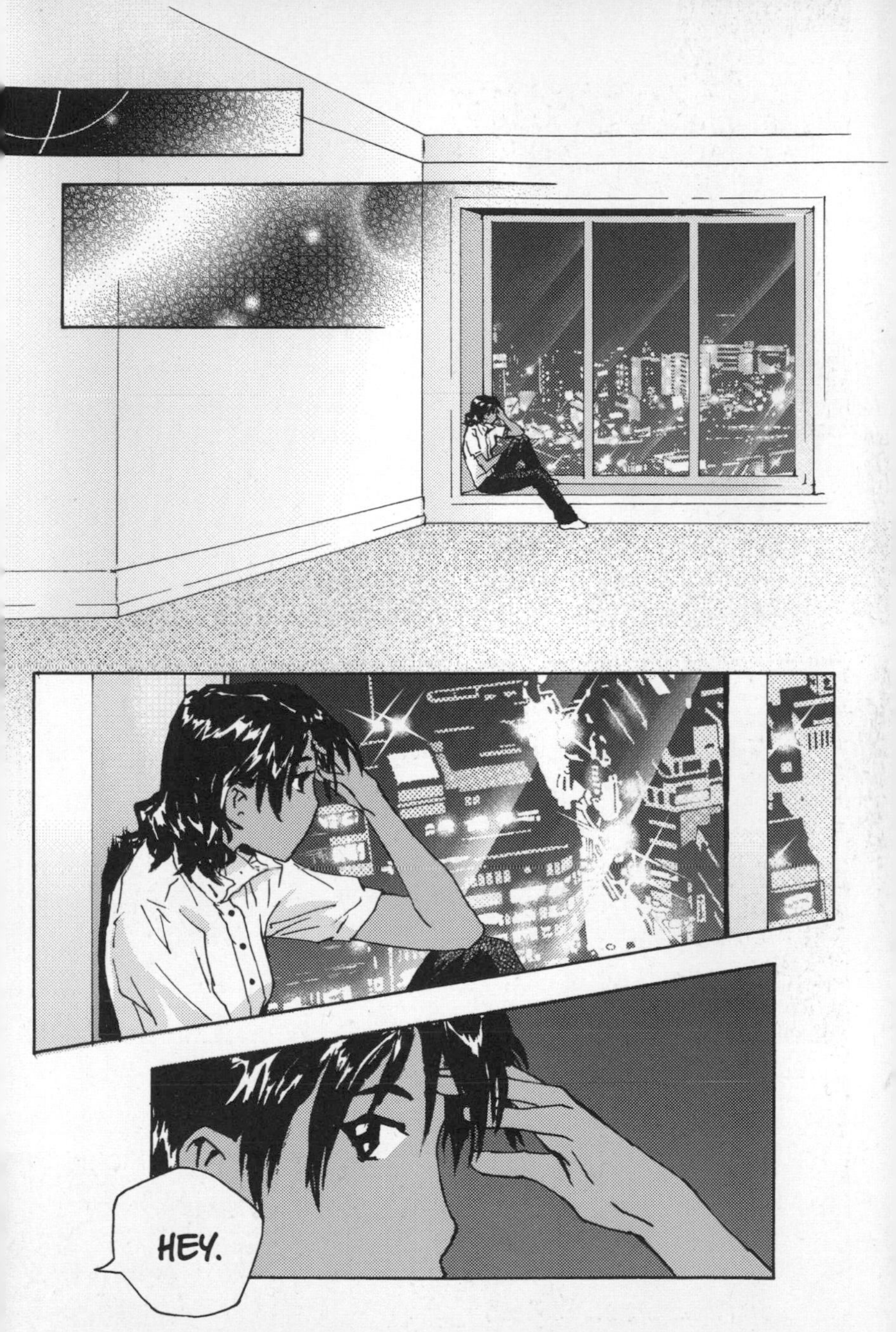
HEY.

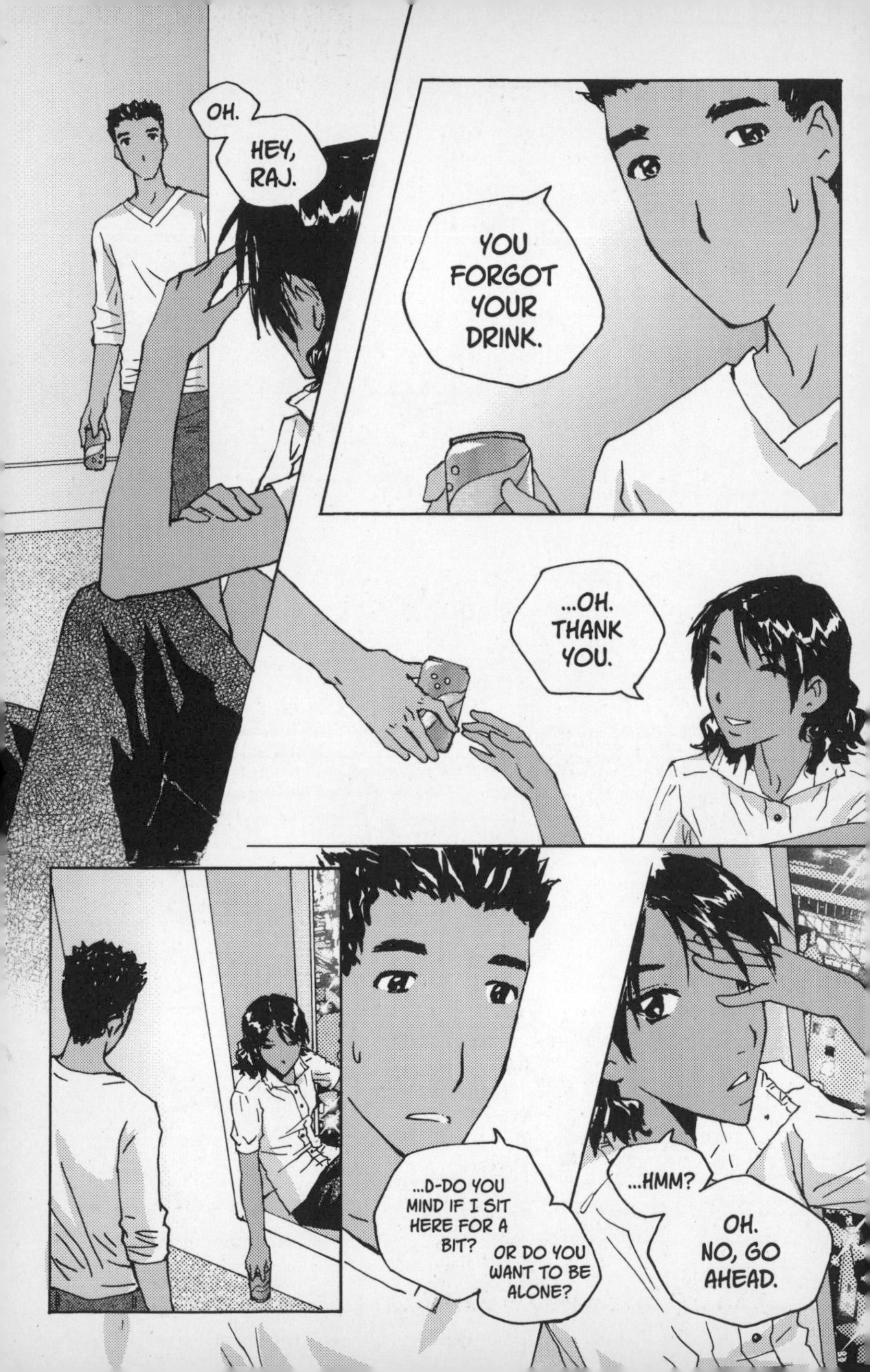
OH.
HEY, RAJ.
YOU FORGOT YOUR DRINK.
...OH. THANK YOU.
...D-DO YOU MIND IF I SIT HERE FOR A BIT?
OR DO YOU WANT TO BE ALONE?
...HMM?
OH. NO, GO AHEAD.

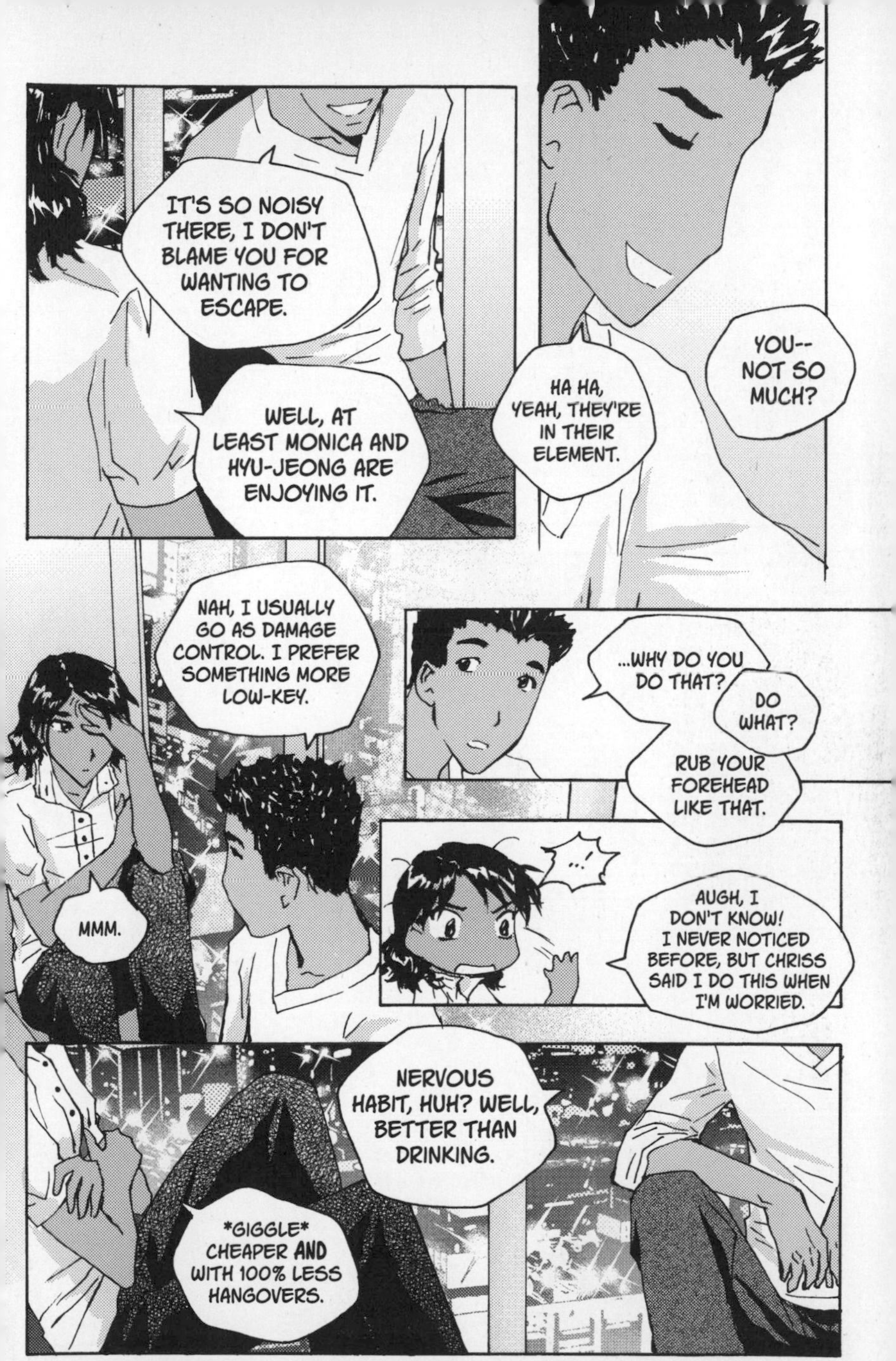
IT'S SO NOISY THERE, I DON'T BLAME YOU FOR WANTING TO ESCAPE.
WELL, AT LEAST MONICA AND HYU-JEONG ARE ENJOYING IT.
HA HA, YEAH, THEY'RE IN THEIR ELEMENT.
YOU-- NOT SO MUCH?
NAH, I USUALLY GO AS DAMAGE CONTROL. I PREFER SOMETHING MORE LOW-KEY.
MMM.
...WHY DO YOU DO THAT?
DO WHAT?
RUB YOUR FOREHEAD LIKE THAT.
...!
AUGH, I DON'T KNOW! I NEVER NOTICED BEFORE, BUT CHRISS SAID I DO THIS WHEN I'M WORRIED.
NERVOUS HABIT, HUH? WELL, BETTER THAN DRINKING.
GIGGLE CHEAPER AND WITH 100% LESS HANGOVERS.

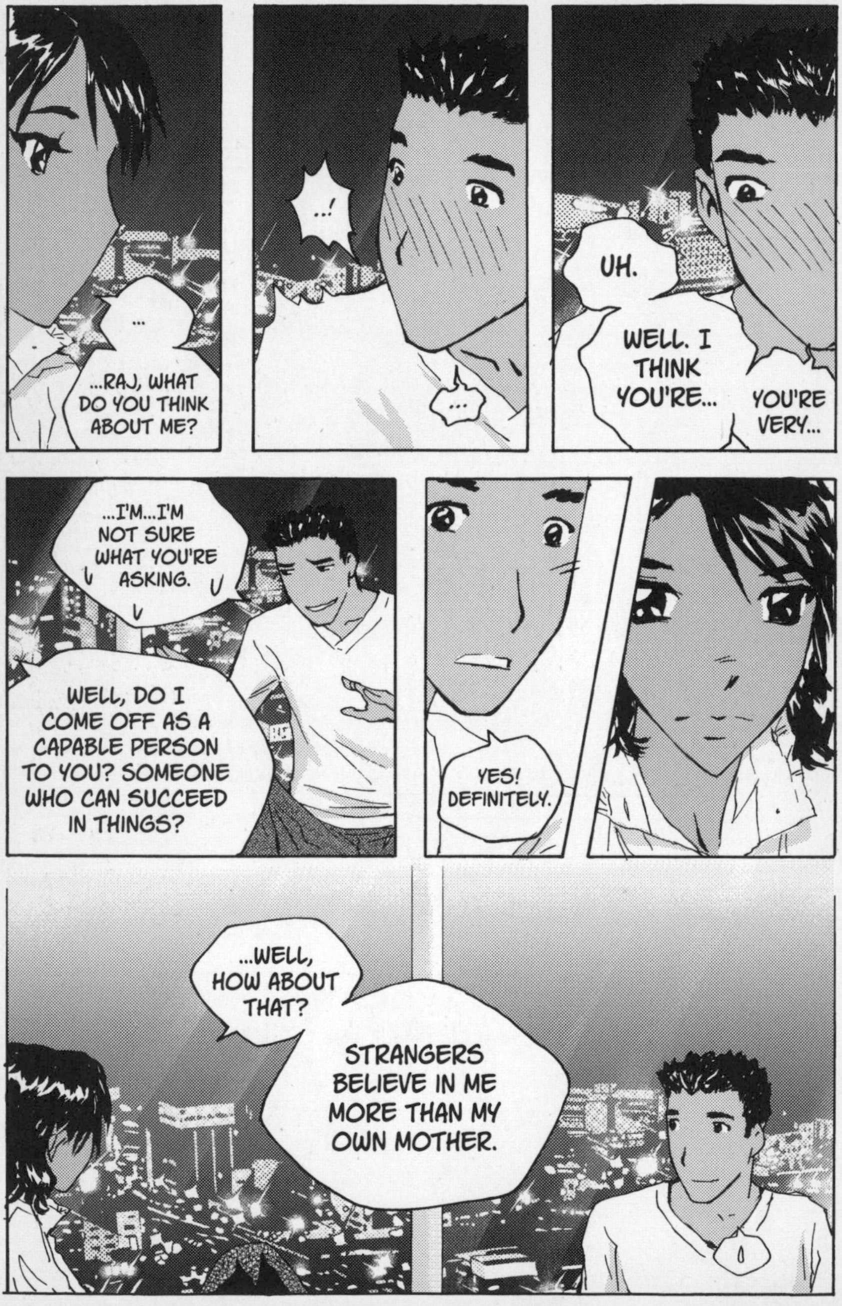
...
...RAJ, WHAT DO YOU THINK ABOUT ME?
...!
...
UH.
WELL. I THINK YOU'RE...
YOU'RE VERY...
...I'M...I'M NOT SURE WHAT YOU'RE ASKING.
WELL, DO I COME OFF AS A CAPABLE PERSON TO YOU? SOMEONE WHO CAN SUCCEED IN THINGS?
YES! DEFINITELY.
...WELL, HOW ABOUT THAT?
STRANGERS BELIEVE IN ME MORE THAN MY OWN MOTHER.

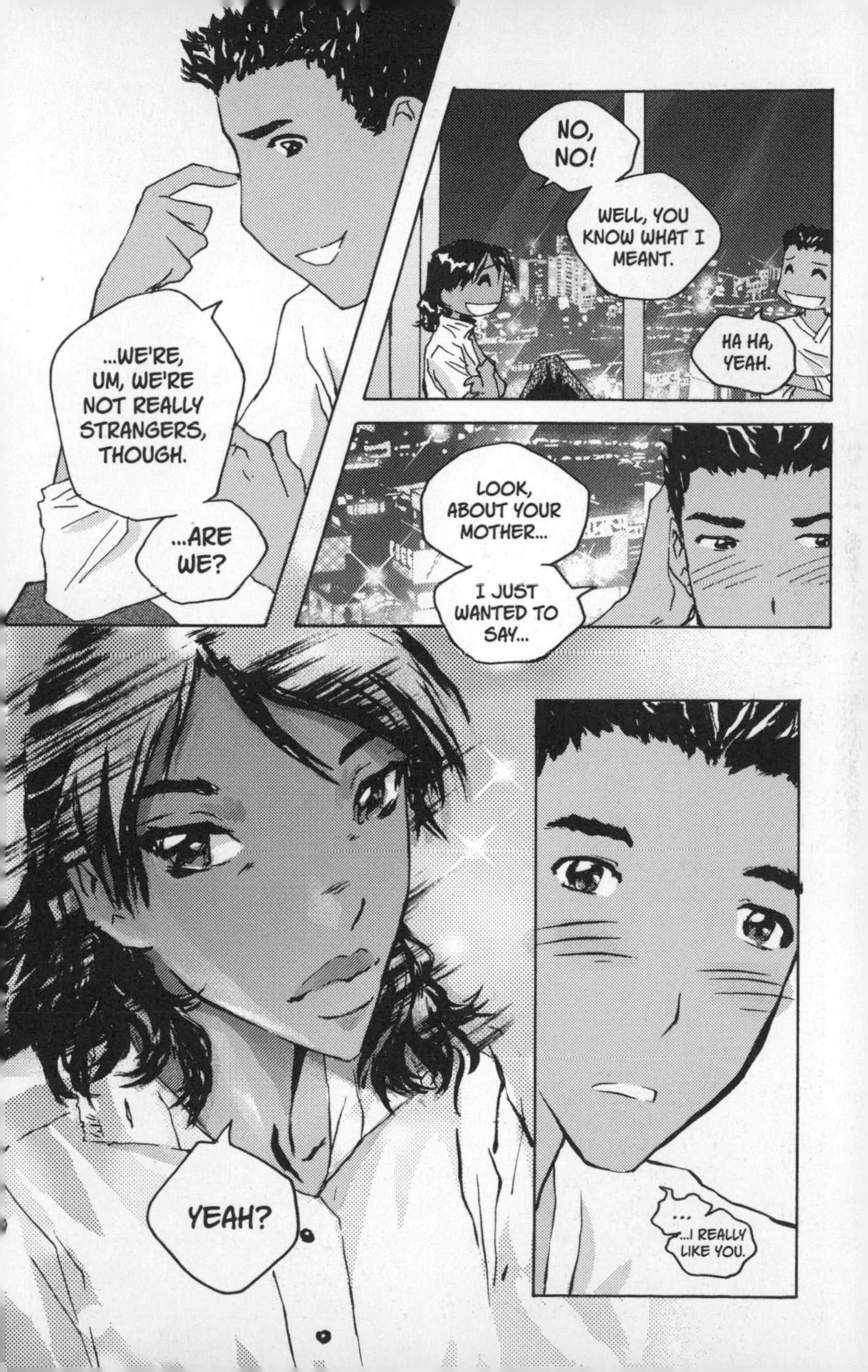
...WE'RE, UM, WE'RE NOT REALLY STRANGERS, THOUGH.
...ARE WE?
NO, NO!
WELL, YOU KNOW WHAT I MEANT.
HA HA, YEAH.
LOOK, ABOUT YOUR MOTHER...
I JUST WANTED TO SAY...
YEAH?
...
...I REALLY LIKE YOU.

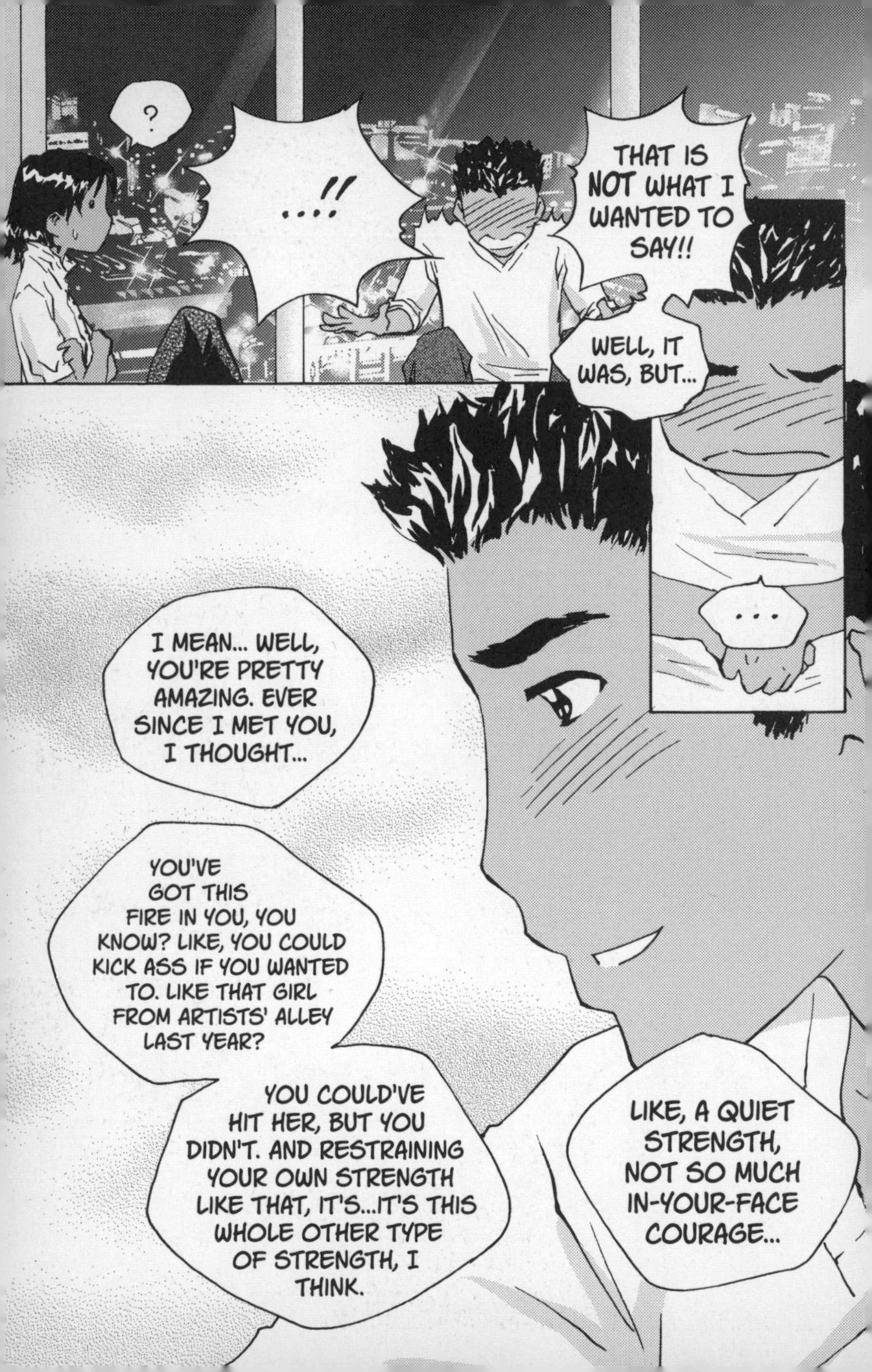
?
...!!
THAT IS NOT WHAT I WANTED TO SAY!!
WELL, IT WAS, BUT...
...
I MEAN... WELL, YOU'RE PRETTY AMAZING. EVER SINCE I MET YOU, I THOUGHT...
YOU'VE GOT THIS FIRE IN YOU, YOU KNOW? LIKE, YOU COULD KICK ASS IF YOU WANTED TO. LIKE THAT GIRL FROM ARTISTS' ALLEY LAST YEAR?
YOU COULD'VE HIT HER, BUT YOU DIDN'T. AND RESTRAINING YOUR OWN STRENGTH LIKE THAT, IT'S...IT'S THIS WHOLE OTHER TYPE OF STRENGTH, I THINK.
LIKE, A QUIET STRENGTH, NOT SO MUCH IN-YOUR-FACE COURAGE...

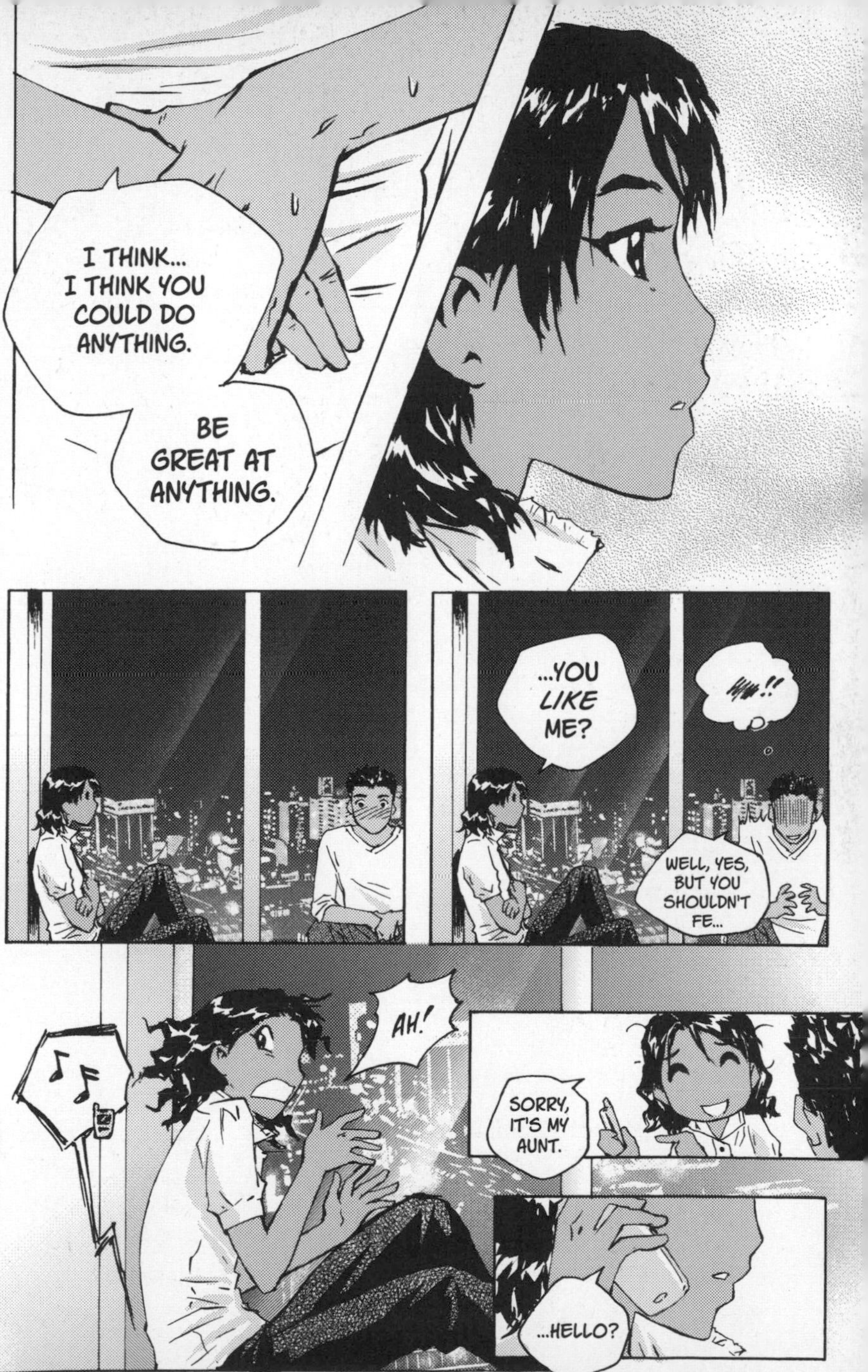
I THINK... I THINK YOU COULD DO ANYTHING.
BE GREAT AT ANYTHING.
...YOU LIKE ME?
WELL, YES, BUT YOU SHOULDN'T FE...
AH!
SORRY, IT'S MY AUNT.
...HELLO?

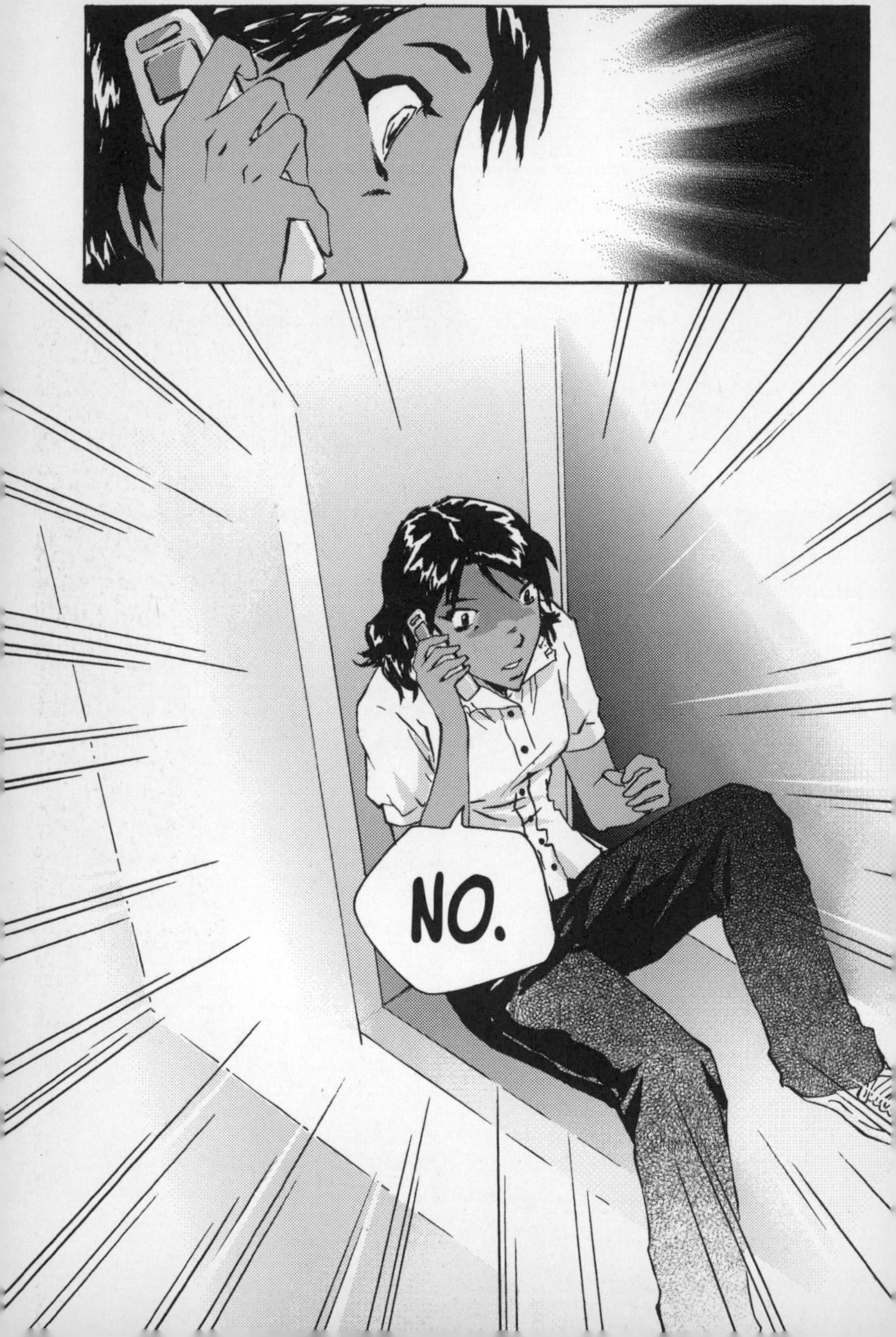
NO.

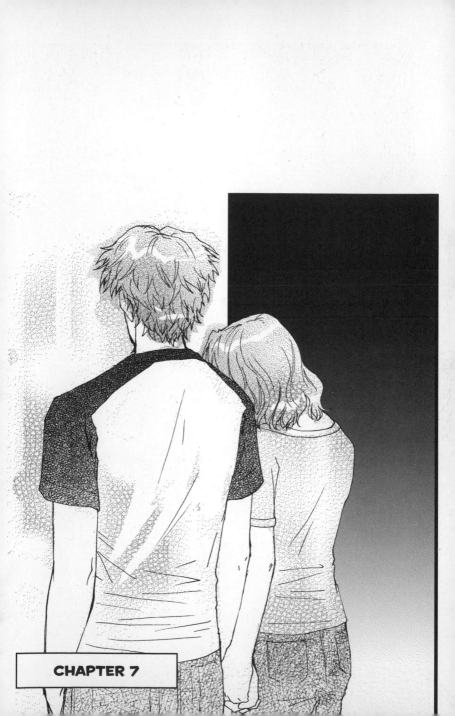

CHAPTER 7

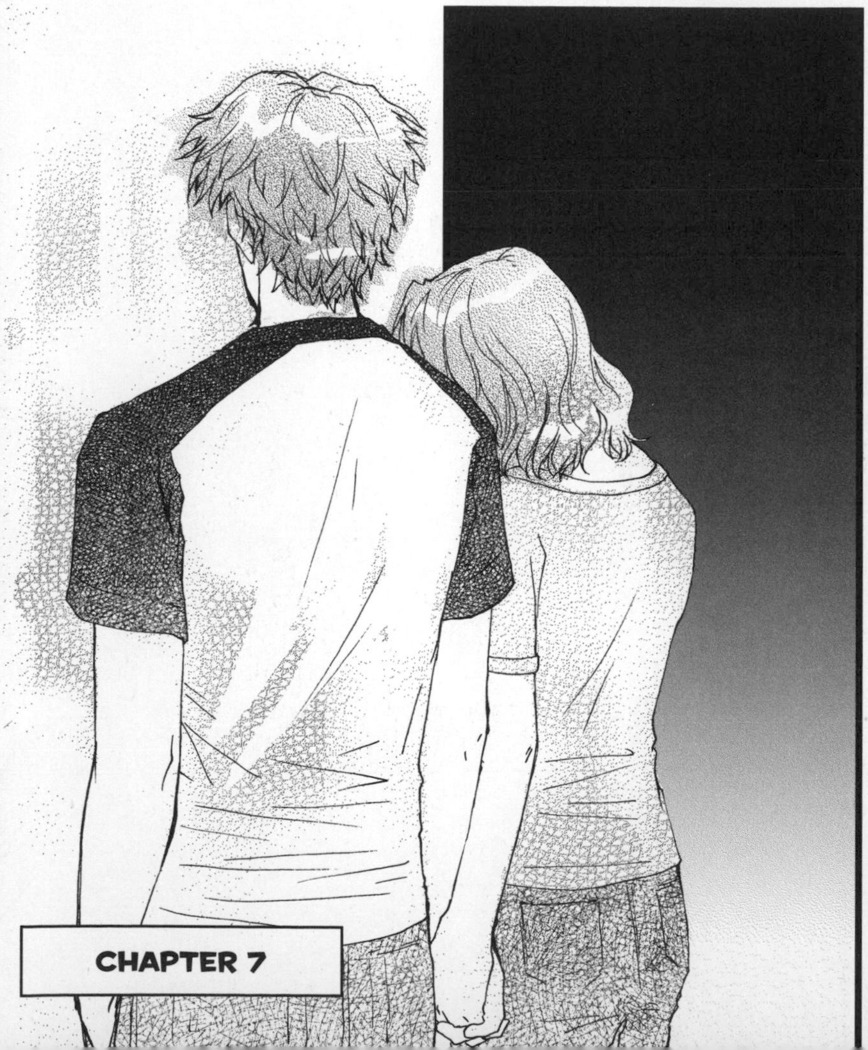

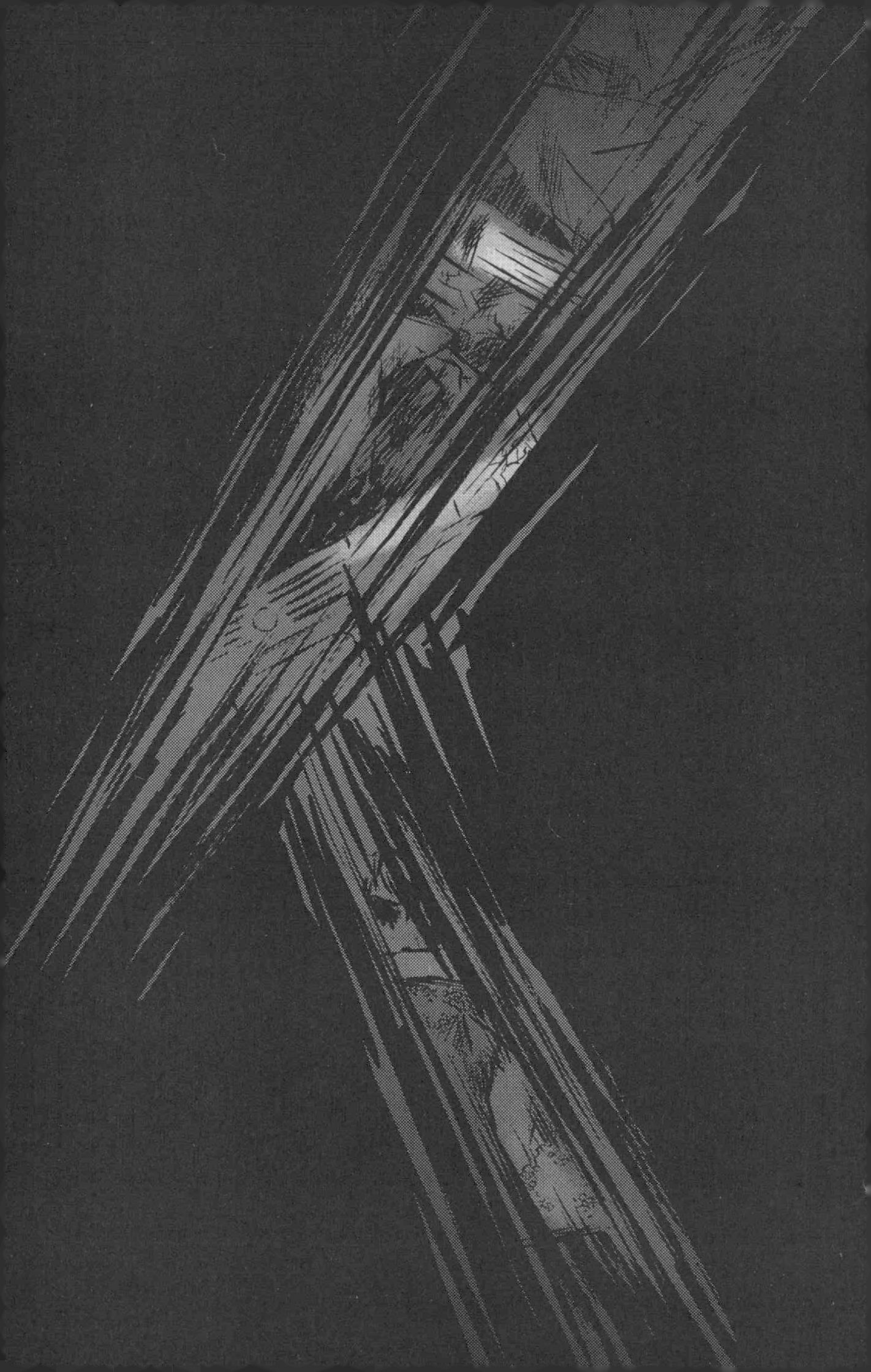

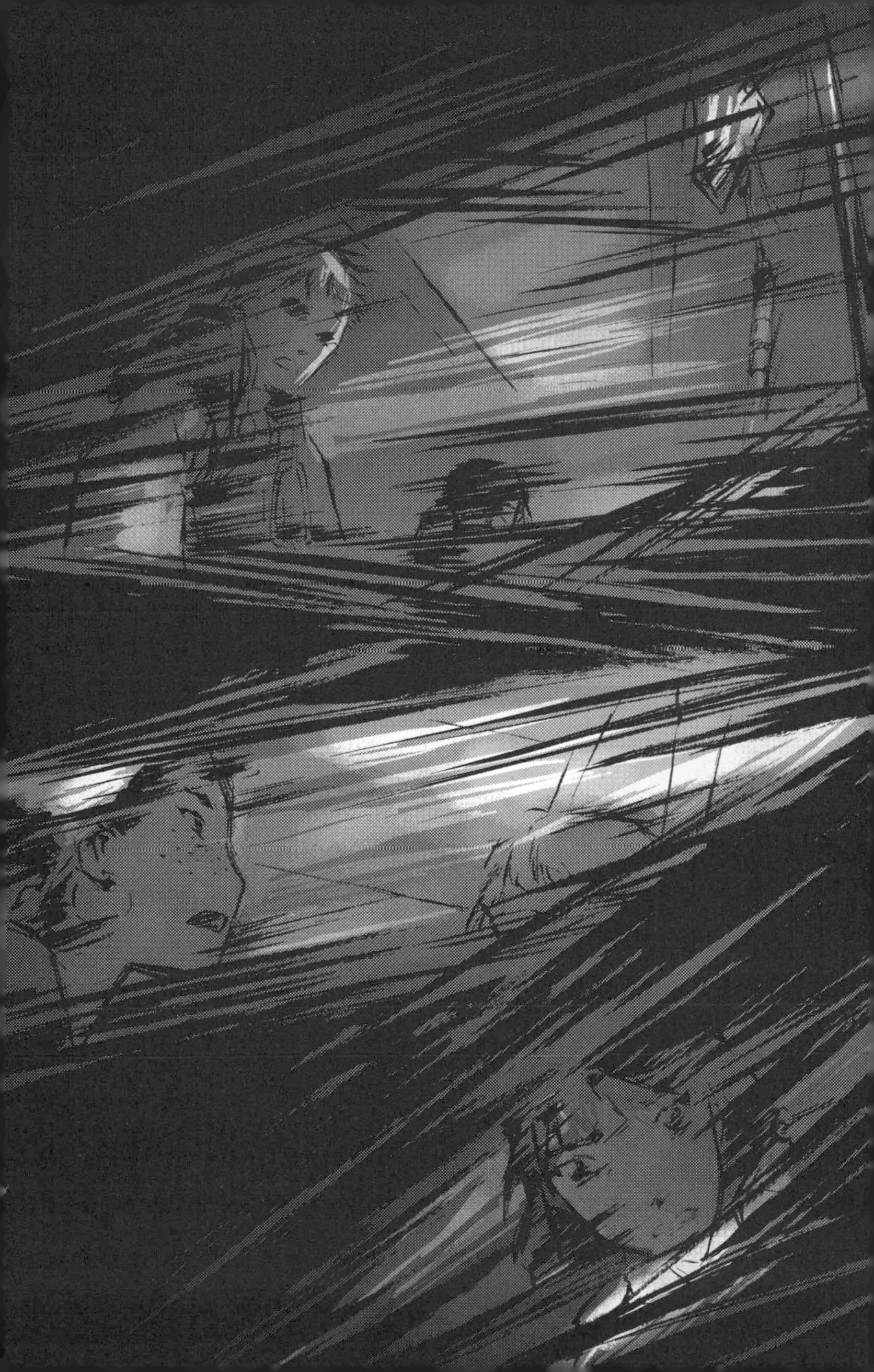

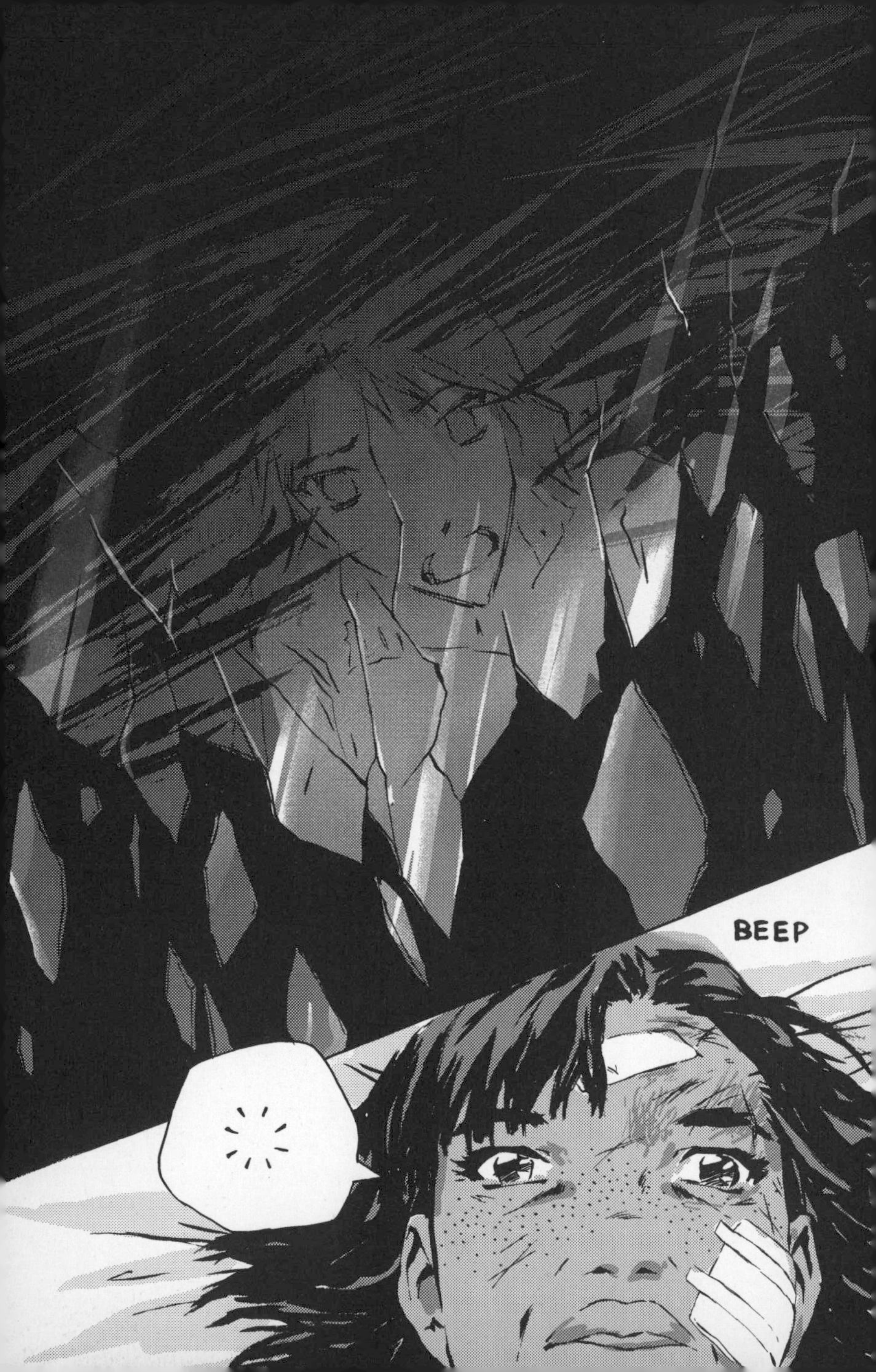
BEEP

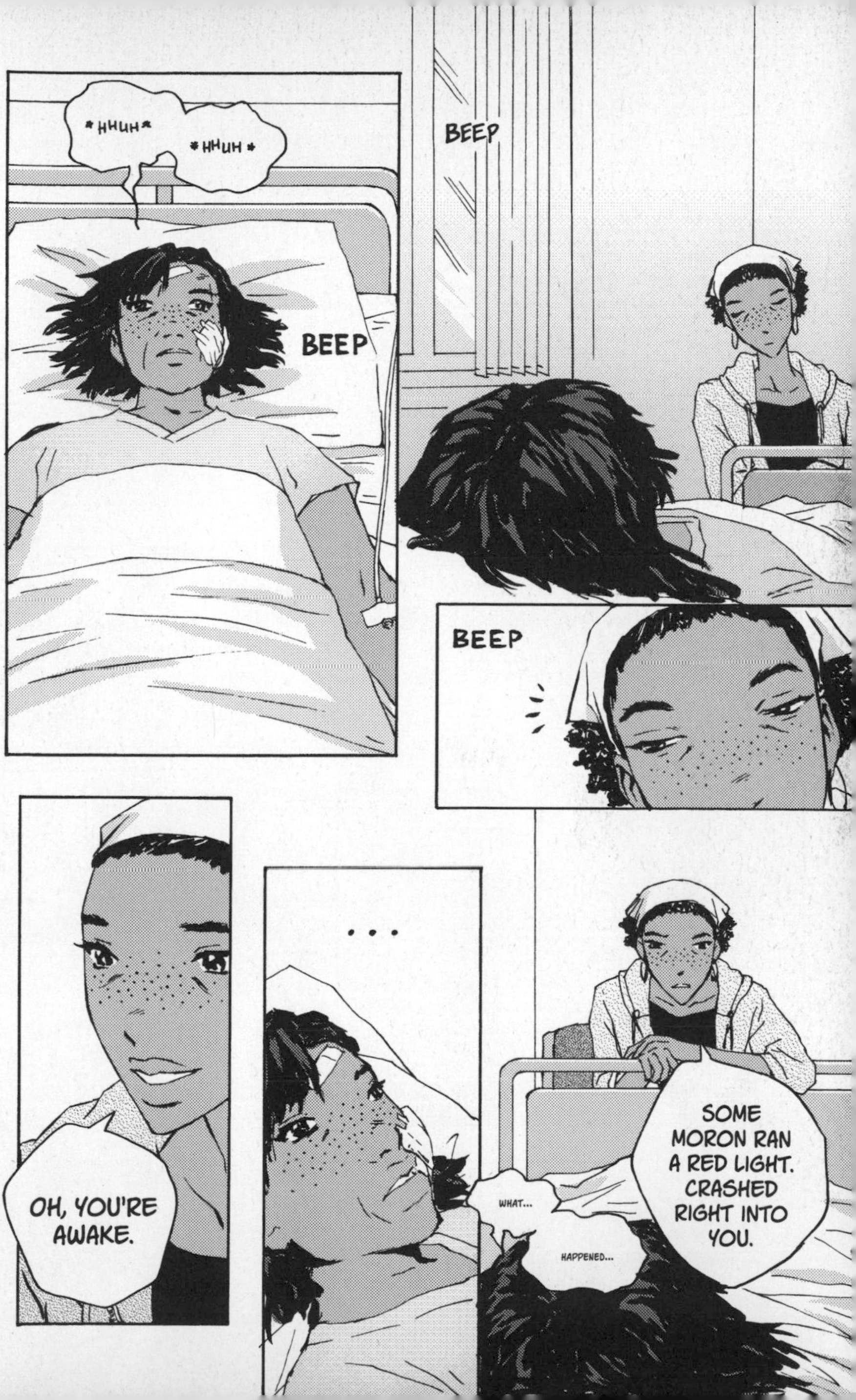
HHUH
HHUH
BEEP
BEEP
BEEP
OH, YOU'RE AWAKE.
...
WHAT...
HAPPENED...
SOME MORON RAN A RED LIGHT. CRASHED RIGHT INTO YOU.

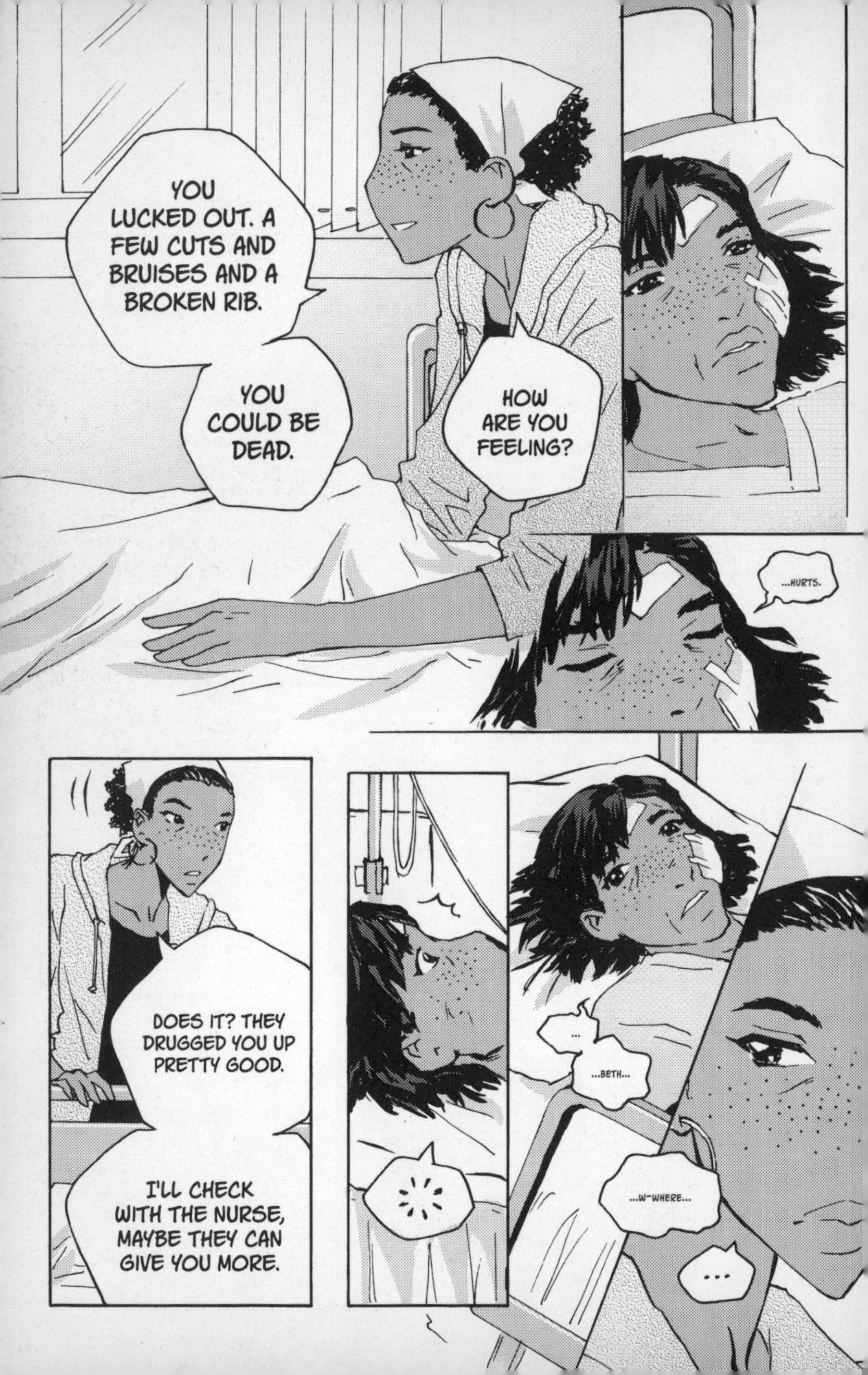
YOU LUCKED OUT. A FEW CUTS AND BRUISES AND A BROKEN RIB.
YOU COULD BE DEAD.
HOW ARE YOU FEELING?
...HURTS.
DOES IT? THEY DRUGGED YOU UP PRETTY GOOD.
I'LL CHECK WITH THE NURSE, MAYBE THEY CAN GIVE YOU MORE.
...
...BETH...
...W-WHERE...
...

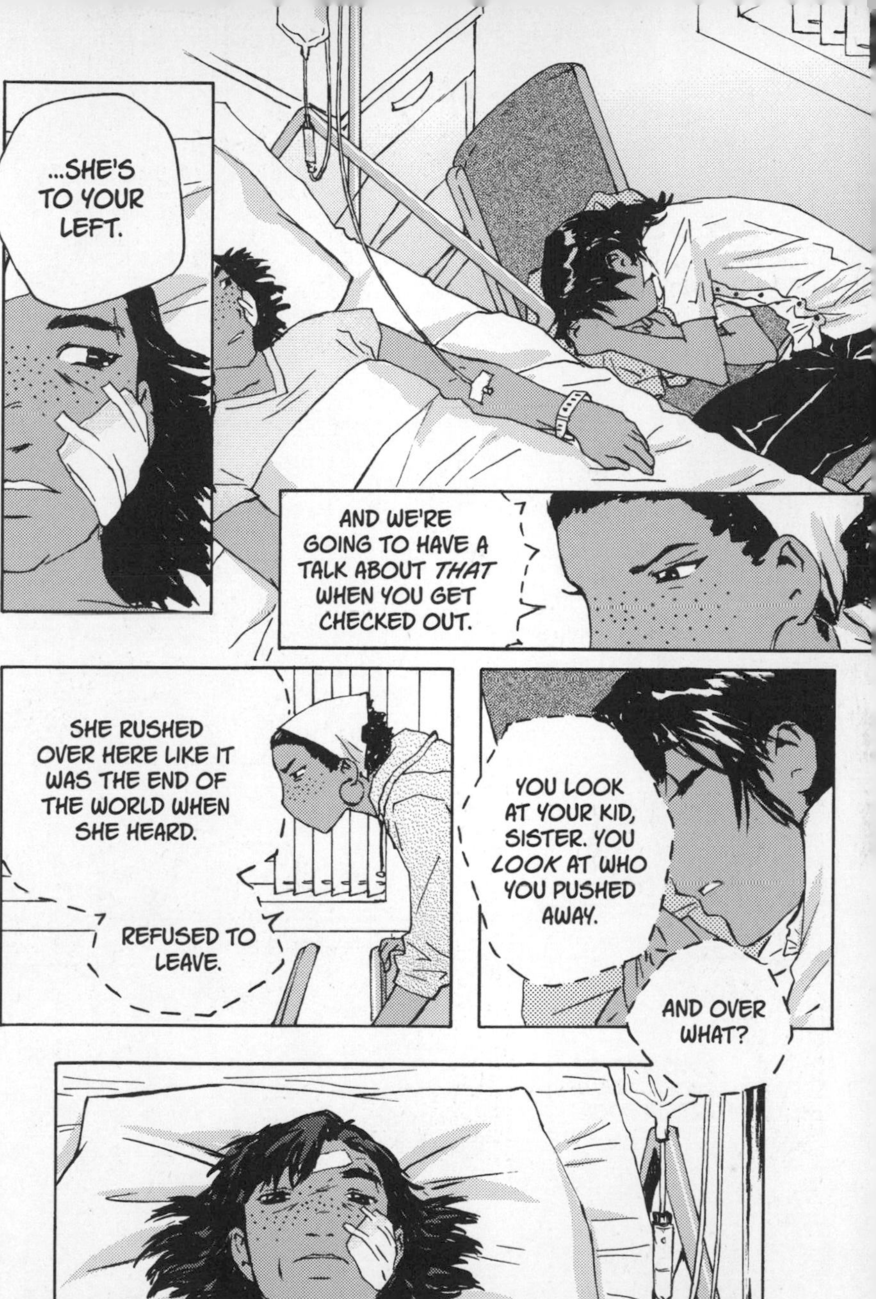
...SHE'S TO YOUR LEFT.
AND WE'RE GOING TO HAVE A TALK ABOUT *THAT* WHEN YOU GET CHECKED OUT.
SHE RUSHED OVER HERE LIKE IT WAS THE END OF THE WORLD WHEN SHE HEARD.
REFUSED TO LEAVE.
YOU LOOK AT YOUR KID, SISTER. YOU *LOOK* AT WHO YOU PUSHED AWAY.
AND OVER WHAT?

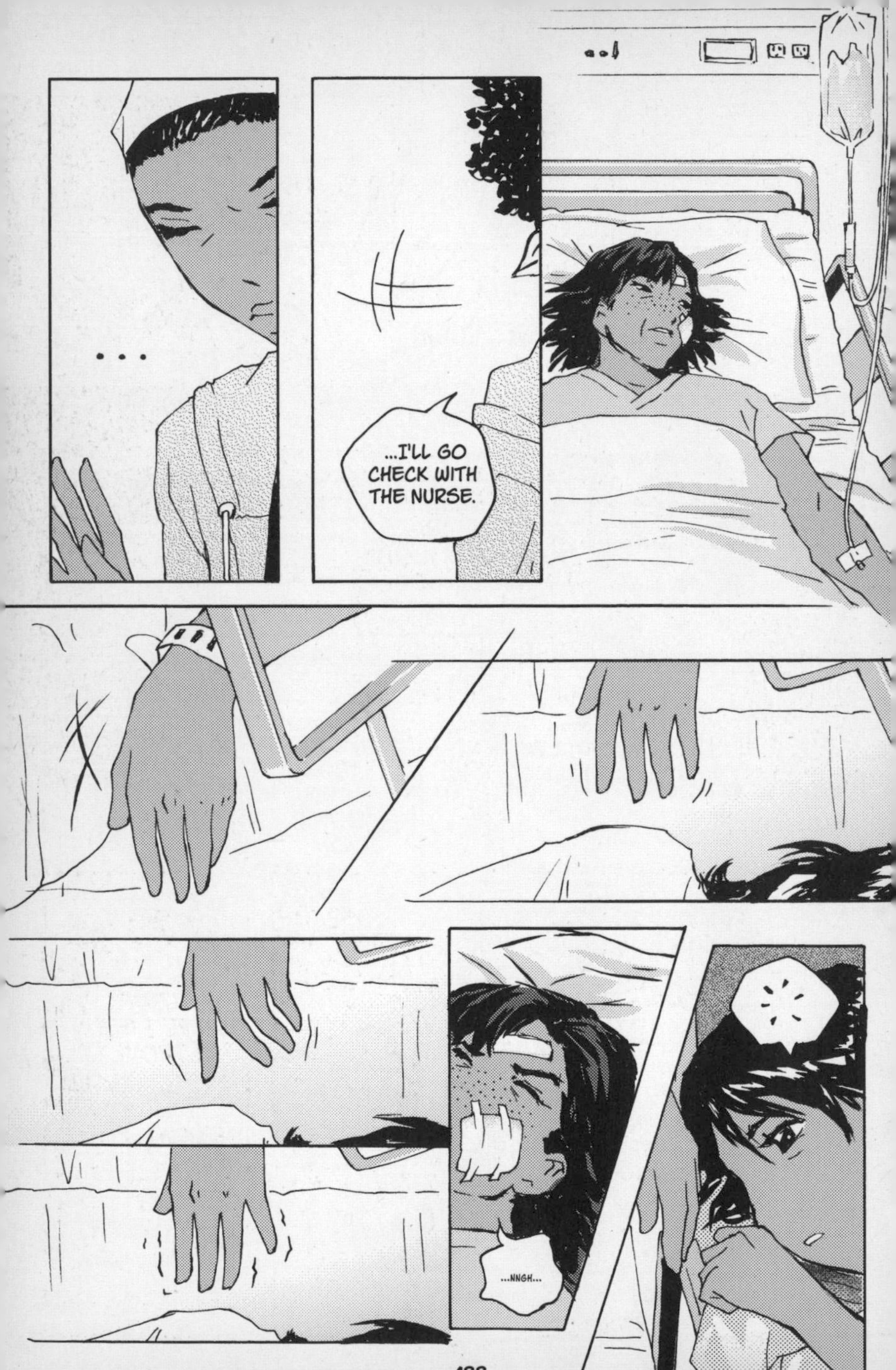
...
...I'LL GO CHECK WITH THE NURSE.
...NNGH...

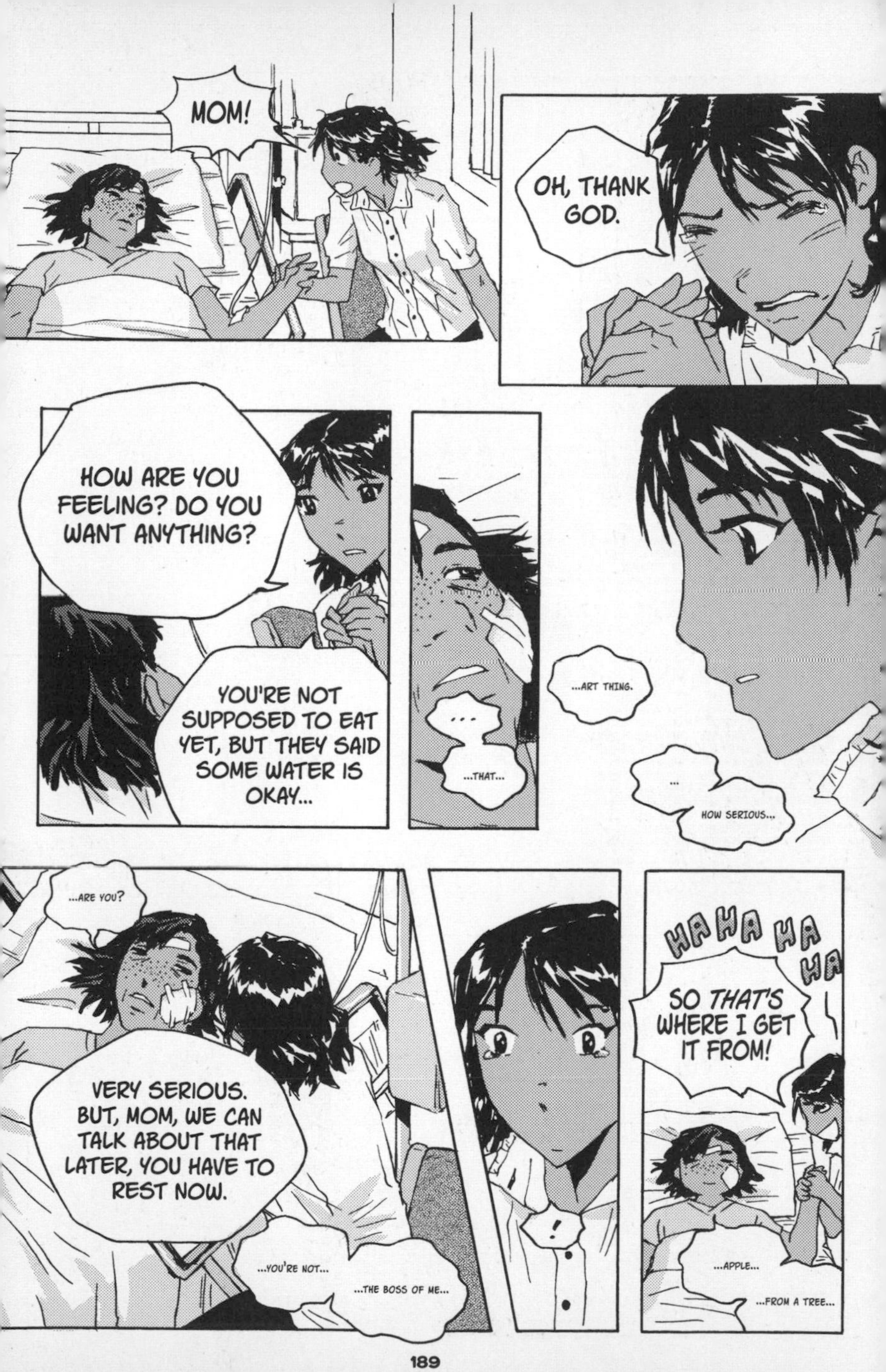
MOM!
OH, THANK GOD.
HOW ARE YOU FEELING? DO YOU WANT ANYTHING?
YOU'RE NOT SUPPOSED TO EAT YET, BUT THEY SAID SOME WATER IS OKAY...
...
...THAT...
...ART THING.
...
HOW SERIOUS...
...ARE YOU?
VERY SERIOUS. BUT, MOM, WE CAN TALK ABOUT THAT LATER, YOU HAVE TO REST NOW.
...YOU'RE NOT...
...THE BOSS OF ME...
!
HA HA HA HA HA
SO THAT'S WHERE I GET IT FROM!
...APPLE...
...FROM A TREE...

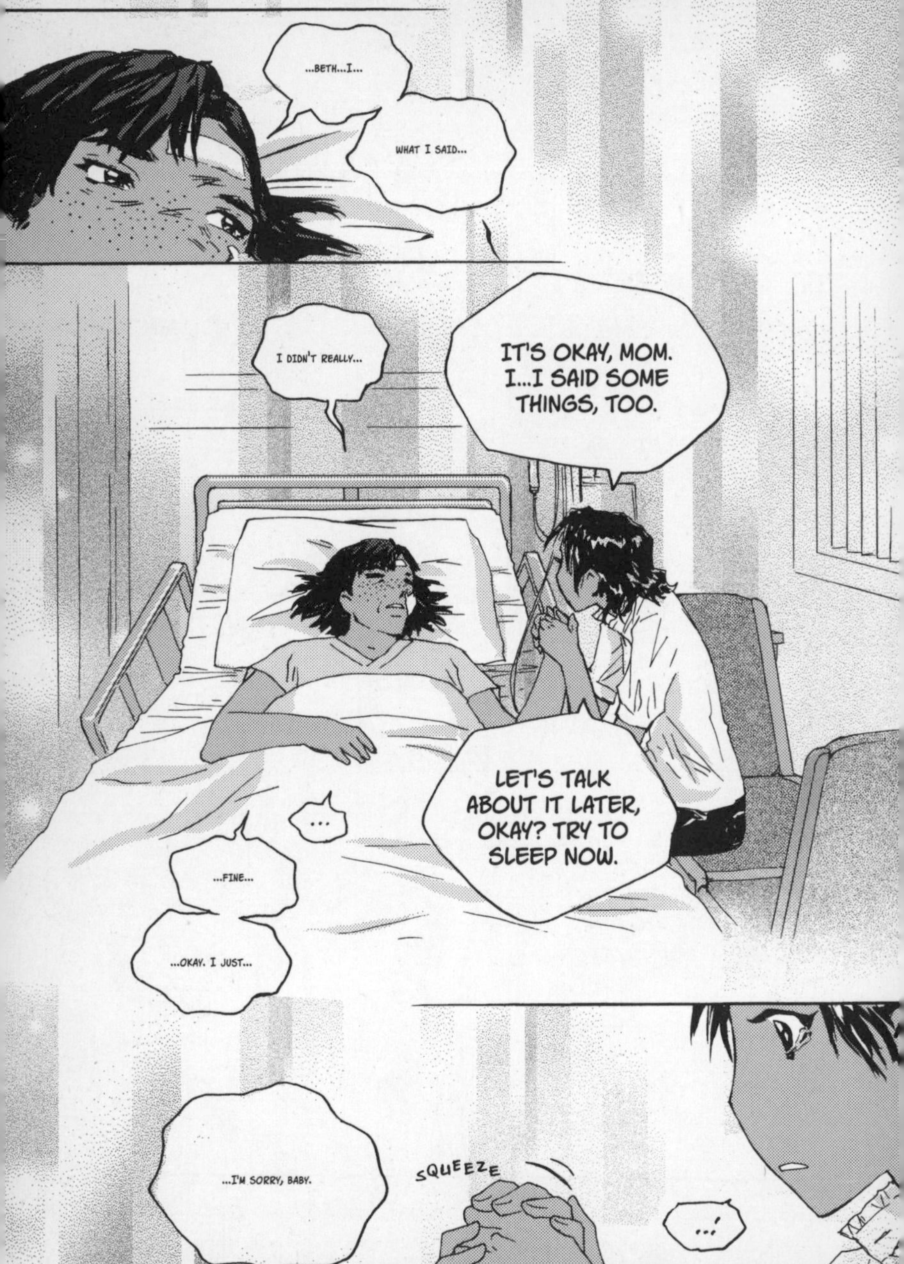
...BETH...I...
WHAT I SAID...
I DIDN'T REALLY...
IT'S OKAY, MOM. I...I SAID SOME THINGS, TOO.
LET'S TALK ABOUT IT LATER, OKAY? TRY TO SLEEP NOW.
...
...FINE...
...OKAY. I JUST...
...I'M SORRY, BABY.
SQUEEZE
...!

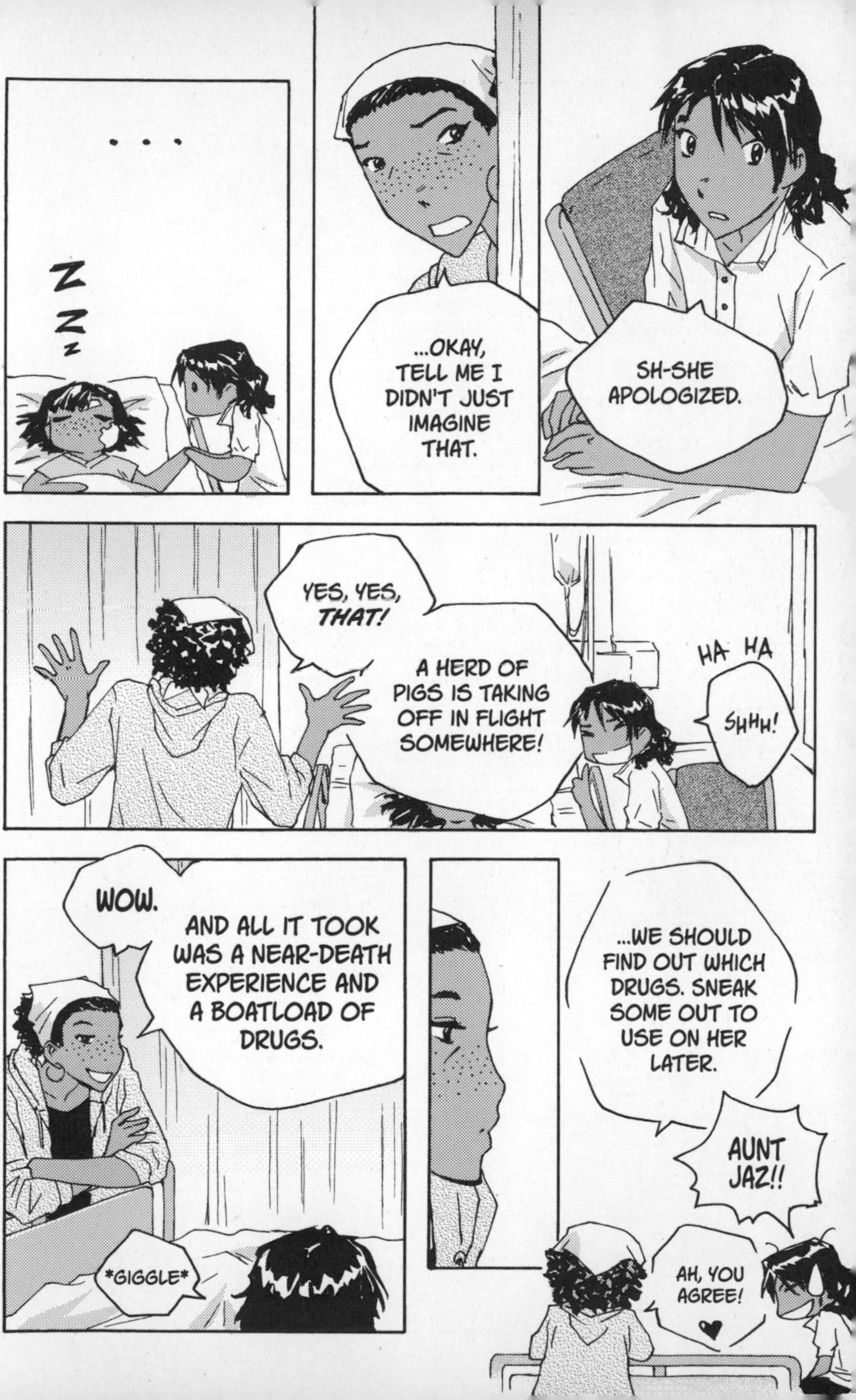
. . .
Z Z z
...OKAY, TELL ME I DIDN'T JUST IMAGINE THAT.
SH-SHE APOLOGIZED.
YES, YES, *THAT!*
A HERD OF PIGS IS TAKING OFF IN FLIGHT SOMEWHERE!
HA HA
SHHH!
WOW.
AND ALL IT TOOK WAS A NEAR-DEATH EXPERIENCE AND A BOATLOAD OF DRUGS.
GIGGLE
...WE SHOULD FIND OUT WHICH DRUGS. SNEAK SOME OUT TO USE ON HER LATER.
AUNT JAZ!!
AH, YOU AGREE!

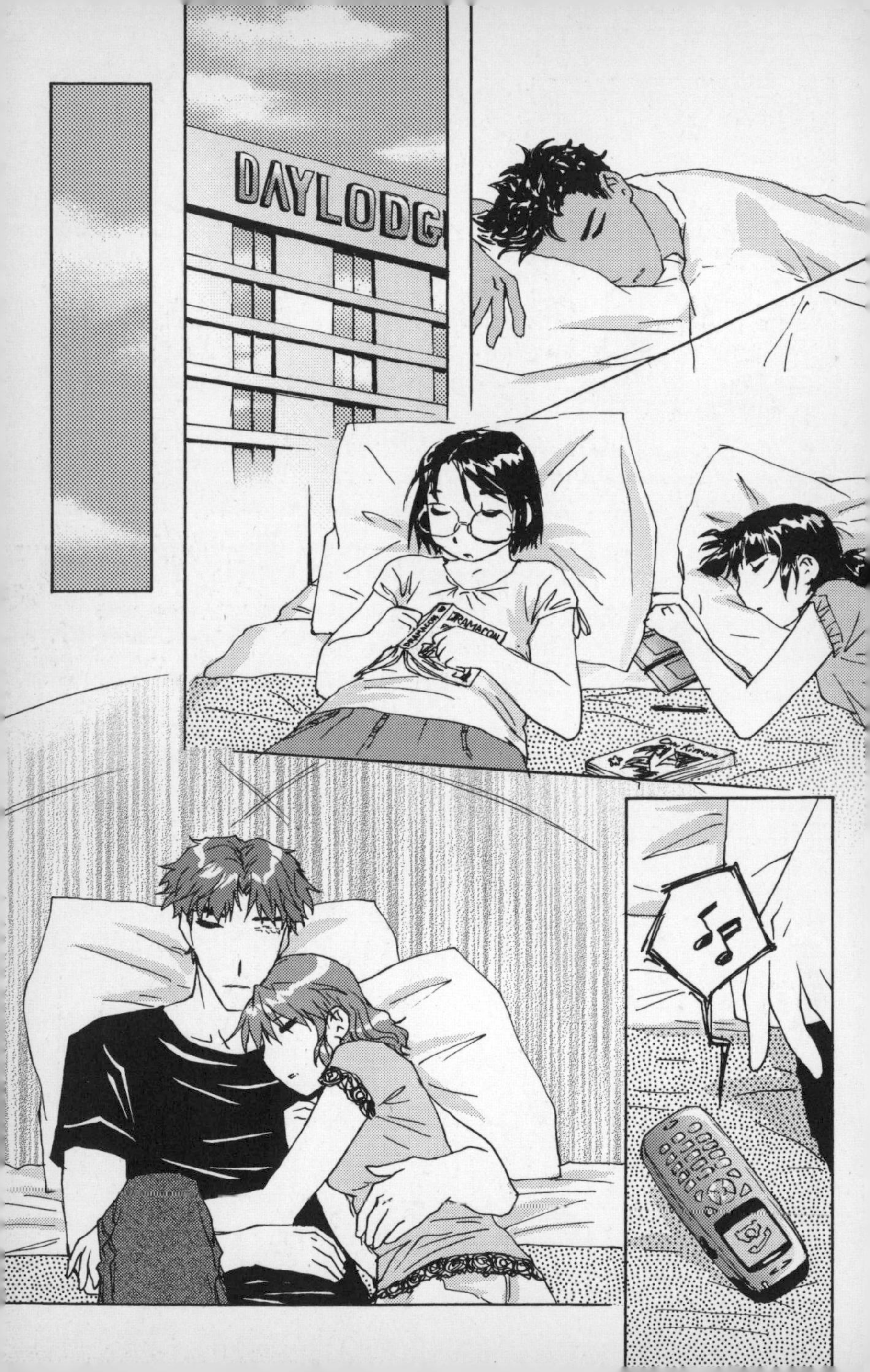
DAYLODG
DRAMACON

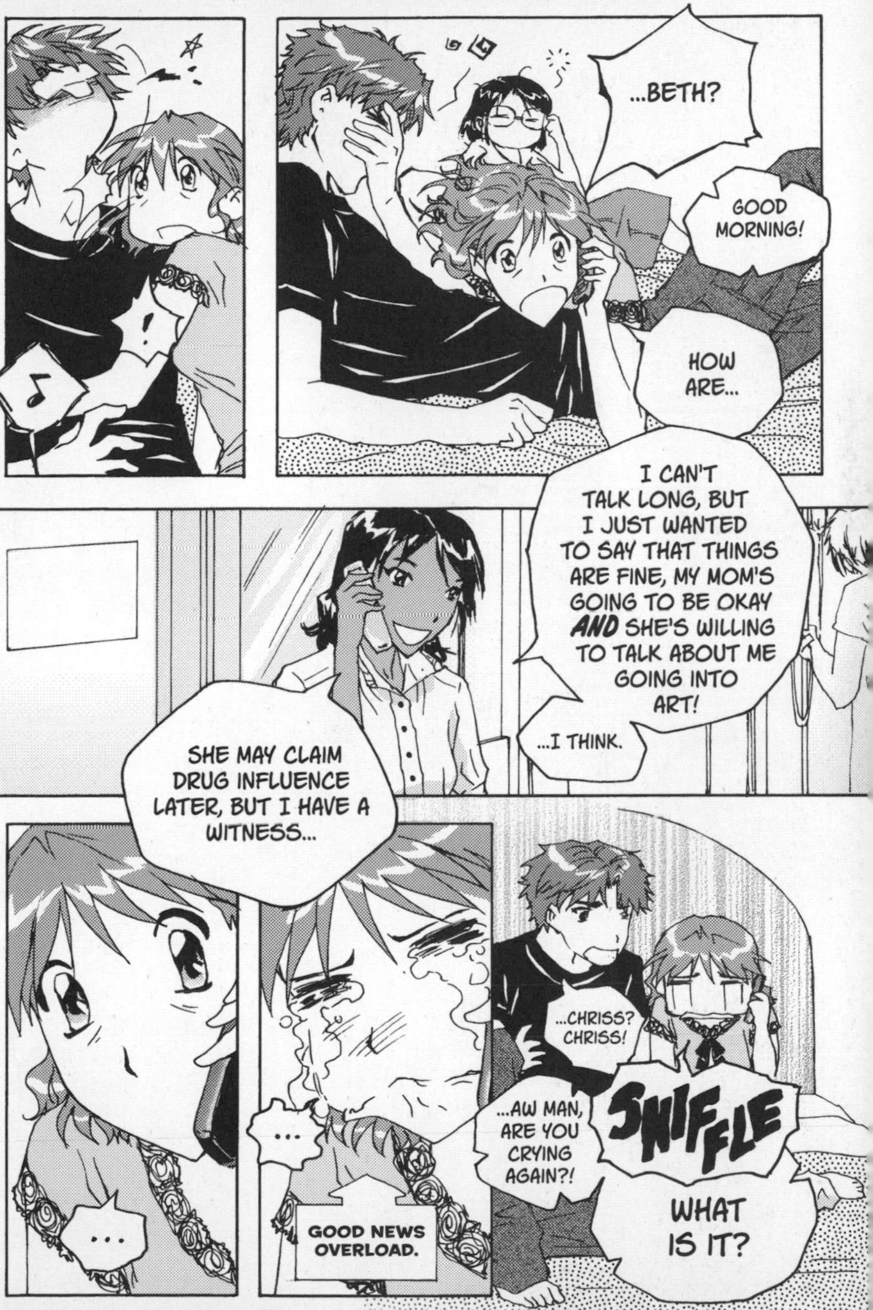
...BETH?
GOOD MORNING!
HOW ARE...
I CAN'T TALK LONG, BUT I JUST WANTED TO SAY THAT THINGS ARE FINE, MY MOM'S GOING TO BE OKAY AND SHE'S WILLING TO TALK ABOUT ME GOING INTO ART!
...I THINK.
SHE MAY CLAIM DRUG INFLUENCE LATER, BUT I HAVE A WITNESS...
...
...
GOOD NEWS OVERLOAD.
...CHRISS? CHRISS!
...AW MAN, ARE YOU CRYING AGAIN?!
SNIFFLE
WHAT IS IT?

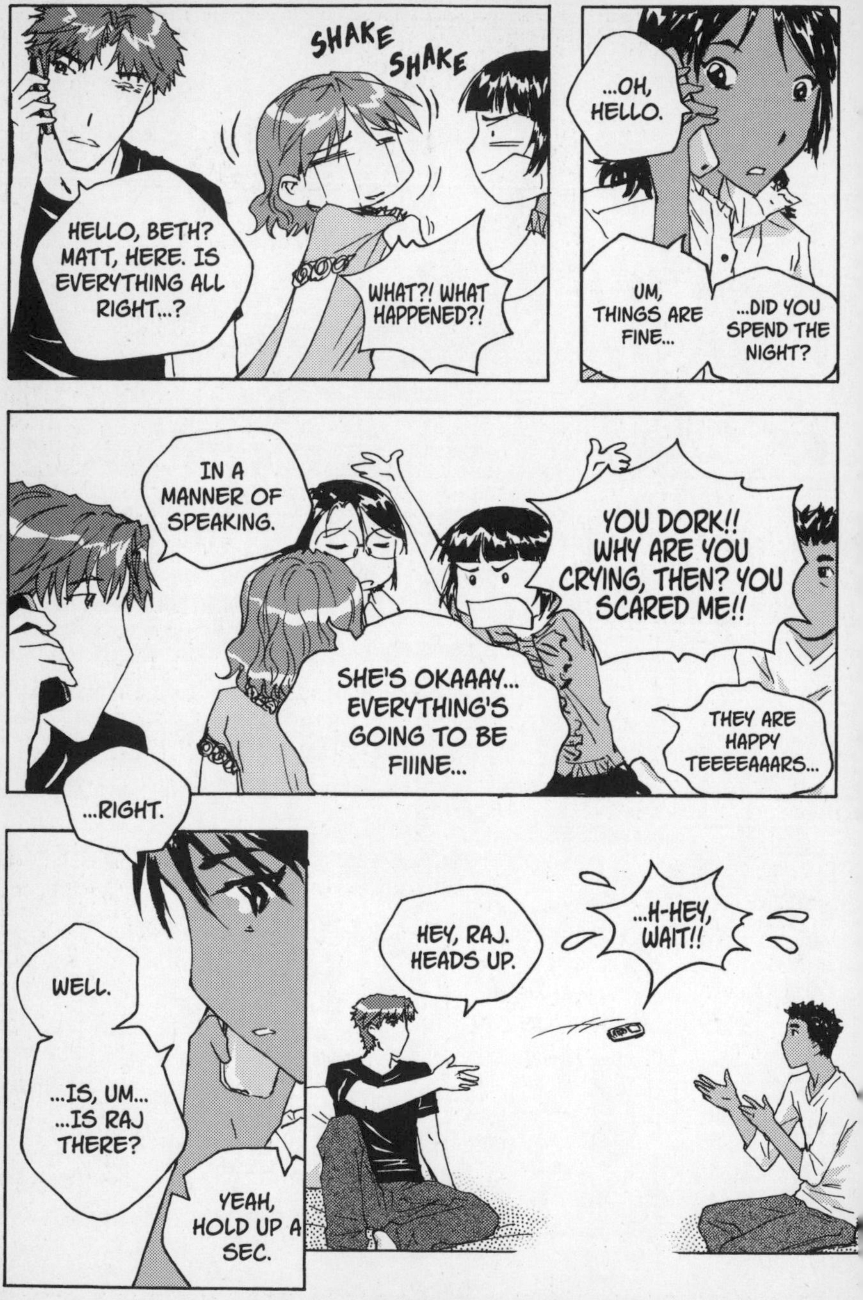
SHAKE SHAKE
HELLO, BETH? MATT, HERE. IS EVERYTHING ALL RIGHT...?
WHAT?! WHAT HAPPENED?!
...OH, HELLO.
UM, THINGS ARE FINE...
...DID YOU SPEND THE NIGHT?
IN A MANNER OF SPEAKING.
YOU DORK!! WHY ARE YOU CRYING, THEN? YOU SCARED ME!!
SHE'S OKAAAY... EVERYTHING'S GOING TO BE FIIINE...
THEY ARE HAPPY TEEEEAAARS...
...RIGHT.
WELL.
...IS, UM... ...IS RAJ THERE?
YEAH, HOLD UP A SEC.
HEY, RAJ. HEADS UP.
...H-HEY, WAIT!!

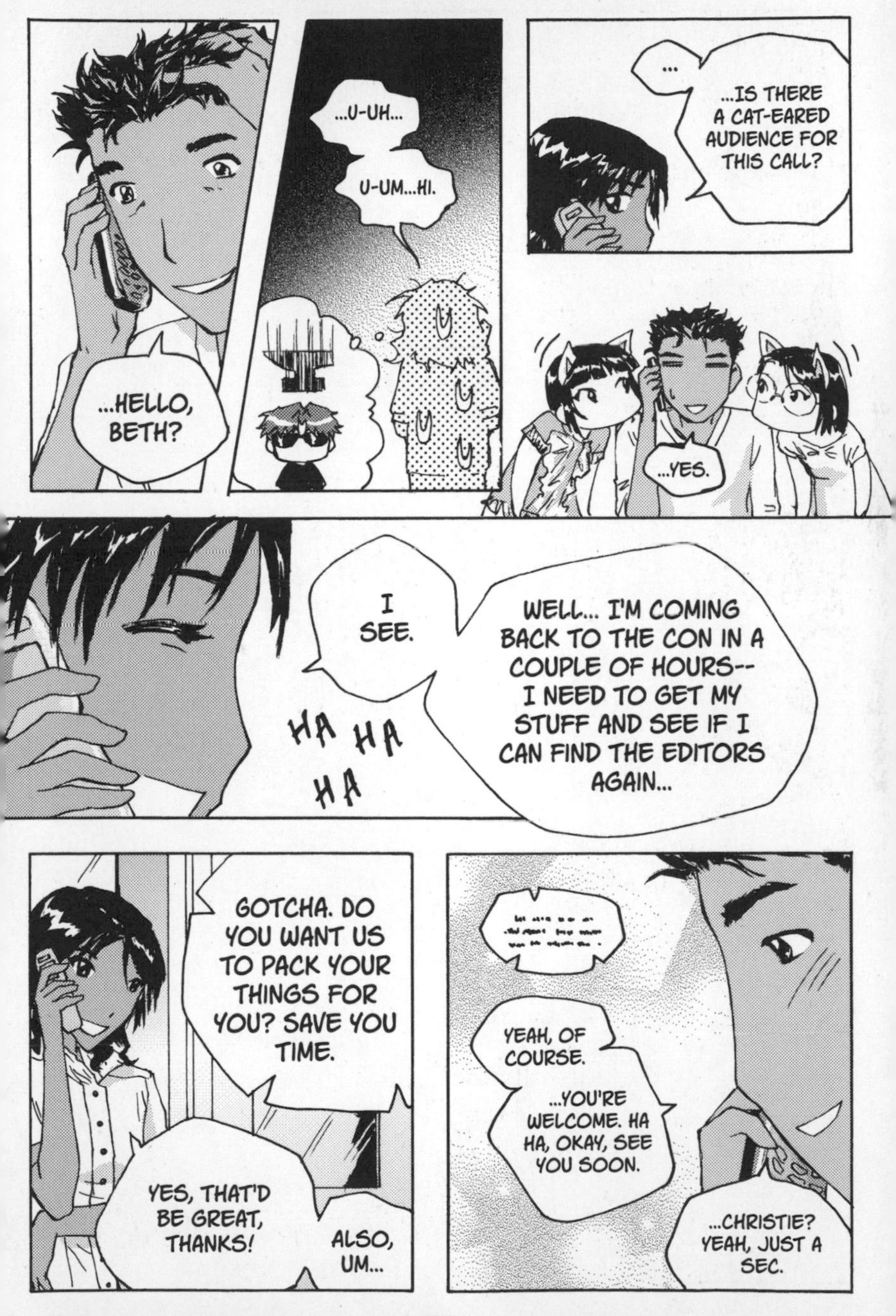
...HELLO, BETH?
...U-UH...
U-UM...HI.
...
...IS THERE A CAT-EARED AUDIENCE FOR THIS CALL?
...YES.
I SEE.
HA HA HA
WELL... I'M COMING BACK TO THE CON IN A COUPLE OF HOURS-- I NEED TO GET MY STUFF AND SEE IF I CAN FIND THE EDITORS AGAIN...
GOTCHA. DO YOU WANT US TO PACK YOUR THINGS FOR YOU? SAVE YOU TIME.
YES, THAT'D BE GREAT, THANKS!
ALSO, UM...
YEAH, OF COURSE.
...YOU'RE WELCOME. HA HA, OKAY, SEE YOU SOON.
...CHRISTIE? YEAH, JUST A SEC.

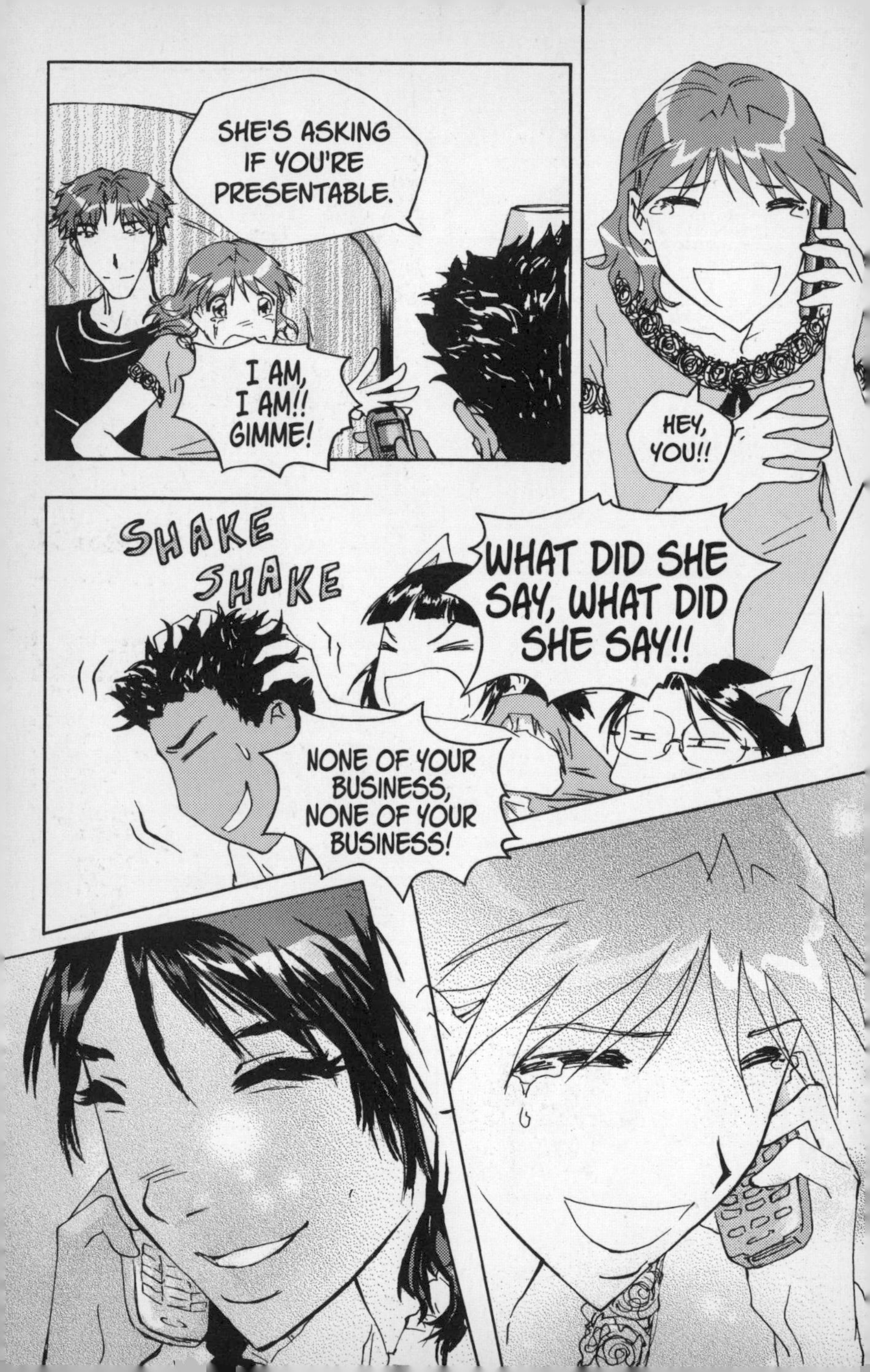
SHE'S ASKING IF YOU'RE PRESENTABLE.
I AM, I AM!! GIMME!
HEY, YOU!!
SHAKE SHAKE
WHAT DID SHE SAY, WHAT DID SHE SAY!!
NONE OF YOUR BUSINESS, NONE OF YOUR BUSINESS!

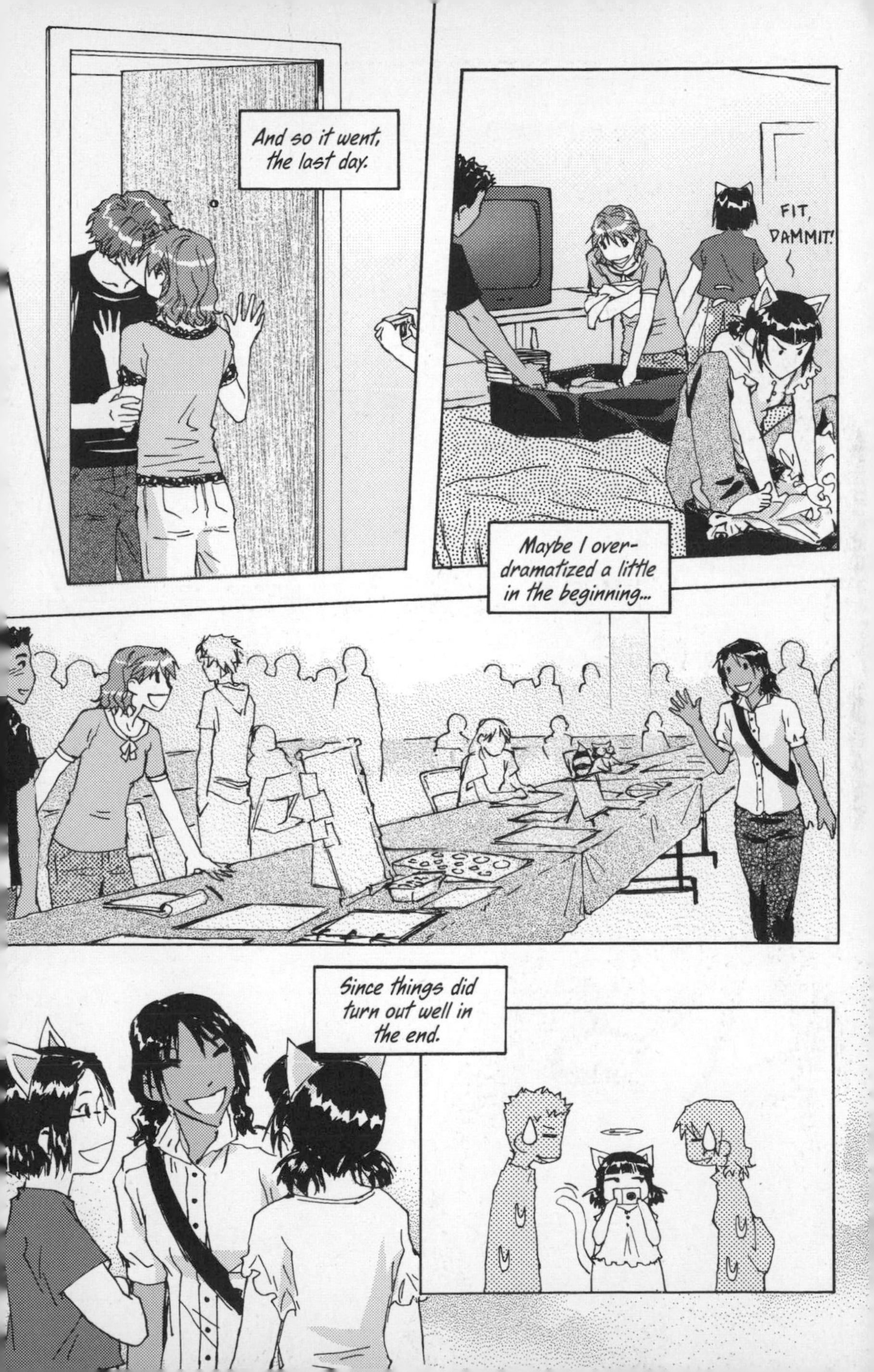
And so it went, the last day.
FIT, DAMMIT!
Maybe I over-dramatized a little in the beginning...
Since things did turn out well in the end.

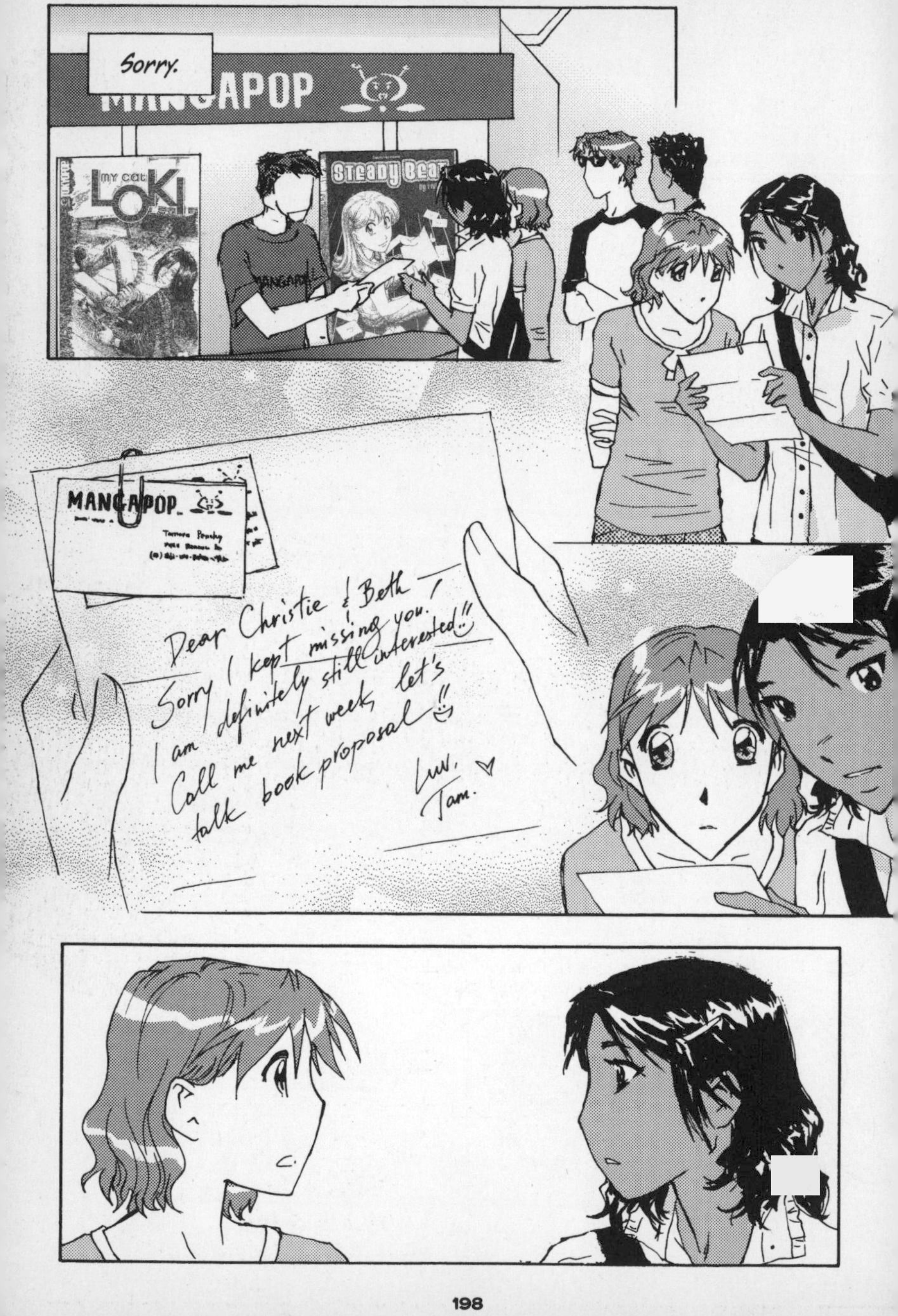
Sorry.
MANGAPOP
MY CAT LOKI
STEADY BEAT
MANGAPOP
Dear Christie & Beth
Sorry I kept missing you!
I am definitely still interested!!
Call me next week, let's
talk book proposal!!
Luv,
Tam.

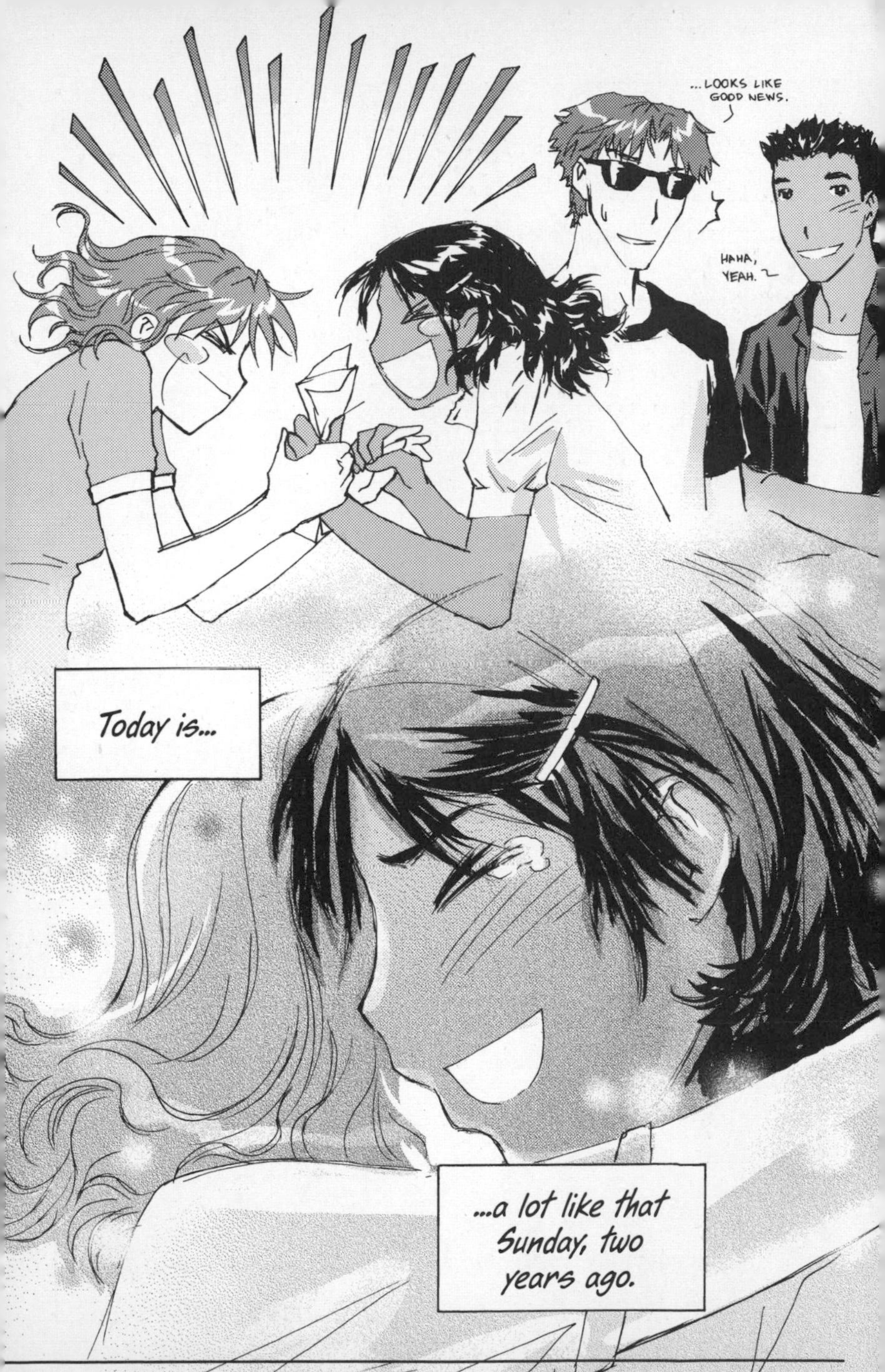
...LOOKS LIKE GOOD NEWS.
HAHA, YEAH.
Today is...
...a lot like that Sunday, two years ago.

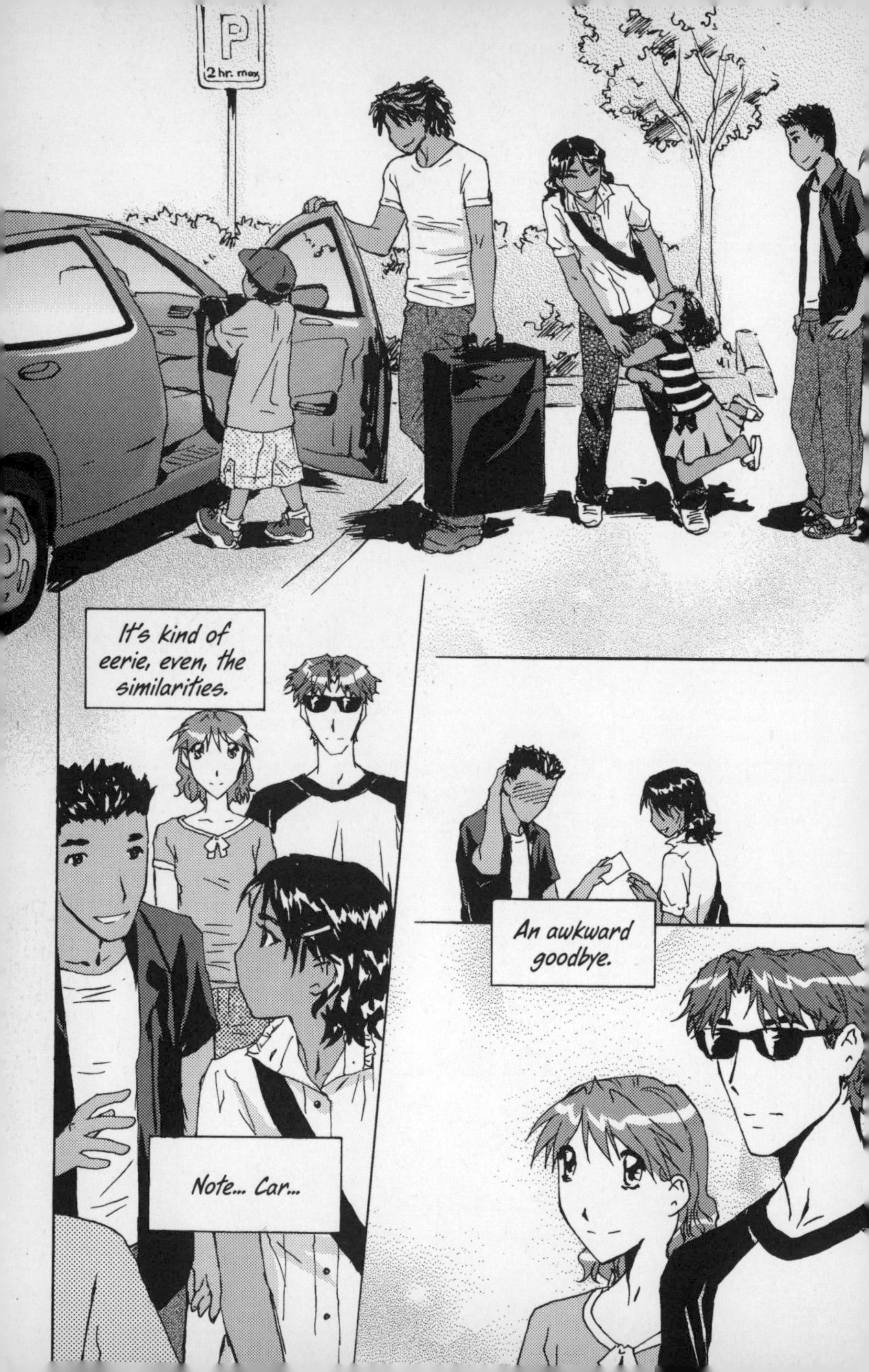
P
2 hr. max
It's kind of eerie, even, the similarities.
Note... Car...
An awkward goodbye.

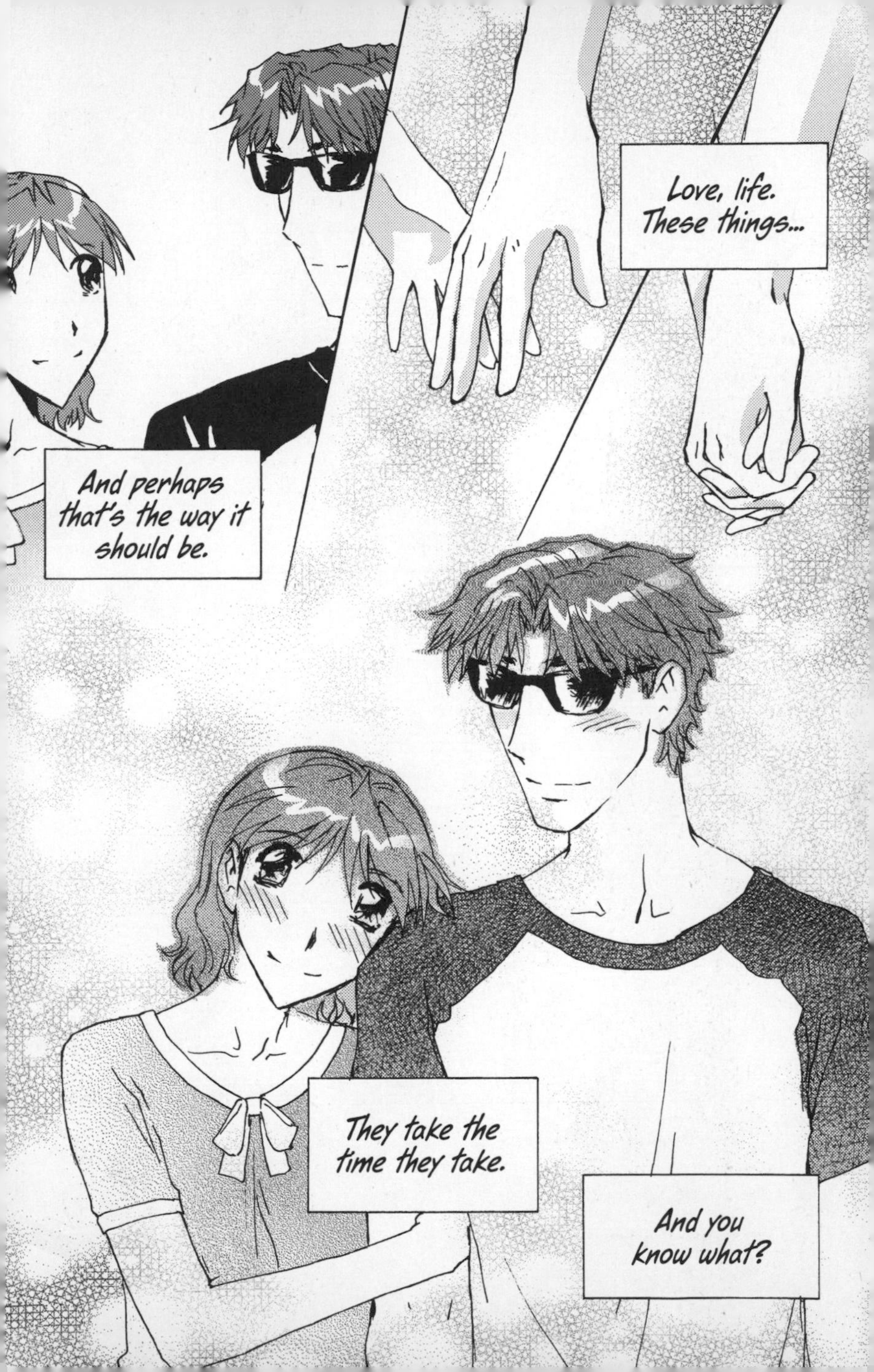
And perhaps that's the way it should be.
Love, life. These things...
They take the time they take.
And you know what?

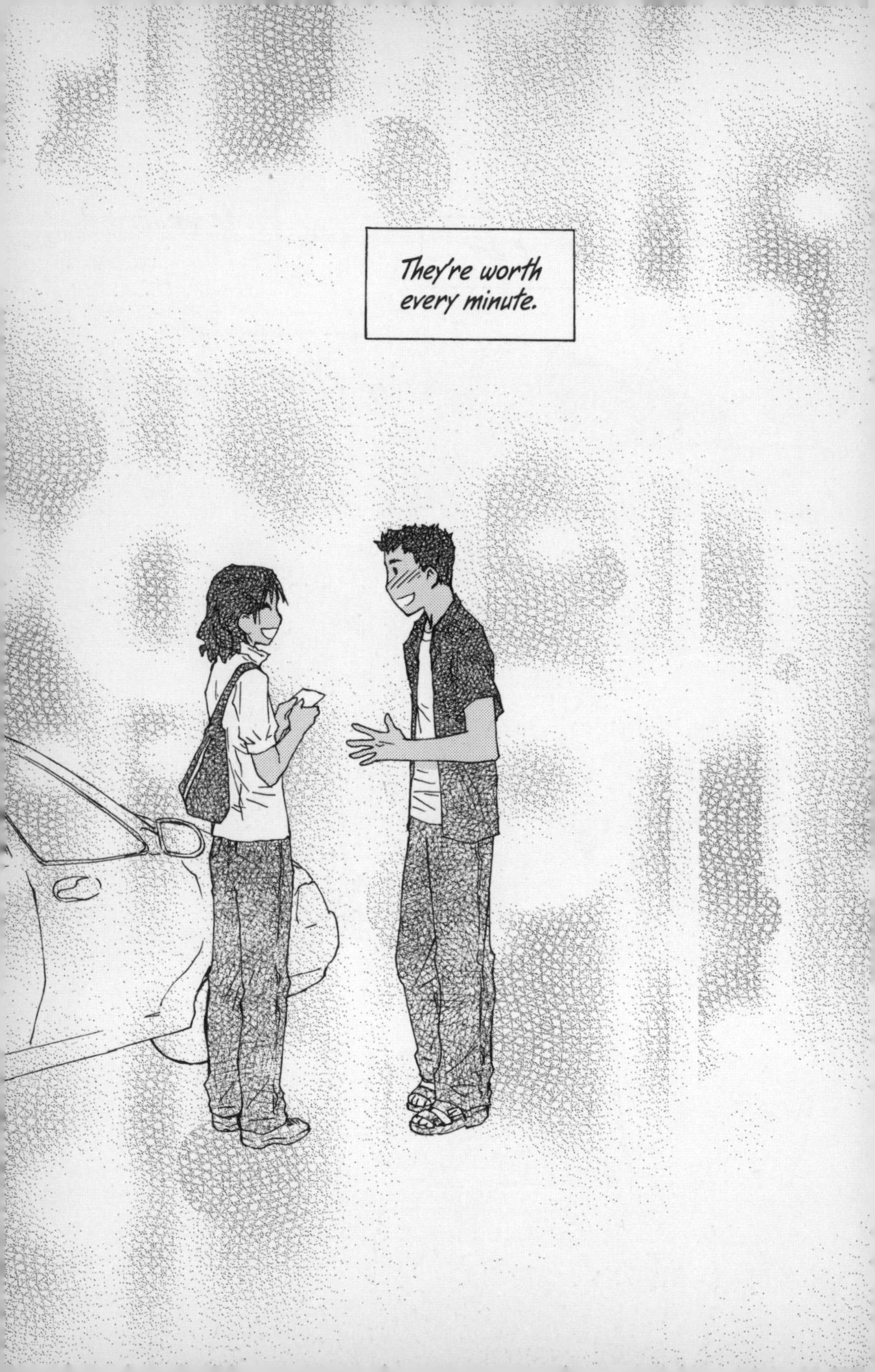
They're worth every minute.

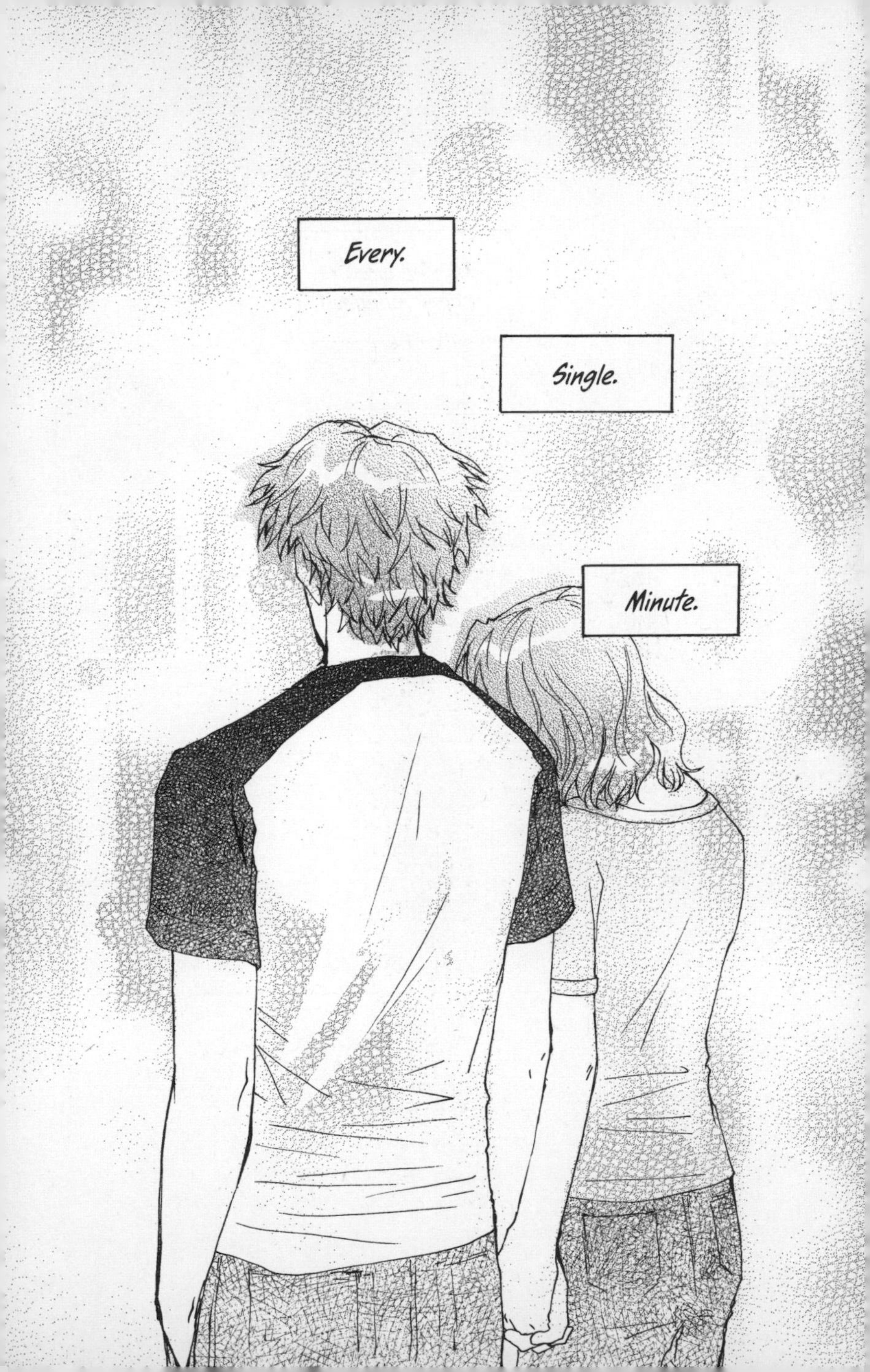
Every.
Single.
Minute.

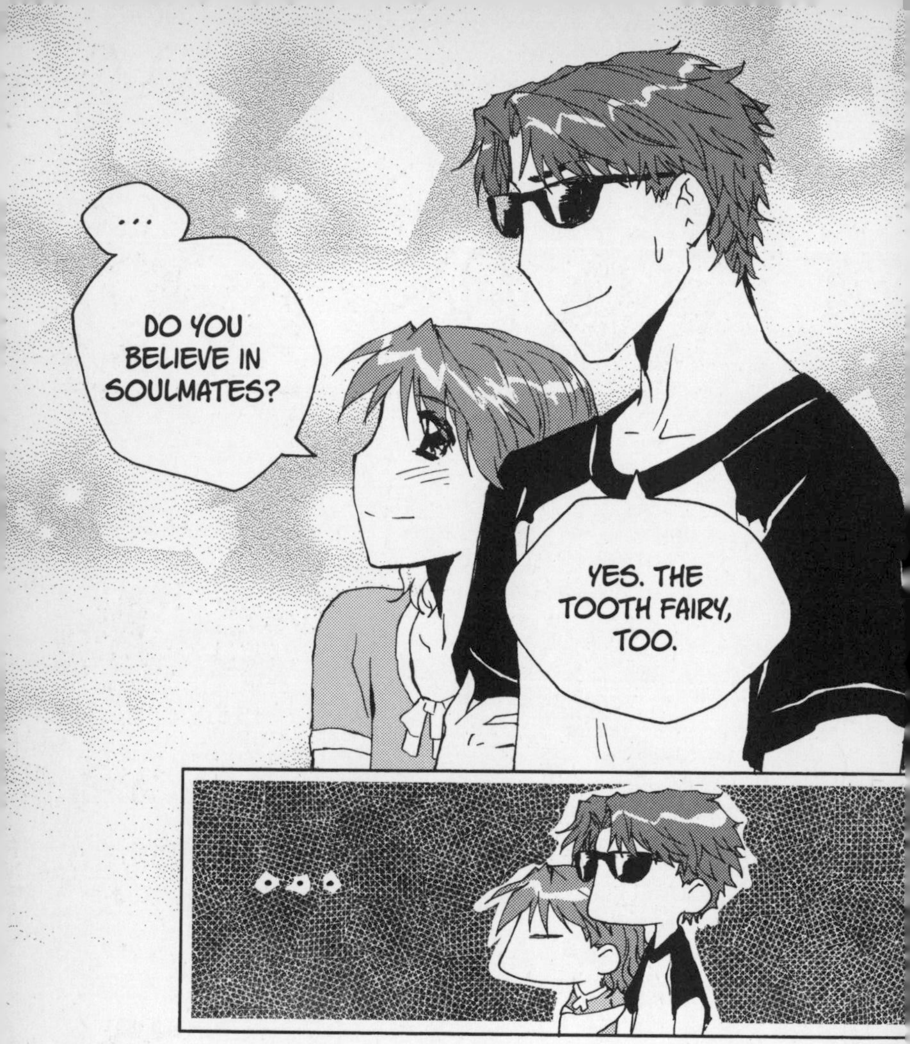
...
DO YOU BELIEVE IN SOULMATES?
YES. THE TOOTH FAIRY, TOO.
...

...Let me revise that.

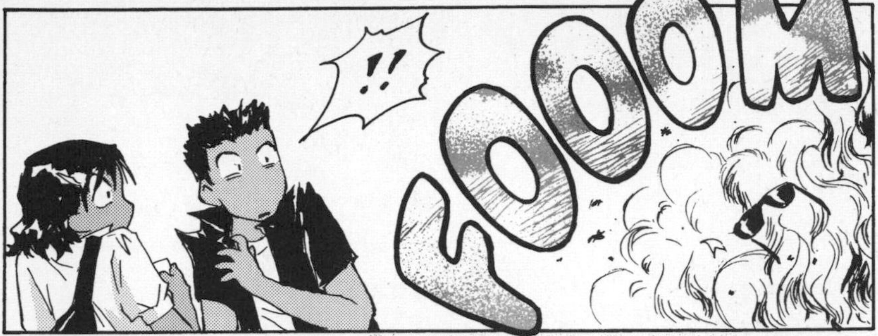
!!
FOOOOM

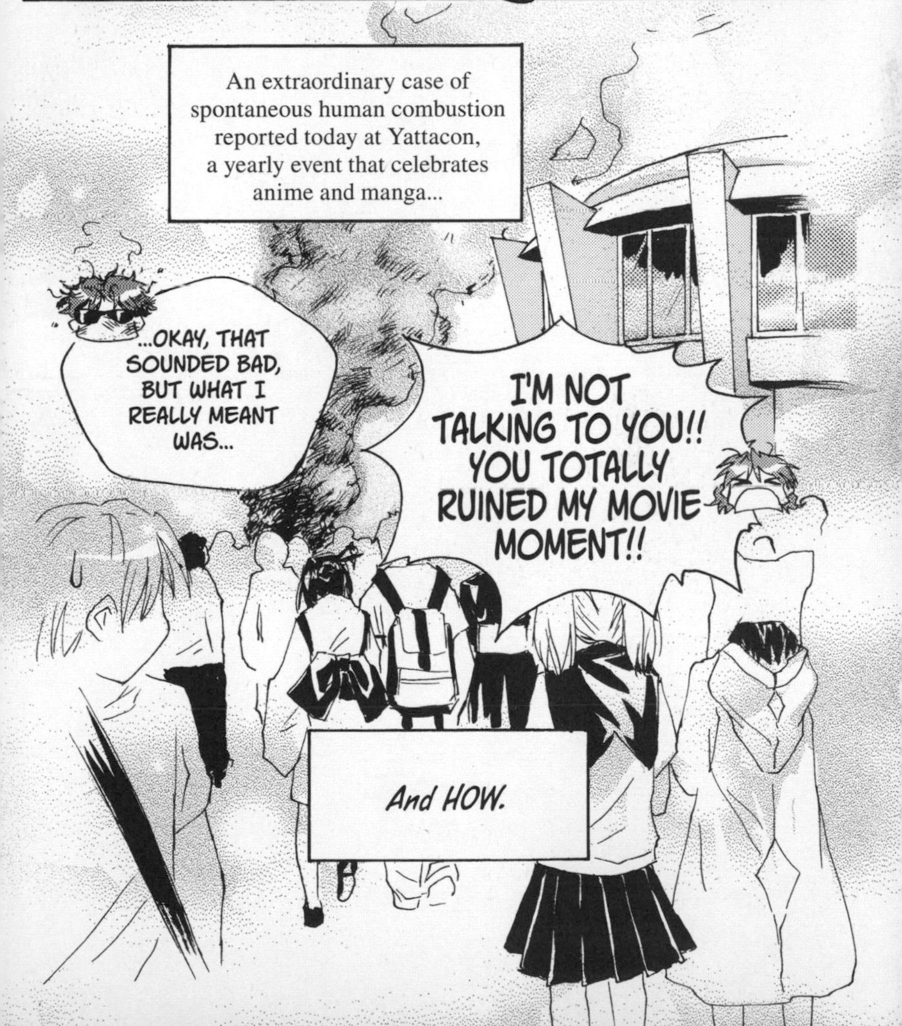
An extraordinary case of spontaneous human combustion reported today at Yattacon, a yearly event that celebrates anime and manga...
...OKAY, THAT SOUNDED BAD, BUT WHAT I REALLY MEANT WAS...
I'M NOT TALKING TO YOU!! YOU TOTALLY RUINED MY MOVIE MOMENT!!
And HOW.

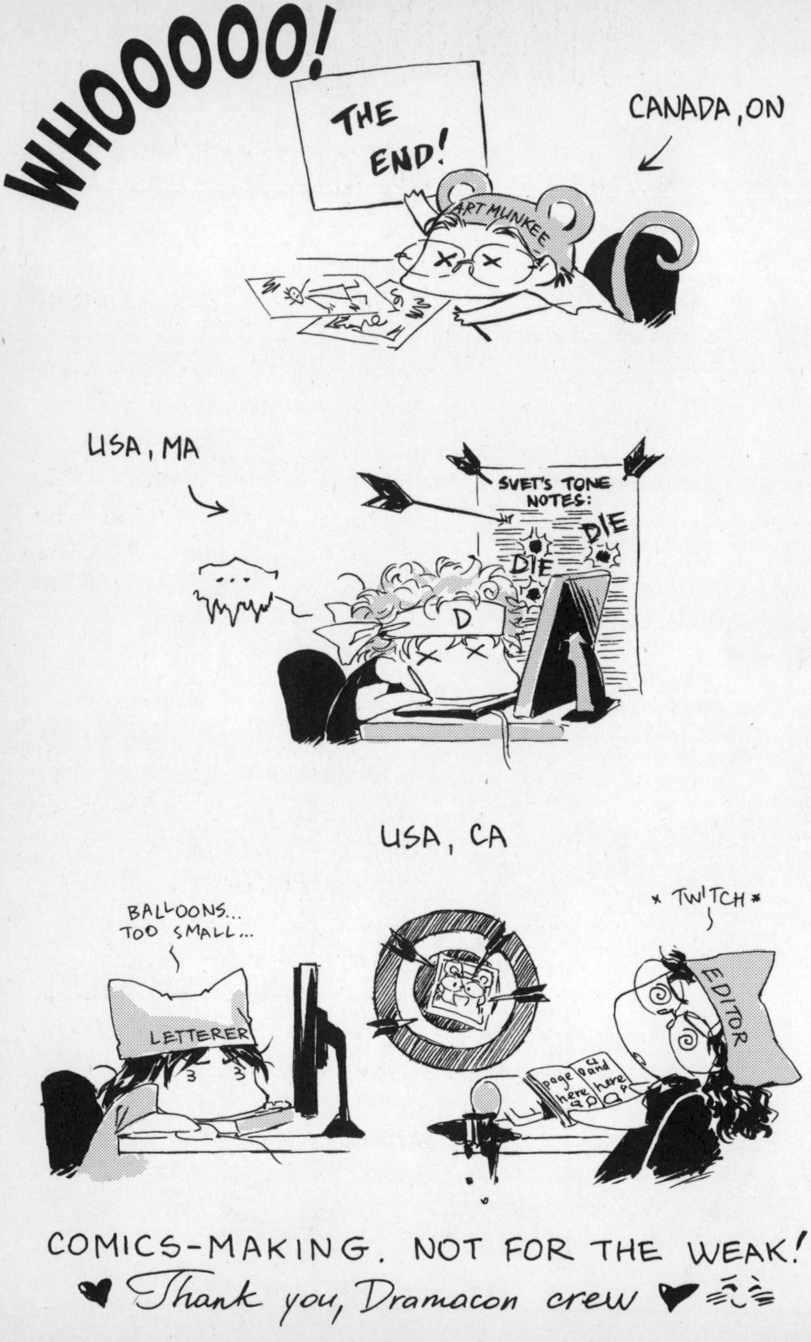
WHOOOOO!
THE END!
CANADA, ON
ART MUNKEE
USA, MA
SVET'S TONE NOTES:
DIE
DIE
D
USA, CA
BALLOONS... TOO SMALL...
LETTERER
* TWITCH *
EDITOR
page here
and here
COMICS-MAKING. NOT FOR THE WEAK!
Thank you, Dramacon crew

~THANQ'S~

The list is long and I won't be able to mention everyone here... Those omitted but still very much appreciated — you know who you are ♡

My family and friends — I LOVE YOU!! YOU'LL SEE ME SOON!!
attempts to crawl out of studio

Dee — selflessly rescued the book AGAIN from the jaws of deadlines. Send this woman chocolate!!!

TOKYOPOP — for giving me the opportunity to make this story (especially to Lillian and Erika, for staying overtime to get this book out on time).

♥ MY READERS ♥ — I HAVE THE BEST FANS EVER.

AWWW...

Thank you for reading, thank you for writing such thoughtful letters — sorry if I did not have time to reply!! I read them all without fail and look approximately like this while doing so (circles under eyes and zombie-like complexion edited out for vanity reasons). Thank you for the wonderful fanart and the gifts! I treasure them all and will be making a section on my website to showcase as much as I can ♥

... And with this, I have exactly 5 minutes left to send this page in before the book goes off to the printer... Cutting it close, you say? Ho ho ho!
... Yes, I am ☺ *rushes off*
See you in my next series!
Luv, Svet.

~ F.A.Q. ~

I've received several recurring questions and figured
here would be a good place to write down the answers,
in case anyone else out there is curious to know...

Q... IS LIDA SUPPOSED TO BE ME?

A: Nope! I wrote Lida as sort of an 'ideal pro', a mentor
figure and an amalgam of all the wonderful pros who
took the time to give me some feedback and encourage-
ment back when I was just starting out. I guess Lida
is someone I would like to be when I grow up!

Q... HOW DID MATT LOSE HIS EYE?

A: In a childhood accident. He doesn't like to talk about it.

Q... IS DRAMACON INSPIRED BY "PHANTOM OF THE OPERA"?

A: I wish I could claim to be that well-read... But no, the
similarities in themes and Christie's name are a coincidence.
(One of my special powers is to appear smarter than
I actually am... But I promise to read the book one day!!)

Q... WHY WAS LIDA CRYING IN BOOK 2?

A: That morning she received news that someone she once
called a good friend is claiming they are a co-creator
of one of her books. In a lawsuit. As of book 3 the
claim has been resolved in favour of Lida, but it hurt
her very much to face this from a friend.

Q... IS CHRISTIE SUPPOSED TO BE ME?

A: No again! ☺ Though we do share some personality quirks
and struggle towards a similar goal. Now go look at
the last panel of second last page of ch. 4 — the geeky
girl in glasses talking to Lida? That's me in high
school, down to the backpack and the scrawny build.

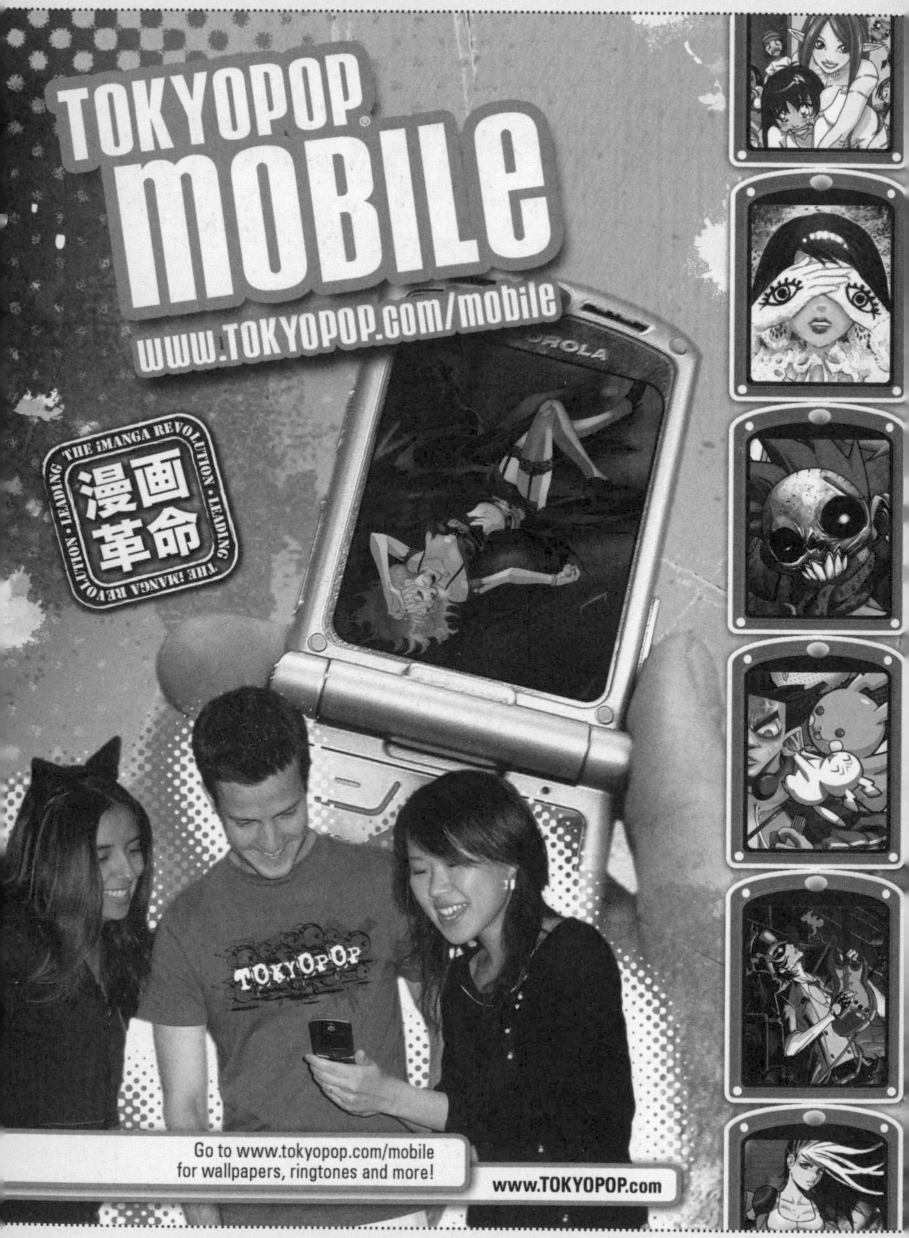
TOKYOPOP®
MOBILE
www.TOKYOPOP.com/mobile
THE iMANGA REVOLUTION · LEADING THE iMANGA REVOLUTION · LEADING
漫画革命
TOKYOPOP
Go to www.tokyopop.com/mobile
for wallpapers, ringtones and more!
www.TOKYOPOP.com